Capitalism and Apartheid

To my parents, Fay and Charles Babrow, my husband, Michael, and to Kenneth Younger, former Director of Chatham House – all of whom made this study possible.

Capitalism
and
Apartheid
South Africa, 1910–1986

MERLE LIPTON

Wildwood House

First published in Great Britain in 1985 by
Gower Publishing Company Ltd
Published in paperback with new Epilogue
in 1986 by Wildwood House Ltd
Gower House, Croft Road,
Aldershot, Hants GU11 3HR,
England

Lipton, Merle
Capitalism and apartheid.
1. Capitalism 2. Blacks—South Africa—
Segregation 3. South Africa—Economic
conditions—1918–1961 4. South Africa—
Economic conditions—1961–
I. Title
306'.342'0968   HC517.S7

ISBN 0-7045-0517-7 Pbk

Typeset in Imprint by Paston Press, Norwich
Printed and bound by Billing & Sons Limited, Worcester

Contents

Acknowledgments and Terminology

The research for, and writing of, this book have been done in stages, interrupted by other projects, by family and domestic activities and by illness. The central Section B was completed and accepted for publication by 1978. The argument of these chapters was strengthened by subsequent developments and it has only been necessary to update them for publication now. I delayed publishing them because they seemed incomplete without the accounts of the general evolution of policy, and of the broader political struggle, that comprise Sections A and C.

This book was mostly written at home but, at various stages, a much-appreciated working base was provided by the Royal Institute of International Affairs at Chatham House, the School of African and Asian Studies at Sussex University, and the School of Advanced International Studies at Johns Hopkins University. A semester at the Wilson Center in Washington DC, although on a different project, stimulated some rethinking about the international aspects of this study. The Nuffield Foundation Small Grants Scheme contributed towards the cost of preparing the manuscript for publication.

I am deeply indebted to the many South Africans who generously spent time talking to me about the issues discussed in this book. Most of them are referred to in the pages (text or footnotes) that follow. Michael Lipton and Maurice Temple Smith closely read and constructively commented on earlier drafts. Judy Toureau, Linda Freston and Margot Woodcock transformed an almost illegible manuscript into a manageable typescript.

Terminology is a minefield in the study of South African society. Many people understandably resent the arbitrary and compulsory racial classification of the population by the 1950 Population

Registration Act. Unfortunately, as all authors discover, it is impossible to analyse government policy without using these categories. The use of these terms does not, however, imply that they provide any justification for discriminating against people, or for fostering differentiation among them.

The 'racial' components of the South African population, set out in Table 1 (p. 378), comprise the ruling whites (sometimes, inappropriately, referred to as Europeans) and the various sub-categories of blacks (sometimes termed 'non-whites') – viz., the indigenous Africans, the mixed-race coloureds and the Indians or Asians.

Confusion is caused by the changing official designation of Africans – partly a reflection of their unsettled status in SA society – who were once termed 'Natives', then (in 1953) 'Bantu' and finally (in 1978) 'blacks'. This was accompanied by changes in the nomenclature of legislation and departments dealing with them. I have used the designation current at the time, hence the 1951 Native Building Workers Act, the 1953 Bantu Education Act and the 1982 Black Local Authorities Act. The old Native 'reserves' are referred to here as Bantustans or homelands, but not as 'national states', which implies recognition of their independent status and hence a denial of the SA citizenship of Africans.

Another source of terminological confusion is the frequent renaming of unpopular departments and legislation. Thus the Department for Native Affairs was transformed into Bantu Affairs, then Plural Relations and, finally, Cooperation and Development. The much attacked Physical Planning Act became the Environment Act; the Department of Labour became 'Manpower'. The pace of change in SA may be slow, but the rate of change in nomenclature is phenomenal – and bewildering.

Abbreviations

AAC	Anglo-American Corporation
AHI	Afrikaanse Handelsinstituut (business organization)
ANC	African National Congress
Assocom	Associated Chambers of Commerce
BAAB	Bantu Affairs Administration Board
BAD	Bantu Affairs Department
Cusa	Council of Unions of South Africa
CP	Conservative Party
CPSA	Communist Party of South Africa
FCI	Federated Chamber of Industries
Fosatu	Federation of South African trade unions
HNP	Herstigte Nasionale Party
HSRC	Human Sciences Research Council
IC Act	Industrial Conciliation Act
ICU	Industrial and Commercial Union
IDC	Industrial Development Corporation
Iscor	Iron and Steel Corporation
MWU	Mine Workers Union
NP	(Afrikaner) National Party
Nationalists	Members of the National Party
OAU	Organization of African Unity
OFS	Orange Free State
PAC	Pan Africanist Congress
PFP	Progressive Federal Party
PWV	Pretoria/Witwatersrand/Vereeniging
SA	South Africa
SAAU	South African Agricultural Union
SABC	South African Broadcasting Corporation

SABRA	South African Bureau of Racial Affairs
SACOL	South African Confederation of Labour
SACCOLA	South African Employers Consultative Committee on Labour Affairs
SACTU	South African Confederation of Trade Unions
SAP	South African Party
SAR	South African Railways
SEIFSA	Steel and Engineering Industries Federation of SA
SWA	South West Africa (Namibia)
SWAPO	South West African Peoples Organization
TUCSA	Trade Union Council of South Africa
UP	United Party
UDF	United Democratic Front

Glossary of Afrikaans Words

baantjies vir boeties – jobs for pals
baaskap – domination
bruin – brown
Handelsinstituut – business organization
kragdadig(e) – forceful
platteland – white rural areas
sjambok – whip, baton
swart gevaar – black danger
verkramp(tes) – reactionary, conservative
verlig(tes) – enlightened
verswarting – blackening

Section A
THE ISSUES EMERGE

1
The Debate About South Africa

What happens to a society depends mainly on the perceived interests and the tastes of the people and groups within it and on their power to secure those interests. This book will investigate whether capitalists in South Africa (SA) wanted to retain, strengthen or destroy apartheid and whether they had the power to secure their aims.

By *apartheid* is meant the system of legalised and institutionalised race discrimination and segregation in SA (analysed in Chapters 2 and 3). By *capitalism* is meant a social system in which there is a substantial degree of private, as distinct from state or communal, ownership of the means of production (mines, farms, factories, banks) and in which the owners of these assets hire employees for a wage (or rent out their assets to others who do so) for private gain. According to the classical definition, another essential characteristic of capitalism is a labour market free from major political coercion.

SA has a sizeable subsistence sector with land held on communal tenure (the homelands or Bantustans), and a system of tied labour (Africans subjected to controls over movement). This means that it is not, according to either the neo-classical or Marxist definitions, fully capitalist. However, these are pre-capitalist elements in a system that is predominantly capitalist. It will be argued that these feudal-like features, connected with fundamental aspects of apartheid, became an obstacle to capitalist development and that this led to recurrent attempts to erode apartheid by capitalists.

Like most contemporary societies, SA also has a large state sector. In 1978 this generated a quarter of GDP, and accounted for fifty per cent of fixed investment (railways, telecommunications, iron and steel, oil, armaments). *Pari passu* with the growth

2

of the state sector, a large bureaucracy emerged, with interests and views of its own. It too played a major role in the struggle over apartheid.

If it is assumed that capitalists are a homogeneous group, and apartheid a fixed social system, then there are four possible relationships between capitalists and apartheid:

   (i)   Capitalists do not want apartheid and have the power to get rid of it;

   (ii)   Capitalists do not want apartheid, but do not have the power to get rid of it;

   (iii)   Capitalists want apartheid, and have the power to retain it;

   (iv)   Capitalists want apartheid, but do not have the power to retain it.

These possibilities represent four logical extremes; in reality, there is likely to be a spread of views, with different capitalists wanting to get rid of various aspects of apartheid and to preserve others, and with some limited power to do this. But these four polar positions have been propounded by participants in the debate and are a useful way of illuminating the issues.

The thesis that capitalists are opposed to apartheid and have (or will have) the power to get rid of it was set out by O'Dowd in his seminal 1964 essay 'South Africa in the Light of the Stages of Economic Growth'.[1] He argued that capitalism and apartheid were incompatible and predicted that, by the 1980s, economic growth would erode apartheid and 'usher in' a period of declining discrimination and a Western-style democratic welfare state.

A striking feature of O'Dowd's analysis was the absence of any stress on racism *per se*; he treated it as a purely functional surrogate for class, another means of extracting surplus (or accumulating capital) at a particular stage of economic growth, and due to be discarded at the next stage.

The argument that capitalists are opposed to apartheid, but lack the power to get rid of it was propounded by liberals like Horwitz and Hutt, who maintained that apartheid was costly and inconvenient to capitalists but was forced on them by the superior political power of the Afrikaner National Party (NP), backed by white farmers and workers.[2] Horwitz predicted that 'the uncontrollable

clash between political conservatism and economic dynamism'
would lead to an explosion.

Bromberger and Lipton combined elements of the O'Dowd and
Horwitz theses, arguing that (i) at an earlier stage, some aspects of
racism were functional for growth in agriculture and mining,
though not in manufacturing and commerce; but that apartheid
was nevertheless imposed on these sectors by the superior political
power of other sections of the white oligarchy; (ii) that the erosion
of apartheid likely to take place as its costs to all sectors rose
(because of growing capital-intensity and the need for skills and
mass markets) would not necessarily follow the Western European
pattern of development; deracialization might be limited and need
not be accompanied by liberalization; instead it could take place
via 'authoritarian reform'.[3]

Although the view that apartheid conflicts with the interests of
capital is usually associated with liberals,* this is surely the
position one would expect a classical Marxist to take, on the
grounds that progressive capitalism was destroying feudal relics
such as tied labour. Compare this, for instance, with Marx's third
essay on India in which he pictured capitalism, spearheaded by the
railroad, breaking down precapitalist modes of production and
serf-like labour relationships.[4] However, Marxists analysing
South Africa have not argued along these lines; instead they
emphasized the interest of capitalists in sustaining apartheid, even
if 'restructuring' its form.

The view that capitalists want apartheid and have the power to
retain it was propounded by neo-Marxists like Johnstone and
Legassick in the early 1970s. They viewed SA as having a fully
developed but distorted form of capitalism, which deliberately
kept alive, and benefited from, the 'reserves' and tied labour. SA
thus provided a special case of dependency theory, with capitalists
(especially foreign investors) living off the surplus from pre-
capitalist formations.[5] This view was later elaborated to allow for
the 'restructuring' or rationalisation of apartheid, linked to the
'increasing organic composition of capital' (i.e. capital intensity)
and the emergence of monopoly capital. But it was denied that this

*In SA, 'liberals' generally refers to non-Marxists who oppose both race discrimi-
    nation and authoritarianism; on economic policy they range from free mar-
    keteers to social democrats.

would lead to any fundamental change; on the contrary, apartheid would be strengthened and white rule perpetuated by this greater flexibility and adaptability.[6]

This view of the essentially rationalising and cosmetic nature of the changes in SA was also subscribed to by non-Marxists, and was probably first formulated by Adam in his book, *Modernizing Racial Domination*. Adam did not however root this in the interests of capitalists but rather in the strategy for survival of Afrikaner nationalists.[7] In a qualified version of this thesis it was argued by Blumer (and later Greenberg) that whether or not capitalists wanted apartheid, they readily adapted or 'nestled into' the apartheid structures.[8]

The fourth view—that capitalists want apartheid, but do not (or will not) have the power to retain it—would, presumably, be the *post hoc* position of successful revolutionaries who had destroyed both capitalism and apartheid. It is presaged in the writings of Slovo and No Sizwe.[9]

Until recently, much of the argument about SA has been couched in terms of whether economic forces, usually described as 'rational', would prevail over 'irrational' political and ideological forces such as race prejudice and Afrikaner nationalism. However, the issue is now widely perceived as being a political struggle between different sets of economic interests, rather than a battle between archaic political and progressive economic forces.

An example of the impossibility of separating economics and politics in the old way is provided by the debate on the black-white wage gap. The division on this issue was not between Marxists and liberals: while some neo-classicals argued that the wage gap was the result of the operation of 'natural' market forces, reflecting the scarcity of skilled (white) labour and the abundant supply of unskilled (black) labour, others joined Marxists in arguing that the wage gap was the outcome of political factors, such as the job colour bar and lack of trade union rights for blacks. In reality, labour supply and political constraints must both be taken into account. The scarcity of skilled labour raised its price; but the scarcity itself was at least partly determined by political and institutional factors which excluded blacks from skilled jobs. The abundance of black labour depressed its price; but this abundance was at least partly the outcome of limitations on land ownership by blacks, which prevented many of them from being farmers and forced them onto the labour market. Neither the economic nor the political factors can be treated as 'pure' and independent; they are too closely inter-related. This analysis treats economic and political forces—conceived as respectively the economic interests of various groups and their relative power to advance them—as inseparable.

Much of the analysis of South Africa has been in static terms, with interests seen as fixed over time. The fact that mineowners supported influx controls and migrant labour in 1910 and 1948 is adduced as evidence that they want it now. The analysis in this book is concerned with the dynamics of the situation and with the changes that have taken place in the interests and power of both capital and labour over time.

The argument is as follows:

(i) Capitalists in SA have never been unanimously or wholeheartedly in favour of apartheid. During the first half of this century, the economically and politically more important farmers and mineowners supported some major apartheid policies, which the less important manufacturing and commercial capitalists had less interest in or opposed. Over time, particularly since the mid-1960s, opposition to apartheid increased among all capitalists, particularly those in the fast-growing manufacturing and commercial sectors. Capitalists are still neither unanimous (some are more opposed than others) nor necessarily one hundred per cent opposed to apartheid (some are strongly opposed to economic, but ambivalent about political, apartheid). *But the trend is towards increasing opposition and it has been accelerating.*

(ii) The power of capitalists to achieve their aims has also varied greatly over time, and by sector, size, ethnic affiliation, etc. Until the mid-1960s, agricultural capital was most consistently able to get what it wanted; mining, manufacturing and commercial capital were less successful, both in their conflicts with agricultural capital and with white labour. Since the mid-1960s, however, there has been a convergence of interests of capitalists on apartheid labour policies, and this, together with changes in capital ownership (growth of Afrikaans capital; concentration of capital in a few giant firms), has increased their capacity to get their way. Hence the reforms of the 1970s, though the limited nature of the reforms, and the obstruction of their implementation, demonstrated that capitalists' power had not grown in step with their opposition to apartheid.

The explanation for the changing interests of capitalists (set out in Chapters 4, 5, 6 and 8) is that, for white capital, apartheid always had both costs and benefits. The benefits were provided by a plentiful supply of cheap, unskilled black workers and by the intervention of the state apparatus to ensure their compliance. But losses were incurred because of the restrictions on black competition in the skilled labour market. These forced employers to rely on the limited, and therefore expensive, supply of white skilled labour.

During the last few decades, the SA economy has grown rapidly and changed, shifting from dependence upon mining and agriculture, which needed cheap unskilled workers, to greater dependence upon manufacturing and services, which need more skilled workers. Moreover, these sectors—and more recently mining and agriculture themselves—became more skill and capital-intensive, and their products and capital equipment became more sophisticated. As a result, the importance of skilled workers grew, while that of unskilled workers diminished.

This increasing need for skilled labour was the most compelling reason for the change in the interests of capitalists and for the pressures they applied for changes in labour policy. No longer so dependent upon a large mass of cheap, unskilled black workers, they wanted a free, mobile, competitive labour market, with large numbers of blacks entering skilled and semi-skilled jobs.

The interests of capital in relation to cheap unskilled labour also changed. As industry became more capital-intensive, labour costs as a proportion of total costs declined. At the same time, a rise in the general level of wages would enlarge the domestic market, which could in turn provide economies of scale. This became crucial, partly because apartheid raised the costs of production and made exports uncompetitive, partly because protection of high cost apartheid products against imports favoured production for the protected domestic market (see Chapter 8). That this led the (protected) businessmen to oppose apartheid is a classic 'internal contradiction'. But the small size of the SA market made it essential for manufacturers to break into export markets as well;

and this led to pressures to reduce the high cost structure of SA industry by, among other measures, encouraging more competition and efficiency in the labour market.

In addition, the changing climate of opinion about race discrimination and inequality since World War Two led to growing hostility to apartheid, both amongst blacks in SA and internationally. This posed a threat to export markets, to supplies of foreign capital and technology, and to political stability. International hostility was of particular concern to the multinational companies in SA and to the huge mining-based SA companies with interests abroad. This changing balance of costs and benefits led to growing pressures by capitalists against aspects of apartheid and contributed to the erosion of economic and social apartheid that took place from the late 1960s.

However, there were also important respects in which apartheid was *not* eroded. In particular, political change lagged behind economic and social change. This was partly because capitalists, uncertain about their fate under a black government, were more divided and ambivalent about political change; partly because of opposition to these changes, particularly from white labour and the state bureaucracy, both of which groups wielded considerable political power.

For white labour, apartheid remained beneficial. It provided an effective 'closed shop', with protection from competition and undercutting by blacks. It also provided the white working and lower middle classes with preferential access to resources such as housing, welfare benefits and education, with social status and cheap domestic servants, and with considerable political power to protect their privileges (see Chapter 7).

However, decades of superior education and training had given white workers a great advantage in the labour market, and many professional and skilled whites no longer needed protection from black competition. Even the less skilled whites might gain more from a fast rate of growth, which the relaxation of apartheid would permit, provided they were given compensation and/or guarantees. It therefore became possible for those who gained from the relaxation of apartheid (white capital and black labour) to compensate or buy off the losers and to neutralise the opposition of at least some sections of white labour.

The outcome of these conflicting interests and views within the oligarchy depended on the relative political power of these different groups and classes. It was also affected by the political forms, institutions and processes, through which all political change must be mediated. In SA, these forms and institutions almost totally excluded blacks and gave considerable weight to white workers and farmers. From the late 1960s, this began to change: the power of agriculture declined and the power of progressive capital and of black labour (though still outside the formal political system) grew. Moreover, there emerged within the NP, a significant group of Afrikaans capitalists—nurtured by the Nationalist government since its election in 1948—and they acted as a Trojan horse for capital, whose interest in undermining apartheid labour policies they came to share. This split and weakened the NP. Nevertheless, the power of the declining classes and sectors had been institutionalized and entrenched, and as the challenge to them grew, they shored up their power by authoritarian measures. The ruling NP, and the vast bureaucracy it spawned, had a vested interest in controlling the rate of change, and in slowing and preventing some changes, particularly in the political sphere, which threatened their power and jobs; like the eighteenth-century French administrators of *gabellas* and *octroi*, they therefore resisted reform.

These institutional factors meant that SA did not conform to the Marxist model of the state as the instrument of capital. The power of the bureaucracy and the political establishment lent more support to Weberian views of the nature of state power.[10] Moreover, this tendency was reinforced by the emergence of sister bureaucracies in the huge firms that dominated the private sector and shared many of the interests and attitudes of state sector bureaucrats (see Chapter 5).

The standard question in the debate about SA—whether economic growth shores up or erodes apartheid—is too crude and needs reformulation. The first question is: what kind of economic growth? If it is growth based on cheap, unskilled labour (as in white agriculture until the 1960s or mining until the 1970s) then it could coexist with apartheid and even benefit from it. But growth requiring skills and a domestic market (as has long been the case in manufacturing and commerce) does not require, and has difficulties in coexisting with, apartheid. Secondly, there was no simple correlation between economic and political power in SA;

capitalists often did not get their way in conflicts with the supporters of apartheid, who might still succeed in retaining some aspects
of it, particularly in the political field.

Another major dimension of the debate about SA is the relationship between class and ethnic/racial factors.* On this issue too, the
division between Marxists and liberals has not been clearcut.
Marxists like Simons, Bunting and Slovo argued that racial factors
acquired a life and power of their own, often over-riding class
interests; hence the failure of white workers to perceive that their
true interests lay in uniting with black labour against capital.[11]
Meanwhile, the work of liberals like O'Dowd, Salomon, and my
own earlier papers treated economic interests and classes as the
driving force of history, and stressed the role of racism in securing
white interests, including those of white workers.[12] The main
division on this central theoretical question therefore has not been
between Marxists and liberals, but between those who accord
primacy to economic and class interests (for liberals this means
income maximization for personal utility; for Marxists class
accumulation and power) and those who accord it to ethnic
security and power.[13]

Initially, I attempted this analysis almost entirely in terms of
economic and class interests. In the early chapters, this approach
provided a way of escaping from what had become a sterile
preoccupation with race and ideology in the analysis of SA.
However, its inadequacies were revealed in Chapter 9 on the
political struggle, and I sought to modify it in order to escape from
the unsatisfactory 'either/or' choice between class and ethnicity,
seeking a solution in the close interaction of these two forces, as
with the false choice between economic and political forces.[14]

In Chapter 9 the close interaction between class and ethnicity is
demonstrated and a reformulation of the relationship between
them suggested. The conclusion is that neither the broad class

---

*An *ethnic* group is defined as sharing a common culture and descent (Afrikaners, Zulus); a *racial* group by hereditary physical characteristics such as skin
colour (whites, blacks). A *nation* (which may be ethnically or racially diverse)
shares the same territory and political system. *Class* is defined by relationship
to the means of production (capitalists are owners/managers; workers those
who sell their labour), modified by 'consciousness' arising from political,
cultural and ideological influences.

categories of capital and labour (or even subsectors of them), nor ethnic/racial categories such as Whites, Blacks, English, Afrikaners, provide an adequate means of comprehending the behaviour of individuals and groups. In the competition for resources, class conflicts often took an ethnic form; the lines of cleavage between groups, and the alliances constructed in the political struggle, were usually along ethnic not class lines. Class interests were not submerged, but nor did ethnic/racial feelings fade in face of the supposedly homogenising forces of industrialization and urbanization; rather, as in many other countries, they proved unexpectedly persistent.[15] Both ethnic/racial and class factors are therefore essential for understanding and predicting political behaviour. The fact that political mobilization took place along ethnic rather than class lines helps to explain, for example, why capitalists in SA were less powerful than expected.

The recent shift, among both liberals and Marxists, towards a stress on class interests was a reaction against the former emphasis on race and on ideology, particularly Afrikaner Calvinism, seen by many as the *fons et origo* of apartheid and often linked to a belief in a distinctive psychology and personality that rendered Afrikaners peculiarly prone to race prejudice.[16] It now seems widely agreed among scholars that the behaviour of white South Africans does not, alas, diverge much from the behaviour of comparable groups in other societies, faced with competition for resources from people readily distinguished from themselves by colour, culture or religion, and that the key to their behaviour must be sought primarily in structural (i.e. social, economic and political) rather than in psychological or ideological factors.[17]

As this brief survey suggests, there is more convergence among the various factions of liberals and Marxists than the often vitriolic debate among them suggests, and more continuity with the past than the disparagement of earlier 'conventional' analyses of SA society indicate.[18] The reason for the clamour and dissension lies partly, as Hughes suggested, in the need for 'product differentiation': the more similar the products, the more necessary for manufacturers to stress the differences—as with toothpastes.[19] However, underlying the polemics were deeper, though largely implicit, differences in assumptions about human and social behaviour, notably about the role that self-interest plays in motivating behaviour, the speed at which profound social changes occur, and what it might be possible to achieve in SA in the light of experience in similar societies.

Another reason why the issues are bitterly contested is because this debate (like that between the Mensheviks, Bolsheviks, liberals and nationalists in nineteenth-century Russia) is an integral part of the political struggle over the future of a country from which many of the aspiring future leaders have been exiled; and these issues, apart from their theoretical and scholarly interest, have important implications for policy and strategy towards SA.

If the interests of capital are firmly wedded to apartheid—are indeed the *raison d'être* for it—then obviously the destruction of the one must entail the destruction of the other. But if sections of capital are opposed to major aspects of apartheid, then they are potential allies in the fight against it.

There are five possible strategies that can be adopted:

   (i)   Retain both capitalism and apartheid;

  (ii)   Have less or no capitalism (i.e. a larger state sector) combined with white domination;

 (iii)   Have less or no capitalism combined with black domination;

 (iv)   Get rid of apartheid: i.e. have multi-racial (or non-racial)* capitalism;

  (v)   Get rid of both apartheid and capitalism: i.e. have multi-racial (or non-racial) socialism.

The analysis presented in this book makes possible the consideration of a wide range of options, including that of enlisting progressive white capitalists as allies in the fight to get rid of apartheid. I prefer this option (iv) because I believe it could be achieved with less violence than any of the others; it does not rule out subsequent movement towards more egalitarian, welfare-oriented politics; and it is the only option compatible with the revival of the remnants of liberty and democracy: the degree of coercion required to enforce each of the other options seems incompatible with this.

*The term 'multi-racial' implies recognition of the significance of ethnic/racial differences; though pluralists, who accept the coexistence of different groups within a common society, must be distinguished from segregationists, who believe the different groups should be kept apart or live in separate societies. 'Non-racial' is used by those who deny the significance of ethnic or racial differences and favour assimilationist policies.

However, my primary aim in this book is not to argue for any particular option or strategy. It is to explain why South Africa, the country of my birth, developed the distinctive apartheid system, the cause of pain and trauma to so many of its people; what is actually happening to this system now; and how it might develop in the future. I hope thereby to contribute towards greater understanding of the costs and risks of the various options which might be considered both by South Africans and by outsiders.

The plan of the book is as follows: Chapter 2 describes the evolution of apartheid and Chapter 3 attempts to assess the extent of its erosion. An explanation of these contrary trends is then suggested by an analysis of the changing interests of the white oligarchy (Chapters 4–8) and of the changing balance of political power (Chapter 9).

2
The Evolution of Apartheid, 1910–70

This chapter will first define apartheid and sketch its evolution and particularly that of post-1948 labour policies. The effects of apartheid and how it differs from other social systems will then be discussed.

The definition of apartheid

The recent erosion of apartheid has been accompanied by a tendency to dismiss as 'marginal' changes in what were formerly held to be its core features, such as the job colour bar.[1] It was even asserted by some that if there was full deracialization in SA, this still would not change 'the system'.[2] But what then is apartheid?

The ending of apartheid cannot logically be held to entail the ending of capitalism and/or of authoritarianism, however desirable these are deemed to be, for there are many capitalist and authoritarian societies which do not have apartheid (and many countries without apartheid which are more purely capitalist and/or authoritarian, such as Chile). It is impossible to discuss what is happening to apartheid on the basis of these shifting definitions and without a clear conception as to what it was before about 1970, and agreed criteria by which to judge whether it is being eroded or intensified.

The defining characteristics of apartheid (also known as segregation and 'separate development') were:

(a) *The hierarchical ordering* of the economic, political and social structures *on the basis of race*, identified by physical characteristics such as skin colour. Whites (roughly 18 per cent of the population, see Table I) comprised a ruling oligarchy and privileged elite; coloureds and Indians (12 per cent) and Africans (70 per cent) were second and third class citizens respectively—

14

indeed, Africans were even defined by the government as non-citizens.

(b) *Discrimination* against Africans, and to a lesser extent coloureds and Indians, who were excluded from many of the civil, political and economic rights enjoyed by whites, such as the vote, freedom of movement, and the right to do certain jobs or own property in much of the country.

(c) *Segregation* of the races in many spheres of life: they lived in separate areas, went to separate schools and universities, used separate buses and trains; there was little social mixing; sexual relations and inter-marriage across the colour line were illegal.

(d) *The legalisation and institutionalization* of this hierarchical, discriminatory and segregated system, which was enshrined in law and enforced by the government.

The difference between apartheid and other social systems clearly did not lie in the existence of a privileged elite with a disproportionate share of economic and social privileges and political power, as this is almost universal. However, most contemporary social systems subscribed to principles which, at least in theory, were more fluid, with people able to move up and down the social scale from one class to another. In SA it was illegal to change from one racial category to another. It was thus more like a caste system, to which the hereditary, ascriptive element added rigidity.

But apartheid seemed more rigid than any contemporary caste system, partly because the class/caste line coincided with racial divisions, which made it more stark and inflexible, partly because the hierarchical divisions were enforced by law. Whereas in India the government practised 'reverse discrimination' in favour of the former untouchable castes, apartheid, with its systematic discrimination against the poorest groups, was backed up by law. This made it unique in the contemporary world, though not historically: its legalised nature had similarities with the mediaeval 'estates'—classes whose rights and privileges were entrenched in law—and with the early period of European colonialism, when only citizens of the colonial power could govern and hold key jobs. But while the legalised nature of apartheid was its most distinctive (and to many most offensive) feature, its essence was the hierarchical racial structure, the fact that all whites were above all blacks, and that blacks could never be equal, let alone superior, to whites.

The assessment of whether apartheid is declining or increasing must relate to changes in these defining characteristics (i.e. the decline/removal of discrimination, segregation, the hierarchical racial structure and of their legalization) and not to verbal changes (renaming it 'separate development') or to changes which adapt or modernize it by, for example, shifting the job bar upwards so that blacks—still under whites—can do more skilled work, thus relieving the skill shortage but leaving the hierarchical structure intact.

As with most major social changes, the erosion of apartheid is likely to take place unevenly. There could be considerable social and economic change (the decline of discrimination in employment, less segregation in social life) with little or no extension of political rights, as has happened in SA over the last decade. Conversely, there could be the extension of political and civil rights, without much erosion of economic discrimination or social segregation, as seems to have happened in the Cape colony after the removal of the legal and political disabilities of the coloureds and slaves in the nineteenth century and in the USA after the emancipation of slaves in 1865. There could also be the removal of *de jure* apartheid, without much practical effect; or conversely the retention of the legal framework, while in practice apartheid withers away.

The effects of apartheid must also be distinguished from the often harsh processes (displacement of people from the land; growth of urban slums; extension of state power) accompanying 'modernization'* and an attempt made to identify the features special to, or exacerbated by, apartheid.

The brief historical outline that follows is divided into four somewhat arbitrary periods: (a) the foundations of apartheid, 1910–39; (b) the abortive erosion of apartheid, 1939–48; (c) the consolidation of apartheid, 1948–60; (d) 'separate development': the new face of apartheid, 1960–70.

---

*Modernization generally means increased economic output, particularly by means of industrialization; creation of a centralized, national state; spread of mass education and literacy; the introduction of Western science and technology.

The foundations of apartheid, 1910–39

Apartheid had its origins in legislative and customary measures of all four colonies/republics* which formed the Union of South Africa in 1910. Within each of these, the whites, whose forebears arrived in SA from 1652 onwards, had established their supremacy over the indigenous Africans, the mixed-race coloureds, and the Indians, who came as indentured labourers in the late nineteenth century. In practice, there was not much difference between the Boer republic's explicit doctrine of 'No equality between black and white in church or in state' and the British principle of 'Equal rights for all civilised men'. But, in the Cape, Africans and especially coloureds had more civil rights, including the right to qualify for the vote.[3]

Blacks were virtually excluded from the democratic political system established for the white oligarchy by the Act of Union, which restricted the franchise to white men, except in the Cape province. However, in 1936, African voters in the Cape were removed from the common roll and instead elected three (white) members to the House of Assembly and four to the Senate on a separate roll. An advisory, partially-elected Natives' Representative Council (NRC) was also set up for them. Coloureds**, however, were retained on the common roll, reflecting the conviction of Prime Minister Hertzog that they were 'in many respects closer to the whites, and differed fundamentally from the Africans [and should be included] among the whites industrially, economically and politically.'[4] (Governments and Prime Ministers listed in Table 14).

The enforced social segregation that is a distinctive feature of the SA system was secured by measures such as the 1927 Immorality Act, which forbade extra-marital sex between Africans and whites, and the 1923 Urban Areas Act, which confined Africans to segregated townships or locations.[5]

Economically, discriminatory measures were enacted against black farmers, traders and workers to prevent them from compet-

---

*The British colonies of Cape and Natal, the Afrikaner (or Boer) republics, Transvaal and Orange Free State (OFS).

**The coloureds were partly descended from the whites, especially the Afrikaners; about two-thirds of them spoke Afrikaans and belonged to the Dutch Reformed Churches.

ing with whites and to ensure that they would instead provide a large source of cheap labour for white farms and mines. The 1913 and 1936 Land Acts reserved almost 14 per cent of the land for Africans, who constituted 70 per cent of the population. Outside these 'reserves' (later known as Bantustans or homelands), in the 87 per cent of SA known as the 'white' areas (which included all the large towns and developed agriculture), Africans could not own, or in most cases even rent, land. Black businessmen were hindered by restrictions on their right to own or lease businesses and property and by a licensing system which kept their opportunities to a minimum, even in their reserves and segregated urban townships.

A key feature of apartheid was the extensive system of controls over black labour. They can be divided into: (i) controls over movement, or horizontal controls; (ii) controls over the allocation of jobs, or vertical controls; (iii) other measures restricting workers' rights.

The horizontal or movement controls

The 1922 Stallard Commission laid down the principle that an African should only be in the towns to 'minister to the needs of the white man and should depart therefrom when he ceases to minister'. African men over sixteen years old had to carry a 'pass' or reference book, which recorded their permission to work and live in a particular white area. These pass laws (or influx controls) controlled the flow of African labour into the 'white' areas, particularly the towns, and allocated labour between sectors and regions.

Official policy discouraged African families and favoured the mining industry's system of migrant workers housed in all-male compounds, while their families remained in the reserves, thus keeping down African numbers and retaining their links with the 'tribal' areas. These laws hindered Africans wishing to leave white farms or reserves and to enter, or move between, the towns. Many doing so illegally were fined or imprisoned. Until the 1950s, however, administration of urban areas was largely in the hands of local authorities, so there was considerable regional variation in their application.

The job colour bar or vertical controls

The job bar reserved specific jobs for whites, or provided for the employment of a minimum ratio of whites. After Union the legal job bar (established on gold mines in the Transvaal Republic in 1893) was entrenched in the Mines and Works Acts of 1911 and 1926, which barred Africans from the more skilled mining jobs. In the state sector, the 1924 'civilized labour' policy, designed to protect unskilled whites from undercutting by blacks, provided that whites should be given preferential employment in unskilled jobs at rates of pay 'at a level at which the European employee can maintain his standard of living'.[5]

In private manufacturing and services there was no statutory (i.e. legal) job bar during this period, but preference for whites was secured by other means. First, the 1925 Customs Tariff Act made protection for local manufacturers conditional upon 'satisfactory labour conditions, including the employment of a reasonable proportion of civilized workers'; firms not meeting this requirement were also excluded from the approved list for the Tender and Supplies Board. Second, the 1924 Industrial Conciliation (IC) Act, which provided for the recognition and registration of trade unions, gave a key role to white workers in determining the occupational structure, access to training, and wages.* The Act provided for the establishment of self-governing Industrial Councils to be jointly controlled by the registered unions and employers. The powerful position of the unions on these Councils (and on the Boards set up by the 1922 Apprenticeship Act) enabled white workers to exclude Africans, and often coloureds and Indians, from skilled jobs, and to secure preference for whites in many other jobs by classic (and not explicitly racial) trade union restrictive practices such as the 'closed shop' and control over entry to apprenticeships. Higher expenditure on white education was another means of giving whites an advantage.

Blacks still had the weapon of undercutting; so to prevent the displacement of whites by cheaper blacks, minimum wages and

---

*The IC Act was not explicitly racial, but the definition of employee excluded 'pass bearers', i.e. African men and, after the extension of passes to them in 1952, African women.

'rate for the job' were often enforced.* In industries where whites were not unionised, minimum wages could be enforced by determinations of the Wage Board set up by the 1925 Wage Act.

Other restrictions on workers' rights

In addition to pass laws and exclusion from the registered unions, many African workers were rendered virtually rightless *vis-à-vis* employers and the bureaucracy and police by Masters and Servants Laws, such as the 1911 Native Labour Regulation Act and the 1932 Native Service Contract Act, which made breach of contract by African farm and mine workers a criminal offence and meant they could not legally leave their jobs without their employers' consent.

This discriminatory system was rationalised by a belief in the inferiority of blacks, then widely held to have a biological basis. It was argued, in Darwinian terms, that they were lower on the evolutionary scale than whites and that it would take them hundreds of years to 'catch up' (it was not stated whether they would by then also have changed their colour). Meanwhile, it was the duty of whites to rule them, acting as their trustees or guardians, and to take measures to ensure that their own, more civilized standards were not 'swamped' by greater black numbers. These attitudes were commonplace, not only among whites in SA, but also in Europe and the USA,[6] and these policies, although a frequent cause of dissension among whites, were enacted by governments representing both Afrikaners and English-speaking whites.

The abortive erosion of apartheid, 1939–48

The worldwide challenge to these racist assumptions, and to colonial rule, during the 1930s and 1940s, had an impact on SA. The influence of the new ideas, and the pressures of blacks, the liberal intelligentsia, and urban businessmen, were reflected in the publications of major official commissions, such as the van Eck, Smit and Fagan Reports.[7] The gist of their arguments was that

---

*The 1930 and 1937 amendments to the IC Act extended the application of agreements to cover Africans so that, if they were employed in jobs covered by these agreements, it would have to be on the same conditions and wages as union members, thus preventing undercutting and job fragmentation.

industrialisation, and the poverty of the crowded reserves, meant that increasing and permanent African urbanization was inevitable, and that industrialization required that African workers should be stabilized with their families in the towns and provided with the improved education, pay and prospects of promotion that would turn them into the committed, motivated workforce required by modern industry, as well as providing an expanding market for consumer goods.

The job colour bar, pass laws, and migrant labour were criticized as unjust and inefficient, deterring ambition and competition. The Minister of Native Affairs, replying in 1947 to NP criticism of the African urban influx, argued that industry could not operate efficiently with migrant workers: 'the native must be trained for his work in industry, and to become an efficient industrial worker he must be a permanent industrial worker. On that account he must live near his place of employment'; the major segregation laws had not anticipated the industrial development of the last decade.[8] Smuts, the Prime Minister, concurred that African urbanization could not be stopped: 'You might as well try to sweep the ocean back with a broom.'[9] Jan Hofmeyr, Smuts's second-in-command, went further, denouncing the *herrenvolk* mentality' of whites and declaring in parliament that: 'I take my stand for the ultimate removal of the colour bar from our constitution.'[10]

These sentiments coincided with the halting and, in some respects, erosion of the seemingly relentless trend towards apartheid, particularly in relation to labour policy. The job colour bar was eased, and there was an extension of training facilities for blacks to expand the supply of skilled workers. Occupational advance and government policy, exercised through the Wage Board, led to the raising of black wages at a faster rate than those of whites so that, for the first time since the 1922–25 'civilized labour' package, black-white wage ratios narrowed (see p. 43). The 1945 National Education Finance Act freed African education from its constricting dependence on African taxes; Africans became eligible for old age pensions and for inclusion in the Unemployment Insurance Fund; and there was some easing of restrictions on black businessmen.[11]

In 1942, the Department of Native Affairs recommended the abolition of the pass laws: their implementation was relaxed and the number of prosecutions fell markedly. In 1947, an amendment to the IC Act was tabled, providing for the recognition of African unions, though this was not to be under the same machinery as for white and coloured unions.

The reforms of this period—like those of the 1970s—were limited to socio-economic policy; politically, there was little progress and even a tendency towards authoritarianism (see Chapter 9). Within the United Party (UP) there were conflicts over the reforms, and the effect of conservative pressures could be seen in the tightening of the pass laws towards the end of the war and the breakdown of relations between the government and the Natives' Representative Council over the brutal suppression of the 1946 African mineworkers' strike.

Nevertheless, the UP went into the 1948 election committed to the Fagan Report, which accepted the principle that African workers were a permanent part of SA society and that migrant labour was socially and economically undesirable. Fagan concluded that urbanization was an 'economic phenomenon . . . [which] can be guided and regulated,' but not prevented, and urged that 'the policy should be one for facilitating and encouraging stabilization'.* Fagan specifically advocated that the mining industry be allowed to provide housing for stabilized labour on the new OFS goldmines.[12]

The consolidation of apartheid, 1948–60

Clearly, apartheid was not the invention of the Afrikaner National Party elected to power under Malan in 1948. But the Nationalists reversed the limited, vacillating reforms of the wartime UP and, in defiance of worldwide trends, proclaimed their belief in segregation and racial inequality and their intention of extending apartheid. The rejection of the Fagan recommendations was a major plank in their election platform; instead their Sauer Commission proposed a return to the Stallard principle that Africans should only be in the white areas on a temporary basis, and for a limited purpose; that they should retain their links with the reserves to which they must eventually return; and that the means of enforcing this was by stricter influx control and the extension of migrant labour.[13]

---

*Stabilized workers are settled with their families at or near their places of work, in contrast to migrant workers, who leave their families at their home base.

However, the Nationalists did not (as businessmen and liberals believed) want to halt industrialization but to control it, so as to make it compatible with the traditional hierarchical race structure and the preservation of white (particularly Afrikaner) identity. They believed this required the reinforcement of racial divisions against the social forces released by industrialization and modernization. As a result, they drew sharper lines between whites and all blacks (including coloureds) and resorted to more legal intervention to enforce this than hitherto.

The basis for this more systematic, explicit policy was laid by the 1950 Population Registration Act, which classified the whole population by race, based on appearance, descent and 'general acceptance'. Borderline cases, affecting mainly coloureds, would be investigated by a race classification board.

Politically, the NP moved first against the coloureds. The 1956 Separate Representation of Voters Act removed coloureds from the common roll in the Cape, in breach of the entrenched clauses in the Act of Union requiring a two-thirds majority for this. Instead they were allotted four (white) representatives in Parliament, elected on a separate roll. For Indians, described in the Sauer Report as 'a strange and foreign element which is not assimilable,' repatriation was envisaged.[14]

The basis for the completely separate political system for Africans, which eventually converted them into foreigners in the land of their birth, was laid by the 1951 Bantu Authorities and 1959 Promotion of Bantu Self-government Acts. The parliamentary representatives and Council created for them in 1936 were abolished; instead each of the eight African tribes or 'nations'— Khosa, Zulu and others (see Table 1)—was to exercise its political rights in its own tribal homeland. But while blacks were subdivided, the English and Afrikaners remained politically one 'nation' although they were segregated culturally (see Chapter 9).

The Nationalists reversed the erosion of economic apartheid that took place during the war and pushed back the black middle and skilled classes. In 1957, the government stopped all trading by Africans outside the reserves and townships, and discouraged trading within the latter, in the hope of encouraging businessmen to return to the reserves.[15] The 1950 Group Areas Act further restricted the residential and trading rights of all blacks, including, for the first time, the coloureds in the Cape. By 1980, 115,000 coloured and Indian families, involving over a quarter of all coloureds and Indians, had been forced to move, often losing their homes and businesses at derisory rates of compensation.[16] The Nationalists therefore rejected the 1940s policy of encouraging the emergence of an urban black middle class, of which coloureds and Indians comprised the vanguard.

Labour Policy

Both the vertical and horizontal controls were tightened. In the state sector, the 'civilised labour' policy was reaffirmed: hundreds of blacks were dismissed and replaced by whites at higher wages. In the huge expansion of the state sector that took place, job preference was given to whites, especially Afrikaners.[17]

In the private sector, the NP supported white labour on the job bar, tightening it on the mines and, for the first time, extending the statutory job bar to manufacturing and commerce. Section 77 of the 1956 IC Act enabled the Minister of Labour to reserve jobs for specific racial groups 'in any industry, trade or occupation'.* The aim was to secure preference for whites and 'to preserve complementarity' between the races and stop the increasing reliance of industry on African labour.[18] In 1959, a further Amendment to the IC Act provided that determinations could even be made against the wishes of the self-governing Industrial Council for the industry, to overcome the resistance of employers and some of the unions to the introduction of legal job reservation.

Educational and training policies underlined the intention of ensuring job preference for whites. In his speech on the 1953 Bantu Education Act, Verwoerd, the Minister of Bantu Affairs, spelt it out:

> There is no place for [the Bantu] in the European Community above the level of certain forms of labour . . . it is of no avail for him to receive a training which drew him away from his own community and misled him by showing him the green pastures of the Europeans but still did not allow him to graze there . . . . [This led to] the much-discussed frustration of educated natives who can find no employment which is acceptable to them . . . it must be replaced by planned Bantu education . . . [with] its roots entirely in the Native areas and in the Native environment and community.[19]

*The legal job bar was first extended by the 1951 Native Building Workers Act, which exluded Africans from skilled building work except in their own areas and townships. This exception enabled them to be trained for skilled work in these areas. In practice it proved difficult to prevent them from using these skills in the white areas as well (see p. 208).

This Act centralized control of African education (formerly managed by the provinces and churches) and pegged expenditure to the level of African taxes, limiting the annual contribution from general revenue to R13m. To promote tribal cultures, the Nationalists made vernacular (mother-tongue) education compulsory in African primary schools; in senior schools both official languages, English and Afrikaans, were added. With his penchant for Orwellian language, Verwoerd named the Act excluding blacks from the open English universities (they were never admitted to the Afrikaans universities) the Extension of University Education Act.* Separate ethnic universities (nicknamed bush colleges) were set up for each 'nation'.

The Nationalists applied themselves energetically to 'sweeping back the ocean with a broom'. The pass laws were tightened and extended to African women, and an elaborate, centrally-controlled system of labour bureaux was grafted onto them to control and direct the flow of African labour.[20] The number of prosecutions under the pass laws rose steeply and many of the offenders were hired out to farmers as convict labour. The intention of giving priority to the needs of the low-wage farms was spelt out by Verwoerd, who said that, 'Emigration control must be established to prevent manpower leaving the *platteland* [white farming areas] to become loafers in the city.'[21] To facilitate this the Nationalists attempted 'to identify Bantu farm labour and divorce it from urban labour . . . and to prevent the infiltration of farm labour into urban areas'.[22]

The means for reconciling urban capital's need for African labour with the NP's determination to limit African numbers and prevent their permanent urbanization was migrant labour, which became one of the centrepieces of 'native' policy. In 1952 Verwoerd refused the request of mining companies to house a higher proportion of African workers with their families on the new OFS gold mines, saying it was the government's intention not only to retain migrant labour on the mines, but to extend it to industry: 'Migratory labour is the best . . . system. Its strengthening and expansion . . . to most of the other spheres of labour would be in the interests of the Bantu . . . fully-fledged Bantu townships . . . are

*Other examples were the 1959 Promotion of Bantu Self-Government Act expelling the Native Representatives from parliament and the 1952 Bantu Abolition of Passes and Co-ordination of Documents Act extending the pass laws to African women.

not in accordance with government policy. There is also good reason to believe the Bantu prefer . . . the migratory labour system to removal to the European areas.'[23] Verwoerd also attempted to discourage the employment of Africans in urban areas by measures such as the 1952 Native Services Levy Act which imposed monthly taxes on employers of urban Africans.

Policy towards Africans already in the urban areas was frequently spelt out by Verwoerd and Eiselen, his Secretary of Bantu Affairs: 'the Bantu have no claim to permanency in the European areas, they are in these areas as workers, and therefore own no real estate and can claim no political rights outside of the Bantu reserves.'[24] Accordingly, the rights of 'Section 10' Africans* were whittled away, for example by the 1954 Western Areas Scheme which moved thousands of families from freehold houses in Johannesburg to short-term leasehold houses in townships further away.

But while the Nationalists rejected the Fagan policy of 'encouraging stabilization' and the emergence of an African middle-class with property and business rights in the towns, they gave preference to Section 10s over newcomers. Verwoerd appealed to employers to stop giving jobs 'to work-seekers who stream in from outside [instead of] those who have grown up in the cities,' and declared that the only way 'to combat this evil is the closing of the urban labour market until the young urban seekers for work have been absorbed'[25]—a precursor of the later Riekert policy.

Influx controls had a number of different aims: (i) to restrict the number of Africans entering the 'white' areas, especially the

---

*The Section 10(1) amendments to the Natives (Urban Areas) Consolidation Act in 1952, 1955 and 1957 provided that Africans could only remain in a prescribed area for longer than 72 hours if he or she (a) had resided there continuously since birth; or (b) had worked there continuously for the same employer for ten, or for more than one employer for fifteen years; or (c) was the wife, unmarried daughter, or son under 18 of a man with Section 10(1)(a) or (b) rights who 'ordinarily' resided with him and had entered the area lawfully. Their rights were only granted for a particular prescribed area and were not transferable. Africans without (a), (b) or (c) rights could only work or reside legally in a prescribed area with special permission granted under Section 10(1)(d) of the Act, and technically they were all migrants. But the term 'Section 10' is popularly applied only to those with (a), (b) or (c) qualifications.

towns; (ii) to limit the terms of their presence there, preventing permanent settlement; (iii) to allocate labour, channelling a large proportion of it towards white farms; (iv) to facilitate social control—reducing urban unemployment, crime and slums, and as a weapon against political 'agitators': Section 29 of the Urban Areas Act, enabling the government to endorse 'idle and undesirable' blacks out of the towns, was used against political opponents; (v) to facilitate enforcement of residential segregation, not only for social but also for security purposes. In his speech on the Group Areas Act, Verwoerd stressed that the black townships must be 'an adequate distance from the white township . . . preferably separated by an area of industrial sites . . . [with] suitable open buffer spaces around . . . and a considerable distance from the main, and more particularly national roads'.[26] Security was also a major consideration behind the strict enforcement of influx control in the Western Cape (west of the Fish and Kat rivers—see map). In 1955, Eiselen announced that the government's intention was 'the ultimate elimination of Natives' from this area, in which coloured labour was to receive preference (though not against whites, of course). 'Surplus' Africans (women, children, the aged) would be sent back to the reserves and henceforth only migrants allowed in.[27] Verwoerd and Eiselen seem to have envisaged this as an area of retreat for whites in the event of an 'emergency' (see p. 31).

The Nationalists rejected the recommendation of the 1951 Industrial Legislation Commission that African *trade unions* should be recognised.[28] The 1953 Natives (Settlement of Disputes) Act explicitly barred Africans from the registered unions and provided for them a separate system of plant-level 'works committees', combined with mediation by state-appointed labour officers. African unions were not made illegal (although strikes by Africans were) but the government urged employers to ignore their unions, so that they would 'die a natural death'.[29] When some employers continued to recognise them, it was made illegal to deduct dues for African unions. Coloureds and Indians could remain members of the registered unions, but no further mixed unions were registered and racial segregation within the existing unions was encouraged.* Many trade unionists were 'named' as

*If they remained integrated, they had to be organised into separate racial branches, hold separate meetings, and have executive committees consisting of whites only.[30]

communists and banned or detained.* By the early 1960s, most of the African unions had been smashed.

The extension and institutionalization of *social segregation* was a feature of Nationalist rule. The Sauer Report stressed the need for 'the preservation of the white people in SA as a pure white race'. J. G. Strijdom, Prime Minister from 1954–58, explained to parliament that: 'If the European loses his colour sense he cannot remain a white man . . . and you cannot retain your sense of colour if there is no apartheid in the everyday social life.'[31] One of the NP's first measures was to extend the restrictions on sexual relations to coloureds and whites and to prohibit mixed marriages.[32] The tightening of legalized social segregation blocked off a major avenue of coloured advance—'passing for white'. It was estimated that in 1936 almost 40 per cent of whites in the Cape were of mixed descent.[33]

The 1953 Reservation of Separate Amenities Act legalized the provision of *un*equal facilities for different races, to counter the decision of the courts in 1952 that separate facilities must be equal. This was one of many measures eroding the power and discretion of the courts.** It was followed by a plethora of measures, such as the 'church clause' of the 1957 Native Amendment Act, extending compulsory segregation into churches, places of entertainment, clubs, buses and sport. Professional, sporting and cultural organizations refusing to comply were threatened with the withdrawal of their subsidies and licences. Provisions under the Group Areas Act and the Liquor Laws made social mixing difficult; people who ignored them attracted the attention of the security police. Legislation also required the provision in factories and offices of separate canteens and lavatories for workers of different races.[34]

The Nationalists did not share the concern of the wartime UP with African wages and welfare. The extension of job reservation

---

*The 1950 Suppression of Communism Act defined communism as any doctrine or scheme aimed at promoting any political, industrial, social or economic change in SA. The absurdity of this definition, and the credit which accrued to communism from its identification with opposition to apartheid, led to its being renamed the Internal Security Act in 1976. The power to ban and detain without trial, however, remained intact.

**Among others were the 1952 High Court of Parliament Act, the Suppression of Communism Act, the 1956 Natives (Prohibition of Interdicts) Act.

and suppression of African unions contributed to the reversal of the favourable wartime trends (see p. 43). Their indifference to African welfare can be seen in the pegging of funds for African education and the removal of Africans from the Unemployment Insurance Fund, and in numerous petty measures such as the curtailment of the school feeding scheme for African children, while that for richer whites was extended.[35]

However, the greater energy and interventionism of the Nationalists had some unexpected results, such as an increase in the number and proportion of African children at school (even though the principle underlying their education was abhorrent) and in slum clearance and new housing schemes (even though the houses were occupied on less secure terms). The number of family houses for Africans in Johannesburg increased from 9,938 in 1946 to 62,475 in 1965. The liberal SA Institute of Race Relations commented that 'within a static—if not regressive—state welfare policy, there has been one outstanding achievement in the past decade; African housing has been tackled with vigour and determination'.[36] These few positive policies had political effects, reducing opposition to the government (see Chapter 9).

The difference between the Nationalists and the wartime UP was not simply one of degree. The UP accepted the principle that Africans were a permanent part of SA society and committed themselves to a cautious policy of 'encouraging stabilization'. The Nationalists—representing the interests of a different section of the oligarchy—were determined to reverse this trend, to prise loose the ties of Africans with the white areas and strengthen their links with the tribal reserves, with all this implied for a whole range of socio-economic and political policies. Unlike the UP, the NP did not wish to blur the divisions between whites and coloureds, but to reinforce them. This was partly because of their obsession with race; partly (as will be shown below) because of the economic and political interests of Afrikaner nationalists.

'Separate development': The new face of apartheid, 1960–70

The Sharpeville shootings in March 1960, when police fired on unarmed demonstrators against the pass laws, killing seventy, provoked widespread unrest in SA, the flight of foreign capital and a storm of protest internationally, with UN resolutions of condemnation culminating in the 1963 voluntary arms embargo, supported by the UK and USA. When SA became a Republic in 1961, it withdrew from the commonwealth to forestall expulsion. Despite his granite response, Verwoerd was shaken by these reactions and concluded that a policy of unending white domination was untenable and that account must be taken both of the moral objections to apartheid and of complaints by businessmen that it impeded economic growth.

The resultant 'separate development' policy proclaimed that SA was not a multi-racial society, but consisted of many 'nations', each of which should have the right to control its destiny and preserve its identity. White SA would undertake to 'decolonise' the various African nations (Xhosa, Zulu, etc), each of which would get independence in its own homeland (nicknamed Bantustans by their critics). The territorial base for the homelands would be provided by the reserves, that 14 per cent of the land spread around SA in a fragmented horseshoe, comprising 81 large and 200 smaller blocks of land (see map). Each homeland would have as its citizens its *de facto* population, plus members of its tribe in 'white' SA, the *de jure* citizens. A separate dispensation would be worked out for coloureds and Indians, who would have to be accommodated within the white 'homeland'.

However, although the Tomlinson Report, which provided the blueprint for the policy, argued that 'no middle course' was possible in SA,[37] the need for African labour meant that only political, not economic, separation was envisaged. In 1950, Prime Minister Malan stated that complete territorial segregation, though 'ideal . . . was impracticable . . . [because] our whole economic structure is to a large extent based on native labour'.[38] This was reiterated by Verwoerd,[39] who stressed that it was not the aim to stop economic growth, but to control it and make it compatible with apartheid and white security.

The economic problems caused by limitations on the number and skill level of blacks in the white areas would be solved by the continuation of migrant labour and by the *decentralization of labour-intensive industries* to the borders of the Bantustans, where blacks could do more skilled work (and live with their families), thus easing the skill shortage and halting the urban influx. Industries in the white metropolitan areas would become more capital-intensive and less dependent on black labour. As Verwoerd argued:

Industry is the magnet which draws the Bantu into . . . 'European South Africa' . . . . This is the reason why . . . industry should be developed in close juxtaposition to Bantu areas suitable for this purpose . . . . The development of industry, under European ownership and control, must take place within a European area. But, if the labour needed for that industry can be housed in its own Bantu area, then a whole Bantu superstructure of social life and administration can be built there . . . . We do not want to stop the economic development of SA . . . [but] to reconcile the economic and social needs of the country . . . . [In the white areas, there should be] well-mechanized industries controlled by whites and staffed mainly by whites. Then one would at least have a chance of industrial peace in the heart and soul of the country, even though you may not have it in some border areas. The danger of economic disruption is much greater when there is a mixed fatherland with the same labour mass present everywhere. I would *prefer to have a smaller white state* in South Africa which will control its own army, its own navy, its own policy *. . . in the event of an emergency* . . . than a bigger state which has already been surrendered to Bantu domination. [But] this essential political independence here, just as in Europe where they are striving for a European market, is fully compatible with economic interdependence.[40]

There was a modification of the racist assumptions about black inferiority, which were now widely regarded as unscientific and morally reprehensible. The argument for racial separation was no longer based on claims about biological or genetic differences, but on cultural or ethnic differences and the right of each group to maintain its identity.

It was conceded that discrimination against Africans in the white areas was a negative aspect of the policy; but it was argued that Africans would be compensated by positive measures providing equivalent opportunities for them in the Bantustans, and by the discrimination against whites in these areas.

The Nationalists' unprecedented action in voluntarily fragmenting the country probably represented, as Bromberger suggested, an attempt to escape from (or externalize) the third world problems of poverty, population explosion and rising expectations, exacerbated by colour conflict, with which the white oligarchy—an outpost of the first world—found itself confronted within its own body politic.[41] In adopting this strategy, they were influenced by the independence of other African countries, particularly the nearby British territories of Botswana, Lesotho and Swaziland, which the Nationalists had initially hoped to incorporate into SA, as was provided for in the Act of Union but refused by the British government.[42]

Initially, it was denied that independence was envisaged for the SA homelands.[43] Verwoerd made the first public reference to the possibility of full independence in 1959, but this hint was not taken seriously either by his supporters or by his critics, and the grant of self-government to the Transkei in 1963 came as a shock to both groups.[44]

Land and economic development were obviously crucial for a policy of partition, but the launching of separate development was not accompanied by additional grants of land to the Bantustans. The prospects for economic development were dampened by Verwoerd's veto on the entry of private white capital and his rejection of the Tomlinson recommendation that £104m be spent on developing the reserves over ten years, on the grounds that this was based on 'the old system which this government inherited of doing everything for the native: the system of spoonfeeding'.[45] However, the Bantu Investment Corporation was established and began to buy out white traders in the homelands and to provide loans and technical assistance to set up Africans in their place. As an added incentive to African businessmen to move to these areas, further restrictions were placed on them in the white areas, where only businesses which provided the 'daily essential necessities of the Bantu' would be allowed (excluding, for example, dry-cleaners and garages); and Africans could not carry on more than one business, form partnerships and companies, nor alter business premises.[46]

The separate development policy led to a proliferation of new political institutions. The 1963 Transkei Constitution Act set up a Legislative Assembly (half elected, half chiefs) with powers to legislate on a small list of topics, subject to a SA veto. In 1968 the coloured parliamentary representatives were abolished and a partly-elected Coloured Persons Representative Council set up; a wholly appointed Indian Council was also established.* In addition, the 1968 Prohibition of Political Interference Act made racially mixed political parties, and even inter-racial political cooperation, illegal.

---

*In 1962, the Nationalists accepted the Indians as a permanent part of the SA population, accepting that voluntary repatriation was unworkable.

Labour Policy

The post-Sharpeville economic boom intensified the pressures from urban employers for the use of Africans in greater numbers and at higher skill levels. By the late 1960s the government believed it had evolved a labour policy which would permit 'the more effective utilization of Bantu labour' without undermining apartheid. The main elements of this supposedly more flexible policy were the 'floating' job bar and the decentralization of industry.

The floating bar involved the fragmentation and/or reclassification of traditionally white jobs, with the less skilled part being done by blacks while whites moved upwards to more skilled work. But it was stressed that: black advance had to take place in an 'orderly and controlled manner'; no white worker could be replaced by a black worker; no white should work under a black; there must be proper separation on the job between the races; if there was a recession, jobs that had been opened to blacks should, if required, revert to whites; and, finally, that the white unions must agree.[47]

Furthermore, black (particularly African) advance was to be limited and must not extend to skilled work, which Africans could only do in their 'own' areas, or in the service of their own people (as doctors or officials). A ceiling was thus placed on black (particularly African) advance in the white areas, and the training of Africans for skilled work (as builders, electricians, plumbers) was not allowed there.

An indication of the determination to keep Africans out of skilled jobs was the 1970 Bantu Laws Amendment Act, the most far-reaching measure of job reservation yet. It made possible the prohibition of the employment of 'a Bantu' in any job, in any area, or in the service of any employer. In 1967, Froneman, the deputy Minister of Bantu Affairs, rejected compulsory education for Africans on the grounds that there would not be enough jobs for them. In view of the acute skilled labour shortage, this underlined the point that Africans were not eligible for these jobs in white areas.[48]

A number of alternative strategems were officially advocated to ease the skill shortage, including (i) the expansion of the supply of white skills by retraining and upgrading white workers (if the floating bar was to remain intact *all* whites had to float upwards into more skilled and senior jobs); (ii) greater use of white women, who were encouraged to take on such traditionally male jobs as crane drivers at Iscor; (iii) increased white immigration: in 1948, the Nationalists had abandoned Smuts's ambitious immigration policy; but they now set up a well-funded Immigration Council and from 1960–70, there was a net gain of 250,000 white immigrants;* (iv) as a last resort, if no whites were available, coloureds and Indians (but not Africans) could be used in skilled jobs, provided the white unions agreed.

These stratagems, set out in the 1958 Viljoen Report and 1971 White Paper on decentralization, are evidence of the serious effort made to keep blacks out of skilled jobs.[50] It is necessary to stress this because of later claims that the job bar was so flexibly applied that it never inconvenienced businessmen.[51] The government's fear that the entry of Africans into skilled jobs would lead to greater pressures to stabilize them was borne out by subsequent events.

The quid pro quo for the 'floating bar' was the tightening of controls over black numbers and permanency in the towns. 'It remains Government policy,' said the Minister in charge of the Bantu Affairs Department (BAD), 'that our white cities, our metropolitan areas, will, in future, become whiter and not blacker . . . the Government deems the survival of the whites to be far more valuable than any temporary economic benefits'.[52] To ensure this, the controls had to be 'streamlined',[53] (i) to meet the complaints of businessmen about the costs and inconveniences of restrictions on labour mobility; and (ii) to get a more effective grip over the labour force in the face of a gradual but fundamental shift in labour supply, as the former acute labour shortages gave way to a surplus of unskilled black labour. This was due to rapid population growth,** overcrowding in the reserves, and the growing gap between rural and urban incomes.

A new instrument for the achievement of this was the decentralization of manufacturing industry to selected 'growth points' on the Bantustan borders. At first, the policy relied on inducements to businessmen—loans, subsidies, tax relief and concessions

---

*This compared with a total of 100,000 for 1935–58 and a net loss of 3,000 in 1960.[49]

**African population growth from 1960–70 was 3.57 per cent annually.

regarding the use of black labour in these areas. But the government soon resorted to coercion: sections 2 and 3 of the 1967 Physical Planning and Utilization of Resources Act (later renamed Environment Act) gave government wide powers to control the establishment and expansion of factories in white areas: expansion being defined as any increase in the number of African employees.

However, despite threats and inducements, businessmen remained unresponsive and few new jobs were created in the decentralized zones (see Chapter 3). In 1969 the Minister of Planning warned that, unless businessmen were more helpful, restrictions in the metropolitan areas would be tightened and 'not another acre' of land there would be proclaimed for industrial use.[54]

The squeeze on urban Africans intensified. The government stressed that even Africans legally in the towns were there on a temporary basis only. Section 10 rights were whittled away: from 1968 Africans could no longer own their own homes on thirty-year leasehold plots, but could only rent them. M. C. Botha, Minister of BAD, threatened 'to remove all and every one' of these sought-after rights, and it was decreed that the urban areas should not be made too attractive by the provision of 'luxuries', hence the low expenditure on urban amenities: the construction of family housing practically ceased by the mid-1960s.[55]

The Deputy Minister of BAD, Froneman, declared that of the six million Africans in white areas, only two million were economically active; the rest were 'surplus appendages' who should be deported to the Bantustans: it was the object of government policy 'to rely on migratory labour to an increasing extent'. The notorious 1968 Bantu Labour Regulations provided that, henceforth, Africans without Section 10 rights would be given work contracts for a maximum of one year only; at the end of each year they had to return to their homeland. These enforced breaks were then legalistically interpreted to mean that they were not working 'continuously' and could not therefore qualify for the much-coveted rights to greater security and family housing conferred by Section 10.[56] The pass laws were tightened: in 1968 prosecutions reached a peak of 700,000, affecting one in twenty Africans, although their incidence fell heavily on a specific group—those trying to work and live illegally in the towns.[57]

To manage the huge flow of migrants on annual contracts, the long-envisaged Labour Bureaux were activated.[58] These were also extended to Africans in the white rural areas, whom Verwoerd had previously left to the devices of white farmers and their District Labour Control Boards.[59] Renewed efforts were made to end the labour tenant system, which had persisted despite repeated attempts to abolish it (see pp. 46 and 89). The aim was to convert tenants into full-time labourers, or to resettle them and their families in the Bantustans. More generally, the government was concerned about the *verswarting* of the *platteland* (blackening of the white rural areas), due to the rapid growth of the black population there and the decline in the number of whites.[60] The attempt to ensure that Africans moving off the land went to the Bantustans and not to the white towns led to the extension of the Labour Bureaux and to other forms of state intervention such as population removals (discussed in Chapter 3).

This heavily bureaucratized and monstrous system was in place by 1970, reaching its zenith in the Bantu Labour Regulations (setting up the Labour Bureaux and reducing Section 10 rights), the Physical Planning Act (controlling the horizontal mobility of both capital and labour) and the 1970 Bantu Labour Amendment Act (extending job reservation).

The aims of this ever more complex network of controls had by then altered. The function of enlarging the supply of cheap unskilled labour, especially for white farms, gradually became superfluous, as the former labour shortages gave way to an oversupply of unskilled labour (coexisting with the shortage of skilled labour). Other functions of the horizontal controls then became more important, particularly (i) avoiding the social problems attending rapid urbanization, and (ii) the political/strategic role of keeping down African numbers in the white areas and keeping Africans tied to their 'homelands'. What remained constant, however, was the desire to retain control over the social forces unleashed by the most profound agricultural and industrial revolution in Africa.

Verwoerd's post-Sharpeville policies brought some material benefits to black labour. In contrast to the 1950s, the real wages of urban blacks rose, although the skilled labour shortage, and the strength of white unions, pushed up white wages even faster, so that black–white wage ratios widened. A similar pattern was evident in expenditure on education and welfare, with the absolute level rising, but the ratio with whites widening (see p. 43).

But suppression of the black (particularly African) middle class was unchanged, with continuing restrictions on entry to skilled jobs and on business and property rights. Instead, Verwoerd nurtured an alternative African elite, based on the Bantustans and heavily dependent on government support and favours.

The effects of apartheid

There are both Marxists and liberals who argue that, if the elaborate ideology is stripped away, apartheid is simply a harsh class system and that SA's development path is similar to that of many other countries in the early stages of industrialization. Others maintain that the impact of apartheid has been exaggerated and that the job bar, and restrictions on the availability of black labour, were frequently not implemented. The claim by the Minister of Labour in 1970 that only 2.9 per cent of the total labour force was potentially affected by job reservation determinations was cited as an instance of this.[61]

A striking correlation between occupation, income and race is shown by Tables 5 to 7 and 9 to 16. By 1970, whites were concentrated in the secondary and tertiary sectors (manufacturing, commerce, services) and the more skilled and white collar jobs; Africans dominated the primary sectors (agriculture, mining) and the low-wage, unskilled jobs; coloureds and Indians occupied a middle position.

This pattern could be the outcome of differing racial/ethnic capacities; of 'natural' market forces (reflecting the higher skill levels of scarce white labour); of the struggle between capital and labour at this harsh, early stage of capital accumulation; or of apartheid policies. Other societies also have wide income differentials and unequal distribution of educational, health and other resources, so that not all the inequality and other evils found in SA can be attributed to apartheid. Nevertheless, it will be argued here that apartheid played a crucial role in shaping the socio-economic patterns revealed by the Tables. Its effect was not to make SA a uniquely different society, but to shift the incidence of poverty systematically onto blacks. This exacerbated many of the usual social evils and denied blacks the chance to escape from them, which equality of opportunity, and various stages of the life-cycle, usually allows to at least some of the poor.

The impact of apartheid will be examined in relation to: the occupational structure, income distribution, and mobility and population distribution.

Apartheid's effect on the occupational structure

The job colour bar must be seen in relation to access to training and education. If blacks are excluded from engineering faculties, they will not become engineers, even in the absence of a formal job bar. Moreover, even when the job and training bars are relaxed, the advance into jobs requiring high skill levels cannot take place rapidly. Some observers missed the significance of successive relaxation or tightening of the job bar because they saw little immediate impact from this; but it obviously requires time for training and 'graduation' to take effect.

The mere existence of the institutionalized job bar is surely evidence that the racially ordered occupational structure was not the outcome of 'natural' economic or genetic factors. If these were the cause, the racial ordering would have come about of its own account, without the need for political intervention to establish the bar and then continually shore it up. This suggests that the job bar was established to prevent the occupational structure being shaped by market forces or individual aptitudes.

This elementary logic is borne out by an examination of what happened when the bar was absent or relaxed, or alternatively tightened. One extreme case was provided by white agriculture, where (despite high unemployment among whites before World War Two) the absence of the job bar led to their rapid displacement by blacks, even in skilled and managerial jobs (see Chapter 4). At the other extreme was the rigid, legal bar in mining, where the proportion of white workers was maintained, and even increased, despite a growing racial wage differential (which increased the inducement to substitute blacks for whites) and tremendous pressures by capital to erode the bar (see Chapters 5, 7 and 9).

In the state sector a similarly perverse tendency towards the employment of (more expensive) whites was evident after the proclamation of the 1924 'civilized labour' policy. Between 1924 and 1933 the number of whites employed by South African

Railways (SAR) rose from 4,760 to 17,783, or from 10 to 39 per cent of employees, while the number of blacks fell from 37,564 to 22,008, or from 75 to 49 per cent. In central and local government the proportion of whites rose from 45 to 64 per cent, while the number and percentage of blacks fell.[62]

The job bar was more difficult to enforce in private manufacturing, construction and commerce, with numerous small firms and lower levels of unionization, than in the mining industry with its few large employers and strong, vigilant unions to police the bar, or in the government-controlled state sector. Nevertheless it had an impact, not only on skilled jobs, for which training was required, but also on those semi-skilled and unskilled jobs in which minimum wages or closed shop agreements could be enforced by means of the 1922–5 labour legislation. Their combined effect could be seen in the perverse trend in these sectors during the depression, when the proportion of blacks in manufacturing declined from 44 to 40 per cent, while that of more expensive whites rose from 38 to 42 per cent. The proportion of whites in protected industries* was also higher: 57 compared with 42 per cent for all industries.[63]

The relaxation of the job colour bar during World War Two also had an impact on the occupational structure, even during this brief period. The view of many observers that blacks advanced into more skilled jobs and that there was a blurring of the former sharp division between skilled and unskilled workers, with the emergence of a racially mixed area of semi-skilled jobs, is borne out by the evidence of the 1951 Industrial Legislation Commission that whites in baking, furniture, millinery, sheet metal and electrical industries were being displaced by blacks despite minimum wages (i.e. even when the 'rate for the job' prevented undercutting), and that blacks 'largely dominate the semi-skilled market and have already penetrated the sphere of skilled labour to a not inconsiderable extent'.[64] At the same time, about 20 per cent of whites (and a much higher proportion of Afrikaners) were still in low skill jobs in 1948.[65] The black vanguard was thus overtaking the bottom group of whites, thereby undermining the hierarchical racial structure.

*The granting of protection was dependent on 'satisfactory' labour policies (see p. 19).

The Minister of Labour, Jan de Klerk, made similar claims about black advance, when justifying the extension of the legal job bar to manufacturing, construction and commerce in 1956. His own account suggests that the effects of the job bar have been underestimated and that, while it was never fully effective in these sectors, it went far beyond the 2.9 per cent of jobs that were formally reserved. This can be illustrated by the struggle over job reservation in the metal industries.

Job Reservation Determination No. 3 of 1958 reserved fifteen different operations for whites. The reason given was that some firms threatened to replace their white workers 'because of the competition experienced from firms who employed Bantu [at lower wages than were paid to whites] on such manufacture'. When the Industrial Council, representing both the employers and the trade unions, vetoed the determination, the government amended the IC Act in 1959, enabling it to over-rule decisions of the Industrial Councils.

The Industrial Councils, particularly employers, disliked statutory job reservation, which encroached on their powers to determine their own job and wage structures and introduced legal complications into the labour market. Minister de Klerk's comment on the reaction of the metallurgical industry to this increasing state intervention is illuminating:

> The introduction of work reservation caused employers to reconsider their attitude and gradually they became more amenable . . . so that it was no longer necessary for the determinations to remain in operation. With a few exceptions, wages were considerably increased so that the way was paved for the employment of white persons, and employers will in future also give preference to the more skilled white persons . . . . The parties to the Industrial Council have now solved their work reservation problems and it is trusted that the *spirit of cooperation* will prevail and that it will not again be necessary to use the machinery of section 77 in respect of the engineering industry . . . . It has always been the intention that industries should endeavour to solve their own problems and that section 77 should be put into operation *only as a last resort.*[66]

The case of the metal industries shows that the existence of statutory job reservation had a more far-reaching 'halo' effect[67] than the limited number of determinations (26 by 1970) suggests. The threat of legal investigation and statutory determinations persuaded employers to show 'that spirit of cooperation' which usually made it unnecessary to use the legal machinery to reserve jobs for whites.*

But even if 'only 2.9 per cent' of the total labour force were potentially affected by formal job determinations, this meant 217,500 jobs in 1970,[68] or 15 per cent of the 1.5 million employed whites. Add to this the 'halo' effect of the legal bar, and the effects of the 'civilized' labour policy in the state sector (which employed one-third of whites in 1970), and the number must be substantial.

In addition to this protection provided by official and statutory apartheid measures, the white unions used traditional trade union restrictive practices, such as the closed shop and control over entry to apprenticeships. An indication of their effectiveness was the virtual elimination of skilled coloured workers, who dominated the artisan trades in the Cape until the 1922–25 labour package. These measures did not explicitly discriminate against coloureds, but the white unions were able to use their power on the Industrial Councils and Apprenticeship Boards to freeze coloureds out: from 1932–5, out of 641 apprentices entering into contracts in Cape Town, only 36 were coloureds.[69]

The effects of apartheid in accounting for the virtual absence of blacks from the ranks of entrepreneurs and commercial farmers is unquantifiable. But the argument that this reflects lack of aptitude is unconvincing in view of the wide-ranging discrimination against them. This obvious point needs to be made because this rationalization is heard not only from racists, but also from free marketeers who turn a blind eye to history and to the institutional obstacles. It is true that Africans lacked an entrepreneurial tradition.** But the Afrikaans entrepreneurial tradition, particularly outside the Cape, was also weak compared with that of the English, and this did not preclude them from entering these professions. Many of them failed, as no doubt many Africans would also have done in the unstable economic conditions before World War Two. But

---

*This view was strengthened by my discussions with employers in 1970, before the legal constraints were relaxed. These revealed a large number of jobs in which they would have liked to employ blacks, if they did not fear that the white unions and labour inspectors would resort to legal means against them.

**According to Kuper, 'Neither the trader nor the industrialist was part of the traditional structure of southern African Bantu societies'[70] unlike those in West Africa.

many marginal whites must have been aided, and many blacks handicapped, by apartheid measures affecting businessmen and commercial farmers.

It is reasonable to assume that, without apartheid, many whites would have been unable to hold their own against the top group of blacks and that there would not have been such a close correlation between race and occupation, and that the wide racial wage differentials would have been narrower, because of the substitution of cheaper black for expensive white labour.

There were, however, also cases in which job reservation was not enforced. Until the acute shortages of skilled labour of the mid-1960s, these applied mainly to attempts to enforce a ratio of white to black workers, of which the best example was the clothing industry.

Job Reservation Determination No. 1 of 1957 laid down complicated racial ratios for the clothing industry in different parts of the country. The Department of Labour declared that its object was to prevent the increasing dependence of the industry on African workers and to protect not only whites, but also coloureds and Indians from being replaced by them.[71] In the Transvaal, 70 per cent of the jobs were reserved for whites, the rest for coloureds.

However, faced with growing evidence of the shortage of white, and even coloured, workers (moving out of this traditionally low-wage industry) the ratio was later reduced to 25 per cent of white workers and 37½ per cent of coloureds. The impossibility of meeting even this target (there were few coloureds in the Transvaal) led to large-scale evasions or exemptions. In 1969, only 8 per cent of the jobs were filled by whites; about a third by coloureds; the remaining 60 per cent by Africans, whom the government had therefore failed to eliminate from the Transvaal clothing industry.[72] This was not for want of trying, and they did not give up, but resorted to the Physical Planning Act in an attempt to force this labour-intensive industry to decentralize, so as to reduce the number of Africans in the Transvaal metropolitan areas.

The metallurgical and clothing industries were thus at opposite ends of the spectrum; but both cases—the government's success in imposing its policy on the former and its failure to do so with the latter—refute Blumer's view of economic forces 'nestling' into the apartheid structures (see p. 5). Either the institutional structure had to be shored up by legal means, which then had to be continually tightened against evasion and loopholes; or the policy was unenforceable and had to be changed. In neither case (and these two industries accounted for over 40 per cent of manufacturing employment) did economic forces readily accommodate themselves to the socio-political structure. On the contrary, the *raison d'être* for apartheid was to counter the natural tendency of market forces to substitute cheaper (black) for more expensive (white) workers.

Apartheid's effect on income distribution

Tables 9 to 12 show that racial income distribution was highly unequal; among the most highly-skewed in the world according to some analysts.[73] Whatever the difficulties of comparing national income statistics, there was no doubt about widespread poverty among blacks, nor about rising affluence among whites after World War Two, when the serious 'poor white' problem had been solved.

This inequality did not simply reflect market forces (i.e. the scarcity and abundance of various kinds of labour or other factors of production). First, income distribution was obviously influenced by apartheid measures affecting the occupational structure and ownership of assets. Second, the differential did not narrow over time, as was the case in most other industrializing societies;[74] on the contrary, it was wider in 1970 than in the pre-war period. Third, there were variations between periods and sectors and these were correlated with the strength of apartheid. During the war years, when apartheid was relaxed, the differential narrowed; thereafter as apartheid was tightened, it widened (see Table 10). The differential was much narrower in manufacturing and commerce, where apartheid was less effectively enforced, than in gold mining with its rigid job bar, where the ratio of white to black wages was most extreme, and widened from 12.7 to 1 in 1946 to 20.9 to 1 by 1971. Yet this ultra-wide differential did not reflect skill differences, for the skill levels of the average white miner were not high, requiring low educational qualifications and a short period of training (see Chapter 7). In the state sector, in accordance with the 'civilized labour' policy, whites were paid more than blacks for the *same* job and qualifications, for example as teachers, nurses or policemen.

The effect of apartheid on racial shares of income and wage

differentials seems incontestable. But the claim that in absolute terms blacks, and particularly Africans, gained nothing from SA's rapid economic growth, that it even led to their immiserization, must, with some qualifications, be rejected.[75] The evidence available shows that during this half century, a growing number and proportion of blacks, including Africans, gained from SA's rapid economic growth, particularly from the movement out of the low-wage primary into the higher-wage urban sectors and from rising real wages in the latter.[76]

In 1921 approximately 496,000 Africans (out of a total African population of 4.7m) were in these urban jobs. By 1970, the number had risen to 2.3m out of 15m Africans. If it is assumed that roughly one-third were economically active, this accounts for 31 per cent of economically active Africans in 1921 and 46 per cent in 1970—a rising proportion at a time of rapid population growth. Urban sector jobs for coloureds and Indians grew from 155,000 jobs in 1921 to 676,000 in 1970, or from 56 to 75 per cent of the economically active.[77]

Table 10 shows that in manufacturing and construction (which set the trend for urban wages) African *real* wages (allowing for inflation) almost trebled between 1916 and 1970. There were similar trends, at a higher level, for coloureds and Indians. The rise was uneven, with real wages falling, for example, during the first decade of nationalist rule; but they rose over the half-century as a whole. Moreover, these increases were not limited to a small elite: wages for unskilled Africans also rose, particularly during World War Two, when there was a flat-rate increase for all workers, which favours the lower-paid.[78]

The main exceptions to these rising real wages were the primary sectors. There is little information on the wages of Africans in white agriculture until the 1960s, when real wages rose by about a sixth, though from a much lower level than urban wages[79] (see Table 12). However, during the preceding period, real farm wages may, as some observers believed, have been static or even declining. This was certainly the case on the gold mines where, as Wilson showed, real wages of Africans declined over the period as a whole (see Table 11). But the gold mines were not typical of the SA economy, because of their heavy dependence on foreign African labour, with lower opportunity cost (that is, lower potential earnings from alternative jobs). SA Africans would not take the arduous, low-paid mining jobs: in 1970, 80 per cent of Africans on the mines were foreign (see Table 8). Moreover, while the mines were once a major employer of African labour, by 1970 they employed 370,000, 7.4 per cent of economically active Africans.

There is least information on the 25–30 per cent of Africans in (largely subsistence) homelands agriculture or unemployed. Static or declining output and rising population growth in the reserves must have led to declining per capita incomes, except to the extent that these were offset by remittances from migrants, on which these areas became increasingly dependent.* Recent research shows that, at least from 1960, remittances from rising urban wages led to rising per capita incomes;[81] though this poorest group seems likely to have gained least from economic growth.

These material gains must be seen in the context of low absolute standards, glaring racial inequalities and other costs of discrimination; but they should not be ignored, both because of the light they cast on the nature and possibilities of the social system and because of their relevance to political behaviour.

Apartheid's effect on mobility and population distribution
It is notoriously difficult to enforce controls which conflict with powerful economic interests (capital's need for workers; labour's need for jobs). Even Stalin failed to achieve full control over mobility in the USSR.[82]** In SA, the controls over mobility were a continual source of dissension within the oligarchy (see Chapter 6). Despite a huge bureaucracy to enforce them, there was large-scale evasion and their net effect on mobility and population distribution is difficult to gauge.

Tables 2 and 3 show that African movement into the white areas, particularly the towns, was not halted, but that it lagged behind that of all other groups. According to Cilliers, the growth rate of African urbanization slowed from 6.4 per cent in 1946–50 to 3.9 per cent in the 1960s.[84] From 1960–70, while the absolute number of Africans in the white areas continued to grow, the

---

*In an earlier paper I argued that the output of black agriculture has been underestimated and that this explained why many blacks were able to turn down jobs on the mines and white farms. But while this would lead to an upward revision of the absolute level of subsistence derived from black farming, it would not alter the trend over time.[80]

**And see Locke on interest rates.[83]

proportion there declined from 63 to 54 per cent. In the absence of the controls, rising population growth in the Bantustans, and the growing gap between rural and urban wages, would normally have led to *increased* migration into the white areas, particularly the towns.

Likewise, although the Nationalists did not succeed in reversing or even halting the stabilization that took place under the wartime UP (the proportion of women legally in the towns rose from 36 per cent in 1946 to 42 per cent in 1970),[85] they nevertheless slowed it down. By 1970 an estimated one-third of African workers in the white areas were still migrants and sex ratios remained highly unbalanced, both in white areas, where the ratio of males to females aged 20–49 was 160 to 100, and in the Bantustans, where the ratio was 40 to 100.[86]

Migrancy is common in the early stages of industrialization, particularly among the young, with levels of about 10 per cent;[87] but the level usually declines as workers marry and settle down with their families. Apartheid restrictions on stabilization obviously contributed to its unusually high level and persistence in SA.

Apartheid thus had a major impact on black mobility and population distribution; but even during the 1960s, when the controls were at their zenith, the absolute number of Africans legally in the white areas increased from 6.8 to 8 million. In the Cape peninsula, where the policy was most strictly enforced, the census showed that black numbers officially increased by 70 per cent.[88] It was moreover widely agreed that the *illegal* increase was much greater: officials acknowledged that the black population of the Cape peninsula was far greater than the census figure; similar estimates were made for other parts of the country.[89] 'White' SA had not therefore become whiter.

Furthermore, the 'shift' to the Bantustans was overstated by the legalistic device of incorporating a number of townships, such as Mdantsane and Kwamashu into them: the inhabitants did not move but were simply reclassified as being part of the Bantustan. There was also a much fuller enumeration of homeland Africans in 1970 than in earlier censuses,[90] thus exaggerating their population increase, while in 'white' areas illegal Africans evaded the census.

An example of the constraints on the government's ability to enforce its policies was the persistence of African labour tenancy in the white rural areas, despite repeated edicts since Union to get rid of it. In 1970, when it was 'finally abolished', there were still over half a million illegal tenants in Natal.[91] Tenancy was by then a dying institution; but it had proved remarkably resilient in the face of the enormous coercive power of the SA state.

Migrancy and other evils associated with apartheid are generally not unique to SA, but government policy perpetuated and exacerbated them. Their severity was lessened by large-scale evasion, which makes it difficult to assess their effects; but the degree of implementation was sufficient to intensify suffering among the poorest groups and to cause perverse economic trends.

Apart from their devastating human effects, the elaborate system of horizontal controls had far-reaching economic and political consequences. The SA labour market did not conform to the two-sector model of many industrializing societies with labour moving from the 'undeveloped' (or at least low-income) rural sector into the higher-wage modern sector.[92] Instead, there was a highly fragmented and rigid labour market, with the state intervening in an attempt to channel labour from the reserves in three separate streams (to white farms, mines and towns) and to prevent movement between them, especially from the white farm to the urban streams. The state also attempted to keep separate a fourth stream of foreign black labour which, from the 1960s, was channelled almost exclusively to the mines.*

As economists continually point out, rigid and fragmented labour markets impose costs; they also, however, confer benefits. The costs and benefits of this system to various segments of the oligarchy will be a major theme of this book, as will the profound political effects—the creation of an elaborate system of authoritarian controls with a huge bureaucracy to administer them and with a vested interest in their survival.

By 1970, apartheid had been intensified by all the criteria set out above: there was more segregation and discrimination; the hierarchical race structure had been reinforced; and apartheid was more thoroughly institutionalized and legalized. To enforce this, there was also increasing authoritarianism and brutal crushing of opposition (discussed in Chapter 9).

However, there had been some indications of other, less bleak

---

*In accordance with the recommendations of the 1962 Froneman Committee that foreign black labour be phased out, except for the mines.[93]

possibilities, notably the limited erosion of apartheid during the war years (and to a lesser extent in 1920–24*), and the material benefits which an increasing number and proportion of blacks derived from economic growth. These suggested that, despite the gross inequalities and ideological rigidity, there might be possibilities for the extension to blacks of the good things in life and their fuller incorporation into society, and that Bromberger's concept of the queue—with whites at the head, followed by coloureds and Indians, and then Africans—might be a better key to understanding SA development than an unbridgeable line which blacks could never cross.

At the same time as apartheid reached its zenith during the late 1960s, these more hopeful possibilities unexpectedly revived, with the first signs of the erosion of the job colour bar and of social apartheid—trends which belong logically in Chapter 3.

---

*The modest signs of some less racist policies during this period were too swiftly reversed to be dealt with in this brief survey; but they are revealing for the analysis of interests and power and will be briefly referred to in Chapter 9.

3
The Partial Erosion of Apartheid, 1970–84

'Reform, that you may preserve.'

Macaulay, in the House of Commons debate on the 1832 Reform Act

'The narrow policy of preserving without any foreign mixture the pure blood of the ancient citizens, had checked the fortune and hastened the ruin of Athens and Sparta. The aspiring genius of Rome sacrificed vanity to ambition . . . . The grandsons of the Gauls who had besieged Julius Caesar in Alesia . . . were admitted into the Senate of Rome. Their ambition, instead of disturbing the tranquility of the state, was intimately connected with its safety and greatness.'

Edward Gibbon, *Decline and Fall of the Roman Empire*, vol. 1

'The more a ruling class is able to assimilate the more prominent men of a ruled class, the more solid and dangerous is its rule.'

Karl Marx, *Capital*, vol. 3

Observers disagree as to whether the changes taking place in SA reform or merely modernize apartheid. The debate is confused by a preoccupation with motives, which are often ambivalent or hypocritical, and therefore difficult to gauge, and may in any case have unintended consequences.* It will be argued here that what is actually happening is a contradictory and confusing mixture of reform (particularly in the socio-economic sphere) and mainten-ance of apartheid (especially politically).[1]

Ideological shifts
Vorster's departure from the rigid, clearcut Verwoerdian doctrines was abrupt. But he presented it as part of 'the natural evolution of separate development' by the device of *multinationalism*. This

*The relevance of self-interest in assessing the significance of the changes is discussed in Chapter 10.

49

doctrine, first applied in social policy, continued to give priority to ethnic groups over individuals, but maintained that once the identities of the various black and white 'nations' of SA were securely established, they could mix and cooperate with each other as they did with other nations. Apartheid measures to protect their identities and 'prevent friction' could then wither away. Multi-nationalism thus provided a way round apartheid.

Whereas observers once overlooked the pragmatic elements in the policies of Malan and Verwoerd—particularly their recognition that total economic separation was impossible—they now overlooked the role of moral factors in Vorster's policies, terming them entirely pragmatic. But while Vorster stressed that economic imperatives, and black and international hostility, were compelling reasons for change, he repeatedly preached, to an electorate schooled in racism, that blacks were as good as whites, that 'one does not have the right to belittle and ridicule the human dignity of others,' and that blacks must be treated not 'as labour units but as human beings with souls'. He declared that 'Africa has been good to us [whites] and we are prepared, as far as our means allow us, to return to Africa a measure of what we have so generously received' by contributing to its development and by extending opportunities to blacks.[2] In a speech to the UN Security Council in October 1974, the SA Ambassador acknowledged that racial discrimination existed in SA, that it was unjust and should be removed. Despite the failure to live up to these principles, they had an impact on the norms of whites and expectations of blacks.

But, although Vorster confronted the white electorate with these moral and political problems and took the first steps towards socio-economic reform, he also reassured the electorate that the changes could be accommodated by modifying, rather than jettisoning, apartheid. Indeed this was essential, as he did not have a vision of an alternative society, but continued to believe in the need for a 'racially differentiated' society, with measures to protect separate identities, such as the Mixed Marriages and Immorality Acts, residential and educational separation, the Land Act, and separate political institutions.

P. W. Botha, who succeeded Vorster in 1978, had some idea of an alternative society, and a greater sense of urgency: 'We are moving in a changing world, we must adapt otherwise we shall die.' He urged Afrikaners to learn the lessons of their own history:

'the moment you start oppressing people . . . they fight back . . . .
We must acknowledge people's rights and . . . make ourselves free
by giving to others in a spirit of justice what we demand for
ourselves.'[3]

Botha argued that people should not become 'too emotional'
about white or Afrikaner identity, and that if they did not have the
will to preserve their identity 'no law can do it for them.' He was
strongly committed to the incorporation of the coloureds, referring to them and the whites as 'relatively one nation' and reportedly
said he wished to devote his life to improving relations between
white and coloured Afrikaners.[4] His intentions towards Africans
were obscure and they suspected that his aim was to exclude them
and to divide blacks more effectively by 'creaming off' coloureds
and Indians, thus prolonging a more diluted form of white rule.

Botha called for more far-reaching changes, declaring that laws
such as the Land Act and the Mixed Marriages and Immorality
Acts should not be treated as 'holy cows; if circumstances make
changes necessary, I will change laws.' His government propounded the principle that, 'A white monopoly of power is
untenable in the Africa of today . . . a meaningful division of power
is needed between all race groups.'[5] 'Our dilemma', he said, 'is to
maintain effective and orderly government on the one hand and to
satisfy the legitimate aspirations of people on the other . . . an
atmosphere must be created [favourable to reform which was a
long-term] process that could not be introduced all at once.'[6]

Botha's 'total strategy' for survival and 'free enterprise' values
(necessitating the withdrawal of state intervention from many
areas of life) provided conservative slogans for further deracialization, involving a shift from a race-based to a more class-based
society, and for the creation of a new national identity. But it is not
yet clear how inclusive this will be: his 1983 constitution included
coloureds and Indians in separate houses but still totally excluded
Africans.

Political change

Political changes exemplified the ambivalence of multinationalism, involving some expansion of political participation but on an
ethnically separate basis, and in a form so complex and bizarre that
it was difficult to gauge its effect or even workability.

The reincorporation of the coloureds into the white political system was achieved via a circuitous route. First, in 1968, separate coloured and Indian councils were set up (see p. 32). These proved unworkable, but Vorster rejected the 1976 Theron Commission recommendation that coloureds be granted direct representation in parliament. Instead, the coloured and Indian councils were in effect converted into elected chambers in the new three-chamber parliament established by the 1983 constitution.* They were thus incorporated into the central parliament in the context of an elaborate restructuring of the political system (rather than by a straightforward extension of the franchise as in nineteenth-century England), including strengthening of the power of the executive president at the expense of parliament.

For Africans, there was a different dispensation. Vorster adhered to Verwoerd's scheme of separate political institutions based on the homelands, through which Africans living in the 'white' areas must also exercise their political rights. The process of Bantustan development was accelerated: Legislative Assemblies (partly elected, partly nominated chiefs) and Executive Councils were rapidly set up for the remaining Bantustans; more powers were transferred to them culminating from 1976 in 'independence' for Transkei, Bophutatswana, Venda and Ciskei.

As the homelands became independent, Africans belonging to the relevant ethnic group (Xhosa, Tswana, etc.) became for-

---

*A House of Representatives for the 2.5m coloureds and House of Deputies for the 0.8m Indians were added to the House of Assembly for 4.5m whites. Members of the three Chambers are directly elected by universal suffrage, except for the President's right to appoint 4 members to the white house and 2 each to the coloured and Indian houses. The 178 white MPs, 85 coloureds and 45 Indians—a ratio of 4:2:1—formed the basis for their votes in the electoral college which chooses the President for a 5-year term. In effect, the dominant party in the white parliament has the majority.

Each ethnic chamber has a Minister's Council and Chairman and is responsible for its 'own' affairs (education, local government). 'General' affairs (defence, African affairs) are conducted by the State President and his appointed cabinet. 'General' legislation is discussed in 'joint standing committees' and requires the assent of all three chambers. Disputes between the chambers will be settled by the President and the President's Council (partly elected by the electoral college, and partly appointed by the President).

eigners in SA.[7] Connie Mulder, Minister of Bantu Affairs—or 'Plural Relations' as he rechristened it—explained that when the policy reached its 'full logical conclusion . . . there will not be one black man [i.e. African] with SA citizenship' and the problem of their political rights in SA would disappear.[8] By 1984, 5m Africans in the Bantustans had lost their SA citizenship as well as an additional 3.5m of their respective ethnic groups in 'white' SA. This denationalization was the main reason why some of the Bantustans, led by Kwazulu, refused independence, and why the 'independent' Bantustans were not internationally recognised.

Botha continued the Bantustan policy, but there were some signs that this too might be a circuitous path en route to some form of incorporation into a common political system. First, despite denationalization, Botha recognised the permanence of the urban Africans (see below), stopping the erosion of Section 10 rights and extending property rights and local government* to them. Second, Botha said he understood African fears about loss of citizenship and would not press independence on unwilling Bantustans, and that, while he would prefer urban Africans to exercise their political rights via their homelands, if 'for practical reasons' they cannot be accommodated like this, then the local authorities could be upgraded and they could 'receive a say in some coordinated form or other in this Council of States where the Constellation of States deliberate on matters of common interest.'[9]

Finally, Botha and his close advisors regarded the new constitution as transitional; Chris Heunis, the minister responsible, frequently emphasised that it was not a final solution to SA's problems. The Prime Minister declared: 'We do not know what tomorrow will bring. We are not prophets. This is a step in the dark. We can only proceed into the future with faith.'[10] This curious (to many disconcerting) admission, was a signal that further changes in the basic political framework were envisaged; though Botha, faced with a right-wing breakaway over the limited

---

*The 1982 Black Local Authorities Act established Community Councils for Urban Africans with powers comparable to those of white municipalities, although there were problems about their financing because the lack of freehold property rights for Africans reduced the normal major source of revenue for town councils.

political incorporation of coloureds and Indians, was evasive about the form this would take.*

The Constellation of States

Botha was more forthcoming about his belief that new political arrangements for blacks must take place within a restructuring of the whole southern African region. This regional dimension, and its connection with internal changes, formed a vital element of his thinking.

Vorster had reluctantly retreated from the isolationist policies of Verwoerd, who disliked foreign influences, was glad to leave the Commonwealth in 1961, and refused the offer of diplomatic relations with Ghana in 1958 and Zambia in 1964. Vorster became convinced that the key to ending international hostility towards SA lay in closer relations with African states, hence his attempts to establish 'detente' with them.[12]

These ideas were enthusiastically pursued by Botha, who believed that regional relationships were linked not only with SA's international, but also with its internal, problems. His Constellation of States, stretching as far north as Zaire, would provide the enlarged common market favoured by SA business interests, as well as an institutionalization of the degree of economic integration which already existed: 'more than a mere Common Market or trading bloc is envisaged . . . a full package of trading links, technological links, transport links . . . the exchange of knowhow, capital and credit.'[13]

The Constellation would also have a security function: 'non-aggression pacts' would help to neutralize subversion and the threat of international sanctions against SA. Botha was vague about the Constellation's political form, both because of the fears and suspicions of neighbouring African states and because of opposition from his right wing. For the present, 'it would not be possible to establish common consultative structures and secretariats . . . . The political will to cooperate is ultimately decisive in allowing cooperation to thrive fully. This political will can often

---

*The 1982 breakaway by the *verkramptes* under Andries Treurnicht was precipitated by Botha's advocacy of 'power sharing' between the races and his refusal to disown the statement made in an NP policy document that 'there can logically only be one government in a country'.[11]

be significantly strengthened by expanding relations in non-political technical and economic fields . . . [this could] lead to the creation of a climate conducive to development and regional solidarity.'

The abortive 1982 proposal for the cession of SA land (and one million black citizens) to Swaziland was an indication of the radical steps Botha was contemplating.* Such physical restructuring became more comprehensible if seen as part of a longterm process in which the various parts of the region that were being separated came together again in a new form. This new form, said Botha, could be 'a federation or confederation';** 'people can call it confederation or whatever they like'—statements which hardly seemed compatible with the assurance that members of the Constellation would 'maintain their individual sovereign status'.[14]

This obscurity, disconcerting to left and right alike, seemed to reflect the uncertain, experimental nature of Botha's policies as much as his political difficulties. The most coherent explanation of this tortuous policy—which seemed to have as its goal the eventual reunification of the numerous ethnically based structures and polities—was given by the Prime Minister's economic advisor, Simon Brand. Acknowledging the contradiction between increasing socio-economic integration and continued political separation, Brand said it would be 'naive' to think that African political demands could be defused by economic concessions alone but that, 'by satisfying the economic aspirations of Africans, we could play a major role in changing the climate in which political demands are made.' African demands might then be made 'in a more constructive and peaceful way,' while whites, used to the experience of economic cooperation, would also react differently. Brand concluded: 'There can only be one overall goal—greater emphasis on the things we have in common and less on the areas of conflict. If we progress along this road, it becomes a lot easier to think in terms of political solutions.'[15] In the meantime, Africans are excluded from the central political system and fearful of the practical consequences of denationalization; while the incorporation of coloureds and Indians remains limited.

*This included the Ingwavuma region of Kwazulu, which successfully challenged in the SA Courts the cession of its land and citizens to Swaziland.
**A confederation is an association of independent, sovereign states; a federation is a closer association under an over-riding central authority.

Socio-economic changes

It is curious that apartheid was first officially relaxed in the *social* sphere. Usually social advance follows economic and political advance. (The external pressures which contributed to this inversion of the normal process are discussed in Chapter 9.) The manner in which sport was deracialized was typical of the Nationalists' step-by-step approach, with each stage accompanied by the declaration that no further changes were intended, and by the initial attempt to contain the changes within the tortuous multinational framework.

In 1967, Vorster reversed Verwoerd's refusal to accept Maoris in the visiting New Zealand rugby team or to permit a mixed team to represent SA at the 1968 Mexico Olympics.* The prohibition on multiracial sport within SA remained, but in 1971 it was decreed that multinational sport would be allowed: each group must play sport separately at club, provincial and national level, but the various black and white 'nations' of SA could compete against each other at special 'open international' events, both inside and outside the country.[16]

In 1976 it was announced that the separate sports clubs, to which members of each race must belong, could play against each other. In 1977 racial restrictions on club membership and use of club amenities were relaxed,[17] and in 1979 a single state department was created to cater for the sporting activities of all races.

In 1980, the government accepted the recommendation of the Human Sciences Research Council (HSRC) that discriminatory legislation was unacceptable in sport and that sporting organizations should have the autonomy to determine their own membership, including the right to differentiate on the basis of race. The aim, said the Minister of National Education, Gerrit Viljoen, was not to compel integration or segregation, but to 'depoliticize' sport.[18] Amendments were made to the Group Areas, Liquor and Urban Areas Acts, removing remaining legal barriers to multiracial sport.

The question of inter-racial school sport then became a conten-

---

*Vorster's decision was one of the reasons for the first breakaway by the *verkramptes* under Albert Hertzog in 1969.

tious issue, causing public dissension between cabinet ministers. In 1980, P. W. Botha supported the entry of coloured, and in 1981 of African, teams into the Craven school rugby tournament and other sporting events.

There was variation in the progress made in different sports, with more deracialization in athletics, soccer and boxing than in rugby. However, by 1982, the Verwoerd sports policy had been reversed; an increasing number of sporting events were being integrated down to club level, and in some instances even at interschool level.

There were similar trends in regard to *social mixing*. In 1971, during the state visit of President Banda of Malawi, a 'multi-national' banquet was given at which whites sat alongside not only foreign, but also local, blacks. Multinational mixing was soon extended to cover all foreign blacks (being courted as part of the detente policy), the Bantustan leaders, and the urban black elite (businessmen, journalists, trade unionists, etc.). After two decades during which social contact had become increasingly difficult, it became fashionable for whites to mix with the black elite at conferences, meetings and social gatherings. To get over the awkwardness caused by the special permission required for these occasions, a few select hotels and restaurants were awarded 'international' status in 1975. By 1983 over a hundred had received this classification and South Africans belonging to the different 'nations' could then mix with one another as equals—if they could afford the prices.[19]

Public amenities were gradually opened to blacks. Vorster stated that, in principle, the NP remained committed to the provision of separate amenities, but where this was not practical, they could be shared.[20] Some town councils, such as Krugersdorp, announced their intention of taking action in consultation with local blacks; others, such as Boksburg were non-committal or resisted. The Johannesburg City Council took a leading role in opening libraries, parks, art galleries and the zoo, which were soon being used by thousands of blacks. As part of the campaign against 'petty apartheid', many 'whites only' signs on lifts, entrances and park benches were removed and blacks could join the Automobile Association and use the same ambulance service as whites. During the mid-1970s, and again in the early 1980s, backlashes against reform, particularly in the Transvaal, led to local attempts to resegregate some amenities, such as the Pretoria parks, but the overall trend was towards gradual desegregation.[21]

Soon after Botha became Prime Minister, he startled party activists at the traditionally conservative NP congresses by questioning the need for the Mixed Marriages and Immorality Acts and by his statement that people of different colours could 'really love each other and want to get married'. He pointed to biblical precedents for mixed marriages which were 'not a sin'. This was not, however, an encouragement to permissive behaviour: 'Immorality of any sort must be fought in a Christian country. If we can improve the Immorality Act, not only in connection with people of different races, but in all areas, I will be amenable to the suggestion.'[22] (It is not clear whether Botha meant that the Immorality Act should be 'improved' by the prohibition of *all* 'immorality', regardless of colour or creed . . .) Botha allowed some Indians and coloureds with white wives to return to SA,[23] but the resistance to reform within the NP meant that in 1984 the old measures were still on the statute book.

Residential segregation was also retained. However, the first exceptions were made for black diplomats, including those from independent Bantustans, who could reside in white suburbs. In SWA/Namibia, the disputed UN trust territory controlled by SA, the 1979 Abolition of Racial Discrimination Act made provision for the opening of all public amenities and residential areas to all races. Penalties were prescribed for infringements of these provisions—apartheid became a crime!

The international status of Namibia meant it was not necessarily a precedent for the rest of SA. Residential segregation is, however, a key issue for coloureds and Indians. As their representatives entered the new parliament in 1984, it seemed likely there would be growing pressures from them over this.

It is a measure of the extent to which apartheid had been systematically extended to envelop the most personal, and often trivial, aspects of life that this huge structure had to be so laboriously dismantled and that these issues—which most democrats would regard as outside the legitimate sphere of state control—were so strenuously contested and of such symbolic importance.

The Erosion of Economic Apartheid

There were major erosions of the vertical colour bar (business opportunities, job bar, access to training and education) and of discrimination in the related areas of income distribution and workers' rights. The arguments of businessmen and liberals about the costs of apartheid were now reinforced by the government's concern about security and the need to give blacks a stake—'to open the system in order to save it and build on it'.[24] This involved a departure from the Verwoerdian policy of suppressing the growth of black skilled and middle classes.

Restrictions on coloured and Indian businessmen and farmers were eased. Botha accepted the 1979 Riekert Commission's recommendation that restrictions on African businessmen in the townships should also be eased and that designated 'free trade areas' be established, both in the white areas and in the African townships, where businessmen of all races could operate.[25] The Industrial Development Corporation (IDC), which had assisted many white businessmen, extended its mandate to cover blacks, and the Small Business Development Corporation was set up to provide training and aid. Property ownership was extended by huge house-building programmes: in 1983 almost half-a-million state-owned houses were put up for sale, mainly to Africans, at bargain prices.

However, by 1984, there was still not complete freedom of operation for blacks in white areas (nor for white capital in black areas) and there was still a long way to go in dismantling the formal apartheid structure, let alone in neutralizing the effects of decades of exclusion of blacks from the market place.

The job bar

In major speeches in 1973, Vorster and the Finance Minister, Nico Diederichs, announced that blacks, including Africans, would be allowed to do skilled work in the white areas, 'with the concurrence of the white unions'.[26] As will be seen below, they began to do these jobs whether or not the trade unions concurred. In 1979, Botha accepted the Wiehahn Commission's recommendation that Section 77 of the IC Act (providing for job reservation) be abolished and the existing determinations phased out.[27]

Also abandoned was the sacred rule that the hierarchical structure (or ratchet) must be kept intact, with blacks always working under whites. The first official inroad into this was in the army: in

1975, the military disciplinary code was amended giving blacks in the defence force the same status as whites of equal rank: henceforth whites would have to take orders from, and salute, senior black officers;[28] and Nationalist politicians began to tell whites that they would have to be willing to work under 'non-whites'.[29] In 1977, when businessmen issued Codes of Conduct committing themselves to equal employment opportunities, including merit-based employment and promotion (see Chapter 6), the government stated it no longer objected to this principle.[30]

The conventional colour bar was also undermined, with attacks on the 'closed shop' by Fanie Botha,[31] Minister of Manpower Utilization (as the Department of Labour was renamed) and the expansion of black education and training, notwithstanding resistance by white unions.

Education and training

In 1972, the Minister of Labour was still reiterating that: 'The policy of this government . . . is to refrain from training and using Africans as skilled workers in white areas.'[32] The turning-point came in the 1973 speeches by Diederichs and Vorster, who declared that: 'it would be of little avail if new, more advanced job opportunities were opened up for non-white workers who were not equipped to take advantage of them because of a lack of suitable training.'[33] The Van Zyl Committee was appointed to determine the need for training facilities for black workers in 'approved work categories'. Its report led to the establishment of government-run industrial training centres in the townships, as well as centres managed and financed by private industry in white industrial complexes, with hundred per cent tax rebates on training costs incurred by employers.[34] Training was supposed to be limited to skills released to blacks with the concurrence of the white unions, but often took place without this.*

To prevent blocking of black training by the unions, the Wiehahn Commission recommended that blacks be trained in

---

*For example, the Motor Industry Employees Union used its power on the Apprenticeship Board to prevent the entry of coloureds to the trade and threatened to expel immigrant motor mechanics training coloured apprentices. In 1974, a separate training course was set up for coloureds, enabling them to be trained independently, outside the control of the Apprenticeship Board and the unions.[35]

separate institutions, and that a National Training Board be established to examine the 'representativeness' of the apprenticeship committees. However, while separate training centres bypassed the white unions, they also entrenched segregated training and were therefore opposed by blacks and by many employers (see Chapter 6). The Minister of Manpower threatened that he would act against white unions which obstructed the indenturing of black apprentices.[36] Their opposition slowed the admission of blacks to apprenticeships: of the new apprenticeship contracts in white areas in 1982, only 5 per cent were for Africans and 21 per cent for coloureds and Indians.[37] However, these centres, and those already operating in the Bantustans* were beginning to produce the skills that could make a reality of black job advance.

In 1972, the Verwoerdian principle of pegging expenditure on African education to direct African taxes was scrapped.[39] Henceforth, finance came from general revenue and expenditure rose very fast. However, there was continued school segregation and enforcement of mother-tongue education (to bind the various ethnic groups to their homelands), as well as insistence on the equal use of Afrikaans (along with English) as a medium of instruction in black senior schools. This requirement sparked off the 1976 Soweto riots. In their aftermath, the insistence on Afrikaans was dropped, and wide-ranging concessions were made, including the commitment to introduce compulsory education for Africans,** and to equalize the quality of education for all races, the government declaring that its aim was 'to make the most of the potential' of all children and to maintain 'the same standards as those established on a national basis for all groups'.[40]

But unrest simmered on in the schools. After the 1980 riots by coloured school children in the Cape, P. W. Botha acknowledged that they had 'justifiable grievances' and said that the government 'pledges itself to the goal of equal education for all population groups but emphasizes that the historical backlog cannot be overcome overnight'. He also said he had an 'open mind' on the question of whether there should be one system and one education department for all races.[41]

---

*Technical and trade schools for Africans had been established there from 1969.[38]

**Compulsory education was introduced for Indians in 1973, and for coloureds in 1976.

However, while the government accepted the 1983 de Lange Committee's principle of 'equal opportunities for education, including equal standards for every inhabitant, irrespective of race, colour or creed', it baulked at accepting its recommendation of a single education department and autonomy for schools to decide whom to admit. Instead the commitment to separate education was reiterated[42] (although no action was taken against private white schools which, in defiance of official policy, accepted black pupils: by 1981, there were 1,500 black children at forty-one subsidized private schools in the Cape).[43]

Increasing expenditure on black education had preceded the riots; but they led to further and faster increases. The education budget for Africans rose from R50m in 1970 to R160m in 1975 and to R1,168m (including the homelands) in 1983. The number of African children at school increased from 2.7m in 1970 to 5m in 1981; the per capita ratio of expenditure on white and African children narrowed from 16.6 to 1 in 1968 to 7.2 to 1 in 1983[44]—still disgracefully wide. However, over these 13 years the number of African schoolchildren almost doubled and per capita spending rose three times as fast as the cost of living index and about twice as fast as the index of African teachers' salaries.

In 1961 it was estimated that only 2,200 Africans in SA held university degrees. By 1980, there were over 25,000 Africans and 21,000 coloureds and Indians at university, accounting for 29 per cent of total enrolment, as well as a big increase in the numbers at technical colleges. The white universities were being reopened to blacks and the English universities anticipated that within a couple of decades they might outnumber white students.[45]

The changing job structure

The recent erosion of the job and education bars will take time to make a substantial impact on the job structure, especially in highly skilled jobs. But the effects can already be detected in recent surveys: Tables 5, 6 and 7 show the movement of blacks out of the low-wage, unskilled jobs in the primary sectors into more skilled jobs in the higher wage manufacturing and services sectors.

Black advance, moreover, was not limited to the ratchet. The black vanguard was overtaking the significant minority of whites still in low-skill jobs (see p. 211) and moving into the skilled, technical and white-collar jobs in which the bulk of white workers were concentrated. Except for the managerial/administrative category, the black share of the more skilled and white collar jobs had increased significantly since 1960.

In the initial stages of black advance, considerable efforts were made, especially in the state sector, to retain the hierarchical race structure and prevent the breaking of the ratchet by retraining and upgrading white workers.[46] As it became clear that many whites did not want, or were not able, to move into more advanced jobs, attempts were made to shield them from the direct impact of black advance by devices such as renaming the jobs blacks moved into and according them lower status and pay. Thus on the railways whites were termed 'train marshallers' and blacks 'shunters'; whites were 'ticket collectors', blacks were 'ticket examiners'. Also, efforts were made to ensure that whites did not work directly under blacks; in large establishments separate workshops, offices or rooms were established, like separate pyramids, entirely manned by blacks. After Wiehahn, there was less resort to these devices; but the tendency to overgrade whites and downgrade blacks probably understated the extent of black advance.

Instances of whites working directly under blacks were less common; but a 1979 survey found that in 22 per cent of companies, blacks (including, in 3 per cent of cases, Africans) supervised whites.[47] Observers believe that this trend has since increased. Recent surveys have also confirmed increasing racial integration on the factory floor and in canteens and washrooms.[48]

Black advance has been very uneven in its extent, pace and manner, depending largely on the strategies and strength of the white unions concerned. (On their differing responses see Chapter 7). The mining unions, for example, ensured that, by 1984, the job bar was still largely intact on the mines; but the building unions failed to halt its erosion, instead they lost control of the process and the 1983 Manpower Survey showed that blacks outnumbered whites in most of the building skills.*

The steel and engineering unions were prepared—at a price—to negotiate an 'orderly' pace of black advance, and this was one of the first sectors in which job reservation was formally scrapped, although the unions retained a considerable degree of control over

*With 23,000 white artisans and apprentices to 37,000 coloureds and Indians and 11,000 Africans (excluding those in independent homelands).[49]

skilled jobs.* The steel and engineering sector (with 500,000 workers in 1978) provides a classic example of that step-by-step manner in which apartheid was so often eroded, and illustrates how the 'floating bar' got out of control, going beyond the limits set for it by government and white unions, with the entry of Africans into skilled jobs and the breaking of the ratchet.

This sector suffered from severe skill shortages (see Chapters 6 and 8). From 1968, African advance was secured by 'productivity bargaining': in return for 'rationalization' (reorganization, fragmentation and reclassification of jobs), white workers received higher wages, fringe benefits and retraining schemes. This deal meant that the initial stages of African advance were often accompanied by a widening of the wage gap, and even by the *extension* of formal job reservation, as the unions demanded 'closed shop' provisions to protect the remaining white jobs against any further African advance. This misled some observers into believing that Africans would gain nothing from the floating bar.

Yet, by 1978, all categories of work, including the artisan grades, were opened to blacks, including Africans. Formal job reservation was therefore eliminated in this sector before the 1979 Wiehahn reforms.** Moreover, black advance frequently ran ahead of the formal IC agreements, although this was concealed by the downgrading or reclassification of jobs taken over by them (see Chapters 6 and 7). The fact that this advance was taking place on the factory floor increased the pressures on government and white unions to recognise the process, and therefore exert some control over it.

---

* 132,000 white artisans and apprentices to 19,000 coloureds and Indians and 5,500 Africans.[50]

** The key steps were as follows. The 1968 IC Agreement for the Iron, Steel and Metallurgical Industries (the SEIFSA group of employers) regraded jobs into eight categories. The closed shop applied to the top four categories, A to D, from which Africans, who could not be union members, were excluded. In return, many white jobs were downgraded into the lower categories, which could be done by people of any race. The 1972 Agreement opened 10,000 jobs in the restricted category D to Africans, followed in 1973 by 8,000 jobs in category C. By 1976, Africans could be employed 'under authorization or exemption' on selected operations in AB and B jobs, but not in the top A (artisan) or AA grades. These were opened to them by the 1978 IC Agreement.[51]

The changes in official policy on the job bar and access to training and education have therefore already had an impact which the official figures probably understate. However, as the Tables show, occupations are still largely structured along racial lines, due to the historical legacy, to continuing educational inequalities, and to restrictions on African urban rights, which puts them at a disadvantage in the job market. Future progress will depend on the further lessening of discrimination and on economic growth and technological developments which will determine the level of demand for skilled workers.

Income distribution

The change in policy on wages had a marked impact on income distribution, accelerating the rising real wages blacks had received since Sharpeville and narrowing black–white wage ratios.

In 1970, the 'traditional' policy that whites should be paid a higher, 'civilized' wage than blacks, even for the same job, was reiterated in parliament.[52] But, in 1971, Theo Gerdener, Minister of the Interior, expressed anxiety about low black wages and instructed the Public Service Commission to prepare a report on how to close the wide wage gap in the public service, warning that 'such gigantic differences in living standards . . . would lead to murder and violence.'[53]

Gerdener's opponents used this dramatic speech to drive him out of the cabinet and the NP; but his successor and rival, Mulder, continued his policy of closing the wage gap in the public sector. From 1971 Africans received larger percentage increases than whites,* and the process was accelerated after the 1973 Durban strikes and the international campaign against 'poverty wages', which included an enquiry by the House of Commons in the UK into the wages paid by British companies in SA.[55] By the mid-1970s, both government and employers' organizations (see Chapter 6) were publicly committed to moving to the rate for the job, thus ending the official 'civilized labour' policy on wages.

The impact on income distribution was dramatic: from 1970–82, real wages for Africans in manufacturing and construction rose

---

*22 compared with 11 per cent in 1972. In that year, in all urban sectors combined, African wages increased by 19 per cent compared with 10 per cent for whites.[54]

by over 60 per cent, compared with 18 per cent for whites; on gold mines real wages for Africans quadrupled, while those for white miners rose by 3 per cent; on white farms real wages for Africans doubled between 1968/9 and 1976. As a result, the white share of personal income declined from over 70 to under 60 per cent, while the African share rose from 19 to 29 per cent (see Tables 9 to 12).

As the Tables show, there were variations between sectors. African wages rose most slowly on white farms, fastest in the gold mines, where the white–African ratio narrowed from 20.9 to 1 in 1971 to 5.5 to 1 in 1982. This occurred despite the fact that the job bar on the gold mines barely shifted. The narrowing of the ratio was not therefore only due to black occupational advance, but to the change in policy and to concern about the low level of unskilled wages, which rose at a faster rate than skilled wages.* In manufacturing and construction (typical of other urban sectors such as government and commerce) the ratio narrowed from 6 to 1 in 1970 to 4.4 to 1 in 1982.

The 1980 Census showed that the black vanguard was overtaking the bottom group of whites, 200,000 of whom were in the 'low income' category (under R290 per month), while over 800,000 blacks (including 465,000 Africans) were in the middle/high categories. But only 35,000 blacks (including 10,000 Africans) had 'high' incomes (R1,000 plus monthly), compared with 719,000 whites.[56] The degree of inequality therefore remained very wide and was even more extreme in the ownership of capital assets.[57]

Rising real wages and economic opportunities in the towns, and overcrowding and unemployment in the Bantustans, led to increasing class differentiation among blacks, particularly to a widening of the urban/rural gap. As mentioned above, it is much more difficult to assess the situation of blacks outside the modern wage sector because of uncertainty about the unemployment level and lack of information about incomes in subsistence farming and in illegal and informal-sector employment. The 1981 current population survey showed African unemployment at 8 and coloured at 5 per cent; but other estimates were higher, putting African unemployment at about 20 per cent.[58]

---

*E.g. the 1974 SEIFSA Industrial Council Agreement provided increases of 15.4 per cent for unskilled workers, compared with 8.6 per cent for skilled.

However, recent research also shows that, even in the Bantustans, real per capita incomes rose,[59] due to remittances from rising African wages (particularly those of mineworkers), the stimulation of some homeland economic development, and state welfare payments: R205m was paid to half a million pensioners in homelands in 1981.[60]

Nevertheless, absolute income levels, especially in the Bantustans, remain very low and contrast starkly with white affluence. African poverty is, moreover, compounded by the social dislocation caused by labour controls, migrancy and population removals. Among their results were exceptionally high levels of malnutrition and infant mortality, reaching 130 per 1,000 live births in the worst rural areas.[61]

A narrowing of racial ratios was also evident in government expenditure. Education was referred to above (p. 62); state old-age pensions provide another example. In 1948, the ratio of pensions for whites, coloureds and Africans was 100 to 53 to 27 respectively. During the next couple of decades, the relative, and in some years even the absolute, position of blacks declined, reaching their lowest point in 1960, when the ratio was 100 to 40 to 16. By 1980, the ratio had improved to 100 to 57 to 30—better than in 1948,[62] but still very wide. These figures illustrate the setback for blacks in the first couple of decades of Nationalist rule.

The daunting cost of making up the huge housing, education and welfare backlogs for blacks, particularly on the lavish scale provided for whites, led to attempts by the government to shift some of the responsibility to the private sector, for example, by making employers responsible for training costs and charging white parents school fees.[63] This trend accorded with the stated desire to decrease government intervention and would make more manageable the financial cost of extending state welfare; but it could obviously result in continuing large inequalities, though on a class rather than an explicitly racial basis.

Trade unions

The extension of full trade union rights to Africans was one of the most important areas of reform; but it was only achieved after the failure of the government's attempt—in response to the 1973 Durban strikes—to establish a separate, alternative 'committee' system for Africans.* Within a couple of years almost 2,000 committees, covering over half a million workers, had been set up.[64] The 1973 Act, unlike that of 1953, was not merely a paper Act. The government seemed convinced of the need for action and wanted its alternative to trade unions to work.

Over the next decade, in response to continuing pressures from blacks and from progressive capital (see Chapters 6 and 9), the government accepted the 1979 Wiehahn Commission recommendation that Africans be included in the IC Act's definition of 'employees' (who could join registered unions). Initially, they attempted to restrict union rights to 'permanent' African workers (Section 10s) and to exclude 'temporary' workers (migrants and foreign blacks)—a similar distinction to that made in the Riekert Report. The formation of racially mixed unions was also prohibited. But, step by step, this stance was modified; by 1984 the definition of employee had been extended to include all workers— black and white, local and foreign—and mixed unions were allowed. Registration procedures were also simplified to encourage the black unions to register and the new Industrial Court was making decisions favourable to black unions fighting for recognition and protection against victimization by some employers.[65]

However, restrictions were also placed on the political activities of trade unions, which were not allowed to give financial aid to political parties;** attempts were also made to curb the growth of *un*registered unions, whose officials were subjected to police surveillance and, often, detention and banning, even when employers were willing to negotiate with them (see Chapters 6 and 9). This contradictory policy seemed partly the result of conflicting pressures within the NP and bureaucracy; partly of a deliberate strategy to control the growth of the African and non-racial trade union movement.

The horizontal controls
This was a complex and difficult area of change. A sharp distinction was made between Section 10s, to whom limited concessions

*The 1973 Bantu Labour Relations Regulation Amendment Act provided for two types of plant-level committee: wholly-elected works committees, and liaison committees, partly elected and partly appointed by management. The Act also gave Africans a limited right to strike.
**The 1956 IC Act had placed similar restrictions on white unions.

were made, and other Africans (migrants, illegals, commuters), subjected to yet another 'streamlining' of the controls, which required reinforcement against the growing demographic and economic pressures driving Africans out of the homelands and into the 'white' areas.

A concerted effort was also made to implement the separate development alternative to full African economic incorporation by developing the Bantustans, largely by the decentralization of industries to them. Vorster hoped this would provide jobs for their inhabitants and act as a 'suction force' attracting Africans back from the white areas,[66] thus reducing the need for influx controls.

The reason for this controversial policy, with its horribly complicated network of controls and mechanisms (pass laws, labour bureaux, population removals, Physical Planning Act, etc.) was its role in keeping down African numbers in the 'white' areas and providing the physical/geographical base for separate ethnic political entities. However, the attempt to put into practice the apartheid master-plan revealed its difficulties and costs and led to its reformulation by Botha. His recasting of the policy in a regional framework was ambiguous, but appeared to move away from the geographical/ethnic base which was its essence. However, while these elements were diluted, they had not been abandoned by 1984, partly because of their connection with the fundamental question of political rights, partly because of opposition from the huge bureaucracy which administered the system.

Concessions to the 'Section 10s'
Vorster stopped the erosion of Section 10 rights; instead they were reinforced, albeit in the Nationalists' typically ambiguous and tortuous manner.* These concessions culminated in the accept-

*In 1972, Piet Koornhof, then Deputy Minister of BAD, promised that more Africans would be allowed to bring their wives into the urban areas, provided housing was available. This was confirmed by his successor, Punt Janson. In 1975, M. C. Botha, Minister of BAD, said there was a major rethinking of policy and that the thirty-year leaseholds would be reintroduced, except in the Western Cape; but he linked these concessions to Bantustan citizenship, stating that only Africans who became homeland citizens would receive 'privileges' in the white areas. After the 1976 Soweto riots, the citizenship proviso was dropped from the leasehold scheme and M. C. Botha announced that Africans could buy their houses 'for all time' and could sell them or

ance of the recommendations of the 1979 Riekert Report that the permanence of the Section 10s be accepted and that they should be granted business and property rights* and increased local self-government and be allowed to have their families with them, provided housing was available (the Western Cape was excluded from these concessions).[69]

Riekert also urged increased mobility for Section 10s. This had already been attempted in 1971, when the numerous 'prescribed' municipal areas, to which Africans were confined by their passes, were replaced by twenty-two larger zones controlled by Bantu Areas Administration Boards (BAABs). In theory, Section 10 rights, previously limited to single municipalities, were to apply throughout these expanded zones. In practice, the BAABs failed to improve mobility, so Riekert recommended that Section 10s should have 'blanket authorization' to change jobs and accommodation within their BAABs and to transfer their rights to other BAABs, provided 'suitable housing' was available.

This recommendation seems to have freed Section 10s from the clutches of the Labour Bureaux, but the housing provision left officials with a lever to control their mobility between BAABs and to make it difficult for them to bring in their families. In the 1980 Komani case, the Appeal Court upheld the right of a Section 10 worker to have his family with him and reprimanded officials who had obstructed this. Because of bureaucratic delays, by 1981, six years after the restoration of leaseholds was first announced, less than two thousand had been registered and there were continual delays in the extension of facilities such as electricity and phones to the townships.

---

bequeath them to their children. But nothing was done to give effect to these concessions. When Mulder became Minister of BAD in 1978, he amended the Bantu (Urban Areas) Act, allowing ninety-nine-year leaseholds; but he also introduced an Amendment to the Bantu Laws Act which appeared to dis-qualify the children of Section 10 Africans who were born after the indepen-dence of their 'homelands' from inheriting such rights, on the grounds that they were foreigners! Again, practically nothing was done to implement this ambiguous concession.[67]

*These were granted on ninety-nine-year leaseholds but in 1983 it was stated in parliament by Koornhof that the leaseholds would continue 'in perpetuity'.[68]

Nevertheless, there was gradual progress with stabilization, facilitated by a shift towards a more flexible housing policy, including the site-and-service schemes and upgrading of squatter housing, that were the only realistic ways of providing cheap mass housing. Government expenditure on African housing in white areas increased from R6m in 1976 to R82m in 1981/82 and more land was earmarked for family housing (for instance, plans to convert Alexandra township in Johannesburg to migrant hostels were scrapped; instead it was redeveloped for family housing).[70] In 1983, to encourage home ownership and raise further funds for housing, almost 400,000 township houses were put up for sale at bargain prices. Employers were permitted to build family housing for their workers and by 1984 thousands of houses were being constructed, not only by employers in manufacturing and commerce, who had long pressed for stabilization, but also by the mining industry and by state corporations such as SAR (see Chapters 5, 6 and 8).

The Riekert proposals marked a turning-point for the Section 10s (estimated at 1.8m urban African workers in 1978).[71] However, these changes did not yet constitute equality: Africans were still excluded from full mobility and freehold tenure, and residential segregation remained intact. As with many of the reforms, movement in the right direction illuminated the enormous task that was still entailed in dismantling the all-embracing and highly-institutionalized apartheid structures.

Maintenance of controls for Africans without Section 10 rights
Africans without Section 10 rights were subjected to yet another 'streamlining' of the controls. Officials evolved an extraordinary hierarchy according to which work permits were allotted.

First in the pecking order were *commuters*, living in townships within the Bantustans, from which they commuted daily to work in 'white' areas. In 1983, there were 740,000 commuters,[72] concentrated in Natal, the Eastern Cape and around the Pretoria/Witwatersrand/Vereeniging (PWV) triangle, where the Bantustans abut major industrial centres (see map). The government favoured this system because it kept down the number of Africans officially living in 'white' areas, while reducing labour turnover and enabling workers to live with their families.

But the number of commuters does not tell the full story of the mushrooming growth of commuter townships, which became magnets for the growing number of people with nowhere to live. The bits and pieces of Kwazulu surrounding Durban, for example, became a vast squatters' town of over one million people and there were similar conurbations throughout Natal and Transvaal.

Riekert confirmed the continuation of *migrant labour* and added an ominous new condition to those under which migrants could be in a prescribed area for longer than seventy-two hours— the non-availability of suitable local work-seekers (i.e. job preference for Section 10s, as there once was for white workers).

Riekert also urged 'streamlining' of the Labour Bureaux to reduce red tape and inefficiency. This had been recommended ad nauseam since the 1958 Viljoen Commission, by means of devices such as 'call-in cards', introduced on the Kimberley diamond mines during the 1960s. These enabled the worker to return automatically to the same employer after his annual leave. If this system was widely adopted it might produce 'stable migrants', thus reducing the high turnover costs of migrancy, but it would also mean more intensive migrancy and family separation—*unless* workers were able to qualify for Section 10(b) rights after the required ten or fifteen years of regular work (see p. 26).

The Riekert Report and the 1981 Rikhoto judgement by the Rand Supreme Court—that migrants could not be excluded from qualifying for Section 10(b) rights on the legalistic grounds that they did not work 'continuously'—appeared to reopen this loophole, which would enable migrants (about one third of African workers) and their families gradually to acquire Section 10 rights.* But the bureaucracy is attempting to prevent this: in 1981, the Courts censured officials of the West Rand Administration Board for refusing to endorse the passes of Africans in accordance with the Rikhoto and Komani judgements. There were also pressures within the NP for legislation to over-ride these judgements.[74]

---

*There is disagreement among observers as to whether migrancy increased during the 1970s. The trends towards stabilization and commuting suggest it did not. However, the number of *SA* migrants may have increased as, from 1974, they replaced *foreign* migrants from neighbouring African states on the gold mines. This did not mean an increase in the total number of migrants, but in the number of SA migrants, especially from Transkei (see Chapter 5).[73]

If the Court's more liberal interpretation of Riekert does not prevail, the Riekert policy could worsen the migrants' situation, because its 'preference for local labour' principle puts them at a disadvantage in competing for jobs. This is aggravated both by high unemployment and, paradoxically, by the trend towards stabilization. When employers switch to stable labour, as many are now doing, officials insist that this must be to local labour (with Section 10 rights). Thus the long-serving migrants are not stabilized, but lose their jobs and are replaced by locals.

Furthermore, the increased demand for Section 10s raises their wages, thus intensifying the trend towards labour-replacing mechanization and reducing the chance of alternative jobs for the migrants and their descendants, who are then repatriated to the Bantustans as foreigners. The 'local labour' policy thus gives a vicious twist to the normally desirable process of stabilization and illustrates the limits of reform within a framework that retains restrictions on mobility and denies citizenship to Africans.

The consequences of mechanization and unemployment were most serious for the bottom category: workseekers and families *illegally* in the white areas. Riekert advocated tightening the controls over them, but by a new method—shifting the penalties onto employers, who should be subjected to heavy fines in the hope that this would prove more effective (and reduce the opprobrium attached to the pass laws). The White Paper accepted this recommendation, but retained the penalties on African workers as well![75]

Fines on employers of R500 per illegal worker were announced. The 1982 Orderly Movement and Settlement of Black Persons Bill proposed increasing this to R5,000 per worker, as well as imposing a R500 fine on anyone accommodating illegal blacks. The outcry over this led to the redrafting and withdrawal of the legislation on three occasions. This crucial issue remains a major battleground between the bureaucracy, backed by the *verkrampte* political establishment, and their black and liberal opponents, including capitalists (discussed in Sections 2 and 3).

There is disagreement about the practical effects of recent changes on the illegals. Some observers believe that controls over this group were tightened during the 1970s, but it was my impression, based on field work for a study of migrant labour, that the controls became less effective. First, the number of Africans in white areas continued to grow and the illegals took more visible form in the squatter townships that sprang up within the white areas, even in the Cape peninsula, where influx controls were most strictly applied and enforcement easier because of the relatively small size of the African population.

Second, prosecutions under the pass laws declined from 700,000 in 1970 to 206,022 in 1982,[76] despite rapid population growth, which would otherwise have led to an increase, merely to maintain the situation. Third, the abolition of the Masters and Servants Laws in 1974 enabled workers on white farms and mines to leave their jobs legally without the permission of their employers. They were then supposed to go to the Bantustans and register for work with the Labour Bureaux. But, fourth, it was widely agreed that the Bureaux had failed to establish an effective grip over the labour force. Both the Riekert Commission and independent researchers confirm widespread evasion and bypassing of them. Surveys found that less than 3 per cent of rural, and 16 per cent of urban, African unemployed sought work via the Bureaux;[77] even legal workers tended to use them merely to rubber-stamp independently arranged employment rather than to find work.

The declining effectiveness of the controls seemed partly deliberate (hence the decline in prosecutions), partly inadvertent (incompetence of the Labour Bureaux). It was facilitated by bureaucratic infighting and disarray as Koornhof presided over the withering away of the Bantu Affairs empire (see p. 320).

However, while influx control declined, there was, confusingly, an increase from the late 1960s of *forced removals* of Africans to the Bantustans. Some of this was the result of sporadic attempts to clear squatter townships, particularly in the Western Cape, but mostly it took place in the rural areas. Its aim was to divert to the Bantustans, and away from the towns, the huge stream of Africans pushed off the land by the abolition of labour tenancy and 'black spots' (land occupied by blacks in white rural areas), by the redrawing of Bantustan boundaries, and by mechanization on white farms (see Chapter 4).

The shortage of farmland in the Bantustans meant that most of the displaced people were dumped in 'resettlement camps', rural slums remote from economic opportunities, which the able-bodied soon left to live in the mushrooming commuter towns or to seek work (legally through the Labour Bureaux or illegally on their own) in the white areas. The resettlement camps were inhabited mainly by old people and children, living off remittances and government welfare payments.

It is difficult to gauge the magnitude of this process, as the disconcertingly wide range of estimates of between 1 and 3½ million people demonstrates.[78] At a time of agricultural and industrial revolution, large numbers of Africans were bound to move off the land, as did many whites and coloureds, especially after the abolition of the Masters and Servants Laws which had tied them to the farms. This movement off the land was not special to SA, nor did it *per se* indicate a worsening of their situation, which was hardly idyllic before. What was special to SA was state intervention to direct them towards the overcrowded and poverty-stricken Bantustans and away from the white towns, with their greater economic opportunities. This intervention was inhumane, authoritarian, and economically harmful, distorting relative factor prices, because an influx of labour would tend to reduce its price relative to capital, thus encouraging more labour-intensive invest-ment and more jobs, which were desperately needed.

Forced removals were probably the worst feature of SA policy during this period. For many observers, the reforms paled into insignificance compared with this outrage against the poorest groups in SA, who lost their homes and were forced to abandon property such as cattle. Moreover, as the *Surplus Peoples Project* argued, this process could not be viewed as 'an aberration', but was an 'inevitable consequence' of apartheid,[79] which denied Africans free mobility and citizenship.

The separate development alternative

The reason for persisting with policies which led to such suffering and conflict, and brought the Nationalists such ignominy abroad, was their fear that an African majority, permanently settled in the 'white' areas, would lead to loss of political control and threaten white security. The separate development policy aimed to provide alternative political outlets for Africans, for which the homelands would form the physical/economic base. They were to be developed mainly by the decentralization of about a quarter of new manufacturing investment to designated 'growth points' and away from the major industrial centres of PWV, Port Elizabeth/ Uitenhage and the Western Cape. In those metropolitan areas (accounting for two-thirds of industrial output*), expansion would only be permitted of industries that were 'locality bound', or had a white–African labour ratio of less than 1 to 2.5.[80]

The decentralized zones would provide jobs for Africans in their 'own' areas, where they could live with their families, and enable white capital to escape from the high costs and restrictions of apartheid labour policies by allowing the freer use of labour there (similar to the export processing zones in developing countries like Malaysia).

The original growth points, such as Rosslyn and Hammarsdale, were virtual extensions of existing (white) industrial areas (see map). But Vorster also established growth points inside the Bantustans and lifted Verwoerd's prohibition on investment by private white capital within them, even undertaking to compensate investors for losses incurred as the result of independence.[81] Development corporations were set up which established industries, often in partnership with private (including foreign) capital. It was hoped that, in addition to the industrial jobs directly created, there would be a multiplier effect stimulating development and thus indirectly creating more jobs.

The unresponsiveness of businessmen led to subsequent increases in the incentives** and also to more use of sanctions: from 1968–78, formal applications to employ an additional 107,674 Africans in the white areas were refused.[82] The 'halo' effect of the Act was greater, as many employers were discouraged from even applying by the red tape, and by informal indications of disapproval. Section 3 of the Physical Planning Act was applied particularly strictly to the Transvaal clothing industry: labour-intensive and heavily dependent on African women, it seemed to Pretoria's planners an ideal case for decentralization. Not only were applications for additional African labour refused, but firms were zealously prosecuted for employing illegal Africans or for being in excess of the 1 to 2.5 white/African labour ratio.[83]

The Physical Planning Act was thus not a paper tiger, as some alleged. Claims by employers and trade unionists that factories were forced to close and thousands of jobs lost were borne out by

---

*Durban/Pinetown in Natal (accounting for about 13 per cent of output) was excluded because of its proximity to Kwazulu.

**They were doubled in 1975 and greatly increased in 1982, when employers were, for example, offered cash payments amounting to 80 per cent of the wages of African workers.

the finding of the Riekert Commission that employment in the Transvaal clothing industry declined by almost a quarter in the decade following the introduction of the Act: over 5,000 jobs were lost.[84] The damaging effect on jobs and business confidence at a time of high unemployment led the Riekert Report to recommend that Section 3 be scrapped. The Riekert White Paper accepted this in principle, once alternative ways of securing decentralization were found.[85]

While the Physical Planning Act demonstrated a formidable capacity not only to halt industrial expansion, but to cause contraction, it proved less effective at generating new jobs in the growth points. There are varying estimates both of the number of jobs actually created for blacks in the decentralized zones,* and of the number required to halt the influx to the white areas.** But even on assumptions most favourable to the policy, it seems that this provided jobs for less than a third of new work-seekers from *within* the Bantustans, and certainly could not absorb the additional work-seekers repatriated from the white areas (partly as a result of the slower growth and mechanization accentuated by the Physical Planning Act itself). It is also widely agreed that the multiplier effect has been weak, as workers crossed the border to spend their earnings in the better-equipped white towns.[90]

The policy's damaging effects on economic growth and employment in the metropolitan areas, and its disappointing performance in creating alternative jobs in the decentralized zones, were acknowledged by the Riekert and Reynders Commissions (see Chapter 8) and led to Botha's 1980 promise to abolish Section 3 as soon as it could be replaced by price mechanisms—both increased incentives to decentralize and increased levies ('disincentives') on African labour in the white areas.[91] By 1984, Section 3 was still on the statute book, but decentralization was being recast by Botha into a regional framework (see below).

---

*It was officially estimated that, by mid-1977, 63,595 additional industrial jobs for blacks were created in the border areas and within the Bantustans,[86] but independent researchers claim the number of jobs actually created was less.[87]

**It was officially estimated that, to provide jobs for all *new* entrants to the labour market in the Bantustans alone, 21,000 new jobs had to be created there annually.[88] Over the decade 1968–77, this would equal 210,000 new jobs, compared with the 64,000 jobs that were actually created. Unofficial estimates of the number of jobs required are even higher.[89]

Other aspects of Bantustan development were even more disappointing. Expenditure was greatly increased under Vorster and Botha, amounting in 1984 to R2.2bn (for the non-independent and independent Bantustans together).[92] But the bulk of expenditure went on the provision of social services (education, health and welfare payments) and on the bureaucracies and political establishments that grew rapidly in each Bantustan. Little remained for productive investment and self-sustaining growth, particularly not in agriculture, their main potential resource.[93]

With the possible exception of mineral-rich Bophutatswana, sited within commuting distance of PWV, the Bantustans remained economically stagnant. In most cases, over half their economically-active inhabitants, and a higher proportion of the men, officially worked in SA as migrants or commuters (and large numbers worked there illegally).* Earnings from these workers accounted for the major part of their GNPs: at least two-thirds in the case of Transkei.[95]

This dismal economic performance did not add to the credibility of the Bantustans; nor did the failure to match their hectic constitutional development with geographic enlargement and consolidation. Vorster refused to go beyond the 1936 Land Act, although he acknowledged that in discussions with Bantustan leaders the issue that cropped up continually was 'land, land and land again'.[96] However, greater efforts were made to purchase the remaining quota of land (1.2m hectares in 1975) still owing to the homelands and to consolidate them. But the 'final' 1975 consolidation proposals would, if implemented, still leave the Bantustans highly fragmented, with Kwazulu in ten pieces, Bophutatswana in six, and only the tiny QwaQwa and Swazi homelands in one bloc each.

Reformulation of the separate development policy

P. W. Botha was prepared to go beyond the Land Act, arguing the African 'nations' must either be granted self-determination on the basis of their own land, or a share of power within SA. However, as his administration examined the problem, the costs and difficulties of consolidating and developing the Bantustans became

*For example, it was estimated in 1970 that the number of migrants from Transkei was 60 per cent higher than the official figure.[94]

clearer. They were spelt out by senior Nationalists such as Gerhard de Kock, Governor of the Reserve Bank and Chairman of the Constellation Commission, and Hennie van der Walt, MP, Chairman of the Commission on Land Consolidation, who acknowledged the failure of Bantustan development and the hopelessness of achieving significantly greater geographic and economic viability for them.

Van der Walt said that 'the time is past in SA to speak about consolidation in terms of drawing lines and borders . . . . If we wanted to carry out consolidation on a geographic basis, then we could possibly have succeeded forty years ago but today it is no longer possible.' He argued, moreover, that the addition of the 3m hectares required for geographic consolidation of the Bantustans would cost R6,000m and would barely increase their economic potential: 'therefore the addition of land is not the answer . . . . Economic development is the answer and economic development that is not necessarily based on the policy of separate development—because it is as plain as a pikestaff . . . that there cannot be nine or ten economics in southern Africa.'[97] This assessment was reinforced by the arguments of leading Nationalist economists like Jan Lombard and members of the semi-official Bureau of Economic Research in Pretoria.[98]

This reassessment led to a recasting of the decentralization policy in a *regional* framework. The aim was no longer to decentralize to growth points in or near each Bantustan, but to eight economic regions, which sometimes cut across the Bantustan borders and/or brought them closer to the metropolitan centres.[99] But what does this leave of the Bantustan policy, whose *raison d'être* (as conceived by Verwoerd) was to push outwards the horseshoe of Bantustans from the white 'heartlands'? Is this one of the NP's typically tortuous manoeuvres en route to a policy reversal?

Meanwhile, the Nationalists cling to this downgraded Bantustan policy, partly because there is no consensus within the NP over its dismantling (hence the failure to abolish Section 3) and partly because it continues to serve certain functions. These include (i) a legal/constitutional rationale for the exclusion of Africans from the central political system on the grounds that they have their own alternative political institutions; (ii) the creation of divisions between blacks, both on ethnic/tribal grounds and in terms of their legal status (Section 10s, migrants, commuters, farm workers, illegals); (iii) the provision of dumping grounds for the unemployed, aged and children: SA provided some finance for social security, health and education (plus big pay-offs to the elites who administer these funds), but these needy groups were tucked out of sight in the Bantustans and the responsibility was less direct. This was illustrated during the severe 1982/3 drought, when many observers claimed the suffering and malnutrition was worse than in the rural areas of a much poorer country like Botswana, where the government accepted full responsibility for its citizens.

Effects of the horizontal controls

The network of controls did not succeed in halting—let alone reversing—the increase in the number of Africans in the 'white' areas, which officially rose from 8.5m in 1970 to 9.5m in 1980 (see Tables 2 and 3). However, the increase was slower than it would otherwise have been; much of the flow being diverted to the commuter townships, which were the fastest-growing areas in SA and contributed towards the fact that the proportion of Africans in the homelands increased (officially) from 47 per cent in 1970 to 53 per cent in 1980. This appeared to give some support to Verwoerd's prediction that the flow to the white areas would peak in 1978 and then be reversed.[100] But the significance of the commuter townships is problematical: they clearly do not promote Verwoerdian grand apartheid, i.e. they do not push the horseshoe of black areas away from the white heartlands. On the contrary, the reclassification of townships like Mdantsane and Kwamashu as part of the Bantustan facilitated the rapid growth of black towns close to the white cities they serviced. They acted therefore as a legal fiction, providing a way round apartheid. However, this legal fiction also resulted in the classification of Africans as Bantustan citizens and was a double-edged sword in the struggle over their politico-legal status.

Many observers dismiss the idea that the Bantustans could form the basis for a more drastic partition and deny that this was the reason for the maintenance of much stricter influx control in the Western Cape, arguing that the economic integration of SA has gone too far and that the Western Cape would be unattractive as a white redoubt because it is less developed industrially than the Transvaal and Natal. But why was the policy of keeping down African numbers so strictly adhered to in this region,* despite its high costs both economically (the sluggish growth rate due to the scarcity of African labour) and politically (adverse worldwide publicity over the removal of squatters from Nyanga and Cross-roads)? The huge investment during the 1970s in the Saldanha/ Sishen iron ore port and railway line (see map) was widely criticised as uneconomic; but it becomes more explicable as part of a strategy to strengthen the industrial infrastructure of the North-West Cape, the 'whitest' region in SA. This suggests that there lingered on in some circles the idea of a geographical base, with access to the sea, which 'in an emergency'—as envisaged by Verwoerd—might form the basis for a radical geopolitical parti-tion—however impracticable this seems to the economically sophisticated.

Conclusion
Measured against the criteria for assessing the erosion or intensifi-cation of apartheid (see pp. 14f), the changes during this period form a confusing, contradictory picture. There has been some erosion of:

> *segregation*—in social policy, especially sport, in integration at the workplace, and in public amenities such as transport;
> *discrimination*—in the job, training, business, trade union and wage bars, with a commitment to equality in government expenditure on education, health and welfare;
> *hierarchical race structure*—acceptance of the principle that blacks can be in equal or superior jobs/positions to whites;

---

*This policy was reiterated by the 1976 Theron and 1979 Riekert Commissions. The first sign of an official retreat from it was the announcement by Koornhof in 1983 that a large new African township would be built at Khayelitsha near Cape Town. This concession was marred by the fear that Africans from the existing townships (Langa, Nyanga and Guguletu) would also be forced to move there—again reflecting the security concern to keep black townships at a distance from white cities (see p. 27).

institutionalized/legalized apartheid—abolition of Masters and
Servants Laws, of Section 77 of the IC Act, and of other
legislation affecting the above changes.

However, vast areas remain of institutionalized segregation (residential and educational) and of discrimination (restrictions on African landholding and mobility, exclusion from political rights). Indeed many view denationalization as an intensification of apartheid; whether or not this is its practical effect, the remaining areas of apartheid, for example on mobility, often constrain the extent to which Africans can take advantage of the job, business and other reforms. This partly explains why many blacks deny there has been any reform. It is not simply a matter of rising expectations: a person's life is a whole, and what happens at the workplace cannot be sharply divorced from the rest of life.

The conclusion is that, while the reforms have made significant inroads into apartheid, and created hopes and possibilities that seemed inconceivable fifteen years ago, SA remains a racially-ordered society, especially in those areas perceived as affecting white security—population distribution, mobility, political rights. Furthermore, outside the workplace, many of the changes have taken a peculiar form: even concessions to the coloured and Indian vanguard have not yet amounted to full incorporation; they remain segregated in housing and education, while political rights have been extended on an ethnic basis.

For these reasons, Koornhof's frequent analogy with the period of reform in nineteenth-century England does not fit. It is true that the extension of the franchise took a long time,* but those to whom it was extended were fully incorporated and the process was eventually universal. Thus far in SA, incorporation has taken place on an ethnic basis (and on terms designed to ensure the NP's continuation in office) and the African majority has been excluded. On an optimistic reading of Botha's present intentions, Africans might eventually be included, but on the basis of (unequal) ethnic units, which would form the building blocks of the new federal or

---

*The 1832 Reform Act enfranchised 18 per cent of adult males; the 1867 Representation of the Peoples Act, described at the time as 'the leap in the dark' increased this to 36 per cent. 'One man one vote' followed in 1918, and the enfranchisement of women from 1918–28.[101]

confederal system.* This will be fiercely resisted by many blacks, as well as by white *verkramptes*.

The evolution of policy is likely to depend less upon the 'hidden agendas' some believe exist than on the unpredictable course of events and the changing interests and power of the white, black and external actors involved. Sections B and C will examine the interests and power of some of them, particularly of capital.

*This interpretation was confirmed by Botha's speeches after his election as State President in September 1984. He spoke of the urgent need to find a solution to the problem of 'nine million' Africans whose presence in the white areas was irreversible and announced that the 'coloured labour preference' policy in the Western Cape would be scrapped and the ninety-nine-year leasehold system extended to Section 10 Africans living there.[102]

In early 1985, Botha offered to release Mandela and negotiate with the ANC, provided they abjured violence. This was followed by the abolition of the Prohibition of Political Interference Act and the sex laws, and by the announcement that policy on African urbanization and mobility would be reformed. However, these measures were in stark contrast to harsh police action against black organizations and demonstrations, leading to the death of nineteen people at Uitenhage in March 1985. These contradictions led to continuing confusion and suspicion about the direction of policy.

Section B
THE WHITE OLIGARCHY'S INTERESTS CHANGE

4
The Interests of Agricultural Capital

The changes in SA society since Union are most dramatically illustrated by the agricultural sector. Their essence was the shift from a system which, though capitalist, had features which could usefully be called feudal—a tied, serf-like labour force on the white farms and a black agricultural sector that was kept in an undeveloped and pre-capitalist state, so that it would not compete with white farmers and would instead serve as a source of cheap labour for white farms and mines. The political power of white farmers enabled them to shape the social organization to their needs in the crucial post-union period, when many institutional structures were established.

From about the 1960s, white farms became much larger and more mechanized. One of the key questions in the debate about SA is whether this shift to more capital-intensive farming increased or diminished the support of farmers for apartheid. Here it will be argued that as farming became more capital-intensive, farmers wanted to dispense with the feudal features and shift to a 'free' labour market. This process led to improvements for workers remaining on the farms; but those moving off found their freedom to look for work impaired by the labour controls which even made it difficult for them to find a place where they could legally reside.[1]

The struggle to develop white agriculture
By the late nineteenth century, the whites had conquered the whole of SA and taken possession of the greater part of the land. Much of this was agriculturally poor, with low quality soil, erratic rainfall and little natural irrigation. At the turn of the century, tens of thousands of farmers, white as well as black, were driven off the

85

land by droughts, locusts and cattle diseases. In the wake of the devastating 1899–1902 Anglo-Boer war, they swelled the exodus to the towns at a time of high unemployment. Much of the developed and commercialised (as distinct from subsistence) agriculture in the more fertile coastal areas was geared to the export market and subject to wild international price fluctuations. The steep drop in prices during the 1930s drove another wave of farmers off the land.

The development of a flourishing agriculture in these difficult circumstances was achieved at high cost—lots of cheap, coerced black labourers and huge state subsidies, financed by mining taxes and dearer food. But the results were impressive: the gross value of output increased from R58m in 1911 to R382m in 1948 to R6.6bn in 1981. SA was able to feed its growing population and have a surplus for export. The net contribution of agriculture to total exports (including gold) since the 1920s was usually between one fifth and one third.[2]

It has long been agreed that white farmers, with their acute production problems, were a major source of support for apartheid, but there is controversy about the impact of the shift to large-scale, mechanized farming.* The changing interests of white farmers will be analysed in relation to the following aspects of apartheid: controls over black labour; measures to reduce competition from black farmers for land and markets; and the exclusion of blacks from political rights.

Controls over African labour

White farmers were consistent advocates of controls over African labour. Their battles over this were not only against Africans, but also against competition from other employers, willing to pay higher wages. Ironically, farmers succeeded in preventing the establishment of the job colour bar in agriculture, although they

---

*In 1936 there were 6,019 tractors on white farms; in 1967, 170,000 or almost two per farm. The value of capital assets in agriculture attributable to machinery, vehicles, tractors and implements grew from R134.7m in 1947 to R763.1m in 1971. The capital–labour ratio, in real terms, more than doubled between 1950 and 1970. The number of white farms declined from 116,848 in the 1950s to 89,785 in 1969, i.e. by 23 per cent. Ownership also became more concentrated, with an increase in the area occupied by farms of 5,000 *morgen* and over.[3]

supported the struggle of white workers to impose it on employers in other sectors.

The absence of the job bar

The only sector to which the job bar never applied was agriculture; white workers were almost entirely driven out of this sector at a time of high unemployment among them. White *bywoners* (landless tenants) and failed farmers, instead of taking on jobs as tractor drivers, mechanics and farm managers, were forced to find work in the towns. By 1970, there were less than 20,000 white employees on the farms.

The 1960 Commission of Inquiry into European Occupancy of the Rural Areas complained that:

> White men and their families are ousted from the farms and replaced by non-whites and their families . . . . The majority of older whites who from 1936 onwards have emigrated to the cities, consisted of foremen, 'bywoners' and share-croppers who were often also employed as supervisors or foreman . . . . Previously the non-white foreman was simply a leading labourer in charge of a labour gang, but . . . in numerous cases such foremen can be regarded as farm managers rather than mere leading labourers.[4]

Despite the Commission's concern with *verswarting* (see p. 36) and decades of lip-service by politicians to the ideal of keeping whites on the land, nothing was done to halt this process. Indeed, white farmers were specifically exempted from the prohibition on employing skilled African builders by Section 15 of the 1955 Amendment to the Native Building Workers Act. The absence of the job bar in agriculture has attracted little comment; but the things that do not happen are sometimes as significant as those that do, and it was important that farmers, who gained so much from apartheid, escaped one of its major costs to other employers.

Curiously, although farmers employed blacks in senior jobs, they were generally opposed to black education, regarding it as likely to make their workers 'cheeky'. But, as farming became mechanized, farmers began to feel the effects of inadequate black education and of the shortage of trained and skilled workers to drive and maintain machines and cope with more sophisticated and scientific farming methods. The rising costs of illiteracy and lack of training were confirmed by the 1971 du Plessis/Marais Commission, which found that only 10,000 of 180,000 tractor operators in SA had any formal training. The maintenance costs of agricultural equipment (despite lower labour costs) were eighteen cents per hour, against five cents in the UK. It was estimated that training could cut the 1968–9 expenditure of R105m by twenty per cent and reduce the high accident and injury rate. At a certain stage in the development of capitalism, cheap untrained workers become a burden to employers, not a boon. Farmers began to develop an interest, which urban employers had long had, in a literate, trained workforce, and pressed the government for an expansion of training facilities and farm schools.[5]

Measures affecting the availability, mobility and price of African labour

The pages of SA history books resound with the cries of white farmers for more cheap labour. Farmers, like mine-owners, used arguments based on the 'backward-sloping supply curve'* as an excuse for not increasing the supply by raising wages. The hunger for cheap labour was partly the consequence of the labour-intensive process of clearing the land for farming; partly because of intense competition for unskilled labour from the goldmines, for the construction of railways and roads and, after World War One, for manufacturing industry. Until the 1950s, economic and demographic pressures within the 'reserves' had not reached the point at which they drove out Africans in sufficient numbers to satisfy this huge demand (see pp. 25 and 36).

Before Union, farmers (like mineowners) looked abroad for cheaper sources. In 1869 Natal sugar farmers imported thousands of Indians to work on their plantations, and seasonal labour was recruited from Mozambique and other surrounding areas. It was estimated that, in 1964, 14 per cent of the agricultural labour force was foreign.[6] However, this did not solve the labour shortage for farmers, who became the major pressure for alternative means of swelling the labour supply.

Restrictions on African land ownership and farming

One of the major objects of the Land Act (see p. 18) was to swell the

---

*This assumes that workers aim at a specific 'target' income; therefore if wages are increased they will work less and the supply of labour, instead of increasing in response to rising wages, will decline.

supply of African labour, which would obviously be increased by restricting their opportunities as independent producers. The restrictions on tenancy (i.e. hiring of land to Africans) were explicitly connected with this. Van der Horst documented how 'tenancy, share farming, and the renting of land to Natives for cash were all severely criticised on the grounds that they reduced the supply of labour.' For farmers who had tenants, they served as a reserve labour force; but farmers without tenants complained that 'the squatting system . . . reduced the supply of labour by enabling Natives to live without working for Europeans.'[7] The 1903–5 Native Affairs Commission, which profoundly influenced the 1913 Land Act, sympathised with their complaints and recommended strict measures against 'squatting' in order to increase the supply of labour.[8]

The effect of these restrictions on land ownership and tenancy, and the difficulties for blacks compared with the advantages for white farmers, reduced the opportunity cost (or alternative earnings) of blacks, thereby increasing the supply and lowering the cost of their labour. And these are amongst the classic methods used by farmers to solve the problem of labour shortage. For, as Marx wrote, 'independent producers who work for themselves instead of for capital, and enrich themselves instead of the capitalist gentry, react very perversely on the conditions of the labour market . . . leaving it always understocked.'[9]

Conflicts over tenancy

However, the issue of tenancy was less straightforward than the restrictions on land ownership, and there were conflicts of interest among capitalists over this. The leasing of land, whether for cash, share of crops, or part-time labour, is a standard way for land-owners to earn income and supplement their labour supply. Many white farmers and African tenants resisted and evaded the restrictions on tenancy, particularly in areas where farming was less intensive, such as the Northern and Eastern Transvaal and upper Natal. The system was also favoured by mineowners, who could draw on the large communities of tenant farmers for migrant labour.[10]

There were repeated attempts—at the behest of farmers who did not have tenants, or wanted their tenants converted into full-time labourers—to abolish the system. The difficulties of doing this were illustrated by the first attempt to apply the restrictions on tenancy in the Leydenburg district of the Transvaal in 1937–8, when tenants were given a choice between moving or working full-time. This led to such an exodus from the area that farmers pressed the government either to extend the provisions to the whole Transvaal (so that tenants would not have the option of moving) or to suspend them—which it did.[11]

These conflicting interests accounted for the repeated attempts—and failures—to abolish labour tenancy. As late as 1976, when tenancy had been 'finally' abolished on numerous occasions, some Natal farmers, struggling to compete for labour with the gold mines, reintroduced tenancy in an effort to hold their labour, as in Leydenburg forty years earlier.[12] However, this was exceptional; by the 1970s, the interest of farmers in tenancy had declined as the labour shortage turned into an oversupply and as farmers shifted to more mechanized, larger-scale production and wanted to farm their land themselves. Moreover, the population on the tenant holdings had grown rapidly, while the able-bodied men among them increasingly looked for jobs elsewhere, leaving behind the women, the children and the aged. Farmers therefore became more amenable to pressure from the government (concerned about black numbers in white areas) to get rid of tenancy. Indeed, by the late 1970s, the wheel had turned full circle: farmers wanted the large communities removed from their farms, but restrictions on the entry of blacks to towns, and overcrowding of the Bantustans, meant that there was often nowhere for them to go, and that officials sometimes insisted that they remain on the farms until they could be accommodated elsewhere.[13]

To sum up the complex pressures for and against tenancy: it was opposed by farmers who did not have tenants, on the grounds that it led to labour shortage (or 'unfair' distribution of labour). Farmers and landlords with labour tenants supported it, unless and until they wanted to farm their land more intensively themselves and to replace part-time labour tenants with full-time workers. However, if, when phasing out tenancy, they were faced with a large exodus of tenants, who preferred to leave rather than be converted to full-time labourers, then farmers were forced to waive or postpone measures against tenancy or risk losing their whole labour force.

Today, few farmers have a strong interest in the retention of the system, and certainly not in the large, unproductive communities living on their farms which are its legacy. But the government—and the whole society—is faced with the problem of accommodating elsewhere the communities released by the brutal destruction of the labour–tenant system.

Competition among capitalists for black labour

The restrictions on black land ownership and tenancy (and the discouragement of black commercial farming and imposition of taxes to force them to earn cash wages) swelled the supply and lowered the cost of black labour, but did not guarantee that this labour would be available for *farmers*. This required measures to tie down workers on white farms and protect farmers against competition from higher urban wages. In many rural areas, the mines and even government departments were prevented from recruiting labour, lest they compete with farmers.[14] No black farm worker could get a 'pass' to work in a town unless he had permission to leave from the District Labour Control Board, on which local farmers served. It became an offence to employ such workers without written permission from the farmer. Terms of service frequently tied the whole family to the farm: under the 1932 Native Service Contract Act they could all be evicted if one member failed to render the service liable. Penalties, including whipping, were imposed for breaches of contract. Many workers were furthermore tied to the farmer by indebtedness.[15]

Despite these harsh measures to increase, and tie down, the farm labour force, farmers complained bitterly of labour shortages during the 1930s and 1940s. The Native Affairs Department referred to 'a crippling shortage of farm and mining labour,' and to the increasing reliance of both these sectors on foreign labour, which was becoming scarce.[16] These complaints were made despite the *increase* in the farm labour force,[17] presumably because of greater demand for labour due to the expansion of the area under cultivation and the enormous increase in output. This intensified the demand for labour at a time when the urban areas provided a growing counter-attraction, and farmers could not get the additional labour they wanted, especially during World War Two, when the UP relaxed the pass laws (see p. 20).

The South African Agricultural Union (SAAU) demanded the tightening of pass laws and their reinforcement by other measures, such as Labour Bureaux to control the flow of labour. They also wanted a permanent division of the urban and rural workforces, to prevent farm workers from moving out of agriculture to urban jobs.[18] The 1948 Nationalist government, put into office by the rural vote (see p. 282), obliged them. The pass laws were tightened and the farm labour force swelled by the addition of convict labourers, largely resulting from pass law prosecutions; by the late 1950s there were thousands of convicts on the farms—a huge, cheap addition to their labour force.[19] The government assured SAAU that farm labour would not be allowed to 'infiltrate' into the urban sector and Verwoerd stated that the intention of the Labour Bureaux was to increase the labour supply for farmers (see p. 25). Even he, however, felt constrained to add that, unless farmers raised wages and improved conditions, it would be 'difficult for the bureaux to supply the *platteland* labour market'.[20] The 1939 Farm Labour Committee had already warned farmers not to apply more coercion as this 'made farm labour unpopular'.[21]

These measures eased the labour shortages of white farmers, despite the substantial differential between agricultural and urban wages (see Table 12). There can be no doubt about the interest of white farmers in the controls over African mobility, nor about their key role in securing the tightening and extension of these controls by the 1948 Nationalist government.

Declining support for horizontal controls

The improvement in the farm labour supply was only partly the result of the tightening and extension of influx control. At least as important was the longterm shift from scarcity to surplus in the labour supply in southern Africa, due to population growth, the declining capacity of the reserves to support their populations, and mechanization.

The effects of mechanization on the demand for agricultural labour are controversial, partly because of unreliable statistics.*

*Due partly to inadequate agricultural censuses, partly to evasion by farmers in excess of their labour quotas or wishing to avoid the increasing fees and taxes on farm workers. In 1978 I came across farmers in Natal who registered less than a quarter of their workers. A study in the Eastern Cape found undercounting of 80 per cent of casual workers in the agricultural census.[22]

Until about 1970 the effect of mechanization was to increase yields rather than replace labour (the people being displaced from the farms were tenants and 'squatters', not farm labourers).[23] Census figures show a huge increase in output, accompanied by an increase in the number of workers, from 1.3m in 1946 to 1.5m in 1970. Thereafter, numbers began to decline, reaching 1.2m in 1978. The labour force on the white farms thus remained surprisingly large in the face of mechanization, perhaps because wages were low.

But mechanization led to a qualitative change in the labour requirements of farmers, who needed younger and more educated men, of whom they were still short. Hence the simultaneous complaint of labour shortage* and the removal of 'squatters' whom previously many farmers wanted to retain. Mechanization usually reduces the demand for casual labour; the du Plessis/Marais Commission- found it was having this effect and anticipated a switch to a smaller, better-trained and better-paid force of regular workers.[25]

All these factors—the readier supply of black labour, the changing labour requirements of farmers, their preparedness to pay higher wages—reduced the need of the more progressive farmers for controls over black mobility. The declining need for these apartheid measures coincided with growing pressures on white farmers to relax the controls over their workers and to improve wages and conditions. These pressures came from a variety of sources, including the mining industry.

After its 1974 decision to shift from foreign to local black labour, the Chamber of Mines pressed for access to the previously restricted rural areas, urging that they should not be a 'closed shop' for farmers and that workers should have the right to sell their labour freely on the best market (see p. 123). Mobility was also increased by the 1974 abolition of the Masters and Servants Acts, precipitated by a threatened boycott of SA coal by US dockers, on the grounds that it was produced by indentured labour.[26] Finally, increased mobility was an unexpected bonus of the Bantustan

---

*For example, a 1969 survey by SAAU reported a shortage of 143,000 male workers, about 14 per cent of total labour needs.[24] In the mid 1970s, there were acute though temporary shortages of labour, particularly in Natal, resulting from increased recruitment of SA labour by the goldmines (see p. 122).

policy, which provided blacks with a 'homeland' to which they could legally go: the tiny Qwa-Qwa Bantustan was crowded with blacks from OFS farms, using it as a stepping-stone to jobs in the mines and towns.[27]

There were bitter complaints from some farmers about these developments. The congress of the OFS Agricultural Union complained that employers were losing control over their labour force and asked the BAD 'to bring to the attention of labour bureaux that young Africans from the country who did not yet qualify should not be allowed to move uncontrolled to the urban areas'. There were complaints in parliament that, although the mines were not supposed to recruit in the OFS, workers were nevertheless getting to them, and some members criticised the repeal of the Masters and Servants Laws, questioning whether blacks were 'mature enough' to use this new freedom and warning that the changes could ruin marginal farmers.[28]

But, by the 1970s, the political influence of farmers had declined and their complaints met with a cool response. In 1974, Raubenheimer, Deputy Minister of BAD, told SAAU that, 'If African farm labourers wanted to live in the homelands there was nothing to stop them'. In 1976, the Minister of Bantu Affairs, M. C. Botha, rejected calls for the reinforcement of the Masters and Servants Laws to stop absconding farm labourers, declaring 'It would be totally wrong to pass laws binding black workers to industries like agriculture and mining . . . . This outdated system was now totally unacceptable. It affected the basic freedoms and rights of the individual.'[29] That statement will startle those familiar with M. C. Botha's own record in restricting 'basic freedoms and rights', but it indicated that farmers had to live with increased mobility—whether or not they liked it. (The declining political leverage of farmers is discussed in Chapter 9).

Progressive and unprogressive farmers
There were farmers who accepted, and even welcomed, the changes. From about 1970, SAAU, dominated by the progressives, urged farmers to raise wages and improve conditions, so that they could compete with other sectors for labour.[30] These farmers favoured a more commercial, less feudal, relationship with their workers. For them, immobility had drawbacks: it often saddled them with workers (or farm residents) whom they no

longer wanted, and made it difficult to get younger, more educated
workers, who avoided the farms because of what SAAU called the
'stigma' attached to farm work. A prime cause of this was the
immobility, and lack of freedom, of farm workers. In 1974, this
was publicly spelt out by a group of Africans to Janson, Deputy
Minister of BAD, when he tried to persuade Bapedi men, who
were being moved from their land, to take jobs on white farms,
where they would be allowed to take their families. The younger
men, especially, were adamant in refusing to be 'forced into
supplying cheap labour' to the white farms, claiming that once
they worked there, they 'would not be able to get permission to
work in urban areas and would be forever classified as farm
labourers'.[31] In the Western Cape, a recent study found intense
resentment among migrant farmworkers at the fact that if they
came on contract they might henceforth be prevented from switch-
ing to urban work.[32] This fear led workers to shun farm work; it
was one of the costs of immobility of which more progressive
farmers were becoming aware.

The progressive farmers were thus prepared to live with these
changes, and might even derive benefits from them, and they won
the backing of the government, which accepted the recommendation of the Marais/du Plessis Commission that marginal white
farmers should no longer be subsidised to stay on the land.[33] The
acceptance of this recommendation marked the first public departure from the traditional SA policy of keeping whites on the land
at all costs. Lip-service was occasionally paid to the ideal of
keeping the 'small farmer' on the land. In 1970, for example, the
Minister of Agriculture, Schoeman (himself one of the biggest
farmers in SA) reiterated that, 'The task of the government is to
protect those who make agriculture their life task against capitalists
who would ruin them and create monopolistic conditions I
am here to protect the small man.'[34] But, in practice, the government abandoned the policy of propping up marginal farmers. It
was thus no longer committed to backing the most reactionary
forces in this sector, because the uneconomic farmer, who was on
the margin himself, obviously resisted paying more to his workers.
He therefore had an interest in retaining controls that ensured him
of a plentiful supply of cheap labour. The efficient farmer could
afford to pay more for his workers: their value or marginal product
was higher to him. Indeed he might have an interest in pushing up

the wage costs of his less efficient competitors, thereby driving them out of business.*

The interests of progressive farmers went beyond easing restrictions and improving conditions. They moved towards the demand of other employers for a mobile, competitive labour market and the ending of controls over mobility. Significantly, this change in attitude coincided with the extension of central control to the rural areas, with the activation of the Labour Bureaux in the mid-sixties and the establishment of the BAABS in 1971 (see p. 36). The District Labour Control Boards, which allocated rural labour, had been dominated by farmers and they had largely escaped the time-consuming red tape and the labour taxes and fees of which urban employers complained. The antipathy of farmers to the extension of central control was vehemently expressed to the Riekert Commission.

Organizations representing Natal Sugar Farmers, among the biggest employers in agriculture, urged the phasing out of the Labour Bureaux and the BAABS, which were of 'no value whatsoever . . . their services are virtually non-existent . . . but their restrictive controls are only too well known.' The farmers recommended that 'the concept of illegal employment . . . should be abolished,' and complained that 'cumbersome procedures for the registration of black employees, restrictions on the grant of permits and complex influx control procedures were the cause of unlawful employment . . . . No action should be taken against employees as all individuals have the right to work.' Instead of the web of restrictions, 'workers should be allowed free labour movement and choice of employer . . . no undue restrictions should be placed on the right of employers to employ whom they like . . . the abolishing of the present system of restrictive legislation and the encouragement of a free system of competition in an open labour market will ensure better utilization of available manpower.'[36]

A further indication of the change in farmers' attitudes was their reply to the extraordinary Riekert questionnaire sent to employers, asking what should be done 'with a view to making Bantu less

---

*The elimination of uneconomic farmers was also connected with another separate process, viz, a marked bias towards large-scale farming and the concentration of ownership exemplified in the 1970 Act on the Sub-division of Agricultural Land.[35]

choosy' about their work and to facilitate control of 'idle or undesirable Bantu'. Once firm advocates of the view that blacks refusing to work for them were idle and choosy, farmers' organizations now objected that: 'It is every individual's right to be choosy concerning his career and job .... Idle and undesirable individuals only arise because of social and economic vacuums. Better basic education linked to economic needs, housing and sophisticated selection and placement, all in a context of freedom of the individual would eliminate the problem.'[37]

The only major aspect of the labour controls which the sugar industry still found acceptable was 'a system of passports' (replacing passes) for workers coming from Bantustans.[38] But, within a few years, as the prospect of land consolidation came closer, they began to voice grave doubts about the whole Bantustan policy and the drastic effects it could have on white agriculture (see below).

The Riekert Report recorded the antipathy of farmers for the Labour Control Boards and Bureaux (which they had once clamoured for) and recommended that the Boards, though not the Bureaux, should be abolished. The government, however, declined to do this 'without further investigation'.[39] White farmers, to defend their interests in the pre-capitalist racism of the past, had created in the 1948 election an army of bureaucrats to perpetuate that racism. Farmers' interests then changed towards 'free' labour markets and progressive capitalism. But by then the bureaucratic Dracula created by the white-farm Frankenstein wanted—and had the power to retain—the racist policies that kept it in work.

Migrancy

There seems little evidence for the belief that farmers favoured the extension of migrant labour.[40] On the contrary, while they used migrants for seasonal work such as sheep-shearing, the evidence suggests that they increasingly wanted the core of their workforce established on the farms with their families. In the Western Cape, where government wanted to prevent Africans (replacing coloureds on the farms) from bringing in their families, farmers complained bitterly about the costs and inconveniences of high turnover, and the Southern Cape Agricultural Union urged that husbands should be accompanied by their wives.[41] In Natal, where stabilization was restricted to 3 per cent of African workers on the sugar plantations, farmers urged the Riekert Commission to remove this ceiling.[42] SAAU recently stated: 'Our policy is for farmers to employ a hardcore of well-paid, well-housed and well-fed workers who live on the farms with their families. These workers are then supplemented by organised teams for seasonal work'.[43]

The belief that farm workers were being forced into migrancy stemmed partly from a confusion with the removals of whole families of tenants and squatters. But this harsh process—analogous to the eighteenth-century enclosures in England—was not incompatible with a settled family life for workers remaining on the farms. Another reason for this belief was the government's concern with *verswarting* of the rural areas. However, in so far as this led to increasing migrancy (and outside the Western Cape this does not seem to have been implemented), it was due to the government's political and security concerns, not to the interests of capitalist farmers, whose pressures to stabilize their workers increased as skill levels rose.*

Support for rising wages
Farmers could only coexist with the easing of restrictions on mobility if they were prepared to improve wages and conditions. The success of the horizontal controls in keeping down their labour costs can be gauged from the wide differential between agricultural and urban wages. In 1952, for example, average farm wages were 64 per cent of the cash wage in mining; 27 per cent of wages in manufacturing (see Table 12). The immobility of labour also contributed to marked variations in wages between regions, and between employers within the same region: during the 1960s farm wages in the Cape were 50 per cent above those in the OFS.[44]

Even with the controls, however, the rapid growth of urban employment and wages during the 1930s and 1940s, and the attractions of the freer, more stimulating life in the towns, had an impact on rural wages, and there is some evidence that they rose.[45]

*This was confirmed by my interviews with Western Cape fruit farmers in 1978. They said that training and experience were required even for seemingly simple and unmechanised tasks like tree pruning. It was time-consuming and expensive to teach these tasks anew each season, so they wanted workers stabilized.

Even during the 1950s, when the controls were most rigorous and the farm labour force was expanded by convicts, SAAU complained that farmers near large towns were forced to raise wages.[46] The farmers therefore were never as isolated from the influence of urban wage levels as the mines, with their preponderance of foreign workers, with much lower opportunity cost than SA blacks.

From the mid 1960s, real wages on farms followed the rise in urban wages, though at a slower pace and from a much lower level (see pp. 44 and 66). During the 1970s, the rise accelerated, especially in Natal. The sugar industry, in direct competition with the mines for Pondo workers from Transkei, was forced to increase real cash wages by over 50 per cent between 1969 and 1977.[47] Obviously farmers would not have to raise wages to compete for workers if they were immobile. This is another indication of the ineffectiveness of the Labour Bureaux and of increasing mobility, despite the proliferation of bureaucratic controls.

However, from the late 1960s, the rise in farm wages was not only a response to competition for labour; it was also the outcome of changes in the interests and attitudes of many farmers, reflected in the changing policy of the SAAU, whose Director, Celliers, began to urge that wages of blacks should rise faster than those of whites.[48]

The first reason for this volte face in wages policy was the effects of technological change, particularly mechanization, which increased the capital-to-labour ratio, so that labour became a smaller proportion of total costs. It therefore became less critical to keep down the wage bill; but labour shortages or dissatisfaction due to poor wages and conditions could immobilise the greater capital investment, while interest charges mounted up and output was lost. This factor obviously varied among farmers: where labour costs were a small element (as in egg farming, where they accounted for 7 to 10 per cent of total costs) an increase in the wage bill was less important than in irrigated or vineyard farming, where labour accounted for 40 per cent of total costs.[49] Mechanization also meant the shift to a more skilled workforce. To attract and hold younger, more educated workers, it became essential to improve wages and conditions, especially since workers had more mobility and could, as a last resort, escape to the Bantustans.

The second reason for the change in wages policy was the huge expansion in the domestic demand for food due to the increased spending power of blacks. As SAAU and the Minister of Agriculture frequently told farmers, the income elasticity of demand by blacks for food was high, and it was food producers who initially stood to gain most from rising black incomes. The uncertainties regarding traditional export markets for food resulting from UK entry to the EEC underlined the attractions of a growing domestic market.

The third factor was the impact of pressures from outside the agricultural sector, both from within SA and from abroad. The changes in agriculture lagged behind those in the towns, and there was increasing criticism of the low wages and poor conditions on the farms, not only from liberal lobbies and black leaders, but from the *verligte* Afrikaans press and even from the normally *verkrampte* SA Broadcasting Corporation, which ran a series of critical programmes on the subject in 1974. Farmers reacted angrily to these campaigns,[50] but many took the point that traditional labour policies and relationships were becoming untenable. These changes in attitude were helped forward by the interpenetration of farming with mining and manufacturing capital, as large, diversified companies like the Anglo-American Corporation (AAC), Schlesingers and Rembrandt moved into agriculture and rendered it more open to reformist attitudes and more sensitive to the bad image attached to farm work. SAAU organised well-attended meetings at which farmers were lectured by 'personnel relations' experts, including blacks, about how to treat their workers.[51] A decade earlier, this would have been rejected by most farmers as intolerable interference in the relationship between master and servant.

International pressures also had an effect. The export market was important to farmers and, like other SA employers, they became aware of the threat which international hostility to apartheid could pose to their markets, for example to the sugar industry's USA quota. The (coloured) Labour Party threatened that it would call for an international boycott of agricultural products unless wages and conditions improved. The growing importance of Africa as a market for food was frequently stressed by Schoeman, the Minister of Agriculture: 'There is a vast market for us in Africa . . . . Why should Africa import maize from the

United States?'[52] Food comprised a high proportion of the R1bn worth of goods that SA exported to African countries in 1981.

Other measures affecting the rights and conditions of farm workers
Farm workers were even more rightless than mineworkers, who could leave at the end of their contracts and be sure that minimal conditions, including payment of wages, were enforced by government inspectors. Agriculture was, moreover, specifically excluded from such inadequate protection as was afforded to urban workers by the Wage, Industrial Conciliation, and Bantu Labour (Settlement of Disputes) Acts. Trade unions were anathema to farmers: when their workers joined the Industrial Commercial Union (ICU) in the 1920s, farmers dismissed them, confiscated their stock, and demanded a sedition law. In their evidence to the 1951 Industrial Legislation Commission, they opposed the extension of trade union rights to Africans.[53]

The power of employers over the lives of their workers meant that there was considerable variation in conditions. Some workers were harshly treated and bullied, others had fairly good personal relationships with conscientious, if paternalist, employers, often sustained over a lifetime or even over generations. The position of farmworkers bore similarities to that of the serfs in Russia before their emancipation in 1861,[54] particularly in the restrictions on mobility, which tied down the worker and his family and gave the farmer power over them backed up by the law, while placing on him some obligations—to accommodate the families, provide some education and allow them to remain in their old age. Other feudal features were the widespread persistence of labour tenancy and the high proportion of payment in kind.*

Many of the harshest features began to decline. The tot system (payment of wages in wine) and convict labour were phased out; the Masters and Servants Acts were abolished. Indebtedness became less effective in tying workers.[56] Trade unions spread to farmworkers, particularly in sectors vertically integrated with the processing of agricultural produce, as in sugar milling and timber manufacturing. Farmers began to press for state assistance for improved housing, clinics, schools and pensions for their workers.

---

*The censuses show this amounting to between a half and a third of total earnings; but microstudies suggest higher levels of between 50 and 85 per cent of total earnings.[55]

The spread of capital-intensive, mechanized farming, then, did not lead to the intensification of apartheid and worsening of conditions. However, reforms lagged behind those in the towns. Moreover, while many farm workers and their families gained, this was not the case for the sizeable tenant communities, whose departure from the land was accelerated by mechanized farming. The death of feudalism, as Marx noted, has painful side effects.[57] In SA these were exacerbated by the large remaining segments of apartheid, which prevented the displaced tenants from seeking work in the towns, or from setting up as farmers on their own account.

To sum up, the web of apartheid laws affecting the supply, mobility, price and disciplining of farm labour ensured white farmers of a larger supply of unskilled labour, at a lower price, than they would have secured in a free market. They got this artificially enlarged and cheap supply at a time they most needed it. From the mid-1960s, there was a decline in the serf-like controls tying workers to the farms, and an improvement in the pay, conditions and treatment of many of them. The explanation for these trends lay partly in changes within the farming sector, which meant that efficient, profitably-run farms could coexist with, and even benefit from, reforms and improvements: their prosperity no longer depended on cheap, forced labour.

However, the pressures for reform within this sector were not as compelling as those in manufacturing, commerce and services. Many farmers could have continued comfortably with feudal relics, such as restrictions on mobility. The pressures emanating from outside agriculture—because of the need and greater power of manufacturing and mining capital to get rid of many aspects of apartheid—were therefore crucial. They were strengthened by the penetration of these outside capitals into agriculture itself.

The process of change in white agriculture illustrates the key role played by conflicts of interest among capitalists, both within agriculture and between the farming and non-farming sectors. The huge, coerced farm labour force—unlike workers in the urban areas—has, as yet, played little part in the erosion of apartheid.

Measures protecting white farmers against black competition

The transformation of SA agriculture was almost entirely confined to the *white* agricultural sector, which produced about 95 per cent of total 1970 agricultural output. The remaining 5 per cent was produced by thousands of Africans farming small-holdings in the Bantustans and grazing their cattle on the communal land. Until the late 1970s, there were few signs of modernization and little increase in output from this sector.

The striking difference between the large-scale, capital-intensive, commercialized white farms and the mainly subsistence, small-scale African farms led many observers to describe SA as a 'dual' economy, with two apparently separate agricultural sectors. It was widely believed that the poor performance of African farmers was due to their adherence to 'irrational' tribal practices and customs (communal land tenure, religious attitudes to cattle) which, together with resistance to modern farming methods, made it increasingly difficult for them to feed themselves or compete with white farmers.

It was furthermore argued that Africans were unambitious; that their aim was to produce enough food (or work for enough money) to feed themselves. If they produced more than they needed, they would not exert themselves to farm or work the following season.[58] This 'backward-sloping supply curve' argument was used both as an explanation of why Africans allegedly did not respond to the growing market opportunities for farmers in southern Africa, and to justify paying them low wages.

This diagnosis confused cause with effect. It was like the argument (which used to be common) that Africans were incapable of doing the skilled, as distinct from 'repetitive', jobs in industry. The fact that so few Africans were doing these jobs was cited as evidence of this, without any reference to the discriminatory measures preventing them from acquiring the skills or doing the jobs.

The claim that Africans were hopeless farmers who could never compete with whites overlooks the historical evidence that, at the turn of the century, some African farmers were increasing production, 'in response to the more favourable terms on which they could dispose of their produce. The growing use of the plough, replacing the hoe, was one of the factors in increasing production.' This led to complaints from whites that the supply of labour has 'year by year become more inadequate as the Natives become richer and yearly cultivate a greater acreage with the plough'.[59]

Case-studies of the Ciskei, Lesotho and Rhodesia provide evidence of responses to market opportunities for food production; at the turn of the century Lesotho was known as 'the granary' of the OFS.[60]

But these examples do not dispose of a puzzle: despite the Land Act, Africans were left in possession of a substantial amount of land: about a quarter of SA's arable land, much of it along the fertile south-east coast, and a higher proportion in surrounding countries like Botswana, Lesotho and Swaziland. What accounts for the conversion of Lesotho, and other food-producing areas, from granaries to stagnant rural slums, exporting manpower and importing food?

Our understanding is still too limited to answer this complex question fully. Social and cultural factors may have played some part; but in view of systematic discrimination it is unnecessary to resort to ill-established racial and cultural generalizations. There are more concrete and straightforward economic and political explanations for the failure of African agriculture in SA.

The 1913 Land Act destroyed a class of African tenant farmers in the 'white' areas, and led to increasing population pressure in the homelands which, combined with taxes, converted many African farmers into labourers, migrating to white areas to work. Second, African political and institutional arrangements were adapted (like those of many whites in the nineteenth century) to a situation of plentiful land. Their failure to adapt to land scarcity was at least in part the outcome of the deliberate policy of white governments to retain and prop up many of the traditional institutions, such as the communal grazing system and the power of chiefs over land allocation. An example of this was Verwoerd's veto of the Tomlinson recommendation for the introduction of freehold tenure.

Third, the economic incentives were rigged, so that it was not worthwhile for Africans to develop their land. From 1910 to 1936, state expenditure on white agriculture was roughly R225m; practically nothing was spent on black agriculture. Per farmer, the ratio was even wider, as there were many more black than white farmers. Recently, expenditure on African agriculture has increased; but, in 1973, the state was still spending twice as much on the 90,000 rich, developed white farmers, who had decades of favourable treatment behind them, as it spent on over half a million poor African farmers.[61] Apart from discriminatory state expenditure, white farmers had easy access to subsidized Land Bank loans; but it was practically impossible for Africans, who could not mortgage their land, to raise private bank loans. White farmers were able to use this capital to invest in fertilizers, new seeds and machinery, all of which multiplied their yields and output. Important, too, was the fact that white farmers got heavily subsidized irrigation; lacking this, crop farming in semi-arid areas is risky and low-yielding. Africans were also seriously disadvantaged in the provision of transport and marketing facilities, while excellent research and training programmes were geared almost exclusively towards the needs of white farmers.

In addition to the highly unequal allocation of land and capital, extensive measures were taken to ensure that white farmers had a plentiful supply, at low cost, of the third factor of production— labour. The demand of white farmers for cheap labour provided an additional (some would say the major) reason for the suppression of African agriculture. This was always a primary consideration affecting policies towards the reserves. For example, the reports of the Native Affairs Commission during the 1930s, when there was growing concern about the poverty of the reserves, made it clear that no developments would be contemplated which might reduce the supply of labour from them.[62] It was clearly intended that the manpower of the reserves should be exported to plough the fields of white farmers, rather than to develop African agriculture. For all their overcrowding, the reserves were probably short of manpower and underfarmed.

Despite disparaging remarks about African farmers, the fear of competition from them was openly expressed by leading officials, politicians and farmers. In 1938, the Secretary of the Livestock and Meat Industries Control Board argued that:

> In practically all secondary industries and in mining, the labour of the white man is protected against the cheaper labour of the Native. But in agriculture, particularly in the livestock industry, the White man competes with the Native on very difficult terms . . . . The Native . . . has free communal lands, and virtually no direct cost of production. It should be quite obvious that this White agriculturalist is up against one of the most serious problems that faces a White standard of civilization.

The Secretary for Agriculture argued that 'in the interest of the farming community it will be necessary to institute measures to prevent such surplus, with its lower cost of production by Native peasants, being dumped on the market, thereby depressing prices.'[63] The possibility of competition from Africans was not brushed aside by J. G. Strijdom (later Prime Minister) when the reserves were extended in 1936. He objected to the proposed purchase of tractors and ploughs, declaring, 'If the Government went on in this way, natives would soon cease to be labourers and become farmers, with disastrous effects on white farming, where the problem of markets was already serious.'[64] Discussing the extension of irrigated farming in the reserves in 1952, Verwoerd acknowledged the continuing opposition of white farmers to 'unfair competition' from Africans.[65]

The fact that Africans were prevented from competing with white farmers does not, of course, mean they would all have been successful farmers. Doubtless there would have been many Africans (as there were whites) who could not adapt to the difficult conditions in southern Africa, or who preferred urban life. But this is unlikely to have been true of all Africans. The fact that it was felt necessary to take such far-reaching measures against them suggests that (apart from the loss of labour that development of African farming would have entailed) some of them might have been highly competitive.

The reason for this is hinted at in the official statements cited above—the competitive edge that efficient small-scale, labour-intensive family farming has over the large-scale, capital-intensive farm, especially when the latter is based on low-paid, coerced labour. Studies throughout the world have shown that output per acre on the small family unit is often higher than on large farms, especially in vegetable, rootcrop and probably cereal farming.[66] Despite long-held beliefs to the contrary, the economies-of-scale argument that applies to industry often does not work for agricultural production (as distinct from marketing). It is this factor which accounts for the low-cost production and 'unfair' competition feared by white farmers.

This suggests that the development of African farming might have provided cheaper food for the towns, thus lowering the costs of industrialization; though it would have reduced the labour available to the mines and white farms. It would also probably have led to a different pattern of agricultural development, with a larger class of small-scale family producers, combined with large-scale farmers in products in which they have an advantage.

The discriminatory measures against Africans made it impossible for them to compete with the heavily-subsidized and protected white farmers. Despite its inefficiencies, white farming developed, while African farming died what was considered a 'natural' death. It is reasonable to conclude that many white farmers, especially the less efficient ones, were heavily dependent on apartheid and that, far from SA being a 'dual economy', there was a close inter-relationship between the development of white, and the failure of African agriculture.

But recently, white farmers have become less opposed to, and less able to oppose, the development of African farming. The expansion of the market for agricultural products has reduced the fear of competition. Indeed, despite periodic surpluses, for example of maize, SAAU anticipated that unless production was expanded, SA would have to import food for its rapidly growing population. The Bantustans represented an unused resource which SA planners, and even white farmers, came to believe should be developed. Some white farmers hoped to play an active role in this. Further, when the former shortages of labour turned into an over-supply, agricultural development was an obvious strategy for mopping up the unemployment which was of increasing concern to the whole oligarchy. Farmers, like other whites, therefore acquired an interest in promoting at least some development of African farming. The result was increased expenditure on African agriculture and the easing of restrictions on Indian and coloured farmers (see p. 59). Natal sugar farmers set up schemes to aid black farmers; in 1980, the President of SAAU invited all races to join the new North-West Cape Agricultural Union.[67]

However, white farmers made the acquisition of the limited amount of quota land still owing to the Bantustans difficult and expensive. This was not necessarily because they were opposed to it in principle; some did not want to sell land that had been in the family for generations, while others bargained hard in the hope of pushing up the price. This raised the cost of transferring land and reduced the revenue available for development. The opposition of white farmers to land transfers and their attempt to exercise some control over Bantustan production and marketing (for example, the opposition of sugar farmers to the establishment of separate milling capacity for Kwazulu farmers) led to sharp criticism of 'white avarice' by Chief Buthelezi and threatened to undermine the political cooperation the farmers wished to establish with him.[68]

Political apartheid

Until recently, apartheid was vital for the interests of white farmers. It underwrote their possession of the land, shielded them from black competition and provided them with plenty of cheap, docile labour, while not imposing on them the costs in the skilled labour market incurred by other employers. Africans intensely resented the Land Act and 'pass' laws, and their removal has been among the demands of every major African political organization. The exclusion of blacks from political power was therefore vital to the interests of farmers. No other group of employers was so dependent on racial and not just class measures, because the needs of most white farmers could not, initially, have been secured by the operation of 'free' market forces, as could those of many urban businessmen. They required massive state intervention.

Moreover, it was not only against Africans that white farmers desired political intervention. It was also against competing white interests—particularly urban employers, who offered higher wages and who also objected to the large state subsidies for white farmers and the protection imposed against cheap agricultural imports. Apartheid was not, therefore, the only reason why white farmers required a powerful, interventionist state. (These often neglected 'non-racial' aspects of policy, which interacted in a complex way with apartheid, are discussed in Chapters 8 and 9.)

As the interests of white farmers changed, they had less need of the apartheid policies that white political control underwrote. They also became aware of the political costs of apartheid—of the threats that international hostility could pose to their exports and internal unrest to their security. The internal problems impinged directly on farmers. First, they were in the front line in the mounting insurgency by black guerillas.* Second, the implementation of the land consolidation proposals (to reduce the fragmentation of the Bantustans), limited though these were, led to

---

*The government attempted to stem the continuing white rural exodus by offering grants and credits to farmers who remained in strategic border areas.[69]

upheaval and uncertainty for farmers in the regions affected. Alarm was caused by the disastrous impact of consolidation in the eastern Cape, where tens of thousands of blacks were dumped in resettlement camps, agricultural output fell, and unemployment, political unrest and crime (including thefts of stock) soared.[70]

Natal farmers mobilised to prevent a similar course of events in their province. In 1979, the SA Sugar Association urged the government not to go ahead with its plans for consolidation and independence of Kwazulu, declaring that this would have 'a disruptive impact' on sugar-producing areas. Instead, leading sugar farmers joined Natal businessmen in commissioning a study by the Afrikaans economist, Jan Lombard, to explore alternatives to the Bantustan policy. The Lombard Report argued that stable government could not be provided by separate development, but only by 'the emergence of new, legitimate political institutions that allow the effective participation of the governed'. The Report recommended an experiment in 'power sharing' between the races in Natal.[71] Ironically, white farmers, who had supported apartheid more consistently than any other capitalists, were the first among them to confront (as a class) the thorny question of African political rights.

The views of farmers remained diverse. As the results of the 1981 election and 1983 referendum on the constitution showed, farmers in the northern Transvaal remained conservative. But the trend among the leading farmers was in a more liberal or *verligte* direction, aided by the belief that, whatever the historical resentments, the spectre of crippling food shortages throughout Africa would make black governments loath to destroy what had become the continent's most productive agricultural sector.

5
The Interests of Mining Capital*

Mineowners supported some major aspects of apartheid, particularly measures which enlarged the supply of cheap, unskilled, black labour and ensured its docility. However, unlike white farmers, they could not escape the job colour bar which, after an intense struggle during the 1920s, became more strongly entrenched and costly in mining than in any other sector. There was thus a conflict between mineowners' benefits from their monopsony power in the unskilled labour market (and from the inhuman compound labour system) and the costs of apartheid in the skilled labour market. This conflict lay at the heart of the ambivalence and divisions among mineowners over apartheid.

From the 1960s, the costs of the job bar rose sharply, leading to renewed pressures against it, but also intensifying the need for cheap, unskilled labour. However, the economics of gold mining were transformed by the rise in the gold price from 1970. Combined with other pressures (unrest among mine workers, the replacement of foreign by SA labour, public criticism of conditions on the mines) this led to rising real wages and improved conditions for black workers. The job bar and the system of compound labour were retained, however. Apartheid remained more entrenched on the gold mines than in any other sector, and mining capital seemed committed to meliorist or neo-apartheid solutions rather than to reform. It was only in 1982, with the recognition of black trade unions and some progress on the job bar, that deracialization seemed likely.

*This chapter will focus on the gold mines, which usually accounted for over two-thirds of the value of mining production.

110

Mining in the SA economy

Gold and diamonds provided the wealth that transformed SA from an undeveloped, largely subsistence economy into the most industrialized, modern state in Africa. In addition to their major contribution to Gross Domestic Product and employment (see Tables 4 and 5), the gold mines provided a substantial proportion of government revenue and often over half of total export earnings. Because of their pioneering and dominant role, the mines had a profound effect on the forms of socio-economic organization: the job bar and compound labour first emerged on the mines, and the initial battles over trade unionism were fought there.

The peculiar economics of gold mining helped to shape these institutional forms. The geology of the Witwatersrand mines, with low-grade ore, thinly and unevenly spread along a wide surface and at great depth, required elaborate, expensive structures for deep-level mining (some of the mines were 3,500 metres deep) and meant that much drilling and blasting had to be done by hand. They therefore required huge amounts of both capital and labour. The price of their product was moreover fixed at $35 per ounce in 1934 and did not rise until 1970. The extreme sensitivity of the industry to costs was a crucial factor in its labour policies, and it is no coincidence that the shift from cheap labour policies coincided with the rise in the gold price.

The huge investment required for deep-level mining meant that the industry soon came to be dominated by a few giant companies. The difficulties of production, political struggles over the surplus, and insatiable demand for the product, led the mining companies, despite their rivalries, to coordinate their policies through the Chamber of Mines, representing the seven leading mining houses. Through the Chamber they established a monopsonistic system of hiring African labour, which kept down its cost despite the labour shortage, and an efficient system of recruiting and transporting workers, which reduced the high turnover costs of migrant labour.

The changing interests and attitudes of mining capital will be analysed in relation to: the job colour bar; controls over African mobility and wages; other measures affecting the conditions and rights of African workers; general political considerations; and the discrepancy between the progressive views of sections of mining capital and their continued implementation of apartheid.

The job colour bar

There was little disagreement among analysts, following van der Horst's seminal *Native Labour in SA*, about the support of mining capital for many of the controls over black labour. But recently, the belief that mineowners opposed the job colour bar, which was foisted on them by white labour, was challenged by neo-Marxists like Johnstone and Davies, who argued that the job bar was an (over-emphasised) part of a total system, which served primarily the interests of capitalists, who sometimes wanted to shift the bar marginally upwards but basically supported it, because it divided black from white workers. They also maintained that the effects of the bar were exaggerated: it was neither so costly to capital nor so beneficial to white workers, as claimed.[1]

This view is contradicted by the historical evidence. The Chamber of Mines opposed the first statutory colour bar established in the Transvaal in 1893, arguing that a test for miners should be based on competence not colour; responsibility for this measure was claimed by the white Mine Workers Union (MWU).[2] It was logical that white unions should support the establishment of a bar limiting competition for their jobs at a time of high unemployment, and that employers should oppose a restrictive practice limiting the labour pool.

Thereafter, the bar was entrenched in response to pressures from white labour. Their opposition to Lord Milner's plan to import indentured Chinese labourers to restart the mines after the Boer War was bought off by reinforcement of the job bar in 1903 against the possible use of the Chinese in skilled work.[3] The 1907 strike by white workers against erosion of the job bar led the Botha/Smuts government to insist on 'a definite ratio in mining of "civilised labour" to indentured natives.'[4]

After Union, the Chamber opposed the legalisation of the bar in the 1911 Mines and Works Act; but this was again supported by the white unions and their Labour Party.[5] In 1918, under trade union pressure, the legal or statutory job bar (protecting about one-third of white miners) and the customary bar (protecting another fifth) were buttressed by the Status Quo Agreement, whereby the Chamber reluctantly agreed to maintain the existing ratio of African to white miners.[6]

However, rising costs and a falling gold price soon led to pressures from mineowners to relax the job bar, thereby increasing the ratio of (cheap) African to (expensive) white workers. The Chamber's representatives on the 1920 Low Grade Mines Commission recommended total abolition of the job bar; the white miners' representatives opposed this.[7]

The costs crisis and the 1922 Rand rebellion

The sharp fall in the gold price in 1921 precipitated a crisis. Ignoring Smuts's warning that the job bar must be treated as 'sacrosanct' and that a 'frontal assault' on it would lead to violent resistance by the white unions supported by the bulk of the white population of the Rand, the Chamber announced that it would withdraw the Status Quo Agreement and increase the ratio of Africans to whites.[8] In response, the white unions called a strike. There is no clearer illustration of the importance both sides attached to the job bar than the ensuing events, which led to a general strike and the declaration of martial law, resulting in the death of 250 people and the wounding and imprisonment of hundreds more.[9]

The strikes were crushed by the South Africa Party (SAP) government, which was now more sympathetic to mining interests and which permitted the Chamber to erode the bar and increase the ratio of African to white miners. The Chamber also challenged the legality of the statutory job bar in the Courts, which, in 1923, declared the Mines and Works Act ultra vires.

But the 1924 victory of the Nationalist–Labour Pact government, committed to 'civilised labour' policies, reversed the Chamber's brief victory. The ratio narrowed again, and the 1926 Amendment to the Mines and Works Act entrenched the job colour bar against the challenge to its legality. The Chamber financed the campaign against the 1926 Amendment—the first well-financed campaign against segregation measures since Union.[10]

Mineowners and white workers were prepared to precipitate a virtual civil war over the job bar because its effects were substantial for both parties. In 1921 the gold price fell by a quarter (from 130 to 95 shillings), while working costs had risen by a third (from 17/5 per ton in 1915 to 23/9 in 1920). This was due mainly to increased white labour costs: the wages of whites, comprising 11 per cent of the workforce, accounted for 25 per cent of total working costs; African wages for 12 per cent.[11] Many mines faced the prospect of closure unless they could cut costs by substituting Africans for whites.

Mining accounted for a high proportion of formal sector jobs at a time of desperately high unemployment. From 1910–18, the number of whites in mining averaged 22,000 and the ratio varied from 8–9 Africans to 1 white worker. The Status Quo Agreement froze the ratio at 7.4 to 1. During the Chamber's brief victory, the ratio was increased to 11.4 Africans to 1 white—by almost 50 per cent. A third of white miners lost their jobs; the rest had their wages reduced. Working costs fell to 19/7 per ton.[12]

After the 1924 election the number of whites climbed back to 22,000 in 1929, when the ratio was down to 8.8 to 1. In 1953 (when there were over 46,000 whites on gold mines) it reached its lowest point of 6.4 to 1—little over half of what it had been during the brief defeat of white labour in 1922. Obviously white numbers would not have reached this level without the job bar, especially given the growing gap between white and African wages. On the contrary, white numbers would have declined from their 1922 level (and/or white wages would have fallen).

During the 1924 election, white mining unions claimed that, if the SAP won, thousands more whites would be dismissed. This belief seemed confirmed by the Chamber's evidence to the 1930–32 Native Economic Commission that, if they had a free hand, there was 'not the slightest doubt' that they could do with 'a materially smaller' number of whites and could then employ more skilled blacks at 'a higher rate of pay'.[13]

It seems likely that, without the job bar, many whites in this acutely cost-conscious industry would have been displaced by cheaper blacks, as they were in agriculture. Instead, high white labour costs contributed to 'significant disinvestment' in SA mines from 1924–32 and to investment abroad by SA-based mining companies.[14]

The view which dismisses these effects as marginal is both ahistorical and static. It overlooks the importance of mining jobs then, as well as the dynamic and cumulative effects over time of policies which pointed in opposite directions—one towards the erosion, the other towards the maintenance and shoring-up, of the job bar—not only in mining, but in other urban sectors, for which the mines set a precedent.

The fact that mineowners were autocratic and illiberal, disliked all trade unions, and supported racist measures forcing blacks to work for them, does not mean that they wanted the job colour bar. There was no reason why, as on the farms and on Rhodesian mines,[15] many of the supervisory jobs could not be performed by cheaper (and probably more amenable) blacks, rather than by expensive (and 'stroppy') whites—unless it is argued that racist sentiments led mineowners to prefer whites. But this is not the neo-Marxists' argument, and it would be incompatible with a Marxist analysis, which asserts the primacy of class over racial factors. More to the point, it is refuted by the evidence that the 'taste for discrimination' (see p. 250) of mining capitalists, racist though they often were, was insufficient to make them pay the premium wages required for the pleasure of employing fellow-whites. The fixed price of gold meant that white workers were too expensive. Despite their rhetorical assurances to white unions about their belief in 'the need to preserve the white race' (and despite their use of the bar as an excuse for keeping unemployed whites out of unskilled jobs[16]) the mineowners' desire for profits overcame any personal preference they had for employing whites. Hence their repeated attempts to erode the job bar. Their failure was due to their lack of political power (discussed in Chapter 9). The disbelief of Marxists that the leading capitalists could be politically weak largely accounts for their insistence that they must have wanted the job bar.

After the traumatic events of 1922–24, mineowners realised that the job bar was 'simply not an agenda item',[17] and acquiesced in it. But its costs and inconvenience remained high. The two critical factors in the economics of mining are diminishing returns, as the better seams are worked first, and the price of the product. The gold mines were stuck with diminishing returns, a fixed price product and rising costs. These resulted in a falling rate of profit.*

*Frankel showed that from 1935–63 the average rate of return on mining shares was 4.3 per cent, compared with 7 per cent for UK equities; in real terms 0.2 compared with 2.1 per cent.[18] White labour by contrast, did well: white wages in mining, for example during the 1930s and 1950s, were two-thirds to one-third higher than in manufacturing (see Tables 10, 11, 12).

The mines were saved from another costs crisis by the devaluations of 1933 and 1949 and, in the 1950s, by the opening of the rich OFS goldfields and the exploitation of uranium as a by-product.*

The 1948 Nationalist government tightened and extended the job bar on the mines. The ratio of white to African workers fell to its lowest level ever, while the wage differential widened from 12.1 to 1 in 1941 to 17 to 1 in 1961 (see Table 11). In the face of this growing wage gap, it is simply perverse to insist that it was in the interests of mineowners to employ expensive white instead of cheap black workers, especially as labour remained an important part of total costs: 37 per cent in 1956, of which whites accounted for 26 per cent. By the 1960s, gold mining was a declining industry, with many mines kept open by subsidies, amounting to R30m in 1970.

These problems led to renewed pressures to substitute black workers for white and to mechanise. It was estimated that replacement of 70 per cent of white with black workers could save R30m per annum,[19] equivalent to the mining subsidy. But the ratio prevented the innovations and reorganization that led to a growing proportion of semi-skilled blacks in manufacturing and in much opencast mining. Moreover, the rigid bar, and the growing shortage of skilled workers, were a deterrent to mechanization, which increases the need for skilled workers to install and maintain the machines. The mines tried to bend the bar, the unions resisted; and the government Mining Engineer regularly charged and fined mining houses for infringements, usually for allowing blacks without blasting certificates to use explosives.[20]

The growing skill shortage

The mines were badly affected by the growing shortage of skilled (i.e. white) labour during the 1960s. By 1969, they were short of 2,000 skilled men, 5 per cent of the white labour force.[21] If the gold price rose, the skill shortage would act as a constraint on the expansion of mining.

Mineowners mounted an increasing barrage of criticism against the job bar. Demands for its relaxation came not only from Harry

*From 1952–70, uranium sales amounted to R1bn.

Oppenheimer, chairman of AAC, known for his liberal views, but also from Tom Muller, chairman of the Afrikaans firm, General Mining, which had recently acquired a substantial interest in gold mining. He pleaded with white miners to let the bar float upwards, allowing blacks to take over routine jobs (*Kafferwerk*, as it was crudely put) so as to free whites for more specialised work.[22]

The acute problems of the mines, plus pressures from Afrikaans capital, led to covert government support in 1965 for an experiment to raise the colour bar. But when this was attacked by the MWU, the government backed away and the experiment was abandoned (see p. 207). In 1968, mining companies applied for the easing of the job bar on mines in the Bantustans,* as provided for by the official separate development policy;[23] but this was also opposed by the MWU, which refused to back down under pressure from the Vorster government.[24] The MWU's intransigence pointed to another major confrontation over the job bar.

Changes in the economics of gold mining

The situation was transformed by outside factors, notably the dramatic rise in the gold price (which reached $200 by 1975 and $800 by 1978), and the threat of withdrawal of foreign black labour. The rise in price led to the expansion of mining and increased the need for scarce skilled labour. The threat of the withdrawal of foreign blacks was one of the factors leading to a rapid rise in African wages, so as to attract SAs who would not work for the low mining wages. Rising labour costs intensified the incentives to mechanize, which would further increase the demand for skilled and semi-skilled labour. In 1974, the Chamber launched a R150m crash programme of research into mechanization.[25] The pressures to raise the job bar and expand the supply of skilled labour became more urgent.

Calculations by Plewman, of the South African Institute of Mining and Metallurgy, demonstrated the difficulties of meeting the growing need for skills. Until the end of the century, at least

---

*The mines concerned were not gold, but Chamber members (General Mining and Union Corporation) were involved and the issue was relevant to all mining operations.

2,000 additional trained men (fitters, turners, electricians, sur-veyors) would be needed each year, and the mining industry could immediately use five times the current annual output of university mining engineers. Even if all job barriers were lifted, the training requirements meant it would take years to satisfy the huge demand for skills.[26]

The expansion of the mines led to more relaxed attitudes among some white workers, while higher profits made it easier to buy off their opposition to black advance. Modest advance was achieved with the 1973 Artisan Aides Agreement, giving whites a bonus in return for allowing blacks to do previously white work;[27] but progress was very slow in comparison with other sectors. In its evidence to the Wiehahn Commission, the Chamber urged the scrapping of job reservation and adoption of the principle of employment and promotion on merit.

In response to the Wiehahn reforms the MWU threatened 'another 1922'. In 1979 there was a strike against the employment of coloured artisans at the O'Kiep mine in the northern Cape, but the strike failed and thereafter the bar shifted slowly upwards, as the result of deals with the white officials' and artisans' unions, whom the Chamber—by means of big handouts—split from the MWU. The MWU, however, adamantly refused any concessions over the crucial blasting certificates reserved for its members by the Mines and Works Act, even on mines in 'independent' Bophutatswana (see p. 309).

The Wiehahn White Paper urged that the ending of the job bar be negotiated between the Chamber and the MWU. In 1983, the Chamber insisted that 'the reasonable period of time' specified for such negotiations had elapsed and demanded legislation to end the bar and to abolish racial discrimination in employment.[28] These diverse reactions were consistent with the attempts, for almost a century, of white capital to erode, and white labour to shore up, the job bar.

There was an alternative strategy open to mining capital: increased profits could be used to pay for apartheid by raising white wages sufficiently to attract skilled workers from other sectors and countries. This is what they ought to have done in terms of the argument that their main concern was to keep apartheid intact. It was also what some observers believed they would do.* This argument overlooked the historical struggle over the job bar, as well as the fact that a higher gold price meant that more gold was mined than would otherwise have been the case; and the unit cost of mining it increased. Both factors increased the costs of labour market inefficiency even further. These were among the reasons why the alternative strategy was not adopted by mineowners, who used higher profits to buy off white workers and erode the job bar.

Controls over mobility and wages

The expensive job colour bar meant other costs had to be cut. Little could be done to reduce the costs of equipment and stores, especially after the election of the 1924 Pact government, which protected SA manufacturing and imposed heavy taxes and discriminatory freight and pricing policies on the (then foreign-owned) mines. It was only in relation to black labour that the mines were given a relatively free hand, subject to the constraint that they should not compete with white farmers.

The mines, like the white farms, had immense difficulty securing sufficient labour at a price that it was economic for them to pay. Mineowners, like white farmers, therefore tried to find ways of forcing blacks to work for them, and of reducing the competition from higher urban wages. They supported restrictions on black land ownership, as well as taxes to force them to work for cash wages. Cecil Rhodes, leading mineowner and Premier of the Cape Colony, sponsored the 1894 Glen Grey Act. Its land tenure and tax provisions would, he said, act as a 'gentle stimulant' to blacks to work and 'remove them from that life of sloth and laziness . . . teach them the dignity of labour . . . and make them give some return for our wise and good government.'[30] Mineowners supported the 1913 Land Act; the President of the Chamber of Mines arguing that it would ensure that 'the surplus of young men, instead of squatting on the land in idleness . . . earn their living by

*For example, a leading financial journalist argued that, with the pressures on profits removed, the Chamber might become 'less resolute in its effort to persuade the unions to climb down' and the higher gold price would then 'fossilise Black–White labour patterns on the mines and help to maintain the status quo'.[29]

working for a wage.'[31] Chiefs were rewarded for persuading their subjects to earn their taxes on the mines; traders encouraged blacks to buy on credit and then pay off their debts by minework.[32]

Mineowners also supported influx control. The pass laws introduced in the Transvaal Republic in 1895 were actually drafted by the Chamber and gave them, as their spokesman put it, 'a hold on the native'.[33] But the influx controls also had costs for the mines, tying down labour on the farms, where wages were even lower than on the mines, which were prohibited from recruiting in many rural areas (see p. 91).

But the mines remained plagued by severe labour shortages. The problem was solved—and a confrontation with white farmers avoided (or at least postponed)—by the recruitment of labour from outside SA, where a large supply was forthcoming at lower rates. Public pressure led to the repatriation of the Chinese, imported after the Boer War, but thereafter mine workers were increasingly imported from neighbouring African countries, particularly Portuguese East Africa (now Mozambique) and the British Protectorates (Botswana, Lesotho and Swaziland), to which they could be readily repatriated. By 1970, foreign migrants accounted for 80 per cent of black workers on gold mines (see Table 8).

The increasing reliance on foreign migrants, who came for short-term contracts of six to eighteen months, added enormously to the problems of recruiting, transporting, training and housing the huge workforce. In 1896, to reduce competition for labour, central recruiting organizations* for all mining companies were established, accompanied by agreements to *reduce* wages. The notorious 'maximum average' placed a ceiling on black wages; fines were imposed on mining companies paying more.[34] This monopsonistic system enlarged the area from which the mines were able to draw labour and cut recruiting and transport costs. The industry succeeded in reducing black wages and maintaining them at a low level. Hence the stagnant African wages from Union until 1970 (see p. 44). In contrast to the wages of white workers, African cash wages, as a proportion of working costs, declined

*First known as WENELA (Witwatersrand Native Labour Assocation) and the NRC (Native Recruiting Corporation), later as TEBA (The Employment Bureau of Africa).

from 16.4 per cent in 1911 to 8.8 per cent in 1969.* The fact that mineowners produced almost solely for export meant that (unlike manufacturers and later farmers) they were not concerned about the effect of low wages in limiting the size of the domestic market.

These measures enabled the mines to increase the size of their black workforce from under 200,000 in the 1920s to over 300,000 in the 1950s, while holding down wages. Yet mineowners complained that they seldom had their full labour complement—as many workers as it would pay them to employ at the wages offered—and that they could not therefore operate at full capacity. Like white farmers, they cited backward-sloping supply curves as an excuse for not increasing the supply by raising wages (see p. 88).**

The fact that blacks do respond to economic incentives is confirmed by much research[36] and was demonstrated by the ample labour supply available in the towns, where wages were higher. It was also recognised by many mine managers who did not like the 'maximum average', which prevented them from giving wage increases as an incentive to higher productivity.[37] (This is a different question from drawing forth extra workers; but it reveals an awareness of the fact that blacks, like others, respond to incentives).

It is curious that the more profitable mining houses agreed to this system, which protected less profitable companies from having their wages bid up, but prevented more efficient companies from maximising profits by raising wages and operating at full capacity. Whatever the reasons (government pressure to ensure that the maximum number of mines remained in operation; the fact that even profitable mining houses owned some marginal mines; the unlimited demand for gold at the going price?) it was adhered to by all members of the Chamber until the 1960s, when

---

*However, these figures do not reflect the cost of housing, feeding, transporting and training workers; black *labour costs* were much higher than the cost of black wages.

**This view was expressed at a meeting of shareholders of a mining company in 1899: 'It is preposterous to pay a Kaffir the present wages. He would be quite as well satisfied—in fact he would work longer—if you gave him half the amount. (Laughter.) His wages are altogether disproportionate to his requirements.'[35]

AAC, by then the largest and most profitable mining house, tried to loosen the system. After Sharpeville, AAC wanted to raise black wages and urged the Chamber to suspend the maximum permissible average. This was opposed by other mining houses, but a compromise was reached whereby the maximum average was retained for all except the top 15 per cent of black miners.[38] The decision by the newly independent Tanzanian and Zambian governments to stop recruitment by the SA mines also reinforced AAC's desire to increase its proportion of SA blacks by paying higher wages.

Changes in labour supply and wages policy

The rise in the gold price coincided with, and facilitated, a major change in the mines' source of labour, with a shift from their overwhelming dependence on foreign black workers. Between 1974 and 1982, SA black workers increased from 20 to 58 per cent of miners.

Among the reasons for this rapid (and dislocating) shift were the 1973–5 riots on the mines, which led to the departure of thousands of miners; the death of Malawian miners in a 1974 planecrash which led the Malawian government to halt recruitment; and further fears about the unreliability of foreign labour supplies following the independence of Angola and Mozambique. These events led to the Chamber's watershed decision to increase the proportion of SA blacks on the mines, which meant they had to compete with urban wages. It is difficult to envisage how the mines could have coped with the unrest and instability in their labour force, and the switch to SA labour, without the rise in the gold price.

Table 8 shows the dramatic changes in sources of labour. Malawians declined from 110,000 workers (30 per cent of the workforce) in 1973 to less than 20,000 in 1976. Mozambicans rose to over 90,000 in 1975, then declined to 35,000 by 1978. There was a steady increase in Basothos, reaching 100,000 in 1980, and in SAs, whose numbers trebled from 81,000 in 1973 to 230,000 in 1982, many of them Transkeians.

It is noteworthy that even before these events, the mines had increased African wages as the gold prices rose. In 1972 there were the biggest wage rises for Africans in the history of the industry, which began to narrow the huge white/African differential (see

Table 9). By 1973, AAC appeared to have abandoned the 'maximum average' and was paying wages in excess of the maximum, and there were publicly acknowledged differences over wages within the Chamber, which formerly did not air its disagreements in public. Some mining houses, notably Goldfields, opposed the rapid increases for unskilled workers, as they feared a fall in the gold price.[39]

Initially, efforts to recruit SA blacks met with a slow response. This was partly, as surveys commissioned by the Chamber revealed, because of the 'bad image' of mining among SA blacks.[40] But it was mainly, as Oppenheimer acknowledged, because mining wages were not competitive: 'it is largely a question of pay,' he said and hoped that 'we could catch up' with industrial wages.[41] The backward-sloping supply curve, for long an article of faith of the mining industry, was abandoned. Between 1970 and 1978, real wages of Africans more than trebled and accounted for over a quarter of total working costs.

The need for SA workers precipitated the long-averted clash with agriculture. A. W. S. Schumann, President of the Chamber, complained about the opposition of white farmers to mining recruitment. Farmers, he said 'had to be handled with kid-gloves because they were well organized, well represented in parliament and can raise a tremendous hue and cry.' He argued that rural areas should not continue to be a 'closed shop . . . . Aside from the human rights argument—the right of a worker to sell his labour on the best market—I doubt whether we can afford restrictions which prevent the market from finding in the capitalist fashion its own level and a sound balance between supply and demand.'[42] In 1983, Gavin Relly, Oppenheimer's successor as AAC chairman, advocated the ending of influx controls, arguing that Africans, like whites, were entitled to free movement and that this would stimulate economic growth.[43]

The Chamber also persuaded the government to waive the regulation requiring urban Africans to report back to the homelands after each period of service on the mines. This had deterred them from taking mining jobs, as they feared they would lose their urban rights.[44] Thereafter, mining recruitment from the urban areas increased. By 1978, rising wages, and increasing unemployment as a result of the recession, eased the labour shortage. Indeed, many mines had a surplus of labour, as they were obliged to honour the commitment to re-engage all miners with valid re-engagement certificates (see below). Nevertheless, the wage increases continued, as the mines were determined to achieve parity with industrial wages.

By 1982 SA Africans (including those from 'independent' Bantustans) accounted for almost 60 per cent of African miners. Moreover, the supply of labour from within SA was such that dependence on foreign labour could have been further reduced. The reasons why this was not done included an acceptance by the Chamber of some 'obligations to its traditional supplier countries';[45] a desire to encourage economic interdependence in southern Africa; a fear of political instability if this major source of foreign earnings was removed; and a desire to keep their options open and to spread their risks.

The events of the 1970s—the skilled labour shortage, rise in the gold price, mine riots, and withdrawal of foreign blacks—led to considerable changes on the mines, with mineowners (who once drafted pass laws) extolling the virtues of a free labour market and paying higher wages than were needed to ensure adequate supplies of labour! If the shift to SA blacks had not coincided with a rise in the gold price it is possible that the mines would have resorted once again to coercive measures to expand the supply. They would have had to contend with the opposition of other employers and of blacks, as well as international opinion, and this scenario might simply have hastened their decline. But the government might have backed them, especially if there had been a serious shortage of foreign exchange. This intensification of apartheid would have been caused (as in the 1920s) by another costs crisis on the mines; instead the prosperity brought about by the rising gold price led to increased wages and pressure from mineowners for a relaxation of both the vertical and horizontal colour bars.

The sharp rise in African wages, and in housing and related costs, raised the cost of unskilled labour. This, and uncertainty regarding future labour supplies, increased the incentives to mechanize. For technical reasons, mechanization is likely to be difficult and slow on the gold mines, but it will further reduce the benefits of the cheap unskilled labour with which apartheid provided the mines, while increasing the costs of restrictions on the supply of skilled labour.

The costs and benefits of apartheid to the gold mines are

therefore changing, *but not as rapidly or to the same degree as in manufacturing and commerce, or in other types of mining.* This is because the technology of gold mining has changed much less; it remains heavily dependent upon large numbers of unskilled workers, who are still forced to live in the single-sex compounds which have become an integral part of the organization of African mine labour.

Other measures affecting workers' conditions and rights

The compound system
The compound system of housing African migrants originated at the Kimberley diamond mines. It allowed close supervision and screening of workers, thus reducing the risk of theft. Mineowners tried but failed to extend it to white workers. As a director of a diamond mine explained to an official commission in 1908, this was one of the deterrents to employing whites: 'You could not search them and put them in a compound. You could not put them in detention houses at the end of the period of service, to see that they do not take any diamonds out . . . you would have them on strike.'[46] This illustrates the other major function of compounds: on the Witwatersrand theft of low-grade gold rock was scarcely a problem, but mineowners found the compounds a convenient way of controlling and disciplining their huge workforce. Workers could be clocked in and out of work on time and absenteeism kept to a minimum. These were great attractions in a dangerous industry requiring a high degree of discipline and cooperation and relying on young, inexperienced, mainly temporary, foreign migrants.

The compounds were strictly policed; they were also dreary and depressing. Workers were provided with the bare necessities: a concrete bed, food and medical attention. The system of enforced migrancy separated men from their families and from normal social life for long periods; the all-male barracks encouraged the spread of both prostitution and homosexuality. There were high rates of drunkenness and violence, including 'faction fights' between different tribal groups, who were separately housed, thus emphasising group differences. Recent studies have confirmed these and other ill-effects long claimed by their critics.[47]

The compounds had both costs and benefits to mineowners. The obvious benefit was that of control and discipline over the workforce. Housing and food could also be economically provided, while ensuring that a high proportion of labour costs was spent on feeding workers, rather than their families. It was also assumed that a true proletariat would have been more effective in pressing for higher wages and for housing and other social overheads, which would have led to increased taxes (though not all these would have fallen on mineowners). The high turnover in the compounds made it difficult for workers to organize and establish solidarity, especially as they came from such diverse backgrounds.

But the system also had costs. The mines had to house and feed their entire African workforce, while reliance on migrants meant very high labour turnover—more than a hundred per cent annually. The constant need to recruit, transport and train huge numbers of workers was expensive and wasteful. It was made tolerable by the efficient and ingenious system of recruitment and training, ruthless economy and discipline, and skilful management.[48] The exclusion of Africans from skilled jobs was crucial, because the training required for those jobs would have been too expensive an investment at these rates of turnover. Not surprisingly, therefore, pressures for stabilization were invariably accompanied by pressures to raise the job bar—and vice versa.

In 1947, when the development of new OFS mines began, AAC pressed the government to let it build family housing, as they were then doing on their Rhodesian copper mines, for their more experienced 'bossboys', whose turnover rates they wished to reduce. The chairman, Ernest Oppenheimer, stated that, for Africans 'coming from territories outside the Union the compound system must be continued . . . but I feel sure our ultimate aim should be to create, within a reasonable time, modern native villages [i.e. with family housing] which will attract natives from all over the Union and from which our mines will ultimately draw a large proportion of their native requirements.' It was intended, as a first step, to stabilize 10 per cent of African miners.[49]

However, Verwoerd's intention was to extend migrancy to the urban sector, not to phase it out (see p. 25). He reluctantly agreed that the mines could stabilize a maximum of 3 per cent of Africans, all of whom had to be SAs. But most long-serving, experienced

Africans were foreigners and, in practice, stabilization was limited to a mere 1 per cent.

During the 1970s, the expansion of the mines and the increased need for skills intensified concern about high turnover. Discussing the need for expanded training, Plewman argued that, 'No industry could embark on such a programme unless it were going to benefit by continuing to employ a major proportion of the trainees. Similarly the trainees would be unlikely to undertake the training programme unless there were a career opportunity. The migratory labour system does not fit either of these requirements.'[50]

This questioning of migrancy was reinforced by the 1973–5 mine riots, during which 135 men died and over 500 were injured. The mining companies, especially those with world-wide interests, were embarrassed by the growing public criticism and jolted by the riots, which took place at a time of rising wages and improving conditions. Investigations revealed that in their abnormal social environment, the men had little to spend their money on except alcohol. It became questionable whether compounds were still an effective way of controlling the better-paid, more educated workforce whom the mines were attracting. The 1972 Ovambo strike in Namibia was based on Katatura compound and migrants were prominent in the 1973 Durban strikes.

Meliorism or reform?
But faced with the difficulties and expense of dismantling this highly institutionalized aspect of apartheid, mining companies resorted to meliorism to mitigate the worst effects of migrancy, rather than reform. Millions of rands were spent on upgrading and improving the compounds, providing better facilities and food, and enabling the men to see their families more frequently: buses, trains, and planes were laid on by the companies so that men at the OFS mines, for example, could visit their families in Lesotho and Transkei for weekends. But, despite improvements, they were still single-sex compounds, in which over 97 per cent of African miners (unlike whites) were compulsorily housed, separated from their families.

Progress in stabilizing the workforce was more limited. The Chamber pressed the government to raise the ceiling on stabilization to 10 per cent, and the more progressive companies began to build houses for at least the theoretical 3 per cent. New mines had a higher percentage of family housing and the compounds were planned so that they could be converted to family flats. But even the progressive companies spent less on building family housing than on upgrading compounds.

It was not clear how far and fast gold mining companies wanted stabilization to go. (In this they were unlike employers in other sectors, including other mines.)* Relly insisted that, on gold mines, 'Migrant labour is here to stay . . . and should be accepted as a permanent feature of our economic and social order.'[51]

There were various reasons for the retention of this particularly abhorrent feature of apartheid at a time when much else was changing. First, there was continued opposition from the government, loath to permit the stabilization of this largest group of migrants, the majority of whom were foreigners or citizens of 'independent' Bantustans. Second, there was resistance to stabilization within the mining industry itself, even in the progressive companies. The bureaucracy which managed the migrant labour system (recruiters, trainers, compound managers) acted as a strategically-placed pressure group for its retention. Their interests and attitudes reflected those of the state bureaucracy, from which many of them were drawn, and contrasted with the views of mine managers and production staff, who did not want the continued problems of turnover, especially as the job bar moved up, and favoured a smaller, stabler, better trained and paid, and therefore (they hoped) more contented and manageable workforce.

Third, a major deterrent for head offices was the cost of stabilization, largely because of the (surely extraordinary) assumption that mining companies must bear the full cost of housing, infrastructure and services, and the high housing standards insisted on by the bureaucrats, who opposed cheap squatter housing. Given the instability of the gold price, and the fact that many mines were short-life and/or situated in remote areas,

---

*For example, in 1980, 80 per cent of Africans were stabilized at RTZ's platinum mine in the Eastern Transvaal, and it was projected that a similar proportion would be in family housing at Rand Mines' new Rietspruit coalfields. Progress was easier on these mines because the workforce was smaller and more skilled.

large-scale stabilization at this standard was unfeasible. High housing standards were an excuse for blocking it.*

Fourth, the risks and upheaval of instituting a new system, whatever its long-term benefits, contrasted with the fact that the compound system was in place and that it worked. The companies were daunted by the scale of the problems which stabilization would involve. At a large mine like Vaal Reefs, with forty thousand miners, it could mean the mushroom growth of a township of a quarter of a million people. The prohibition on stabilization had prevented this from happening gradually and it was feared that if the controls were lifted, many people, bottled up in the Bantustans, would flock to join their relatives at the mines, causing enormous social and administrative problems. It was not a prospect welcomed by mine officials accustomed to strict control in their neat, disciplined, hierarchically-ordered company towns. The institutionalization of the compound system served to perpetuate it.

Finally, slow progress with the job bar, and the consequent lack of skills among African miners, remained a key factor limiting interest in stabilization. Moreover, in anticipation of rising levels of skill, the mining bureaucracy was devising schemes to reduce the need for stabilization, by the use of 'call-in cards' and re-engagement certificates. These guaranteed the miner his job back if he returned from his annual break within a specified time. Thus the migrant would depart from the old pattern of twelve to eighteen month contracts, interspersed with long absences, and become a regular worker, taking normal four to six weeks' leave—in other words, a stable migrant. Advocates of this system argued that it would enable migrants to have steady jobs and prospects of promotion. But it would also mean not only the perpetuation, but the intensification, of migrancy, as the men would spend a longer part of their working lives separated from their families.

Historically, pressures to stabilize migrants have accompanied rising levels of skill, as employers found it paid them to contribute

---

*For example, in 1977, houses being built by mining companies cost R10,000 each. At this rate, stabilization of the over 400,000 African miners would cost R4bn. This compared with R2,500 for housing a miner in the new, upgraded compounds, and on most mines the compounds already existed.

towards housing for workers' families in order to reduce labour turnover.[52] If this scheme to perpetuate migrancy in SA works, it will provide an example of neo-apartheid, not of reform. But the rising job bar, growing abhorrence of compulsory migrancy, and the emergence of African trade unions, will increase the pressures to extend to African miners the same right to have their families with them as whites have.

Workers' rights

The bargaining rights of African mineworkers—faced with a powerful, monopsonistic employers' organization—were severely circumscribed by the 1911 Native Labour Regulation Act (making breach of contract by mineworkers a criminal offence) and by the denial of trade union rights. The Chamber only recognised white unions when forced to do so by the Botha/Smuts government in 1915. They did their utmost to prevent the growth of unions among the low-paid African workforce. The consequent 'rightlessness' of Africans suited mineowners; as van der Horst commented, 'There can be little doubt of the superior attractions of Native labourers who were engaged on long-term contracts and subject to penal prosecution for desertion.'[53]

While some urban employers recognised African unions during the 1930s and 1940s, War Measures 145 of 1942 prohibited union meetings on mine property and made strikes by Africans illegal. In 1946 the African Mineworkers Union struck in protest at the Chamber's refusal to accept the recommendations of the official Lansdowne Commission that mine wages should be increased. The strike was brutally suppressed and the Chamber declared that 'trade unionism as practised by Europeans is still beyond the understanding of the tribal Native.' In its evidence to the 1951 Industrial Legislation Commission, the Chamber stated it viewed 'with alarm' the prospect of African unions.[54]

When black unions revived during the 1970s, mineowners showed some interest in alternative means of 'improving communications' with their workers, such as 'personnel relations' and the liaison committees encouraged by the Labour Department (see p. 67). But the pressure of events pushed them towards the acceptance of unions. First, they were jolted by the 1973–5 riots, of which their *induna* system* had given no advance warning. The sudden changes introduced on the mines without consulting the workforce were believed to be among the reasons for the unrest. These had some unintended consequences, for example, upsetting long-established wage differentials. If workers had been involved in negotiating the new wage scales, there would have been forewarnings of these resentments.

Second, the traditional means of disciplining and managing the workforce were becoming ineffective. The more educated SA Africans entering the mines, in response to rising wages and better conditions, were less amenable to the old military-style discipline, barking out orders and wielding the *sjambok* (stick or whip). If assaulted, they might hit back, or even walk out, as they were legally entitled to do after the 1974 abolition of the Masters and Servants Acts. In 1977, there were almost 50,000 'absconders' (workers who broke their contracts) from Chamber-affiliated mines—about 1 in 8 of the workforce. This compared with about 10,000 annually in the early 1970s, when wages and conditions were worse. Absenteeism also shot up: on OFS mines, for instance, it rose from 0.3 per cent before 1973 to 6 per cent afterwards.[55] New means had to be found of managing the huge workforce. Mineowners were unenthusiastic about trade unions, but they offered an institutionalized means of doing this. As Oppenheimer said after the mine riots, without unions there was 'no one to talk to' when problems arose—a classic reason why unions are useful to employers in large companies (see p. 172).

Third, black unions would be allies in the struggle against the MWU over the job bar, while the more amenable white unions began to insist on enrolling Africans entering the same jobs as their members (see p. 208).

Fourth, public opinion was important in shifting mineowners' attitudes. Their hostile stance towards unions was out of step with the willingness of many urban employers to recognise them. This reinforced the bad image they wished to escape from.

In 1974, Oppenheimer called for a commission of enquiry into

---

*The *indunas* were 'tribal elders' who were supposed to represent the miners and convey their grievances and problems. In practice, they were an arm of management.

the question of trade unions for blacks, and was supported by Schumann (see p. 167). In the Chamber's evidence to the Wiehahn Commission, AAC and Johannesburg Consolidated Investments (JCI), in a minority report, called for trade union rights for all African mineworkers, including foreign migrants. The other mining houses supported trade union rights for local Africans only, excluding foreign migrants. It is surprising they went as far as this, in view of the known opposition to unions of the conservatives in the Chamber, including the chairman of General Mining, Wim de Villiers (see p. 174). Trade unions, like wages, were one of the issues over which there were increasing divisions within the Chamber, as the pressures for change grew stronger. The progressives claimed that they were being held back by the conservatives, and Nicholas Oppenheimer, a senior AAC director, warned that the strains could break up the Chamber.[56]

In 1982 the Chamber was the last of the major employers' organizations to extend recognition to African unions. The National Union of Mineworkers (NUM) grew very fast. In 1984, the Chamber was faced with the first legal strike by African miners. The strike was quickly settled, though not without the violence, deaths and police intervention that seem a feature of industrial disputes on the gold mines. NUM general secretary, Cyril Ramaphosa warned that 'This year we were talking for 20 per cent of the workforce. Next year it will be higher and things will be different then.'[57] A more assertive role by African miners will accelerate changes on the gold mines.

Political apartheid

Mineowners were not as consistently opposed to black political rights as white farmers. At the 1909 conference to establish the Union of SA, Sir Percy Fitzpatrick, the Transvaal mineowner, supported the retention of the more liberal Cape franchise.[58] After 1948, some mineowners supported the campaigns against the extension of apartheid and helped to establish the liberal PFP (see p. 329). But, until recently, most mineowners supported many racist policies and, as their attitude to black unions showed, were hardly out of step with many of the Nationalists' repressive policies. It is moreover unlikely that in a system responsive to black political pressure, they would have got away with the large-scale importation of cheap foreign workers who undercut

black South Africans,* or with such extreme restrictions on their
rights as compulsory compounds and Masters and Servants laws.

However, employers elsewhere have got away with restrictions
on workers' rights and the importation of cheaper foreign workers.
The distinctive apartheid measures which affected the mines were
restrictions on mobility, the job colour bar, and closed compounds. Not all these measures were wanted by mineowners, and
even the restrictions on mobility, which they supported, benefited
farmers more. Their need for the compounds was closely tied to
the existence of the job bar and dependence on foreign labour
which, in turn, was a function of the political preference for
farmers.

For mineowners, therefore, apartheid was a more complex
equation than for farmers or for white workers—except *initially*,
when white conquest and reduction of the opportunity cost of
black peasants was probably essential for their operations. Thereafter, they might have managed without extra-economic coercion,
or even made some gains, outbidding white farmers for SA blacks
and avoiding the job bar. Instead the extra costs imposed on them
by apartheid intensified their own need for labour-repressive
measures such as closed compounds.

Mineowners also did not favour as substantial a state apparatus
as farmers. Their requirements were limited to the provision of an
infrastructure of transport, power, water, and an orderly environment for the conduct of their operations. They opposed the large
role assumed by the SA state in the development and protection of
agriculture and manufacturing, for which mining taxes footed the
bill. Curiously, their attitude to both aspects of state intervention
changed. Mineowners now want a free, mobile market in labour,
but are less opposed to state support for agriculture and manufacturing in which they have themselves become heavily involved.

Mineowners, like farmers, have also become concerned about
apartheid's political costs. Many of them, such as Barlow Rand,
Gencor and AAC, have world-wide interests, and they are worried
about hostility to SA in Africa and the West. They want to have
continued access to Western capital and technology, to invest

---

*African awareness of this was revealed very early, for example in the Transkei
Bunga (assembly) during the 1920s, when opposition was expressed to the
employment of blacks from outside SA.[59]

abroad themselves, and to continue selling their products on world markets. They draw much of their labour from the countries of southern and central Africa; some of them have investments in the region, and most SA mining houses would like to participate in the development of the considerable mineral resources of Africa, including those of Marxist states like Angola and Mozambique.

SA mining companies have continued to operate in independent Zambia, Botswana, Zimbabwe and even Angola, and mineowners have been prominent among the businessmen urging the SA government to introduce internal reforms and to pursue detente with Africa. Their regional interests suggest they want an accommodation with black nationalism not confrontation and adherence to apartheid.

Progressive views and apartheid policies

There were thus a wide range of issues—the job bar, wages, mobility, workers' rights and broader reforms—on which there were changes in the interests and attitudes of mineowners. They were summed up in a 1972 speech by W. D. Wilson, Deputy Chairman of AAC, calling for a 'major overhaul' of policies towards black workers. The problem, he said, 'goes very deep, to questions such as whether we will retain industrial peace and whether we will have the human resources to continue the development and expansion of our enterprises.' Urging a rapid increase in black wages, he argued: 'It is true that the mines are not short of labour and that in a strict business sense [wages do not need to be raised] . . . but the situation on other grounds appears untenable, particularly now that the mines are receiving an appreciably higher price for their product.' Black mine wages were 'extremely low in an absolute sense and compare unfavourably with other industrial wages'. Blacks are 'not afforded the same opportunities in relation to basic needs such as housing and education . . . the gap is so great and the need so urgent that it is plain common sense for commerce and industry to divert a small part of their profits to supplementing the activities of public authorities in these fields.' He urged consultation with employees in introducing changes, citing the 1972 Ovambo strike as 'a serious warning on the question of communications' and called for 'far-sighted policies [which often] . . . do pay'.[60]

Significantly, this speech was made in 1972, before the mine riots, or the threat of withdrawal of foreign labour. It was not then simply these pressures that were responsible for the changes, but also internal factors. These were (i) the changing policies and attitudes emanating from the now-dominant manufacturing and services sectors, in which, with the diversification of their investments, the mining companies were increasingly involved; and (ii) within the mining sector itself, the growing skilled labour shortage and slow shift to more skill-intensive technology, which increased the costs of apartheid, while the ample supply of black labour, and rising black wages—made possible by the rising gold price—reduced the need for apartheid in the unskilled labour market.

However, the policies of progressive mining capital since World War Two are puzzling, not only because of the contrast with the more liberal pressures of manufacturing and commercial capital (in which mining capital was itself increasingly involved) but also because of the progressives' failure to bring about changes within the mining industry and even in their own companies. Instead their operations remained based on the highly regimented and institutionalized form of apartheid found throughout the mines. What were the reasons for this discrepancy between their beliefs and actions?

First was the political weakness of progressive mining capital. On a number of occasions, they did attempt to introduce changes—in the job bar, stabilization of African labour, the ceiling on black wages. But they were prevented by the white unions and/or government and/or conservatives within the mining industry. The bargaining power of the conservatives was strengthened by the fact that the Nationalist government and white mining unions often supported the same policies.

Second was the dichotomy in the interests of the progressives, with their operations resting on cheap, coerced labour until the 1970s. This contributed towards their undoubted ambivalence towards reform on the gold mines (though not necessarily in their other operations).

Third, the various elements of the system hung together: only if mineowners got rid of the job bar would they develop an interest in stabilizing black labour. Hence the significance of challenges which, although limited to specific elements of the system, were likely to lead to wider systemic changes.

Fourth, an important obstacle to reform was the resistance to it within the progressive companies themselves. Giant companies like Barlow Rand and AAC (with 250,000 employees) were a cross-section of SA society, and liberal views were as thinly spread among white employees as in the rest of that society. Partly for historical reasons, white miners were hostile to company management. The middle-level bureaucracy, though loyal to the company, was opposed to progressive policies, which often threatened their own jobs and power.

Fifth, the institutionalization of apartheid gave a strategic advantage to those wishing to perpetuate it, while increasing the effort required to erode it. The extent to which apartheid was legalized on the mines, as well as their prominence and the vigilance of the white unions, prevented the informal and gradual erosion of apartheid that took place in other sectors.

Sixth, the consensus decision-making of the Chamber militated against change. This unusually tight and effective employers' organization provided advantages (particularly the efficient monopsonistic recruiting organization) which progressives, no less than conservatives, were loth to sacrifice. This was reinforced by social/class ties, which made individual mineowners reluctant to break rank with their colleagues, fellow-members of the Rand Club etc. The reasons for the policy differences between the progressives and conservatives would make a fascinating study. The profitability of Goldfields suggests that the answer does not lie solely in the economics of their mining operations. Mineowners' interests in other sectors and regions, and their political views and values, were also important.[61]

All these factors—political weakness, ambivalence, institutionalization of apartheid—meant that powerful pressures were needed to push mineowners towards reform. After 1948, there were few such pressures until the 1970s. The progressive companies were by then more numerous (Anglovaal, AAC, Barlow Rand, JCI) and they embarked on programmes of 'reeducation', led by liberal industrial relations specialists like Alex Boraine and Bobby Godsell. White miners were sent on special head office courses to persuade them of the need for black job advance, trade unions, etc. But changing attitudes was a slow, difficult process.

Whatever the reasons for the contradiction between liberal sentiments and harsh apartheid policies, it led to accusations that the sentiments were insincere. Concern about this, in turn, spurred the progressives' campaigns for reform and their substantial grants to black education, housing and community development. These political and moral pressures interacted in complex ways with changes in the gold price, labour supplies and technology to produce the significant, though still limited, changes in the policies of mining capital.

6

The Interests of Manufacturing Capital*

There was agreement between liberals and Marxists that, at certain stages, at least some aspects of apartheid were functional for growth in mining and agriculture. They disagreed, however, about the relationship between apartheid and manufacturing.

Liberals argued that in this sector apartheid was particularly inefficient and costly and predicted that these costs would rise and become an obstacle to continued growth.[1] Marxists argued that manufacturers also benefited from a plentiful supply of cheap, docile labour. Johnstone pointed out that the rapid expansion of manufacturing during the 1960s coincided with the tightening of apartheid and concluded that there must be a close correlation between the two. Legassick argued that apartheid was tailored to suit the needs of industry and constituted an attempt 'to formulate a "native policy" . . . which would actually promote growth in the specific conditions which existed in South Africa,' and that 'the pursuit of economic growth by continued capital intensification and the pursuit of separate development . . . [were] compatible.'[2]

This compatibility was certainly what the framers of separate development sought to achieve; and like the Marxists, they believed in the capacity of the state to shape the economy. However, manufacturing and commerce always posed problems for apartheid: it proved difficult to maintain the job bar in these sectors, which also provided the major impetus for the urban influx. These sectors were therefore at the heart of the struggle to impose apartheid on the economy.

*This chapter is mainly concerned with private manufacturing and construction, but also refers to employers in commerce, who shared many of the same labour problems and policies.

138

The argument here is that manufacturing and commercial capital did not need, and indeed opposed, most apartheid labour policies. The job bar raised their skilled labour costs and so limited their supply of skills that this became a constraint on growth. They were not short of unskilled labour except insofar as this was limited by influx controls, which also involved them in constant bureaucratic hassles. The importance of the domestic market to these sectors meant that they favoured generally higher wage levels, while protection made it easier for them than for mining to pass on costs. Their higher wage levels and less coercive policies also made them less fearful of black unions than the primary sectors. During the 1960s, the costs of both the vertical and horizontal bars rose steeply, partly because of mechanization, partly because of rapid growth,* and this intensified business opposition to apartheid labour policies.

However, while their labour policies led manufacturing and commercial capital consistently to reject segregationist Stallard principles and to press instead for the incorporation of blacks, including Africans, into SA society, they were cautious and paternalist in their social and political policies. Until recently, they mostly shared the general racist belief in the need for white rule to ensure political stability and they did not challenge measures such as residential and school segregation. The argument here is *not* that urban capitalists opposed apartheid because they were liberals—though some of them were—but that they opposed apartheid labour policies because these conflicted with their interests, and that this had dynamic implications for the whole system, as became evident when they achieved some of their aims during the 1970s and were then, logically, driven on to oppose broader aspects of apartheid.

The interests of manufacturing capital will be discussed in relation to the following aspects of apartheid: the job colour bar; the mobility and price of unskilled black labour; trade unions; protection against competition from black businessmen; and general political considerations.

*The contribution of manufacturing to national income rose from 5 per cent in 1911 to 27 per cent in 1970 (see Table 4). The value of output increased from R14m in 1911 to R3.3bn in 1970 and R18.7bn in 1981.

The job colour bar

There was no statutory job bar in manufacturing and commerce until the 1950s; but the 1922–25 legislative package enabled the white unions and government to exclude blacks from skilled jobs and to secure preference for whites in other jobs (see p. 19). The FCI* and Assocom opposed the Pact government's colour bar policies. In 1925 the journal, *Industrial South Africa*, which reflected their views, argued:

> The natives today are more widely educated than in the past . . . . Many thousands have grown up in the towns, many having been born in the cities or brought there in their early youth . . . . It is therefore no easy matter to bring into operation compulsory laws which will have the effect of throwing natives on the streets, where, unemployed, they will become a menace to the community . . . . [Instead, Wage Boards should] lay down the rates of wages to be paid for each occupation, according to the job, and then, no matter what the colour of the man's skin, if he was engaged to do that job, he must receive that wage . . . should any native prove physically and mentally capable of doing a certain kind of work, he will receive the rate of wages laid down for such work . . . . The Native must be given every opportunity to progress in the directions for which he is most fitted.[3]

Businessmen complained that the job bar, by limiting the supply of skilled labour, raised its cost, while the restrictions on black advance, and the lack of education and training for them, discouraged ambition and reduced productivity. Furthermore, the job bar in manufacturing and services was not limited to skilled jobs, but penetrated quite deeply into the semi-skilled and even unskilled categories. Whereas in mining, whites accounted for 10–15 per cent of the workforce, in manufacturing they accounted for almost 40 per cent until World War Two. Thereafter their relative importance declined, but there were still 0.25m whites, 25 per cent of the workforce, in this sector in 1970. The bar also limited

*The Federated Chamber of Industries, established in 1917. By 1970 it had 5,000 member firms, 70 per cent of SA manufacturers. Other major employers' organizations were the Associated Chambers of Commerce (Assocom) representing 17,000 businesses in 1970; and later the Steel and Engineering Industries Federation (SEIFSA) with over 1,600 affiliated firms; the *Afrikaanse Handelsinstituut* (AHI), representing 7,500 Afrikaans businessmen in all sectors outside agriculture. Some firms might of course belong to more than one of these organizations.

employers' freedom to reorganize and change their work patterns, a serious handicap in an industry in which, unlike gold mining, the technology and methods of production changed rapidly.

The manufacturers' argument that the high cost of the white labour they were forced to employ justified protection against cheaper imports was accepted by official commissions, such as the 1925 Customs Tariff Commission (see Chapter 8). Protection eased the problem by passing the costs on to consumers (and other businesses), but it raised the cost structure of SA manufacturing and did not end the complaints of businessmen about the job bar.

In 1931, the President of Assocom (whose membership then included many manufacturers) condemned the 'political interference' which imposed such high costs and inconvenience on secondary industry.[4] The widespread evasion by employers of measures which forced them to employ more expensive and/or less competent whites led to continual complaints by white unions and labour inspectors* and to the tightening of the IC Act in 1930 and 1937 (see p. 20).

However, the arguments of businessmen (and of liberal economists like Frankel) about the costs and inefficiencies of the job bar—and the whole range of labour policies which denied mobility, security, training and decent living conditions to blacks—had an impact on official thinking. This was evident in the reports of the wartime commissions which urged the relaxation of apartheid and rejection of the doctrine that Africans were 'temporary sojourners' in the white areas (see p. 20). The reformist case was clearly set out by the Industrial and Agricultural Requirements Commission which argued that it was essential to nurture manufacturing as a longterm replacement for the gold mines, and accepted the argument of businessmen that apartheid labour policies raised their costs, limited their domestic market, and rendered manufacturing uncompetitive and 'uneconomic'.[6]

*The Department of Labour pointed out that the exclusion of Africans from the IC Act meant that: 'there was no wage regulation for [them] . . . and some employers soon began to take advantage of this . . . by employing persons . . . whose wages were unregulated . . . . In some industries, for example engineering, which permit of various processes being simplified . . . it is possible to conduct the work almost entirely with unskilled and semi-skilled workers, and . . . agreements under the Act were evaded by the employment of uncivilized labour at low wages.'[5]

Reformist pressures were aided by the wartime boom, which aggravated the shortage of skilled workers, who cannot be produced quickly, but require training and experience. The exigencies of war led to relaxation of the job bar and gave employers the chance to reorganise their job structures. Production processes were simplified and fragmented, especially in the engineering and munitions industries, so that they could be done by semi-skilled operatives, including blacks, who were given special crash training courses, such as the three-month Central Organization of Technical Training (COTT) scheme for workers in the metal industries.[7]

The dilution and fragmentation of skilled jobs undermined the effectiveness of 'closed shop' provisions, while the improvement in the quality of black labour (due to training) meant it was increasingly employed in preference to whites, even when the rate for the job applied. These developments led to the emergence of a middle area of operatives' jobs, done by semi-skilled whites and blacks, between the previously rigid skilled and unskilled categories. It was accompanied by a narrowing of the racial wage differential (see pp. 21 and 43). After the war, these trends seemed likely to increase because of the shift to modern mechanized plant and growing capital intensity in manufacturing. But the 1948 Nationalist government reversed these trends.

The entrenchment of the job bar

The 1951 Native Building Workers Act and 1956 Amendment to the Industrial Conciliation Act extended the statutory bar to the secondary and tertiary sectors. The Minister of Labour, de Klerk, explained that this was necessary to overcome the tendency of employers to substitute black for white labour (see p. 40). Manufacturing and commercial capital opposed this major extension of the job bar, but were over-ruled. The 1948 election (like the 1924 election for the mines) was decisive in determining their labour structure for the next three decades.*

---

*A curious account of the pressures for and against this major extension of the job bar is given by Davies, whose claim that it was white capital, not white labour, which wanted the bar (in order to divide the working class) has been widely quoted. He interprets Helen Suzman's speech in parliament *opposing* the bar as evidence for his view. What Suzman said was: 'It would be cheaper to subsidize such Europeans [rather than to extend the job bar] . . . in order

The argument that the job bar had little effect and never inconvenienced employers was refuted above (p. 38); but *once it was in place*, the iron apartheid framework generated pressures for its own extension. For example, once job reservation (or minimum wage determinations) were applied to an employer, he had an interest in ensuring that they were extended to his competitors—or he would be undercut, because they could use cheaper or more efficient labour. But this did not convert those affected to general support for the job bar. Indeed, their continuing objections to it (recorded for example by the 1958 Viljoen Commission[9]) led to warnings from government spokesmen that:

> it is very dangerous for businessmen to enter the political arena in an organized manner. Speeches made at the (FCI) Convention were nothing more than a reflection of the United Party's integration policy . . . . The integrationists among industrialists . . . wish to go against the stream of an overwhelming White Volkswil. The Prime Minister asked them cordially to reconsider. If they continue . . . the Volkswil must be called in against them.[10]

The post-Sharpeville boom and rising costs of the job bar

The 1960 Sharpeville crisis was followed by a tremendous boom in manufacturing: output increased from R1bn in 1960 to R1.7bn in 1965—by 70 per cent in five years. The fact that this coincided with the tightening of many aspects of apartheid was one of the reasons for the argument that growth in this sector was fuelled by apartheid.

However, the relationship between apartheid and the boom was complex. The re-establishment of 'law and order' (which many

---

simply to help a small number of unfortunate European workers who cannot hold their own against competition.' Davies claims that the concern of Suzman, and the businessmen whose view she supported, was 'to prevent any white marginals falling below blacks in that [race] hierarchy,' i.e. to maintain intact the racial division between blacks and whites. But Suzman was obviously attempting to combat the support of white workers for the bar by offering them compensation in return for its dismantling. Davies's account of these events, and also of the crucial struggle over the mining job bar in 1922/4, ignores the explicit pressures for the bar from white labour, simply referring readers to other works 'for an account of the position of labour and of the Communist Party and its ambiguities'.[8] For such an account see below, Chapter 7.

would see as dependent on white supremacy) contributed to it, but so did non-racial economic policies, such as strict exchange controls, which prevented local businessmen from getting their money out; expansionary policies spear-headed by the state sector; and increased protection, via both import controls and domestic procurement (discussed in Chapters 8 and 9).

Apartheid labour policies did not contribute to the rapid expansion of manufacturing and commerce. Instead, the boom raised the costs of these policies, particularly in the skilled labour market and to the balance of payments. This in turn intensified the pressures from businessmen, who eventually succeeded in securing the abandonment of some apartheid labour policies.

The main reasons for the rising costs of the job bar were:

(i) *Technological change*: After World War Two there were enormous technological changes in manufacturing, as worn-out plant was replaced by modern machines. Between 1946 and 1970 the fixed capital stock in constant prices rose from R204m to R938m, and the capital–labour ratio almost doubled. This increased the need for skilled and semi-skilled workers, and reduced the need for the unskilled. It is sometimes claimed that while mechanization increases the need for semi-skilled workers, it reduces the need for skills. In reality its effect is rather to change the 'skill mix': while some of the traditional skilled crafts become redundant, there is increased need for operatives, mechanics and technicians. This, and the exceptionally rapid growth of the SA economy during this period, increased the absolute and relative need for skills, as well as for literate and numerate operatives.

(ii) *The shortage of white labour*: This enormous increase in the demand for skills was not accompanied by a sufficient expansion of the pool of white labour from which employers had to draw their skilled, and often semi-skilled, workers. Up to World War Two, high white unemployment had been the *raison d'être* for the job colour bar. By 1960, there was virtually full employment among whites, who were moving out of manufacturing and into white collar jobs in the tertiary sector. This shrinking of the (already restricted) pool of skilled labour intensified the skill shortage, which was not solved by the government's stratagems to maintain the job bar in the white areas, i.e. white immigration, 'the floating bar', decentralization etc. (see p. 33).

Magnitude and effects of the skill shortage
Surveys by employers' organizations showed that the skill shortage, especially in the vital metal, engineering and construction sectors, was becoming a bottleneck on growth. Extrapolations of future skill needs showed that *a choice had to be made* between retention of the job bar and economic growth.*

The effects of severe and widespread shortages were not limited to the rising cost of skilled labour, but resulted in other symptoms of a tight labour market, such as high turnover. According to the SEIFSA survey, turnover of white artisans reached 150 per cent in 1970; at Dunswart Iron and Steelworks, for example, annual white turnover was over 100 per cent compared with 5 per cent at Thyssen Steelworks in the tight West German labour market.[12]

The job bar and skill shortage also contributed to declining productivity.[13] The lack of competition for white workers led to slackness on the job, high turnover and absenteeism, while the barrier to job advance was a disincentive to hard work, motivation and commitment among blacks. Inadequate education, poor living conditions and insecurity were also believed to contribute to low black efficiency.

The mounting difficulties with both black and white labour led to increasing problems and strain for senior management, already understaffed as a consequence of the shortage of suitable personnel. Many of the surveys commented on this and on the time-consuming red tape and bureaucratic 'rigmarole' caused by the labour laws.

Mobilization of capital against the job bar
As the boom aggravated the skill shortage, employers intensified their campaigns against the job bar, reiterating their longstanding arguments about the need for incentives, competition and promotion on merit. Initially businessmen, particularly the government-supporting AHI, emphasised the more flexible application

---

*Surveys in 1969–71 showed skill shortages of 13 per cent in construction and clothing, 8 per cent in metals and engineering, 11 per cent in motors, 12 per cent in furniture. The acute shortage of apprentices (29 per cent according to an AHI survey) indicated that the shortage would worsen.[11] For extrapolations of future skill needs see p. 238.

of the bar, allowing it to float upwards.[14] But on the eve of the 1970 election, there was an outcry from all business organizations against the 1970 Bantu Laws Amendment Act, giving BAD *carte blanche* to extend job reservation (see p. 33). After the election and defeat of the HNP, prominent Afrikaans capitalists like Albert Wessels of Toyota Motors, Fred Zoelner of Dunswart Metal, Jan Marais of Trust Bank, Anton Rupert of Rembrandt and Jan Hupkes of Federal Volksbeleggings, joined other businessmen in calling for abolition of the job bar.[15]

The fact that employers initially emphasised erosion of the bar, rather than its abolition, does not mean that they 'really wanted' to retain the bar with some marginal adjustments. With the Nationalist government in power, and white unions resistant, it was an obvious tactic to emphasize adjustments to it, while reassuring the white unions, who (correctly) suspected this would be the thin end of the wedge.

However, opposition to the costly job bar did not mean that employers were liberals, rejecting all aspects of apartheid. It was, perhaps, the assumption that people have a consistent and logical set of beliefs that led some Marxists to believe that capitalists must have wanted the job bar. Employers (like other people) did not necessarily think through the consequences of all the policies they advocated. Those who did—like Verwoerd and Oppenheimer— were exceptions, and both of them predicted that the erosion of the bar would have far-reaching effects. When these became clearer, with its actual relaxation in the 1940s and 1970s, businessmen accepted them and moved on to oppose other aspects of apartheid as well; hence the similar reform packages of both these periods.

As the bar was relaxed, examples of savings piled up.* A 1974

---

*In the Transvaal building industry, African operatives were allowed to do artisans' work in 1974: they were paid R1 per hour, compared with the artisans' rate of over R2.[16] In 1976, an agreement with the Diamond Workers Union permitted semi-skilled blacks to work on small stones; until then SA had been unable to compete with the cheaper labour used in India or the machinery used in Israel[17]

At one of the large factories I visited in 1974, management estimated that, while it would take time to train black artisans, they could immediately replace 80 of the jobs earmarked for artisans (20 per cent of their artisan complement) by 150 blacks with 3 months' in-service training. The 150 blacks would each earn R100 p.m. (an increase for them), compared with R425 each for white

wages survey showed that, in a similar category of work, white operators earned R300 per month, coloureds R150, and Africans R100.[18] The differential was wide even where the rate for the job applied, as the skill shortage enabled white artisans to command premium rates, above the minima laid down by Industrial Councils. Considerable gains could therefore be made by employing blacks, even if the rate for the job applied. The enlargement of the supply of skilled and semi-skilled workers would moreover slow down the rapid rise in wages.

The government's 1973 concessions on the job bar (see p. 59) were the fruit of this campaign and the first major victory against apartheid since 1948. Encouraged by this success, businessmen pressed for bolder measures. The FCI complained that the relaxation of job reservation was proving 'too slow'[19]. In 1974, the fragmented employers' organizations reorganized the SA Employers' Consultative Committee on Labour Affairs (SACCOLA), representing almost 90 per cent of secondary industry and commerce, to coordinate their pressures for reform of labour policies. Their first priority was the removal of the vertical bar and creation of a mobile, competitive market in skilled labour—historically a classic demand of capitalists. This would give them a larger pool from which to select workers and greater freedom to organize their workforce. Employers were not content that black advancement should take place by stealth, with resultant uncertainty; they wanted an explicit change of policy.

From 1973, these pressures on the job bar were reinforced by increasing black political activity (evident in the growth of trade unions and the 1976 Soweto riots) and by international criticism of apartheid and of capital's connections with it. These pushed moral and political issues into greater prominence and led to the acceptance by employers' organizations in 1976 of Codes of Employment, committing them to 'the elimination of discrimination

---

artisans. The annual saving to the company would be R240,000. A second group of blacks with 3 months' training could shortly replace a further 20 per cent of white artisans. Thereafter, a two-year hiatus would be needed before blacks could be sufficiently trained to replace—or simply fill vacancies for— further artisans. In this factory alone, the abandonment of the job bar would soon lead to savings of R500,000 p.a. with the prospect of further savings, and an easing of severe shortages within two years.

based on race or colour from all aspects of employment'.[20] These principles, along with their traditional opposition to the job bar, were reiterated in their evidence to the Wiehahn Commission, whose report led to the ending of the statutory job bar.

The second priority of businessmen, closely connected with the advance into skilled jobs, was for improved and expanded *education and training* for Africans and coloureds. The implications of the huge expansion and restructuring of the educational system were underestimated by analysts who envisaged 'smoothly functioning' floating job bars, which could be manipulated at will, allowing blacks to advance 'on a temporary basis' when labour was scarce, and being pushed back when there was white unemployment. This view was shared by Nationalist officials and politicians, who hoped that they could avoid the cost and political difficulties of providing formal training by making companies provide it on an *ad hoc* in-service basis.

Due to inadequate schooling, many blacks were illiterate and innumerate. Companies could do some on-the-job training but formal, systematic training was expensive, time-consuming and possible only for large, wealthy companies; even they were then in danger of losing expensively trained workers to their competitors. The scale and cost of training required by SA industry was such that businessmen pressed for it to be done by the state on a national basis, starting with expanded and improved school education. Afrikaans businessmen like Wessels, Wim de Villiers of General Mining, and Andries Wassenaar of Sanlam, were among those supporting these demands.[21] The enormous expansion of black education that businessmen wanted made heavy demands on scarce resources of capital and skilled manpower. Workers trained at such trouble and expense would not readily be pushed out of their jobs and slotted into some lower category of work when white unemployment rose. As blacks advanced into skilled jobs, and as the educational system strained to train them, talk of 'floating bars' and of doing these jobs 'on a temporary basis only' faded away.

The pressures for the expansion of education and training were powerfully reinforced by the Soweto riots, and state expenditure on black education rose sharply, supplemented by funds provided by large companies for scholarships and for the upgrading of teachers and the construction of secondary and technical schools.[22] The argument then shifted to the question of whether technical training should take place in racially separate institutions, such as those provided for in the 1976 Black Inservice Training Act, or whether it should be on a non-racial basis. The question was complicated by the possibility that non-racial training would be vulnerable to manipulation by the white unions (see Chapter 7). But segregated training was expensive, involving the duplication of facilities, and conflicted with the commitment to remove racial discrimination. Leading businessmen like Mike Rosholt of Barlow Rand called for the opening of the existing training centres and 'a common educational system for all races'.[23] New training centres, such as that established by SEIFSA at Benoni in 1983, had fully integrated training facilities. Many companies also began to integrate facilities such as canteens, toilets and locker rooms at the workplace (the attitudes of both capital and labour to social apartheid are discussed in Chapter 7).

When the first Wiehahn Report and White Paper were published in 1979, the erosion of the job bar was well under way. Despite this, and the mid-1970s recession, there were still severe skill shortages, due to the backlog and long training times required for producing skilled workers. These continuing shortages underlined the fact that SA had run out of its traditional sources of skilled labour, and that the solution was an expensive and longterm process, involving enormous changes in the educational and industrial relations structures. The skill shortage could not be solved by devices like floating bars. *The vertical bar was incompatible with skill-intensive growth*, as distinct from growth dependent on large supplies of unskilled labour.

The victory against the job and education bars was only won after a prolonged struggle, in which urban capitalists played the key role. This victory had immense consequences for other aspects of apartheid, particularly those concerning mobility, stabilization, wages and trade union rights.

The mobility and price of African labour

The pass laws restricted the amount of labour available to urban employers and made it difficult for them to employ whom they liked, where they liked, and to shift workers between worksites and areas. It also rendered their workers liable to police raids and to arrest and imprisonment for pass offences—problems which mine and farm workers generally escaped during their term of contract. Not surprisingly, therefore, the reports of official commissions resounded with complaints from urban businessmen, not of labour shortage, but of the inconvenience of influx controls and their adverse effects on the stability and morale of their workers.

However, urban businessmen shared the dislike and fear of most white townsmen of the problems associated with rapid urbanization and supported some controls over entry, even while they complained about restrictions on the size of the labour pool and the mobility of their *own* workers. Despite this ambivalence, their pressures were consistently for the easing of controls and for less government intervention in the labour market.

During the 1930s and 1940s, relaxation of the pass laws, and acceptance of a stable urban workforce with security of tenure, had been a major demand of urban capital. Even SEIFSA, most conservative of the employers' organizations on broader socio-economic issues,* urged, in its evidence to the Fagan Commission, that migratory labour should be gradually phased out as it was 'sociologically unsound. As an industry we would prefer to see a permanent labour force.'[24] The wartime UP government, responsive to their pressures, moved in this direction (see p. 20); but the Nationalists so tightened restrictions on entry to and stabilization in the towns that urban employers, who had not previously been short of black labour, were faced with increasing problems in the unskilled, as well as the skilled, labour markets.

The Viljoen Commission acknowledged the problems created by the 'manner' in which influx control was implemented, 'reducing the scope for employers to select suitable employees'. It recorded the complaints of employers that the Labour Bureaux regarded blacks as 'interchangeable units . . . an undifferentiated mass,' and conceded that this was inappropriate for jobs requiring aptitude and dexterity, which were 'becoming increasingly important in the selection of employees'; this aggravated high turnover, while the productivity of black workers suffered from insecurity and police harassment.[25]

Business views on the need for reform of the pass laws were

---

*Probably because of the presence within its ranks of the huge parastatal ISCOR and, later, of substantial state shareholdings in heavy engineering and steel firms like Usco, Samancor, Dorbyl and Stewarts and Lloyds.

stressed in the memorandum to the Prime Minister by the FCI, Assocom, SEIFSA and even the AHI after Sharpeville. Verwoerd reacted angrily to these representations, refusing to address a major gathering of businessmen, whom he charged with 'paving the way for black domination'. He denounced Assocom (most liberal and vocal of the organizations) as 'traitors' and, for some years, government departments refused to receive, or even reply to correspondence from, Assocom officials.[26]

The growing conflict between capital and bureaucracy

Instead of 'redressing grievances', as businessmen urged, Verwoerd elaborated his blueprint to reconcile apartheid with economic growth by 'streamlining' the pass laws and supplementing them with Labour Bureaux and by introducing controls over the movement of capital itself (see p. 35). Government planners and ideologists envisaged a system tailored to suit the needs of modern industry, but businessmen claimed they were being forced into a straitjacket which made matters worse, subjecting them and their workers to time-consuming red tape and bureaucratic delays and obstruction.

The anger and frustration of employers, and their growing opposition to the labour control system, was documented by the Riekert Report, which confirmed that the 'overwhelming majority of employers' denied the claim of the Bureaux and BAABs that labour mobility had improved; rather they insisted it had got worse, complaining of 'the inability of Labour Bureaux to provide suitable workers on request or within a reasonable time,' of the 'difficulty and inconvenience' of registering workers, of 'cumbersome procedures linked with voluminous documentation,' and of delays and problems which meant that they were often 'faced with the choice of losing business or contravening the law'.[27]

The problems were particularly acute for smaller firms; they could not afford to hire special staff to deal with recruitment and labour problems, which absorbed much of the time and energy of senior management. Employers were incensed at the steeply rising levies and taxes imposed on them 'to subsidize these uneconomic, bureaucratic institutions',* and commented adversely on the 'high

---

*By 1976/7, the administration costs of the BAABs along were R85m, of which direct levies on employers provided R52m, four times the figure of R13.7 in 1970/1.

salaries of senior officials and the excessively high cost' of administration buildings.[28]

The Riekert Commission observed: 'There is indisputably also
a measure of antipathy to the use of Labour Bureaux on the part of
some employers because the Bureaux would make inroads into
their *freedom of choice* (Riekert's underlining) of workers, or in
general because they simply disapprove of the Bureaux as a
manifestation of the control machinery'. Riekert concluded that
the 'extensive, complicated . . . fragmented and overlapping'
labour measures led to 'all kinds of market failures . . . and to
dissatisfaction and frustration among workers and employers,' but
that control over the rate of urbanization was nevertheless an
'absolutely essential social security measure; even though, as some
witnesses contend, the abolition of such control would lead to
faster economic growth, the price to be paid for it in terms of direct
and indirect social costs would be too high.'[29]

The antipathy of businessmen for the bureaucracy was fully
reciprocated. The Riekert Report recorded the complaints of
officials about large-scale evasion and undermining of the labour
control system by employers, who bypassed the Bureaux,
employed illegal workers, and 'even make provision in their tender
prices for the payment of fines'.[30] The opposition of the bureaucracy, and the Nationalist obsession with black numbers in the
towns, limited concessions on the horizontal bars. Moreover, in
response to the demand of bureaucrats that capitalists 'will simply
have to be compelled' to comply with influx controls, penalties on
illegal workers were reinforced by heavy fines on their employers.*
The outcry which greeted this regulation led to caution in its
implementation, but hundreds of employers were prosecuted and
fined (see p. 73).

Businessmen's pressures for mobility focussed on their workers.
Their views on the broader question of mobility for all Africans
remained less clearly defined and more ambiguous. In 1974,
senior officials of FCI and AHI told me they had not thought
through this 'sensitive' question, on which they wished 'to take a

---

*In their evidence to the Commission bureaucrats went beyond this, demanding
not only steep fines and imprisonment for continued offences, but also 'the
suspension of the offenders' privileges to employ black workers and . . . the
closure of the businesses of persistent offenders'.[31]

low profile, unlike Assocom'. The sensitivity of this question was due to its links with political issues. While none of the employers' organizations, apart from the AHI, even paid lipservice to the separate development policy, they generally avoided explicitly political issues, partly because they did not wish to aggravate relations with the government; partly because of divisions among their members.

But the Soweto riots and growing black militancy jolted them into confronting these broader issues. The 1983 speech attacking the principle of influx control by Relly (see p. 123), indicated a significant shift in thinking.

The struggle over decentralization

The decentralization policy, enforced by Section 3 of the 1967 Physical Planning Act (see p. 35), was a source of intense conflict between capitalists and government/bureaucracy. The restrictions on the location and expansion of industries were not compensated by the incentives (including cheap labour and relaxation of the job bar), which did not work in the way intended.

This policy did not affect all employers equally. Expansion in areas adjacent to Bantustans, like Natal and Ciskei, was not constrained; but in PWV and Western Cape, which together accounted for two-thirds of industrial output and employment, restrictions on the availability of African labour were tightened. Firms which already had large labour complements (or were mechanizing) might not be affected. But labour-intensive industries, such as clothing, and new or expanding companies, began to find it difficult to get permits to employ additional Africans, and this led to increased illegal employment. According to the Riekert Report, two-thirds of clothing factories in the PWV area had contravened the Act and 'there was reason to believe the position was not much different in other branches of secondary industry.'[32] The FCI estimated that 47 per cent of industries in PWV exceeded the 2.5 to 1 ratio of African to white workers laid down in 1971 and that, with the number of whites in blue-collar work diminishing, this ratio could not be achieved.[33]

The policy was most strictly applied in the Western Cape. The Cape Chamber of Industries complained that the 'acute unskilled labour shortage in the Western Cape was restraining the economic growth' of the region, which became one of the slowest in SA, lagging behind Natal. The Cape Chamber of Commerce was also 'totally opposed' to the policy. Both Chambers made repeated representations to the government for the scrapping of this and the related 'coloured labour preference' policy.[34]

The conflict between business and government over decentralization came to a head in the public clash, shortly before the 1970 election, between Oppenheimer, (who had substantial manufacturing and commercial interests)* and the Minister of Planning, Karel de Wet. De Wet threatened that unless Oppenheimer cooperated in decentralizing industry, 'the government will approach his requests for African labour differently from those of other industries . . . . Each Oppenheimer application' for black workers would be closely scrutinised. 'I will not allow him and the Progressive Party to destroy our policy.'[35] Jan Haak, Minister of Economic Affairs, concurred: 'We must accept that the days of uncontrolled influx of Bantu labour into the metropolitan areas are gone forever . . . the decentralization policy will be pursued even if it involves a sacrifice in the overall economic performance.'[36]

After the 1970 election, the FCI and Assocom were joined in their campaign against the Physical Planning Act by the AHI, which had initially expressed support for the principle of separate development and rejected the 'uncontrolled use of non-white labour in pursuit of a maximum growth rate'.[37] But the AHI's enthusiasm for decentralization waned as its implications became clearer and it became apparent that it might be applied to *them*. The AHI then warned that decentralization could only be carried out 'within the limits of the economic laws'; that uneconomic decentralization was undermining the growth of the metropolitan areas; and that 'the government does not always have the necessary knowledge of the practical implications of its policy and does not always realise the importance of the profit motive as a basis of efficiency.'[38]

The refusal of capital to decentralize was deplored by Adendorff, Director of the Corporation for Economic Development, who said that only three hundred companies had responded and

---

*After World War Two, and especially after Sharpeville, when exchange controls made it difficult to get money out of SA, most mining companies diversified into manufacturing and commerce. For example, AAC's industrial investments grew from R40m in 1960 to R640m in 1974 and R3,238m in 1983.

that the 'big names in SA industry were absent'.[39] (Most large investments were by foreign companies, often in partnership with the SA government.) But the Reynders and Riekert Commissions accepted that the policy damaged growth and employment, contributing to the slowdown in growth and the fall in manufacturing investment from 1968 (see Chapter 8). The Riekert Report also recorded that 'the evidence from the private sector was overwhelmingly damning' and in favour of abolition of Section 3 of the Physical Planning Act.[40]

Despite friendlier relations with the Botha government, and the substantial 1982 increase in the decentralization incentives (see p. 76), businessmen were not won over to support for the policy. Oppenheimer argued that:

> Decentralization is just as sure to fail in its new form as it was in the time of Verwoerd . . . . [The increased incentives] will involve costs the country cannot afford; and it will make a mockery of the official policy of relying on private enterprise operating in a free market . . . . By world standards, even Johannesburg is not a major metropolis . . . . What imperative is there to stop or even slow down development in these areas, particularly in a time of recession . . . ? The top priorities for economic growth and social improvement surely lie in and around our existing metropolitan areas.[41]

Why were industrialists not lured to decentralize by incentives, including unlimited supplies of cheap unskilled labour and relaxation of the job bar?

Reasons for opposition to decentralization

Most industrialists had substantial interests in the continued growth of the existing metropolitan areas. The few cases of successful decentralization soon generated opposition from metropolitan employers (and trade unions) fearful of being undercut by 'Hong Kongs' on their borders. After the 1975 increase in the incentives, the Transvaal Chamber of Industries protested that diversion of investment could harm the established industrial areas.[42]

The 'cheap labour' advantages of the policy were undermined by a number of factors. First, low wages in the border areas attracted attention from the anti-poverty lobbies and led to restlessness among the workforce, for example, during the 1973 strikes. Metropolitan employers and trade unions supported their protests against lower wages. This did not necessarily lead to wage increases but created *uncertainty* as to whether significantly lower levels could be maintained there. Second, among the incentives offered to businessmen was cheap capital. This, and the installation of new plant, meant that factories there were often capital-intensive, thus reducing their need for cheap, unskilled labour and the advantages of this aspect of the policy.

Decentralized industries also had problems in relation to skilled labour. White staff were reluctant to move to undeveloped areas and had to be lured there by higher wages; Africans feared they would lose their tenuous urban rights if they once worked there. Furthermore, there was uncertainty over the relaxation of the job bar: for example, in 1970, the government, under pressure from the white unions, reneged on its undertaking that job reservation would not be extended to motor firms moving to Rosslyn.[43] Then, from 1973, the concessions in the metropolitan areas regarding the use of skilled blacks undercut the relative advantage of the decentralized zones.

Political factors were also a deterrent. Businessmen were nervous of the prospect of Bantustan independence, with possibilities of political upheaval and nationalization, and were worried by the consequences of economic fragmentation. In 1975, the FCI stressed the 'imperative' need for the 'harmonization and rationalization of labour policies and legislation' between SA and its bevy of Bantustans.[44] The dreams of the Nationalist planners seemed like nightmares to businessmen, who also disliked the policy's ideological overtones, and the coercion and threats used to pressure them into decentralizing.

Last, but not least, the Physical Planning Act added to the morass of bureaucratic red tape. Riekert noted that 'the continuous stream of applications for the employment of additional black labour takes up much of the time of the top management.'[45] The problems and uncertainty as to whether they would be able to expand or even continue their operations led to a serious fall in business confidence and in manufacturing investment from the late 1960s. The fate of the clothing industry in the Transvaal, where factories were forced to close and thousands of jobs lost (see p. 76), reinforced the conviction of businessmen that the policy was 'moonshine' and the policy-makers 'mad ideologists'.[46]

Stabilization

The question of stability and permanence for urban Africans was long in dispute between urban employers and SA governments. During World War Two, when the job bar rose, business pressures led to the 1948 Fagan recommendation that Africans should be accepted as permanent urbanites, settled with their families in their own homes, on the grounds that 'the constant change in occupation militates against the acquisition of skill.'[47]

Claims by government planners (and their sister bureaucracies in some large companies) that the Labour Bureaux and 'call-in cards' would reduce turnover, and hence the need for stabilization, were not borne out by my fieldwork during the 1970s, nor by the fact that employers continued to press for stabilization. [48]

A striking example was provided by a large Western Cape factory whose personnel department claimed to have solved the turnover problem. This firm has recruited its migrants from the same district in the Transkei for decades. The workers were transported by the company and housed in its own compound, thus avoiding the usual hassles with the Labour Bureaux, municipal compounds, etc. The arrangements were dealt with by a specialised staff, with experience of handling the bureaucracy and red tape. The company's workforce was stable in the sense that workers, once on the books, frequently returned for further contracts; but there were fifty per cent more workers on the books than were currently serving contracts, the rest being at home on leave. Stability thus meant a stable *pool* from which workers were regularly drawn, often after quite long absences; turnover was low only in the sense that recruitment of entirely new workers was low.

Despite the fact that turnover in that sense was low by the usual standards of SA companies—most of whom did not have personnel departments and their own compounds—the company began to shift to stable labour in the mid-1970s. The government refused to let it stabilize its migrants, so they were replaced with local labour, mainly coloured, and therefore more expensive. The company did this because, with mechanization, its labour structure was changing and it needed fewer unskilled, and more skilled, workers. The old system, whereby a man could go off for six to ten weeks' leave, and then send his brother or uncle instead if there were problems at home, became untenable. Brother or uncle might substitute for a worker moving and cleaning equipment or stoking the furnace, but not for a semi-skilled worker operating an expensive machine—let alone a skilled man. These workers must return to their jobs at the agreed time, or others would have to be trained to replace them. Apart from their ability to perform a specific task, they were part of a team, which could lose productivity as members changed. Even a system of relatively stable migrancy will not do for more skilled jobs, which require stable workers housed with their families within commuting distance. Rising skill levels were increasing the costs of migrancy.

This firm had coped more effectively with migrancy than most of those I interviewed. The Transvaal branch of the same company did not have a compound for its migrants, who were housed in the nearby municipal compound. The manager said that conditions there were, from the point of view of productivity, untenable. The men were not properly fed, and they could not sleep at night because of the noise and the constant coming and going of shift workers. He had, however, recently refused the opportunity to erect his own compound and was holding out for family housing, which he was convinced the government would have to accede to. He and his production department heads were adamant that they would not invest time and effort training migrants for the more skilled jobs then being opened to blacks; they would only train workers whom they could stabilize.*

Apart from economic reasons for stabilizing workers, many urban businessmen, who often knew their workers better than mineowners, disliked the enforced separation of families, and became increasingly discomfited by the stigma attached to migrancy. This was one of the reasons for the decision by the Western Cape factory to phase it out. It was partly owned by a foreign company, which did not like the unfavourable publicity abroad. This shift in the thinking of the big companies was important because, outside the mining industry, migrancy existed mainly in large companies and in the state sector (Iscor, the Railways, etc.). Except in the Western Cape, much of the urban African workforce in small/medium factories and offices was drawn from workers settled with their families in the towns.

*Researchers at the National Institute for Personnel Research in Johannesburg confirmed these findings and stressed that smaller firms, which could not recruit and house their own migrants, had tremendous turnover problems.

Businessmen did not, however, fight the government all the time on all issues. Migrancy was not always given the priority it had in the 1940s, and again from the mid-1970s. In 1972, at the height of the struggle on the job bar, the FCI's 'Programme for Sustained Industrial Growth' made scant reference to migrancy. But their 1975 *Aide Memoire* complained that migrancy was 'not conducive to optimum industrial productivity and sound industrial relations . . . . A stable pool of industrialized labour cannot become available through the present migrant labour system and to that extent industry is at a disadvantage.'[49]

In 1976, Assocom reiterated its support for stabilization and home ownership, calling for the phasing out of migrancy, for land to be released for African family housing, and for Africans to be granted secure titles to their property. By 1976, the AHI also supported stabilization.[50]

The doctrine that Africans were 'temporary sojourners' in the towns had socio-political effects that went further than the perpetuation of migrancy. It was partly responsible for the fact that the townships were bleak and drab, lacking shops, entertainment, phones and electricity. People were housed in tiny 'matchbox' houses, which they were not allowed to own or even improve. The townships were sited far from the 'white' areas and inadequate transport meant hours of travelling to work. Periodically, there were strikes and riots over transport bottlenecks and increased fares. In 1972, the (Nationalist-dominated) Pretoria City Council's management committee accused the government of being 'lax and inactive' over this. Referring to the 'frustrations of the Bantu workers', it warned that if there was not soon a fast, reliable service, 'we will have a rebellion on our hands.'[51] Mineowners and farmers generally housed workers on their property and escaped these problems.

Increasingly, urban businessmen wanted their workers to have a stake in society, to live with their families in their own homes, and to be well supplied with shops, amenities, and entertainment. They believed this would reduce black turnover and increase competition for white jobs, and also make for a less explosive situation and a more contented black working and middle class, enjoying higher standards of consumption and providing a larger domestic market for their goods.

The Soweto riots, and international pressures, brought these issues to the forefront. Mining capital, with growing investments in manufacturing and commerce, supported these reforms for urban Africans (though not necessarily for mineworkers). Oppenheimer and Rupert took the initiative in establishing the Urban Foundation, with the aim of 'improving the quality of life' for urban blacks. The Foundation lobbied for stabilization and home ownership, including the 'normalizing of land tenure for all urban residents' and 'direct access to Building Societies and other free market lending institutions for the purpose of financing the purchase of their homes'.[52]

By 1980, the Urban Foundation had raised R73m for house-building and the improvement of township amenities, such as the electrification of Soweto. Companies like Ford also spent millions of rands on housing their own workers. The Foundation's director, Jan Steyn (a former judge), became closely involved in the struggle to overcome the political and bureaucratic obstacles to this programme, playing an active role in protests against the bulldozing of squatter housing at Crossroads in Cape Town in 1979, and lobbying for the more flexible housing policies which were a prerequisite for large-scale stabilization. These pressures contributed to Botha's limited concessions on African housing and urban security (see p. 70). Employers' organizations continued to press for further reforms, such as full freehold tenure for Africans and acceptance of the Rikhoto and Komani judgments (see p. 72) enabling migrants and their families to qualify for Section 10 rights.[53]

Wages and Cheap Labour
The impact of apartheid on urban labour costs is problematical. By limiting African numbers in the towns, apartheid made urban labour scarcer and dearer. Its cost was also raised by levies and taxes to finance Labour Bureaux and other control mechanisms. However, restrictions on trade union organization and lack of mobility hampered Africans from finding the best market for their labour, and this reduced their bargaining power and depressed wage levels.

Given the abundant supply of labour that would have been available to urban employers if influx controls were abolished, it is not clear what effect trade union rights would have had on African wages. Unionization could have led to higher African but lower white wages and a smaller white/African differential (and possibly less total employment). This package would not have suited white workers, but employers could probably have coped with it, as suggested by their recurrent pressures for the general raising of black wage levels, on the grounds that this would lead to higher productivity and expansion of the domestic market.

During the 1920s and 1930s, progressive urban businessmen pressed for higher black wages, complaining that the wages of 'our principle consuming population' are too low and that 'undue economic pressure' was used to force blacks to work on the white farms and mines. Logically, they did not share the opposition of mining and agricultural capital to development of agriculture in the 'reserves'. Rather, as Bozzoli recorded, business spokesmen deplored the failure to support black farmers in developing this 'wasted' national asset, asking whether it would not be 'in the interest of every section of the body politic to turn these sources of wealth to account and thus to enhance the general well being?' It would certainly widen the domestic market; as they plaintively remarked 'even a slight increase' in black incomes would lead to a big increase in demand.[54]

The pressures of progressive urban businessmen, even before World War Two, were therefore for a move away from a cheap labour system and towards the creation of a stable, contented workforce, with rising standards of production and consumption, following the model of West European societies. This was seen as part of a package involving a general rise in black wages and productivity and a long term reduction in the cost of skilled labour as the job bar and other apartheid labour policies were eroded.

Nationalist policies during the 1950s resulted in stagnant black wages and a widening of the black/white wage differential. Industrial unrest and the Alexandra bus boycott (against a penny rise in fares) forcibly reminded employers of the poverty and squalor in which workers lived. Johannesburg employers arranged to subsidize the bus fares of their workers; in 1958, some of them formed the Bantu Wages and Productivity Association to press for higher black wages.[55]

However, the pressures of FCI and Assocom for higher wages were not supported by the AHI, nor by the owners of the small, inefficient factories set up during the war which were hit by the post-war contraction. At the AHI's 1946 conference there were demands that black wages be held down, and the conference also opposed the UP's inclusion of Africans in the Unemployment Insurance Fund.[56] The AHI then represented only 6 per cent of employers in manufacturing and 25 per cent in commerce (see Table 13); but the election of the NP gave them disproportionate political influence.

In their evidence to the Viljoen Commission and again after Sharpeville, major employers' organizations urged the raising of black wages, either by government action or private initiative, or by collective bargaining.[57] This was done, but the lack of regular, institutionalized bargaining procedures for Africans meant that their increases were often erratic and uneven, while the skill shortage and strength of white unions widened racial differentials. These issues were widely publicized during the 'poverty wages' campaigns of the early 1970s and contributed towards the 1973 Durban strikes.[58]

These pressures jolted businessmen into calling for reform of the whole wage structure and wage-regulating machinery. Dennis Etheredge of AAC advocated a unified, non-racial wage scale, with priority for redressing the low unskilled rates and creating 'a properly conceived hierarchy of jobs . . . which paid men adequately and justly for their services and would transform the Republic from a country of very low productivity to at least the average.'[59]

Leading Afrikaans businessmen now supported this view. Wim de Villiers argued that it was not enough to raise black wages; the wage gap must be closed and the redistribution of income towards blacks would have to come partly out of a 'lowering of the profitability' of business.[60] Other advocates of higher black wages were Rupert and Wessels, who argued that: 'South Africa can only realise its hopes for a stable future if, within the capitalist system, it provides for the distribution of wealth to a larger number of people.'[61]

While businessmen favoured raising the general wage level, they wanted to reduce what they regarded as the 'artificial' level of skilled wages. They did not therefore generally support the rate for the job, which was fought for by black unions, supported on this issue by the white unions, which feared undercutting (see Chapter 7). By 1977, the unions and liberal lobbies had won this

argument and the major employers' organizations were committed
to the rate for the job in their Codes of Conduct.

Reasons for support for wage increases

Some of the reasons why urban businessmen did *not* want to pay
their workers as little as possible were touched on above. First,
wage increases were seen as part of a package including erosion of
the job bar, expansion of education and training, stabilization and
improvement in living conditions which were likely to improve
productivity and ease the skill shortage, thus in the long term
cutting the average cost of labour and leading to greater efficiency.

Second, as manufacturing became more capital-intensive,
wages became a lower proportion of total costs. It was also easier
to grant wage increases in manufacturing and commerce as they
were not stuck with a fixed-price product, like the gold mines, or
geared to a competitive export market like agriculture. With
protection, manufacturers could pass on costs; this gave them
more room for manoeuvre over black wages.

However, there were differences in the capacity and willingness
of employers to pay, depending on their profitability and on the
importance of wages in their costs. Wages were lower in labour-
intensive industries like textiles and clothing: in 1971, the unskilled wage in textiles was forty per cent lower than in the rest of
manufacturing. This led to differences over the rate of increase. At
the 1973 FCI meeting at which these issues were thrashed out, the
pace-setting capital-intensive companies got their way, but they
were opposed by low-wage sectors like textiles and clothing.[62]

Third was the need to expand the domestic market, particularly
in capital-intensive industries which require the economies of
scale longer production runs provide. Oppenheimer echoed the
arguments businessmen had long made about the formidable
difficulties faced by manufacturing: 'Our population is small by
world standards and the effective market . . . is restricted by a
rigid, oppressive social and economic system . . . . Prosperity is
indivisible . . . . We must gradually move over to high wages, high
productivity and capital-intensive industry such as exists in the
leading industrial countries of the world.'[63]

As is well-known, the lower-paid consume a higher proportion
of their incomes; raising their wages therefore generally leads to a

greater increase in consumption than is the case with the rich, who have a higher marginal propensity to save. The lower-paid also tend to spend a larger proportion of their incomes on locally produced goods. In SA, locally produced clothes, blankets and furniture were often referred to as 'Kaffir goods' because of their large market among blacks. Protection, furthermore, made the domestic market more attractive to manufacturers than exports. (It is a nice irony that apartheid, by making manufacturing uncompetitive, led to the need for protection, which made the domestic market attractive; and that this, in turn, became one of the pressures to erode apartheid.)

As black wages rose, a wider range of businessmen became aware of their buying power. The prospect of a siege economy following threats of sanctions led to proposals by the FCI for large-scale import replacement and greater reliance on the internal market.[64] There was pressure from estate agents and builders to encourage black home ownership; building societies were among those pressing the government to grant blacks freehold title.[65] Retailers of durable consumer goods (fridges, stoves, electrical equipment), hit by the mid-1970s recession, hoped the electrification of Soweto would lead to increased demand. Some businessmen stood to gain from the removal of social apartheid which kept blacks out of restaurants, theatres and hotels. As black purchasing power grew, the incentives to remove apartheid and improve services and facilities for them increased, and shops and department stores resisted demands by some whites that they should stem the influx of black shoppers into white towns.[66]

Fourth, employers who raised wages had an interest in ensuring that their competitors were forced to do the same. They were usually unwilling to do so unilaterally, for fear they would be undercut (though they might also get better labour). Hence, although employers initially opposed intervention in their affairs by the Industrial Councils and Wage Boards, many of them came to favour wage determinations as a way of raising the general wage level and ensuring that these were extended to other employers.*

---

*The trade unionist, Solly Sachs, writing of the 1930s, when he was fighting for the rights of (white women) garment workers, perceived that efficient and progressive employers were his allies on the Industrial Councils in enforcing wage agreements, sick pay, etc.[67]

SA's extensive system of price controls also required government action on prices, and sometimes on competitive imports, before wages could be raised.

The need for coordinated action in the context of a package of reforms, divisions among businessmen, and lack of pressure from the African workers denied bargaining power were among the reasons why the raising of black wages was often more preached than practised. It invariably took action by workers themselves to jolt employers into action. During the 1970s, these actions were reinforced by international pressures (see Chapter 9) and by the growing conviction of businessmen that reform was essential for the survival of capitalism. These factors were critical in relation to trade union rights.

Trade unions
The belief of many employers in manufacturing and commerce that higher black wages would be in their interests meant they saw some advantages in black unions, which would help to bring about this and other elements of the reform package. But there were also fears that unions might be a threat to political stability, or simply to order and discipline on the factory floor. These reservations meant that pressures in this area (unlike those on the job bar) had to come from black workers. The response to their periodic pressures was diverse, but there always were employers who favoured recognition.

Before World War Two some employers, notably in the garment industry, recognised and negotiated with African unions; others showed a readiness to do so. According to the 1951 Industrial Legislation Commission 'the vast majority of employers' outside the primary sectors supported recognition of African unions. There were, nevertheless, divisions among them; Natal employers were 'not prepared to concede the same degree of recognition' as the Transvaal and Cape Chambers of the FCI and Assocom; while the AHI and SEIFSA were opposed to African unions.[68] These divisions proved remarkably persistent over the next few decades.

The UP's 1947 IC bill extending trade union rights to Africans was a response to progressive pressures; but the election of the Nationalists ensured that the conservatives prevailed. The smashing of the African unions by the Nationalists removed the main pressure for their recognition. In addition, the government discouraged employers from negotiating with them, even making it illegal to deduct union dues for them (see p. 27).

The government's alternative to trade unions (plant level committees and Bantu Labour Inspectors) was ineffective.* The absence of negotiating procedures left a vacuum, filled by periodic strikes, followed by unilateral and uneven wage increases. These were unsatisfactory ways of coping with the complex wage structure of the huge and diverse industrial and commercial sectors. The FCI and Assocom complained about the 'inadequacy and ineptitude' of the government's system.[70]

However, in the security-conscious post-Sharpeville period, there was little business pressure on behalf of African unions. The attitude of the conservatives hardened, SEIFSA even objecting when the Labour Department began a campaign to set up more works committees in factories. The FCI reiterated the principle that legal machinery should be provided for direct negotiations with African workers, but considered that 'the time was not yet ripe for this, but as a first step, black workers should be represented in the Industrial Councils now.'[71]

From the late 1960s, there was a resurgence of unrest among African workers. The lack of machinery for the settlement of disputes meant that strikes could arise over trivial incidents. Employers could (and did) call in the police, but this could lead to the arrest and absence of their entire workforce, as in the 1972 Putco bus strike. A series of widely-publicised strikes, including the Ovambo strike and 1973 Durban strikes, thrust the issue of unionization to the fore. The political context was changing, with right-wing pressures on employers (from government and white unions) now countered by pressures from black workers, supported by anti-apartheid lobbies in SA and abroad.

Committees or unions?

The divisions among businessmen resurfaced in reaction to the government's alternative to African unions—the revamped com-

---

*Only thirteen committees were established in the whole country; and at the Industrial Council and Wage Board hearings, at which other parties were represented by an array of experts, the Regional Bantu Labour Officer, often a retired schoolmaster, was unable to cope with the complex wage negotiations, usually confining himself to appeals 'not to forget the interests of the Bantu workers'.[69]

mittee system (see p. 67). The traditional opponents of unions, the AHI, SEIFSA, and leading Natal businessmen, favoured committees, especially the partly-appointed liaison committees rather than the elected works committees.[72] The FCI and Assocom accepted committees as a step in the right direction, but not as a substitute for unions.[73] Oppenheimer argued that the committees failed to provide 'a means of joint consultation for the maintenance of industrial peace.' He went on:

> There is a grave psychological objection to them . . . . I do not believe that blacks . . . [will accept a separate system, or that we will] be able to maintain quite different systems of representation for black and white workers. It will do no good for the government to refuse to recognise black trade unions, for they are increasingly obtaining power to force recognition by employers . . . . Indeed the best thing in the circumstances would be to encourage the growth of racially mixed trade unions in order to prevent, if possible, political action on a racial basis by black trade unions.

Calling for a commission of enquiry to draw up a plan for effective representation of all workers, he said the traumatic events on the gold mines showed that even favourable changes 'cannot just be imposed by management but must be understood and approved by workers also'.[74]

In 1974, AAC announced its willingness to recognise and negotiate with African unions (at that stage, the offer was clearly limited to its industrial/commercial and not mining interests). But faced with the threat of action against them by the Minister of Labour, Marais Viljoen, Oppenheimer backed down.[75] Wilson of AAC later remarked that Oppenheimer's views were not 'in line with the Government's thinking . . . other prominent industrialists likewise remain concerned over the implications of black trade unionism . . . [moreover] Black unions . . . remain relatively small and inexperienced and it seems clear that an interim evolutionary period will occur before the final shape of black industrial representation will emerge . . . . [Meanwhile AAC would] move along other lines.'[76]

What kind of unions?

The 'other lines' included the establishment of the Institute for Industrial Education to provide a forum in which employers could meet and exchange ideas with African trade unionists. The Institute (and also many of the larger companies) ran training courses in industrial relations for both unionists and management. There was intensive lobbying and debate, with conferences and seminars, including discussions with overseas trade unionists such as the British Trade Union Congress (TUC) and the International Metal Federation, and visits abroad by SA employers to examine industrial relations systems in Britain, Germany, Japan and other countries.

The debate, contacts with African unionists, and experience with the thousands of plant-level committees that were established, provided a learning process for businessmen and managers, who discovered that black unionists were not—as the official propaganda had it—a bunch of 'communists and agitators' and that they could establish useful working relations with them. Capitalists were thus actively preparing for African trade unionism and hoping to influence its development.

The business supporters of black unions assumed that the unions would be incorporated into the established Industrial Council system, which laid down strict requirements for the conduct of industrial relations and strike procedures. This was later to be a source of dispute with the new unions, which were suspicious of the constraints placed on them by the established system. Another source of dispute with some of the unions was the preference, particularly of liberal capitalists, for dealing with one multiracial union, rather than with a variety of white and black unions.[77] This was partly because of their desire to move away from racist policies; partly because of a belief that the multiplicity of unions in, for instance, the UK was inimical to industrial peace.* But the history of trade unionism in SA made many blacks suspicious of the white unions and determined to run their own.

Businessmen showed no interest in the bizarre, bureaucratically-inspired idea of Bantustan-based unions. On the contrary, the intervention by the Kwazulu government in the 1973 strikes led to a sharp reaction from both conservative Natal businessmen and from the progressives. Oppenheimer, who had always

---

*This had long been the business view; the 1951 Industrial Legislation Commission reported that employers were 'overwhelmingly against' the proposed segregation of the trade unions which the Nationalists enforced in 1956 and that they did not want to negotiate with a proliferation of unions.[78]

opposed the Bantustan policy with its 'unforeseen consequences', pointed out that the only answer to Buthelezi's insistence that he must intervene on behalf of rightless Zulu workers was the granting of normal trade union rights: 'Industrial disputes and problems are best settled within industry itself and any system which makes intervention by political leaders . . . necessary, is likely to prove at once inefficient and dangerous.'[79] This incident may have helped to convince the conservative Natal business community of the merits of the more straightforward alternative of negotiating directly with their own workers. In this, as in other areas of economic policy, the Bantustans did not fit the requirements of capital.

Growing support for unions

A 1974 survey found that the majority of businessmen favoured some form of union recognition.[80] However, until 1979, there were few cases of recognition, partly because of continuing opposition by the government and most white unions, partly because of the initially slow growth of African unions (see Chapter 9). Foreign companies were among the first to take the plunge, led by the British firm, Smith & Nephew, which signed a formal wage agreement with the National Union of Textile Workers in 1974.

Gradually, opposition from the conservatives declined. In 1973, Errol Drummond, director of SEIFSA, had insisted: 'In this industry there will be no—and you can underline no—negotiations with African trade unions.'[81] But in 1975 the chairman of Dorman Long, a prominent SEIFSA firm, pointed out that though eighty per cent of the industry's labour force was black, 'their pay is fixed by bodies in which they are not represented and have no say. This state of affairs cannot continue and I believe that orderly negotiations can only take place if blacks are represented by trade unions. Otherwise our industrial peace will be disturbed.'[82]

The shift in opinion was reflected in the stance of the Urban Foundation. When it was set up in 1976, its commitment to ending race discrimination in employment, pay and housing was not matched by a commitment to recognise black unions, as it was 'not possible to get a broad consensus on the matter'.[83] A year later, however, its Code of Employment Practice called for the 'recognition of the basic rights of workers of freedom of association' etc.

By the time the Wiehahn Commission was set up in 1977, there was a broad consensus among urban businessmen in favour of African unions. The evidence of business organizations reflected a spread of views, ranging from Assocom's recommendation of trade union rights for all workers and an end to all race discrimination in SA's labour laws to the AHI's recommendation that migrants be excluded and that the bargaining power of *all* (including white) unions be 'subordinate . . . to the national interest'.[84]

The Wiehahn reforms and growth of African unions

The 1979 Wiehahn reforms were followed by the rapid growth of African unions and by widespread industrial unrest. Employers were taken aback by the internationally publicized 1979 strike at Ford, one of the most progressive companies. Some employers reacted in alarm, dismissing strikers or even calling in the police. But, over the next few years, the trend was towards working out a modus vivendi with the unions and accommodating many of their demands. The progressives, led by big companies like Ford, Barlow Rand, AAC and Chloride (SA), pressed for the series of amendments extending trade union rights to migrants and allowing unions to determine their own racial composition (see p. 68). However, to their surprise, many unions were still reluctant to apply for registration.

Initially, the employers' organizations, especially SEIFSA, urged their members to deal only with registered unions.[85] But the FCI and Assocom (later followed by SEIFSA and AHI) soon amended their stance, recommending a 'flexible and pragmatic' approach, with representativeness of unions rather than official registration as the criterion for recognition. Chris du Toit, President of the FCI and of SACCOLA, urged members to move away from reliance on the authorities and to 'hammer out a mutually accepted structure' for industrial bargaining with workers themselves.[86] All employers' organizations wanted the unions to operate within an official system so that agreements could be legally binding. But they also wanted that system to have legitimacy and were prepared to amend it and, in the meantime, to negotiate with unions outside the official system.

Despite pressure from government (and white unions) against negotiations with unregistered unions,[87] there were, by 1982, at least 150 recognition agreements with unregistered unions.[88] The emergence of this unofficial negotiating system forced the hand of the government and led to the 1982 amendments easing the stringent registration procedures.

Many employers also opposed attempts by the security police to 'break the power of militant' unions.[89] These union-busting tactics led to the detention of many trade unionists, particularly in the Eastern Cape, where they were also persecuted by Chief Sebe's Bantustan administration. The regional Chamber of Industries denounced detention without trial and asserted its belief in 'democracy and the free enterprise system'. The FCI and Assocom called for detention without trial to be reviewed and advised their members not to penalise workers who joined the strike to mourn the death of Neil Aggett, the trade unionist who died in detention.[90] Theo Heffer of Grinaker Holdings said that 'free and independent trade unionism is an essential institution in any country that subscribes to democratic principles. Only totalitarian regimes fail to recognise the right of workers to . . . organize themselves into unions.'[91] Increasingly, faced with unrest, employers preferred 'to hammer out a new structure of industrial relations' with their workers themselves, rather than call in the police.

The continuing disputes over the relative shares of the surplus that should accrue to capital and labour, and over the say which each should have in the running of the enterprise, therefore took place within an institutionalized framework in which employers accepted that they must negotiate with black labour. However, in a situation in which Blacks were denied all other institutional outlets, and were vulnerable to action by the security police, the unions (and their overseas supporters) tended to focus their attention on the progressive companies. In 1983, Rosholt of Barlow Rand complained they were being 'picked on' as soft targets.[92] SA businessmen also felt aggrieved by their expulsion from the International Organization of Employers (the employers' wing of the ILO) in 1983, after a decade of industrial reform. There were therefore sources of resentment on both sides in the emerging relationship between capital and the new unions.

Reasons for recognising unions
Growing support for recognizing unions was partly due to pressures from African workers and their supporters, partly to the benefits to, and growing power of, progressive capital.

Trade unions fulfil important functions, particularly in large enterprises. In a small firm, wages can be negotiated and problems sorted out by the employer personally; in large firms, institutionalized means of communication are required. The alternative to unions is an hierarchical, authoritarian system; but this becomes less effective as skill levels rise and the commitment and active cooperation of workers become more important. Authoritarian managements are also likely to be out of touch with the feelings of workers and less likely to anticipate disruptive strikes.*

Some opponents of unions believed that they would add to industrial unrest; but many social scientists claim that the incidence of strikes is correlated with 'weak labour organizations, rival labour movements and employer hostility'.[94] In SA, the introduction of the IC system in 1924 led to a decline in the number of strikes by whites (from 205 involving 175,000 workers in 1916–22 to 44 involving 16,500 workers in 1923–9, and hardly any thereafter).

The waves of African strikes in the 1920s and 1940s, at Sharpeville, and during the early 1970s, invariably raised the question of alternative ways of handling relations with Africans, who constituted an increasingly important part of the workforce, yet were totally excluded from the institutionalized bargaining system.

Employers were taken aback by the widespread labour unrest in 1973. They were unsure what caused it—dissatisfaction over wages (though they had risen more rapidly than before); the upsetting of differentials due to faster rises for unskilled workers; rising expectations caused by changes in the job structure: or general political unrest? They did not know how to find out and there were no effective leaders with whom to negotiate.

---

*In an illuminating comment on unionization in the USA, Olson remarked that: 'The often violent interaction between employers and employees in the early stages of unionization should not obscure the informal and consensual unionization that also sometimes occurs because of employers' initiatives. This sort of labour organization or collusion arises because some types of production require that workers collaborate effectively. When this is the case, the employer may find it profitable to encourage team spirit and social interaction among employees . . . . When stable patterns of active cooperation are important to production, the employer may gain more from the extra production that this cooperation brings about than he loses from the informal or formal cartelization that he helps to create.'[93]

The view of the Nationalists that businessmen should oppose black unions (and the prediction of Marxists that they would) rested on their shared assumption that unions would support revolutionary policies. During the 1950s many businessmen probably were worried about the alleged connections between the SACTU unions and the SA Communist Party.[95] But there was always a wing of the African union movement which was primarily concerned with industrial issues, including of course the job colour bar and other discriminatory policies, and their goals were reformist not revolutionary, as was recognised by the Industrial Legislation Commission.*

These unions would be allies in the struggle against the job bar and other apartheid labour policies. They would also be useful industrially, because of the importance they attached to professionalism in the conduct of union affairs (partly to overcome the legacy of fear and suspicion among many black workers left by some of the highly politicized but loosely organized 1950s unions).

What was more unexpected was the coexistence of capitalists with unions such as SAAWU, which grew rapidly from 1979, did not share this concern with professionalism, and were explicitly political. The key to this lies in capital's conviction that far-reaching reform in SA was 'inevitable'—a word they constantly used. They seemed resigned to the fact that, until acceptable political institutions emerged, black frustration and anger were likely to spill over into the workplace, that sometimes unions and strikes would be used to express broader 'political, economic and social grievances', and that they would just have to 'sweat it out',[97] hoping that the existence of unions would demonstrate to both workers and government the value of having institutions that would, as Rosholt put it, 'channel conflict'.[98]

Some of those who had predicted that SA businessmen would never recognise black unions, then depicted their willingness to do so as a sinister means of 'social control'. Bringing unions within the

*In its patronising comment that 'there are a number of [African] unions which are well organized and are conducted on correct lines. The leaders of some of these unions have in the past rendered considerable assistance by advising against, and restraining their members from taking, drastic action: they are able to place the case for the workers before wage-fixing bodies, and some of them have shown indications of a measure of ability to negotiate with employers.'[96]

law, subject to legal procedures and constraints, has always been an important element in the attitude of businessmen.* But social controls cut both ways: they also constrain capital and give leverage to labour. Trade unions are subject to these controls in state-owned enterprises like railways and (when permitted) in socialist societies like Poland. The unions both contribute to the functioning of the enterprise and influence its policies. There seems little alternative to these institutionalized means of bargaining and channelling conflict other than anarchy or authoritarianism.

The willingness of businessmen to 'sweat it out' was also related to the level of unrest which, although widely publicized, has so far been relatively low. In 1981, SA lost 365,000 man-days, compared with an annual average over 1972–81 of 8m in Canada (with roughly the same population) and 3m and 12m respectively in France and Britain (with double the population).[100] If this level rises significantly, capital's tolerance might decline.

Pressures from third parties also pushed businessmen towards recognition. Most white unions had opposed unions for blacks, but once blacks entered skilled jobs, white unions developed an interest in unionizing them (in order to prevent undercutting) and, logically, began to demand the right to do so. However, their attitudes remained ambivalent and their pressures weak. More important were external pressures, particularly from the international trade union movement (discussed in Chapter 9).

The marked differences in attitude among companies and employers' organizations cannot be accounted for purely in economic terms. There was not necessarily a correlation between wage levels and opposition to unions. Wages in SEIFSA were much higher than in the clothing industry, partly because this traditionally low-wage industry was heavily dependent on women, but it also illustrates that unions share with employers an interest in staying in business.

Political attitudes were also important, with English and foreign employers generally more liberal on this issue than Afrikaners, including those like Wim de Villiers who advocated higher wages

---

*In the 1940s, the FCI expressed itself 'concerned at the continued development of native trade unions free from any form of control or recognition by the Government and considers it essential for them to be given some form of legal recognition.'[99]

and the scrapping of the job bar. Wessels was one of the few prominent employers in the garment industry who opposed African unions: in 1972, he still considered Africans were 'not yet ripe for trade unions',[101] though other clothing manufacturers had been dealing with them for decades.

Both supporters and opponents of unions were explicit about the importance of political factors. Conservatives argued that trade unions would be 'used by the far-left socialists as a political tool, and not to improve the workers,' and explained that they preferred plant-level committees, because then 'the power base is where it belongs—on the shop floor, and unlikely . . . to be influenced by the political overtones of a national labour movement.'[102] The progressives viewed unions as part of the reform programme to deracialize SA and encourage the emergence of a black middle and working class with a stake in the system.

Government hostility was undoubtedly a reason why practice lagged behind theory. Government wielded great power over the private sector—power to grant protection, licences, tenders and contracts, foreign exchange, labour permits, planning permission—the list was endless. It was easier for businessmen to confront it if they were united; but on unions they were divided. The divisions were not just between, but within, companies. Senior management was more pro-union than line management or white workers. And even the progressives were nervous of the risks—of the unpredictable reactions from black workers, white workers and low-level white management, who had to deal with the unions. Not surprisingly many employers, as the visiting TUC team commented, 'blow hot and cold and . . . lack the will and courage' to confront the government on this issue.[103]

The divisions and hesitations of businessmen over black unions—on which the risks of change were greater, and the benefits less clearcut, than on the job bar or stabilization—meant that black and external pressures were a crucial and necessary condition for change: but they were not a sufficient condition. Until 1979, the African unions were too small and weak to force recognition (see p. 340). Thereafter, despite rapid growth, they still accounted for under ten per cent of the black workforce in 1983 and remained vulnerable to police action. The belief of an important section of manufacturing and commercial capital that black unions were an 'inevitable' part of the reform programme to which they were committed was essential for their survival and growth.

Competition from black businessmen

Competition from blacks was less of a threat to white urban businessmen than to white farmers and workers, particularly in relation to manufacturing, for which few blacks had the necessary access to capital and skill, nor the entrepreneurial tradition (see p. 41). But Indians (like the English and Jews) came to SA from societies with well-established entrepreneurial traditions in commerce, and they provided stiff competition for small-scale white retailers, of whom there were 36,426 in 1970, most with total annual sales of less than R50,000. Both Africans and Afrikaners tried to break into the ranks of these longer-established trading groups. Demands for protection against 'unfair competition' came mainly from aspiring Afrikaans entrepreneurs and from the Natal English, competing with Indians.

In 1930, for example, there was strong opposition in the OFS to a measure enabling the central government to force municipalities to grant trading licences to Africans in the townships. OFS members of parliament and the OFS Municipal Association demanded that the interests of white traders be put first, reminding the government of the policy that Africans should be prevented from acquiring a permanent stake in the towns.[104]

During the 1940s, more licences were issued to African traders, although the Minister of Native Affairs was careful to assure white traders that 'Europeans will not be allowed to buy in the locations [i.e. townships] and native shops will not be able to undermine ordinary shops or business concerns in the towns.'[105] However, the UP was forced by its Natal wing to tighten restrictions on Indians.

The severe tightening of restrictions on black businessmen by the Nationalists in 1963 followed pressure from the Afrikaanse Sakekamer (business chamber), which opposed the granting of licences within locations and recommended instead that white trading areas be established just outside them. In 1958, the Sakekamer had complained that, just as Afrikaans businessmen were beginning to make progress, the government instituted a 'policy of monopoly for Bantu over Bantu trade,' thus placing the Afrikaner at a disadvantage.[106]

The reference here was to the positive side of the separate development policy, which provided for blacks to be given opportunities in their 'own' areas. Whites, particularly the rising Afrikaans businessmen looking for new opportunities, did not want to be excluded from this expanding market. Yet these same whites argued for protection against 'non-white' business. In so doing, they complained of 'unfair competition'; the example usually given was of the Indian family-run business, working long hours, cutting costs, and undercutting whites 'with higher living standards to maintain'.

However, there were also white businessmen who did not oppose opportunities for blacks and supported the wartime relaxation of restrictions. In the 1960s, Assocom and the Johannesburg City Council wanted to provide commercial training and funds to assist black businessmen; but they were stopped by the Nationalists.[107] Later, the creation of opportunities for black businessmen became an important part of the reform programme, and received strong backing from the big chain-stores like Pick-and-Pay and Checkers, which by then dominated retail trade. They were irked by apartheid measures excluding them from SA's fastest-growing market in the black townships, and were confident that they would gain from the scrapping of all trading restrictions and a free-for-all, giving them access to the black areas, still bereft of shops and services. They might also get cheaper, more competitive services (delivery, repairs etc.) in sectors now monopolised by whites.

Assocom's policy was now supported by the AHI, which had come round to the view that: 'Unless the black man is given a greater share of SA's free enterprise system, he will be driven into the arms of Marxism and socialism, as evidenced by events elsewhere in Africa.'[108] Encouragement was given to this belief by the argument of prominent African businessmen like Richard Maponya that a black middle class would 'serve as a bulwark to any political uprising in this country'.[109] The removal of these restrictions also tied in with the general business offensive against political constraints on economic activity.

Assocom, AHI and other business organizations therefore pressed for, and welcomed, the concessions to black businessmen, including the 1980 promise that central business districts in the cities would be opened to trading by all races (see p. 59). The

President of the AHI, Martin van den Berg, commented: 'Although it may imply stiffer trading and might affect AHI members, we believe this is an insurance premium we should be willing to pay to ensure that our non-whites share in our economic prosperity.'[110] Anton Rupert set up the Small Business Development Corporation to train and aid black businessmen.

It was not just big business which supported this change in policy. The vulnerable minority which had once demanded protection felt more secure and believed that the stringent post-war measures, particularly the use of the Group Areas Act against Indians, had not served their interests, leading to the general decline of business centres in small towns like Zeerust and Louis Trichardt. The business community in these *platteland* towns, which had once agitated fiercely against Indians, now pressed government to let them return, and crossed swords with bureaucrats who doggedly continued to force removals under the old policy.[111]

However, black businessmen were worried about the entry of white capital, especially the cut-price chainstores, to the townships. The National African Federated Chamber of Commerce and the Soweto Traders' Association objected to this, especially if it happened without a full quid pro quo for black business in the white areas, and without measures to ensure that they were not undercut in the black areas by whites who had a headstart.[112] It was now their turn to complain about 'unfair competition'. The handling of this issue by white businessmen could obviously alienate their intended allies, or even abort the emergence of a significant class of black businessmen.

Political apartheid

Urban capitalists did not have the same need as white farmers, mineowners and workers to exclude blacks from political rights in order to secure their economic interests. On the contrary, apartheid labour policies were increasingly costly to them, and their pressures helped to secure their erosion. Moreover, their interest in blacks as skilled workers and consumers led to consistent pressures from them for their incorporation into SA society, and for a conciliatory response to their industrial and political protests.

However, most urban businessmen probably regarded white rule as guaranteeing the political stability essential for their business operations and their personal security. This concern (discussed further in Chapters 8 and 9) constrained their opposition to the Nationalists, despite their dislike of apartheid labour policies. But the influence of this factor declined as the political costs of apartheid rose and it became a source of tension imperilling the stability it was supposed to protect.

International hostility threatened manufacturers' foreign markets and their access to foreign capital and technology, on which manufacturing was more dependent than mining or agriculture. Businessmen claimed that pressures on foreign investors, and fears of internal unrest in SA, were responsible for the scarcity and high cost of investment capital (see p. 286). As manufacturing became more capital-intensive, longer production runs and bigger markets were required and manufacturers became more concerned about threats to exports.

Until recently, business organizations avoided the question of political rights, partly because businessmen were divided, partly because they were reluctant to confront the government in this sensitive area. Their occasional sallies into the political arena met with particularly sharp rebuffs—from Verwoerd at Sharpeville and, after the Soweto riots, from Vorster, who told Assocom to stick to business and keep out of politics, warning them that, 'Efforts to use business organizations to bring about basic change in government policy will fail and cause unnecessary and harmful friction between the government and the private sector. You cannot ask me to implement policies rejected by the electorate and in which I do not believe.'[113]

Assocom now persisted; commenting on the 1983 constitutional proposals, it called for 'a clear ruling on black citizenship rights' and for 'common citizenship and labour mobility,' possibly on a confederal basis, for all those who would have been eligible for these rights within SA's original borders.[114]

Industrialists had always been sceptical of the Bantustan policy. In 1980, the FCI chairman, Leo Borman, reiterated their view that the Bantustans 'could not possibly be viable; instead the economy of the whole country should be treated as one unit.'[115] The Soweto riots prodded them into raising the question of the political implications of the Bantustan policy. In a memorandum to the Prime Minister, the Transvaal Chamber of Industries (largest of the FCI's sections) pointed out that urban Africans did not regard themselves as 'homelanders' and urged that they should be recognised as permanent urban dwellers with land ownership rights and the municipal vote in black townships.[116] Both the FCI and Assocom expressed qualified support for the 1983 Constitution, in the expectation that this would be 'a first step in the right direction' and that further changes would follow.[117]

The FCI and Assocom also condemned the strengthening of authoritarian controls. At the FCI's 1982 conference its director, van Zyl, said the organization was disturbed by the 'sweeping powers' given to ministers. Assocom urged the government to avoid creating 'arbitrary powers' which excluded the right of appeal to the courts. Both organizations condemned the detention without trial of trade unionists and expressed concern at the extensive powers of the President in the 1983 constitution.[118] SA urban capital, unlike German capital under the Nazis, did not on the whole support fascist policies.

However, the central argument of this chapter is not that manufacturing and commercial capitalists were liberals (though some of them were) but that *their interests, and the costs (and interconnectedness) of apartheid labour policies drove them to oppose these policies whether or not they were liberals*. Members of the AHI did not share the liberal preferences of Assocom. They would have preferred to make separate development work by limiting African numbers and skill advance in the metropolitan areas and decentralizing industry to the Bantustans, but as the costs and difficulties of this became apparent they were driven to oppose it. The growing need of manufacturing and commerce for skilled black labour, and for a larger domestic market, meant that apartheid was incompatible with continued economic growth in these increasingly capital- and skill-intensive sectors.

The argument that economic growth readily adapted to the requirements of the socio-political structure misses this central economic contradiction, which could not be avoided by the government's stratagems. Certainly some businessmen were willing to conform to the status quo, but they were not free to do as they chose: economic requirements set the limits within which it was possible for them to conform if they wished to remain in business. Apartheid proved too costly and unworkable. Forced to choose, they sacrificed (or changed) their political preferences, not their economic interests.

Within the limits set by these economic requirements (need for skills, stable labour, larger markets) capitalists had certain choices. These were partly determined by their preferences (often conformist and racist, but sometimes liberal); partly by the pressures upon them. Until the 1970s, those from the right were indubitably stronger. For most of this period, employers were looking over their shoulders at the white unions, and at governments which were responsive to those unions and had the capacity to compensate businessmen for the costs of apartheid (by protection) or to punish them for deviations (by withholding licences, permits, contracts). The ability of the left to apply pressures, whether by carrots or sticks, was severely limited; but when exercised (by strikes or political action in the 1940s and in 1960, 1973 and 1976) it had an effect.

Analyses which miss the central economic conflict between apartheid and the requirements of manufacturing and commercial capital give little sense of the prolonged and intense struggle over apartheid labour policy, and often imply that the government was never serious about implementing its separate development policy. This is a misreading of the course of events and of the relative political strength of various classes—in particular underestimating the political power of white labour, white agriculture and the bureaucracy.

Also obscuring the fundamental nature of the conflict was the incremental, ad hoc approach of businessmen, setting themselves limited aims, seeking to avoid conflict with government, and anxious not to alarm the white unions. They did not (as the radicals complained) wish 'to overthrow the whole system', but this did not mean that the changes they brought about were merely 'marginal'. The system hung together, and the limited changes they inaugurated drove them to seek further changes—erosion of the job bar leading to erosion of the education and training bars and to pressures for stabilization, and hence to the demand for a secure and permanent African status in the 'white' areas; this, in turn, raised the question of African citizenship and political rights.

The various elements of reform for which urban capital had pressed since Union became, by the mid-seventies, part of a more comprehensive and far-reaching programme of socio-economic and even political reform. Support for this came not only from the FCI and Assocom (representing the greater part of manufacturing and commercial capital) but also from the AHI, which had not previously supported reformist policies. Important sections of mining and agricultural capital also lent their support; indeed by then the diversification of their investments into manufacturing and commerce blurred the sectoral distinctions among capitalists. The reform programme will therefore be discussed further in Chapter 8.

7

The Interests of White Labour

Liberals viewed white workers as a major source of pressure for apartheid, particularly for job reservation measures protecting them from black and coloured competition. However, while recognising that self-interest underlay white labour's pressures, liberals also described their behaviour as 'irrational', on the grounds that it led to policies which were economically inefficient, preventing growth and output which might benefit society as a whole.

Marxists were ambivalent towards white labour. Initially they saw white workers, battling against the Chamber of Mines, as the vanguard of the proletariat. They even supported their struggle to retain the job colour bar, on the grounds that though 'reactionary in form [it was] progressive in content' and due to false consciousness that could be corrected later. The Communist Party of SA (CPSA) described the 1922 Rand rebellion as 'one of the most glorious episodes in the history of SA's workers' and fought alongside white workers under the banner 'Workers of the world unite and fight for a white SA.' By 1930, however, the CPSA accepted that white labour in SA was a supporter, not an opponent, of apartheid.[1]

Recently, some Marxists have interpreted white labour's support for apartheid as the outcome of deliberate attempts by capital to divide the working class by stirring up racism. Johnstone argued that 'the exploitation colour bars', created by and for capitalists, rendered black labour 'ultra-exploitable', thus leading to the 'structural insecurity' of white workers and their support for colour bars. Davies argued that capital 'assigned privileged places in a racial division of labour' to white workers, in order to prevent an alliance between them and blacks, and that the Labour-Pact policies of the 1920s, generally regarded as a triumph for white labour, had the effect of 'isolating and disorganising the white wage-earning classes and . . . reinforcing the isolation of white from black wage earners, to the political advantage' of white capital.[2] This analysis reverts to the earlier Marxist belief that white workers were victims of false consciousness, failing to perceive that their interests lay in an alliance with black labour against white capital.

The argument here will be that white workers actively promoted many apartheid policies, particularly the job bar, which gave them a monopoly of skilled jobs and preferential employment in other jobs. This policy was costly to white capital (and to black labour), but benefited white workers, *whose interests thus reinforced their prejudices*.

However, the consequent division of the working class also created problems for white workers. The widening gap between black and white wages increased the incentives to capital to substitute blacks for whites, thus leading to continual attempts to erode the job bar. White labour's industrial power was generally insufficient to counter this; their success depended on the exercise of political power.

Rapid growth, and preferential labour policies, transformed the situation of white workers, eliminating the high unemployment among them and creating, by the mid-1960s, an acute shortage of the skills they monopolized. This ensured them premium wages; but the high cost intensified capital's pressures against the job bar and also threatened the economic growth on which white labour's prosperity and security also depended.

White workers were divided in response to these developments. Some resisted the erosion of the job bar; others gradually acquiesced—at a price. The divisions among them and the decline of their political power, meant they became less able to prevent black advance, although they delayed and limited it.

The interests of white labour will be discussed in relation to: (i) apartheid labour policies—the job colour bar, wages, unionization and the 'rightlessness' of blacks; (ii) social apartheid; (iii) other strategies they might have pursued.

Apartheid labour policies

At the beginning of this century, there was high unemployment and poverty among whites, especially Afrikaners, in SA.[3] The closing of the land frontier, agricultural disasters, and the devastation of the Anglo-Boer War drove many whites off the land and into the towns, where they competed for jobs with similarly displaced blacks and with European immigrants, all hoping to find fortunes, or at least jobs, on the diamond and gold fields. In relation to the numerous and even poorer black workers, whites were faced with three possible strategies:

(i) *The incorporation strategy*: Whites could accept that blacks and coloureds could compete for jobs on the same cut-throat basis as themselves, and incorporate those who got jobs into their trade unions, thus ensuring that they received the rate for the job, paid their union dues etc. These were classic means whereby wage-earners controlled entry to their trades and tried to prevent undercutting from the unemployed. The alternative to incorporation was the exclusion of blacks, either by traditional trade union restrictive practices, or by political measures.

(ii) *Exclusion by traditional trade union restrictive practices*: Measures such as the 'closed shop', control over apprenticeships, and rate for the job are not *per se* racist, but they can be used in a racist manner. In SA, whites used these classic trade union restrictive practices to systematically exclude blacks from competing with them for jobs. The practices of the skilled unions adapted readily to this; but they had to be able to enforce a closed shop and control entry to apprenticeships. If capitalists undermined this by fragmenting and reclassifying skilled jobs, then white workers either had to fall back on strategy (i) and unionise blacks entering their jobs, or resort to strategy (iii).

(iii) *Exclusion by political measures*: This strategy used explicitly racial measures to exclude blacks, either reserving specific jobs for whites, or stipulating that a minimum ratio of whites must be employed. This could be done by law (as on the mines), or on a customary basis (the 'civilized labour' policy in the state sector). This explicit, rigid system insulated whites from competition so that they had no need to incorporate blacks into their unions or be concerned about low wage levels. The resort to this strategy indicated that employers were not acquiescing in strategy (ii), and that white workers had political (though insufficient industrial) power to force them to do so.

Logically, each group of white workers must choose between strategy (i) or some mix of (ii) and (iii). Either they must concern themselves with the pay and conditions of blacks in the same jobs and/or industries—which can be most effectively done by unionising them—or they must exclude them, either by traditional trade union restrictive practices or by political measures. However, they could shift between these strategies, excluding blacks by strategy (ii) (traditional trade union practices) at one stage, but falling back on strategy (i) or (iii) if unable to enforce this.

Most white workers opted—indeed fought—for the exclusion strategy, though they disagreed over the means by which it should be enforced, the more skilled tending to prefer strategy (ii). But, whenever they were unable to exclude blacks, white workers were generally flexible enough to fall back on the incorporation strategy.

The job bar

The job bar—the prime instrument of the exclusion strategy— emerged in the course of the bitter struggle over jobs in the mining and state sectors, then the major employers outside agriculture. The struggle over jobs was not only between whites and blacks, but between local whites (mainly Afrikaners) and immigrants (mainly British). Initially, the skilled trades were dominated by the immigrants—engineers, mechanics and miners from the UK. They established exclusive craft unions and tried to limit competition for their jobs by agitating against further immigration,* and by excluding Afrikaners from skilled jobs and from their unions. It was only in 1907, when Afrikaners were brought in as strike-breakers, that they got a foothold in the mining industry.[5] They too protested against the continued inflow of (white) immigrants. In response to these pressures, mineowners discontinued the policy of employing mainly imported workers in skilled jobs.

Skilled whites also resisted attempts to ease the 'poor white' problem by relaxing apprenticeship rules and diluting jobs. Craft unions objected that skilled workers were in danger of being ousted by 'the less-skilled, lower-paid rural migrant'—and it was

* In 1892, for example, there was a large demonstration 'against the attempt of the Chamber of Mines to flood these fields with labour by means of cheap emigration' (from the UK).[4]

whites they were referring to. Engineers and boilermakers refused to organize unskilled whites, and they objected to the increasing number of women working in factories and shops.[6]

These attempts to limit the supply of labour, and to prevent technological and organizational changes involving loss of control over job content, were common trade union restrictive practices, which they struggled to apply at a time of high unemployment. The restrictions were not intrinsically racist and they were not only applied against blacks. However, the numerous, low-paid blacks were seen as the most serious 'threat' of all and were readily identified by the badge of colour, which provided a relatively easy means of erecting barriers against them. Both the (English-speaking) immigrants and local (Afrikaans) whites did their utmost to exclude from the jobs they wanted not only Africans, but also coloureds and Indians who, in the nineteenth century, dominated skilled trades in the Cape and Natal.

The struggle was, moreover, not confined to skilled jobs, but encompassed many semi-skilled, and even some unskilled jobs. The object was not simply to ensure preferential employment for whites, but to upgrade their pay and status, regardless of the skill of their jobs and of the large number of blacks willing to do them at lower wages. This was obviously difficult to enforce on employers who, as white labour spokesmen complained, were only too inclined 'to put their selfish economic interests before the preservation of the white race'.

Even before the establishment of formal job bars, white unions attempted to exclude blacks. The Transvaal unions did so explicitly: in 1911 the Transvaal federation of trade unions called for a boycott of builders and merchants who 'sacrificed the heritage of white people' by employing coloureds.[7] Cape unions, which often had coloured members, usually denied that they supported the job bar, but used devices such as the closed shop, minimum wages and entry to apprenticeships to restrict the numbers (see p. 41). Dr Abdurahman, the coloured leader of the African Peoples Organization, claimed that there was little difference between the blatant racists of the Transvaal and the supposedly open unions in the Cape which 'hounded coloureds out of their workshops'.[8]

The decisive struggle over the job bar was fought in the mining industry from 1893 until 1926, when the bar was entrenched in law against the Chamber of Mines' challenge to its legality in the Courts. Throughout this period, white workers fought unremittingly against mining capital's attempts to erode the bar (see p. 112). White workers won, not because of their industrial power—which was unable to prevail against the Chamber—but because of their political power. This secured the election of the 1924 Nationalist–Labour Pact formed by the mainly English Labour Party (established by the white unions in 1909) and the Afrikaner National Party. The Pact's 'civilized labour' package provided white labour with institutionalized, legal means of securing a monopoly of skilled jobs and preferential employment at higher wages in other jobs. The subsequent declining militancy of white workers was not because they had been politically castrated, but because they could get what they wanted by these easier, institutionalized means.

The representatives of white labour always showed a sharp awareness of the importance of *education and training* in the battle for jobs. The Labour Party majority on the Transvaal Provincial Council voted free secondary education for white children, but opposed schools for blacks. They also proposed that 'the teaching of trades, or the use of tools, to coloured peoples and natives will be sternly discountenanced'. During World War Two, when blacks were admitted to the COTT training centres (see p. 142), the unions threatened to withdraw the membership of whites who acted as instructors.[9] Simons argued that white workers gradually became supervisors, whose jobs were in large part dependent on the lack of skill and experience of blacks. Unlike capitalists, therefore, white workers did not have an interest in the training and education of blacks; their jobs often depended on their ignorance.[10]

Black wages and unionization

Despite the white unions' concern about the danger of undercutting from cheap, unorganized labour, they showed little interest in establishing the rate for the job, or narrowing the wide black–white wage differential. On the contrary, during a costs squeeze on the mines, J. Seddon, the MWU's first secretary, demanded: 'If any wages had to be reduced, let the wages of black labour be cut down'[11]—a strategy which increased the attractions of substituting cheaper black for white labour, hence reinforcing the need to shore up the job bar. Nevertheless, white workers invariably preferred to get a larger share of the cake at the expense of blacks and then defend their jobs by the bar or other means of exclusion.

Sometimes the dangers this posed to their jobs led them to adopt a different strategy. In 1909, Wilfred Wybergh, a leading advocate of 'civilized labour' policies, pressed for the extension of the Industrial Disputes Prevention Act to blacks, warning that their exclusion from industrial laws increased the incentives to employ them, 'because they were being made humble slaves . . . therefore easier to be dealt with and more satisfactory to employers than white people.' Consequently, in 1912, the Labour Party urged parliament to extend the principle of statutory compensation for industrial injuries and miners' phthisis to blacks, because workmen's compensation was raising the cost of white labour and leading to its replacement.[12]

Outside the mining and state sectors, where there was no formal job bar, it was more difficult to prevent undercutting, especially for less skilled whites. They were therefore more concerned with black wages. Africans, though not coloureds and Indians, were excluded from the system of collective bargaining set up by the 1924 IC Act. To ensure that Africans could not be employed at rates below those set by IC agreements, white labour supported the 1930 and 1937 amendments to the Act, enabling the Minister of Labour to extend agreements to cover them, even though they remained excluded from the negotiating process (see p. 20).

White labour also approved of the Wage Board's efforts to raise African wages during the 1930s. Boydell, the Labour Party Minister for Posts and Telegraphs, explained that whites were being ousted from jobs by 'unfair competition', particularly from Indians in Natal; employers must be forced to pay them the same wages.[13] These measures benefited blacks in the same jobs as whites, but reduced the job chances of unemployed blacks.

The IC Act excluded Africans from the definition of 'employee' and from representation on the Industrial Councils. But, until 1956, white unions were not prevented from organizing and representing African workers, nor from cooperating with their unions. Moreover, the 1924 Act included coloureds and Indians and, until 1952, African women. Most white unions, however, did not want African members. The Transvaal unions even refused to include coloureds and Indians in their unions.[14] The Cape and

Natal craft unions often admitted them formally, but, as Simons said,* the fraternal embrace could be deadly. Rutherford, secretary of the Typographical Union, explained to the Industrial Legislation Commission that:

> Up till 1927 we refused to have Indians in the Typographical Union. They then commenced negotiating separately, and eventually eliminated the European printer from Natal. We then took them into our Union to stop that. The result is . . . they have been almost eliminated. That happened because we took them into the Union. But when they were separate, they practically eliminated us. That tells a story.[15]

However, there were cases in which blacks were incorporated into unions in substantial numbers, without this being a ploy to exclude them from jobs. The mixed unions flourished most in the Cape, where coloureds were well-established as artisans and factory workers. Here they, and sometimes Africans, were included in unions such as the Garment Workers, Food and Canning Workers, Sweet Workers, and National Union of Distributive Workers. They were either organized into the same union, or into separate parallel branches, sharing the same offices and secretariat. During the 1930s and 1940s, mixed unions, such as the Garment Workers, spread to the Transvaal. Many of the mixed unions were in low-wage industries such as garment, leather and furniture, and the whites were often Afrikaans women, recently arrived from the *platteland*, working alongside blacks, often at similar jobs and rates of pay.

Greenberg noted that, in the USA, integrated unions were established 'when blacks constituted a sizeable and well-integrated portion of the workforce . . . and demarcation and exclusion were unrealistic possibilities'.[16] In SA too, mixed unions flourished in sectors where blacks constituted a large proportion of the workforce and where their skill and wage levels were closer to those of whites than in mining and engineering, and their bargaining power consequently greater. These industries also attracted able and idealistic white trade unionists, like Solly Sachs, Ray Alexander and Johanna Cornelius, and they provided a minority tradition

---

*Jack Simons was a scholar and member of the CPSA who had no illusions about, and made no excuses for, the racist policies of white labour.

of non-racialism, distinct from the exclusive, often explicitly racist, policies of most of the craft and industrial unions.

Excluded from most of the registered unions, many Africans and some coloureds and Indians set up their own unions, of which the most important before 1948 were the Industrial and Commercial Workers Union (ICU) and the African Mineworkers Union. The question of relations with these unions was highly divisive for the white unions. The Transvaal Federation of Labour did not want coloureds, let alone Africans, in the national federation of trade unions. The TLC/TUC* supported the Cape policy of including coloureds, but vacillated continually over Africans, in 1927, for example, refusing a request for affiliation from the ICU.[17]

The 'rightlessness' of blacks

Apologists for white labour's exclusion strategy argued that it was prompted by the 'rightlessness' imposed on blacks at the behest of capital: pass laws, forced labour measures, the maximum average ceiling on wages rendered blacks rightless and powerless. This made them more attractive to employers and made it difficult for free workers to compete with them, thus giving particular force to the charge of unfair competition and prompting white labour's racist policies.

This argument was first expounded by the Labour Party MP, Frederick Cresswell. In 1914, opposing a petition by the Cape Liberal, John X. Merriman, to remove the job colour bar, Cresswell said he was in principle against the bar and in favour of the rate for the job, but as long as the mining industry depended upon uncivilized, servile and largely imported workers, the abolition of the bar would merely set black and white workers against each other and enable the Chamber to get cheap labour and destroy trade unionism. White workers would lose, and blacks gain nothing from its abolition.[18] Tom Matthews, secretary of the miners' union from 1908, contended: 'seeing that the average Kaffir is bred as a slave he has no right to usurp our position as free

*The Trades and Labour Council was established in 1930; at various times it was known as the Trades Union Congress (TUC). In 1954, it became the Trades Union Council of SA (TUCSA).

men, to drive us from these mines . . . . I hold that the Kaffir should be allowed to get free, but in the interim, as he is here as a semi-slave, I have a right to fight him and to oust him.'*[19]

In reality, white labour played an active part in imposing on blacks the rightlessness they then used as an excuse for their racist strategies. The Labour Party's 'Native Policy' recommended that blacks be segregated in their own reserves and prohibited from owning or leasing farm land in white areas. Their only criticism of the 1913 Land Act was that it would increase the supply of African labour. (However, they did not favour exempting the Cape from its restrictions, nor setting aside large areas of land for Africans, which would reduce the supply.) Cresswell's only objection to the 1911 Native Labour Regulation Act was that, by the increased control it afforded over black labour, it 'narrowed the white man's sphere of employment'; he did not protest against the medieval penalties it inflicted on blacks. Instead, in 1917, the Labour Party suggested to the State Mining Commission that African convict labour be employed on the grounds of cheapness and ready availability—an extreme case of rightlessness, if ever there was one! The Labour Party also opposed the extension of the franchise to blacks and demanded legislation 'prescribing heavy penalties . . . for cohabitation of whites with kaffirs'. On the basis of this policy, Cresswell proudly claimed that the Labour Party was the first to advocate segregation between the races.[20]

For Indians, the Labour Party advocated an even more radical segregation policy—repatriation. But coloureds, who had the vote and were members of unions in the Cape, were a divisive issue for the Party, which resolved to admit coloureds who gave 'practical guarantees that they agree to the Party's policy of upholding and advancing white standards.' To reassure Labour supporters in the north, it was explained that there would be no 'indiscriminate admission of large numbers of Coloured people,' and that 'no social commingling was intended . . . . The racial instincts could have their full sway socially.' There was also no intention of extending this policy to Africans and Indians.[21]

---

*Reminiscent of St Augustine's 'Make me chaste, Lord, but not yet'; or Tom Lehrer on the Israeli policy towards nuclear weapons: 'The Lord is my shepherd, says the psalm. But just in case, we'd better have the Bomb.'

So deep was the commitment of white labour to racist policies, that the socialists and communists* who were their allies against mining capital not only found it expedient to support their struggle for the job colour bar, but also their segregationist tendencies, for example, blaming capitalism for breaking down 'the ethnological tendency . . . [to a] natural social apartness of white and black' and assuring white workers that, under socialism, blacks would be protected from exploitation but excluded from government until they reached maturity. S. P. Bunting, a leading communist, believed that blacks were peasants who would not need to seek work in the white areas if left to themselves, for they were better off than whites and earned wages as a luxury.**[22]

This stance partly reflected what *annales* historians like Lucien Lefebre term *mentalité*—the mental constraints of the society from which practically no one (including white liberals and communists) was free; but it was primarily because support for the job colour bar (and consequently other racist policies) was a *sine qua non* of cooperation with white labour, whose interests (like those of agricultural capital) could not be secured in a 'free market' situation, but required the structuring of a totally racist society. This was clear from their reaction to the erosion of apartheid during World War Two.

The 1940s reforms

The reforms of the 1940s gave white labour a chance to reduce the rightlessness of black workers, thus providing a better basis for worker solidarity. Most unions rejected this opportunity. Only the Cape federation supported the 1943 proposal to recognise African unions (as the FCI and Assocom urged). The TLC argued that Africans had 'not yet reached a stage of mental and cultural development in which they can be entrusted with the rights and

---

*In 1915, socialists broke away from the Labour Party and established the International Socialist League. The break was *not* over the job colour bar, but over Labour's support for Britain in World War One. The League merged into the CPSA, which was one of the first communist parties to be formed outside Russia after the revolution.

**Curiously, the American Communist Party in the 1930s also proposed 'autonomy to the point of separatism if wished for the Black majority areas of the South'.[23]

duties involved in recognition of their unions'.[24] The 1951 Industrial Legislation Commission gave a more candid explanation, acknowledging that many African unions were well run and that many Africans were able and ambitious and, if allowed to secure parity of bargaining power, 'could not be restricted indefinitely to unskilled or even semi-skilled work, but would get an increasing hold on skilled occupations'[25]—one of the reasons why there was more support for African unions from white capital than from white labour.

Mineowners were opposed to African (as they had been to white) unions. Nevertheless, during the 1930s, an African union emerged on the mines. The MWU had the option of working with the African Mineworkers' Union, but instead it spurned its plea for cooperation and, during the 1946 strike, scabbed against African miners and stood by while police drove them down the mines.[26]

White labour therefore opposed the opportunity of moving towards the incorporation of African workers by extending trade union rights to them. Indeed, many white workers wanted to exclude coloureds and Indians from their unions. Their presence in the mixed unions was one of the main reasons for the breakaway of right-wing unions from the TUC/TLC. With the backing of the 1948 Nationalist government, they formed an all-white, Afrikaans-speaking SA Confederation of Labour (SACOL), decisively splitting the white labour movement. Far from wanting to free Africans from servile conditions, they wanted to reduce the rights of coloureds and Indians.

Moreover, the conservative majority in TUCSA (as the TUC/TLC became known), dominated by the English-speaking craft unions, followed a vacillating and ambiguous policy. Put to the test in the 1940s, their slogans of 'rate for the job' and preventing competition from 'unfree, rightless labour' were revealed as rhetoric. They differed from SACOL in preferring to secure their aims by traditional trade union means—strategy (ii)—and disliked the explicitness, ideological overtones and rigidity of Nationalist policy; but, except for a small minority, they did not support the incorporation strategy.

The entrenchment of apartheid

The tendency towards exclusion and segregation was strengthened by NP policy, which, by depriving white workers of the option of incorporating blacks, encouraged them to resort to legal job reservation as a means of controlling competition. But these measures were not adopted at the behest of capitalists, who opposed the 1956 IC Act entrenching the job bar and segregating white and coloured unions (see p. 142). Nationalist policy was closer to the harsh SACOL recommendation that African unions should be 'prohibited outright'.[27]

TUCSA opposed the 1956 Act on the grounds that this was not an effective way of protecting their members:

> Our main [worry] ... is the economic disadvantage involved for workers in the separation into racial trade unions, otherwise we have no objection to racial separation. When the Minister extends [IC] agreements the employer is compelled to pay the same wage to a Native and that, of course, keeps them out .... We regard the existence of mixed trade unions as the only means whereby the standard of the European workers can be maintained because the idea of equal pay for equal work can only be maintained in this way.[28]

So the aims of the 1956 Act accorded with the practices of the TUCSA majority, but they disliked its explicit methods and the removal of the incorporation option, preferring to rely on traditional devices such as 'the rate for the job with realistic minimum wages'.

The liberal minority in TUCSA opposed the 1956 Act and tried to find ways round it, for example by having nominally separate unions that shared the same offices and officials with coloured and, in a few cases, with African unions. But the exclusion of coloureds from the executives of mixed unions faced them with a dilemma; for example the National Union of Distributive Workers, which had a strong commitment to multiracialism, decided to split so that coloured members would be free to elect their own representatives and be directly represented on the Industrial Councils.[29]

Benefits of the exclusion strategy to white labour
Preferential employment policies put whites at the top of the job queue. This, and rapid growth, wiped out white unemployment (less than 5,000 in 1950) and solved the 'poor white' problem. The exclusion strategy also insulated white wages against the downward pressure that would otherwise have been generated by competition from the numerous blacks. White capital repeatedly

demonstrated its unwillingness to pay premium wages for the pleasure of employing fellow whites. A competitive labour market would have led to their replacement by cheaper blacks (as in agriculture), and/or to a narrowing of the white/black wage differential. This tendency was apparent during the 1940s, when black wages rose faster than white, narrowing the wage ratio. This was partly due to erosion of the job and training bars; partly to deliberate official policy: during the war, controls were exercised over the wages and even mobility of skilled workers in key industries, constraining their wage increases despite the skill shortage. Also, to allow for rising prices, a flat-rate cost of living allowance, which favours lower-paid workers, was added to all wages. The limited relaxation of apartheid labour policies, even for this short period, thus had an impact on the occupational structure and on income distribution (see pp. 38 to 45).

The relationship between high white and low black wages was recognised not only by capital and the government,* but also by white labour. The TUC acknowledged in its evidence to the 1935 Industrial Legislation Commission: 'The fact does remain that we use non-European labour to offset a high cost of production and to allow the European labourer the high standard of living which they enjoy today.'[31]

The gains of white labour and elimination of the poor white problem did not convert most white workers to support the reformist policies of the war years. Rather, they resented the setback to what they regarded as their natural right to precedence over blacks, and many of them voted for the Nationalists in the 1948 election (see p. 282).

Nationalist policies once again held back the top group of blacks, and pushed ahead of them the poorer, less-skilled whites in the towns and the last major wave of white rural migrants.** The pressure of black competition was testified to by the Minister of Labour himself, in justifying the 1956 legislation (see p. 40), and

---

*The FCI complained in 1925 that high white wages were 'paid at the expense of the native workers'. In 1924, Smuts said: 'Our wages paid to skilled workers in SA are far in excess of what are paid in any other country, except America, and we were able to do it because we paid the black man such a low wage.'[30]

**From 1946–60, the proportion of whites in the urban areas increased by 50 per cent from 1.7m to 2.5m (see Table 2).

by numerous observers, such as the chairman of the Wage Board, Steenkamp, who explained that devices such as high minimum wages 'proved too flexible to exclude the non-white completely from jobs that had come to be regarded as white preserves . . . . [The problem was] most marked in the marginal areas where the less talented, not to say sub-normal members of the white population came into competition with the more talented . . . members of the non-white sector.'[32]

Nationalist policies promoted the further embourgeoisement of white labour, but this should not lead to the fallacy that there never was a white working class. The 1951 Census shows that even after the advances of the war years, there was still a substantial white working class, with 38 per cent of white male workers (and a higher proportion of Afrikaners) employed as workers in factories, on building sites, in transport, in the mines and so on. Thousands more were in lower-level white collar jobs such as clerks and salesmen.[33] The jobs reserved for them were another indication of their working-class status: from 1956–60, determinations were issued reserving for whites the job of driving sewage vans in Durban, as traffic constables in Cape Town, and as passenger lift attendants in Bloemfontein, Johannesburg and Pretoria, as well as production jobs in the clothing, building, metallurgical and mining industries.[34]

The post-Sharpeville boom led to further white gains. By 1970, 22 per cent of whites were in professional/technical and managerial/administrative jobs. The production/transport/labourer category was down to 26 per cent. The white collar category had expanded to 37 per cent. White educational levels had risen: by 1970, 60 per cent of the white workforce had matriculation or higher qualifications, though there were still almost a quarter of whites with JC (O level) or less.[35] From 1948 to 1970, real white wages doubled in manufacturing and construction and rose rapidly in all other sectors. By 1970 the ratio with African wages reached peak levels of 21 to 1 in mining and 6 to 1 in manufacturing (see Tables 6, 9, 10 and 11).

By 1970, the situation of white labour was thus very different from what it had been before World War Two. Desperately high unemployment had given way to an acute and growing shortage of white labour, and to mounting pressures from employers to relax the job bar.

White labour's response to the skill shortage

White labour leaders took an active part in the public debate over the skilled labour shortage. TUCSA leaders like Arthur Grobbelaar, the Secretary General, and Tom Murray of the Boilermakers, argued that erosion of the job bar was unstoppable; unless white workers cooperated in facilitating it, the 'uncontrolled' employment of blacks would pose a threat to them; however, they could gain from the 'disciplined relaxation' of the bar. They called for the rate for the job, unionization of Africans and, in the interests of economic growth, the expansion of training and education for blacks. They also advocated promotion on merit, reflecting the interests of coloureds and Indians, who constituted the majority of TUCSA members by 1970.[36]

The issue was highly divisive within SACOL. *Verligtes* like J. H. Liebenberg and Wally Grobler, of the Railway Artisans Staff Association, became convinced that it was essential for continued economic growth to allow 'the more rational utilization of non-white labour.' They argued that growth 'would stall within a decade unless the induction of Africans into semi-skilled and skilled industrial work was speeded up . . . . Raising the education level of Africans is a sound investment for the future. If we refuse to make it because of prejudice, fear or any other reason, our economic growth will be seriously inhibited and we will all suffer.' However, they warned that there was 'an enormous gap between the intelligentsia and workers on the shop floor'. They urged white workers to cooperate in drawing up plans for the 'controlled advance' of Africans that would not threaten their security.[37]

Other SACOL unions disagreed. They conceded that economic growth was the issue, but advocated a slower growth rate, geared to the availability of white labour.[38] This policy was supported by Gert Beetge of the Building Workers Union, Arrie Paulus of MWU, and Lukas van den Berg of *Yster and Staal* (Iron and Steel), who said in 1971 that his union would never condone the introduction of blacks into skilled work, except in the Bantustans: 'Whites must do the skilled work in white areas.' But he admitted, 'the position of trade unions is becoming very difficult . . . it is our duty to protect our members, but we cannot allow plants to close because employers can't find white workers . . . . Even with a system of temporary exemptions we cannot continue indefinitely and that explains why the situation is so delicate.'[39]

The majority in SACOL, like their President, Attie Nieuwoudt, gradually and reluctantly accepted the changes in government policy until the Wiehahn reforms. In the interests of the economy, they would countenance some black advance, subject to the provision of guarantees for whites, including the retention of job reservation and the proviso that jobs should, if needed, revert to whites. But the quarrel within SACOL over black advance became increasingly acrimonious and led to the breakaway of *verligte* unions, led by the Railway Artisans, from 1975.

Consequences of black job advance

Erosion of the job bar obviously increased the danger that the wage gap would encourage the substitution of black for white workers, so white unions began to take an unaccustomed interest in black wages. The 1971 TUCSA conference declared that 'sixty per cent of our people live below the poverty line,' and unanimously condemned as too low the minimum wages set by the Wage Board.[40] Professional organizations began to demand the rate for the job: the SA Nursing Association condemned the low wages of black nurses as 'unfair' and adversely affecting 'the status and integrity of the nursing profession'. Some branches of the Nursing Association stated that they would not accept further increases until black wages had been raised.[41]

Even SACOL became concerned about black wages. After the 1972 Ovambo strikes, Liebenberg warned there would be growing industrial unrest among blacks unless the wage gap was narrowed, and advocated the rate for the job.[42] Logically, there was less concern among unions whose members were in legally protected jobs and did not envisage black advance, such as the unskilled railway union, *Spoorbond*, whose leaders declared that though the wage gap was 'large I wouldn't say it's too large . . . . On account of the Christian civilization of the white, he is of a greater responsibility. A man is paid according to what he is worth.' The Durban Municipal Employees Society opined that if blacks were given more money they would simply work less as they 'had not matured to the same state as the white'. Paulus of the MWU did not consider that it was his job to worry about the wages of blacks who, because of 'their low standard of living', did not need more money.[43]

In areas where the job bar was eroded, however, unions increasingly insisted on the rate for the job. In the 1978 SEIFSA negotiations, Ben Nicholson of the Confederation of Metal and Building Unions said that the demand for high minimum wages was 'a test of the employers' sincerity . . . . If they try to keep wage minimums low, the scrapping of job reservation will merely mean an attempt to exploit cheap labour.'[44] A similar stand was taken by the Railway Staff Associations and the Surface and the Underground Officials Association on the mines, which insisted they would only agree to the abolition of job reservation if blacks promoted to officials' jobs were subject to the same conditions as whites, including rate for the job.[45]

This logical concern with black wages added to the pressures forcing capitalists to accept the rate for the job (see p. 162) and contributed to the remarkable extent to which white workers accepted the narrowing of differentials and redistribution of income towards blacks during the 1970s.

Unionization

White workers were more ambivalent and divided over African unionization. SACOL accepted the 1973 revamped committee system, and opposed African or mixed trade unions. Its leaders said it would be dangerous to allow black unions, like putting a 'sharp knife into the hands of a child . . . . He will not only hurt himself, he will hurt you too.'[46]

But there were dissident voices. Liebenberg, Grobler and P. J. H. Roodt (of the Railway Footplate Staff Association), said they were 'open-minded' on the subject of African unions, that it was 'crazy to have so large a mass of unorganised workers who are without the disciplines and the controls of the trade union movement,' and that unless 'experienced white trade unionists' helped blacks establish unions they would be 'trained and manipulated by overseas trade unions'.[47]

In 1975, Nieuwoudt reiterated SACOL's opposition to African unions when he rejected the FCI's support for the 'orderly' development of African trade unions. In a statement reminiscent of those white labour leaders of the 1920s who managed to sound radical while supporting the job bar, Nieuwoudt said he rejected the 'paternalistic' approach of the FCI and that, if African unions were recognised, they should be 'trade unions in the full sense of the word and not at the discretion of the employers'.[48] But, as their respective evidence to the Wiehahn Commission again showed, Africans had more chance of getting support for their unions from the FCI than from SACOL.

TUCSA's constitution excluded unregistered (i.e. African) unions. However, unlike SACOL, it included coloureds and Indians, who soon constituted the majority of its members, although this was not reflected in the executive or secretariat, which remained white dominated. The 1962 TUCSA congress resolved to allow the affiliation of 'properly constituted' African unions and requested official recognition for them under the IC Act. One of the reasons for this change in policy was growing pressure from the international trade union movement, which forced the withdrawal of SA from the ILO in 1964. With a grant from the International Metal Federation, an African Affairs committee was set up under Eric Tyacke and Loet Douwes Dekker to organise African unions. By 1969, thirteen African unions were affiliated to TUCSA.

This change of policy was fiercely attacked by the government. In 1967, the Minister of Labour threatened to deregister TUCSA, claiming that it was out of touch with the feelings of white workers and that its policy was undermining the official committee system. These attacks prompted the disaffiliation of fifteen TUCSA unions, including most of the important craft unions, drastically cutting TUCSA's membership and revenue.[49] In 1969, against the protests of its liberal wing—the Garment Workers, the Distributors, the Boilermakers, and the black unions—the TUCSA congress voted to limit membership once again to registered unions. This affair embittered relations between TUCSA and the African unions, but secured the reaffiliation of the Typographical and other craft unions.

In 1970, TUCSA turned again to the question of African unions, on which the divisions within it seemed so irresolvable. Grobbelaar, commenting on the African job advance shown by the census, warned that the unions' declining representativeness of the labour force would lead to an 'industrial explosion' unless 'institutional forms' were established for African workers.[50] In 1972, TUCSA again resolved to campaign for the recognition and affiliation of African unions. But their continuing ambivalence was illustrated by the speech of Crompton of the Iron Moulders Society:

> . . . already in this industry 70 per cent of the persons employed are people who are not able to belong to a trade union . . . we are becoming more unrepresentative of the workers in the industry every year, and the fact that Africans cannot . . . belong to our unions is something we cannot tolerate. We also cannot open the flood gates to this unorganized horde, that will bring our standards right back to ninety or a hundred years ago.[51]

The 1973 strikes injected a note of urgency into these somewhat academic debates—as did the shift in policy permitting the entry of Africans into skilled jobs. Reacting swiftly to the government's training plans, Murray of the Boilermakers said this made it imperative that Africans be granted full trade union rights, otherwise a 'head-on clash' between them and white workers was inevitable. The training programme would produce thousands of skilled and semi-skilled Africans during the next decade and this large number of workers operating outside the unions would represent 'a dire threat to the security and welfare of white workers' who would be undercut, unless the rate for the job was enforced: 'The future of white workers in this country depends to a very great extent on Africans being permitted to join the trade union movement. Without this we are inviting labour chaos and civil strife'.[52] The movement of blacks into more skilled work thus opened the way to a more integrated labour force, conducive to the growth of mixed unions.

TUCSA rejected the 1973 committee system, Grobbelaar warning that thousands of plant-level committees would prove 'uncontrollable' and lead to 'chaos'. A number of TUCSA unions, including the Typographical and SA Electrical Workers, announced that they intended to organize Africans in their industries.[53] TUCSA appealed to its shop stewards to cooperate closely at factory floor level with stewards of black unions, warning that undercutting and collusion between employers and black workers could be combated 'only through joint policing action by shop stewards of all races at the factory level'.[54]

Despite this logical volte face in policy, there was in fact little recruitment of Africans by the registered unions. Among the reasons was discouragement by the government. Until 1979, considerable pressure was exerted by the police and Labour Department to dissuade registered unions (and employers) from unionizing Africans or dealing with African unions. Second, white capital and white labour were often at cross purposes over this issue: capitalists did not want the sort of unionization that would enable white labour to block job advance and training; but this was precisely what many white unions wanted. The conflicting interests of capitalists and unions (and divisions within the ranks of each) complicated and delayed unionization.

Third, the trade union rank and file felt secure in their jobs and less convinced about the arguments for African unionization than the trade union leadership, whose jobs could disappear if they did not broaden their constituency. McCann, general secretary of the Amalgamated Engineering Union (AEU), said that he was under pressure from his members for paying too much attention to African unionization.[55] There seems little doubt that it was in the *economic* interests of white workers to unionize those Africans moving into the same jobs as themselves, and that they would have done so had these workers been whites (say recent immigrants from Europe); their failure to do so seems a clear example of racism over-ruling self-interest

Finally, there was the reaction of Africans themselves. There had always been African unions which preferred to be independent, though they had usually tried to establish some relationship with registered unions. These attempts had often been rebuffed (for example, the ICU's unsuccessful application to join the TUC; the African Mineworkers attempt to cooperate with the MWU; the expulsion of African unions from TUCSA). The growth of black consciousness, and disillusionment with the vacillating, paternalist policies of TUCSA, led to increasing support for independent black unions, rather than mixed or non-racial unions, and to suspicion of the motives behind the volte face in the policy of hitherto racist unions. Younger Africans were no longer impressed by the example of cooperation provided by the Garment Workers and other mixed unions. They argued that this relationship enabled the shrinking minority of whites in the industry to retain relatively greater influence on the executive, which did not reflect the growing importance of Africans in the labour force, and that relations remained stuck in a paternalist pattern, with whites taking the decisions.

But, while they were suspicious of the white unions, the black unions supported the rate for the job—unlike those coloured unions which, in the pre-war years, saw this as a device to exclude them. They presumably believed that, because of the labour shortage, employers would succeed in getting them into these jobs. They were also concerned about status and equality, areas in which their expectations were disappointed as they moved up the job ladder, because of reclassification and downgrading of jobs (see p. 63). On the question of access to jobs and training, black unions were in agreement with employers. But, once they got into these jobs, they were in agreement with the white unions on the rate for the job, and at odds with employers who, while they favoured redistribution towards blacks, argued that the contrived shortage of white labour had established 'artificially' high wages, which should not be perpetuated. This provided black and white labour with a shared interest.

However, relations between white and black unions were marred by conflict. TUCSA was accused of only bothering to unionise Africans in factories where black unions were active and of then attempting to exclude them by setting up 'tame' parallel unions. They were also alienated by TUCSA's failure to protest when they were harassed by the police and their officials banned and detained.

But while TUCSA policy—and certainly its implementation— was unable to meet the needs and aspirations of Africans, it went too far for some of its members. In 1976, after Murray's death, the Boilermakers, and the National Union of Furniture and Allied Workers, disaffiliated because of the competition from Africans for their largely *coloured* membership during the mid-1970s recession.[56] These conflicts within TUCSA, and the history of suspicion and lack of trust between officials of TUCSA and of the black unions, accounted for continuing tensions in its relations with the struggling black unions.

The Wiehahn reforms

White labour split three ways in response to the Wiehahn reforms. TUCSA signed the majority report recommending full trade union rights for all African workers and supported the later amendments extending these rights to migrants and permitting mixed unions. Grobler and Neethling, representing the large group of unaffiliated (mainly craft) unions, opposed the inclusion of migrants in the unions and wanted measures 'to prevent a flood of black artisans seeking employment in white areas'.[57] SACOL declared that 'the crisis hour had arrived for white workers' and that it had been betrayed by the Minister of Labour, Fanie Botha, who had assured them African unions would never be allowed in SA. They complained that 'people of other colours are consulted all the time, but we were not even given the time to formulate our views on the changes which were introduced'; and they accused the government of 'hasty action which gives rights to those who will not know how to manage them'.[58]

However, the reforms pushed some SACOL unions, like the Technical Officials Association and the SAR Police Staff Association, into opening their ranks to coloureds and even Africans.[59] This led to a sharp reaction from the militants (MWU, Yster and Staal, Building Workers), who drove them out of SACOL and drew up a defiant policy calling for the restoration of job reservation, a prohibition on supervision of whites by 'non-whites', the rejection of African training in white areas, expulsion of African strikers to the Bantustans, prohibition of mixed or even parallel African unions, and the prohibition of all foreign codes of conduct 'since foreign companies had no right to upset SA's social order.'[60] The MWU also broadened the terms of its constitution to enable it to recruit dissatisfied white members of unions which had opened their ranks to blacks,[61] thus making a bid for leadership of a conservative white labour bloc.

The MWU's attacks on the government, and its close association with the HNP, made some SACOL unions nervous of being associated with it (even if they agreed with it). Some of them, including Nieuwoudt's union, resigned from SACOL. The right-wing labour movement was thus seriously split by the Wiehahn reforms.

The break-up of SACOL left TUCSA as the biggest trade union federation. Some of the unaffiliated craft unions, like the Railway Artisans, joined TUCSA, whose membership increased by 1983 to almost 0.5m, 26 per cent of whom were whites. Almost 30 per cent of its members were by then Africans, whom TUCSA unions began to recruit more actively after Wiehahn.

This activity revived the accusation by the independent black unions that TUCSA's recruitment efforts were mainly aimed at undermining them and that many workers were being forced by 'closed shops' to join established TUCSA unions, rather than the union of their choice. They were also angered by TUCSA's lack of support for officials of black unions detained during the widespread 1982 arrests, and by TUCSA's demands that unregistered unions be banned, that employers be prevented from dealing with them, and that illegal strikers be prosecuted.[62]

To the black unions, the difference between SACOL and TUCSA seemed tactical, with the former favouring the retention of strategy (iii) (explicit exclusion), while the latter, especially the craft unions, fell back on strategy (ii) (exclusion by traditional trade union means). However, as in the past, there were also TUCSA unions which favoured strategy (i), non-discrimination and the use of trade unions to incorporate rather than to exclude black workers. After a period of internal turmoil, the Boiler-makers, SA's largest union, emerged as the most important of these.* By 1983 Africans comprised 20 per cent of its members, with proportionate representation on its executive. In that year the Boilermakers left TUCSA in protest against its unsupportive attitude towards the black unions, exemplified in its refusal to condemn the continuing rightlessness imposed on Africans by the Orderly Movement Bill and their exclusion from the 1983 Constitution. SACOL, true to form, never concealed its opposition to the extension of political rights which it warned would follow the Wiehahn reforms.[63]

Varying responses by white unions to black advance

The uneven pace of black job advance was closely connected with the varying strategies and strength of white unions. The steel and engineering sector provides an example of *negotiated black advance*, beginning with the 1968 IC Agreement and culminating in the 1978 Agreement abolishing job reservation in this sector before the Wiehahn reforms (see p. 64).

Among reasons why the unions agreed to this, including hardliners like Yster and Staal, was the increase in the number and proportion of black workers in this sector, which meant that the registered unions represented a diminishing proportion of the workforce. Union activity had moreover been largely focussed on the powerful national Industrial Council. There was little activity at shop floor level and deals were often struck between white workers and employers, especially in smaller factories and work-

---

*In 1983, the Boilermakers had almost 55,000 members. Most SA unions were small: over two-thirds had less than 5,000 members.

shops, where it was impossible for the unions to police black advance effectively. Union leaders were aware that, while they were arguing, black advance was taking place and that they represented an ever-shrinking proportion of the workforce.

Resistance to black advance was weakened by lack of solidarity among the unions. Reasons for the differences between Yster and Staal and the Boilermakers included greater black penetration of Boilermakers' jobs (providing an incentive to recognise and unionize the workers concerned) and the more amenable attitudes of union members (including a significant number of coloureds and Indians) and of union leaders like Tom Murray and, later, Ike van der Watt.

The ending of job reservation in 1978 did not necessarily mean the unions fully accepted black advance. With the notable exception of the Boilermakers, it mostly signalled a retreat from formal exclusion to the use of traditional restrictive practices. After Wiehahn, employers and Africans accused some unions of using their position on the Apprenticeship Committees to block entry.[64] Although the steel and engineering unions were unable to stop black advance, they (and the railway unions, which adopted similar tactics) were strong enough to maintain some control over the process and to exact compensation for their members.

On the gold mines, the MWU fought a *successful rearguard action against black advance*. The tentative 1965 attempt to shift the bar slightly upwards was hastily abandoned when reaction among miners led to the overthrow of the MWU's secretary-general, Grundlingh, and his replacement by Arrie Paulus, who promised to resist with all his might 'the onslaught of Kaffir, Moor and Indian' on white workers.[65] In resisting erosion of the bar, the MWU was able to cite official policy until 1973 (in effect until 1979, as the 1973 concessions were conditional upon 'the concurrence' of the white unions). But their opposition, from 1968, to relaxation of the job bar within the Bantustans (see p. 309) flouted official policy and alienated the government, even though it did not dare to force the issue.[66]

The MWU's position was also gradually undermined by growing isolation from the officials' and artisans' unions on the mines. In 1973, the Chamber of Mines succeeded in splitting the Council of Mining Unions, when the winding drivers (who work the hoists which could bring the mines to a standstill) voted to leave the

Council and accept an offer of official status, a pay rise, and continued reservation of their jobs; they were followed by the reduction workers and the artisans' union. The MWU, which had hoped to unite them all into one union, was isolated.[67] But it continued, successfully, to resist encroachments on its members' jobs and, less successfully, to rally other unions against concessions.

The MWU hoped that its 1979 strike against black advance would prove to be 'another 1922'. In the event, the strike collapsed within a fortnight, both because the MWU did not receive the full support of its members (20 to 40 per cent turned up at various mines) and because 'officials, including shift bosses, have been underground supervising drilling and blasting'.[68]

The failure of the 1979 strike emboldened the Chamber and the other mining unions (mindful of Grundlingh's fate). The Underground Officials Association agreed to phase out job reservation protecting its members, provided it could enrol blacks moving into the jobs concerned.[69] In 1982 the all-white Council of Mining Unions disbanded in favour of a confederation including multiracial unions, thus further isolating the MWU. Nevertheless, by 1984, in defiance of the Wiehahn recommendations, the bar protecting MWU jobs was still intact.

The building unions, by contrast, failed to maintain the job bar. In 1970, almost 40 per cent of white building workers were in jobs reserved by determination No. 28.[70] In addition, the 1951 Native Building Workers Act excluded Africans from training or working as artisans in white areas. However, it proved extremely difficult to enforce the bar in this sector. This was partly because of the pool of blacks trained to work in their 'own' areas (and on white farms) in terms of the 1951 Act (see p. 24), whom it proved impossible to keep out of the white areas; and partly because of the difficulty of policing thousands of building sites. Other factors were public resistance to rising building costs, which were felt directly by white voters, and the lower level of unionization and the split between the TUCSA-affiliated Amalgamated Union of Building Trade Workers, which supported the rate for the job, and the SACOL-affiliated *Blanke Bouwekersvakbond* (White Building Workers Union), led by Gert Beetge, which supported job reservation.

Despite Beetge's protests, large-scale exemptions from job reservations were granted from 1971 on. By 1977 only 29 per cent of building jobs were still legally reserved and many of these were being done illegally by blacks.[71] (In 1974, the Industrial Tribunal reported that it found 'alarming malpractices' on visits to building sites, with blacks 'openly engaged' in nearly all classes of skilled work.) Hundreds of building employers were prosecuted for contraventions of the law—but even larger numbers escaped; and the Minister of Labour became increasingly reluctant to take action against the widespread contraventions, despite accusations from the unions of a 'cold-blooded sell-out' of white workers.[72]

After Wiehahn, job reservation and the Building Workers Act were abolished. The unions' attempts to use the Apprenticeship Committee as a means of blocking black advance (and their demand that blacks who wanted to become artisans should, like whites, be subject to call-up for military training) was hampered by the existence of independent training centres for blacks, outside their control. Manpower surveys confirmed that there was much greater black penetration of the building trades than was the case in engineering or mining (see p. 63).

It was hardly surprising that unions whose members benefited most from job reservation opposed it most doggedly. Unsuccessful rearguard actions were also fought by some of the less skilled unions in the state sector. For example, in 1971 the Durban Municipal Employees Society opposed employment of Indian constables, declaring they 'would not tolerate a situation in which a white constable had to relieve a Non-White'.[73] The South African Postal Union opposed the employment of blacks, insisting, 'We will always be opposed to this—even in twenty years time'. However, within a few years they reluctantly agreed to the appointment of blacks 'on a temporary basis' on the grounds that 'the public had to get service.'[74]

The severe 1974–8 recession led to a backlash against black advance. Railway workers, angry about low wage increases, threatened a go-slow strike over the pace of black advance; the Diamond Cutters Union staged an eleven-week stoppage against black advance in a 'work-starved' industry.[75] Even the Boiler-makers reacted (see p. 204) and, in face of a fall of employment by one-third in the construction industry, the government responded to pressures from building unions by temporarily withdrawing some of the exemptions from job reservation and prosecuting employers for contraventions.[76] The economic recovery once again eased black advance, as can be seen from the 1978 SEIFSA agreement. These provide telling examples of how growth eroded apartheid, while stagnation and white unemployment reinforced it.

The Wiehahn reforms thus precipitated turmoil and a complex struggle in the white labour movement (and a parallel struggle among black workers). By 1983, SACOL, the proponent of strategy (iii), was being overtaken by TUCSA—still torn between strategies (i) and (ii)—in terms of white support; but TUCSA was losing to the independents in the battle for black members (see Chapter 9).

Reasons for differences among white workers

The varying responses of white workers were related to differences of interest among them. Roughly three groups can be distinguished:

(i) Wage-earners with *high skills and qualifications* which require years of post-matriculation training and experience, and which are scarce, not only within SA, but internationally, giving these workers mobility and bargaining power. This group includes experts in mining, agriculture, accounting, electronics, engineering, etc. Their number and importance grew as the economy became more mechanized and sophisticated. Some analysts would classify them with the bourgeoisie; however, it is not the typology that matters here, but their interests, attitudes and power.

(ii) Wage-earners with *middle-level skills and qualifications*, requiring some post-school training, such as teachers, nurses, laboratory technicians, mechanics, craftsmen, computer operators, administrators. They are required in very large numbers and their skills are often scarce in developing countries. The supply can be increased over a few years, provided that the educational system is producing enough school-leavers, that facilities for training exist, and that there is the political will and administrative ability to implement crash training programmes. It would take years to replace the huge number of trained workers required for these jobs in SA. The majority of white wage-earners fall into this category (the number of blacks is growing rapidly as well).

(iii) Wage-earners of *low skill*, who would be relatively easy to replace as their training/induction can be done quickly, frequently on the job: machine operators, clerks, cashiers, telephonists, drivers, traffic wardens. There are others who need, or usually receive, no training: shop assistants, salesmen, receptionists, waiters, lift attendants. The proportion of whites in these jobs has shrunk but the absolute number is still quite large.*

The attitudes towards black and coloured job advance of these three groups varied markedly. Surveys of white attitudes consistently show *a positive correlation between educational and income level and acceptance of black advance* (see p. 308). The professionals and experts of group (i) have been among those members of the oligarchy calling for the relaxation of job bars; the skilled unions have generally been more amenable to black advance than the less skilled, as can be seen by the difference between the mine artisans' and officials' unions and the MWU. The MWU's opposition is often described as irrational, but the officials and artisans had more reason to feel secure. They were well-qualified, while miners required only Standard VI education and sixteen months' training. Much of their work consisted of supervising blacks, some of whom became proficient without formal training and certificates. The miners' fear that they could be replaced, and that their high earnings depended upon barring black competition, was therefore rational. The apparently strong bargaining position suggested by their relatively high wages could be rapidly eroded if they lost their monopoly. Likewise, on the railways, the skilled Railway Artisans Staff Association was less resistant to black advance than *Spoorbond*, union of the unskilled railwaymen, most of whom owed their jobs to the 'civilized labour' policy.

However, once black advance took place, the skilled unions were generally more able to control or limit it. Significantly, by 1983, few blacks were in the Railway Artisans or the Footplate

*In 1971, 76,000 whites in manufacturing were officially classified as 'semi-skilled operators'. In the services sector, 32,476 whites were classified as porters, caretakers, cleaners, lift operators, ushers, waiters, kitchen hands and labourers; 18,000 were chauffeurs or drivers. Many did relatively unskilled white collar work: 83,685 were shop or counter assistants, 40,000 clerks/telephonists/office machine operators.[77] This adds up to 250,161 whites, 17 per cent of those economically-active in 1970, in jobs being overtaken by the black vanguard, often in the same factories, offices or shops.

Associations, which were using their control over apprenticeship to limit numbers. But both *Spoorbond* and the Railway Police Association had significant black memberships, almost 40 per cent in the case of the police.

The 26 per cent of economically-active whites employed in the state sector seemed more resistant towards the erosion of apartheid than other white workers. This can be seen from the policies of SACOL, to which most unionized state sector employees belonged. It was also borne out by observation and by surveys of their attitudes.[78] This was partly because many civil servants owed their jobs to the 'civilized labour' policy and believed their job security was linked to white, or even to Afrikaner, hegemony; partly because of the low calibre of many (though by no means all) civil servants: the number in this category probably increased as the job bar rose during the 1970s, and the bottom group of whites retreated from the private into the state sector. Finally, the jobs of many white bureaucrats, such as those in BAD and the Department of Community Development, consisted of operating the controls over black labour. The erosion of apartheid thus constituted a direct threat to their jobs and power. Indeed they must prefer wide-scale evasion (requiring lots of administrators to control it) to the abolition of apartheid!

Reasons for the changing policies of white labour
White workers' resistance to erosion of the job bar was less effective and less fierce than expected. Among the reasons for this were changes in their interests and attitudes and in their industrial and political power.

By the mid-1960s, the high unemployment and poverty of the pre-war period had given way to security and prosperity. This transformed the interest of white workers and reduced their need for apartheid. The top group did not fear competition; many of them occupied managerial positions and shared the attitudes of employers about the need for black advance. The middle group did not feel threatened by the crucial early stages of black advance. The bottom group, comprising a shrinking but still significant percentage of white workers, was more vulnerable and more resistant; but their opposition was reduced by the considerable efforts made to shield them from its economic and psychological effects. Wherever possible, white workers were retrained and promoted to higher jobs; where this was impossible, they were moved sideways, into separate units, where they would not encounter blacks working at the same or superior jobs (see p. 63). These whites also gravitated out of private industry, where they were operatives or low-level clerical workers, into the state sector, which was more willing to spend money and management time on them (or at least on the men).

Second, white labour was handsomely compensated for agreeing to black advance—at least in the early stages, when their acquiescence was secured by big rises in pay and fringe benefits, or by bonuses which gave them a direct interest in productivity. This meant that the initial stages of black advance were often accompanied by a widening of wage differentials (see p. 64); but in these deals white labour gave away a great deal of 'territory', via fragmentation, dilution and downgrading of jobs, thus permanently weakening their bargaining power and ability to influence the rate of change.

This intensified the third factor—the declining industrial and political power of white labour. With economic growth, whites constituted a declining percentage of the labour force; and the entry of blacks and coloureds into the strategic skilled jobs further eroded their bargaining power. There was also a decline in the degree of mobilization of white labour, due both to prosperity and complacency, and to the centralised Industrial Council system, which discouraged activity at plant level and left much of the work of unionists to Industrial Council officials. The unions thus did not have tight control over developments at shop floor level, where informal deals were often struck between management and white workers. This loss of control over the situation often faced them at the negotiating table with the *fait accompli* of black advance.

The white unions were furthermore deeply divided by skilled/unskilled and particularly English/Afrikaans differences. The favoured Afrikaans unions were probably weakened by their over-close connection with the government, which led them to rely on political support, rather than industrial organization. (In interviews, Afrikaans workers often said they accepted erosion of the job bar and other changes because 'the government says it's OK'.) The non-Afrikaans unions were subjected to bullying and increasing controls which, in the long run, weakened the whole trade union movement.

These measures were aimed at the left; but they set precedents and conferred powers which could be used against all unions. In 1966, the right-wing unions got a taste of the medicine they had been happy to see administered to others. In the wake of the strikes over the Grundlingh-Paulus leadership struggle in the MWU, an amendment to the IC Act prohibited strikes (already illegal for Africans) for any purpose unconnected with the relationship between employer and employee. It also provided that, in future, an order for the deduction of union dues must come from, and at the discretion of, the Minister of Labour, who could therefore deny the docking of dues to any union.[79]

In the mid-seventies, as white unions faced declining living standards, they woke up to the existence of extensive curtailments on the right to strike in 'essential services'. In 1979, railwaymen called for the reinstatement of their right to strike.[80] But the 1982 Intimidation Act gave the government yet more powers to act against trade unions. The Act was passed at a time of widespread African strikes, which also inhibited white unions from adding to industrial unrest.

The declining economic and industrial power of white workers was paralleled by declining political influence, particularly for the bottom group. An example of this was the MWU, whose position had always been heavily dependent on political support. Once, Nationalist politicians were attentive to their every complaint, but they refused to respond to the 1977 revelation in the Union's journal, *Die Mynwerker*, of a secret plan by AAC (which they dubbed the African Advancement Corporation) to weaken the MWU. This was to be done by upgrading its members to official status (thus reducing its numbers), by making deals permitting black advance with individual miners on various mines, and by training blacks and drawing up a contingency plan so that it would be possible 'to operate the mines in the event of strike action by the MWU'.[81] The final element in the AAC strategy was recognition of a black mine union. Without the political support to which it had long been accustomed, the MWU was unable to counter this systematic undermining of its position.

The gradual, incremental nature of the changes—the fact that, initially, they took place by exemption rather than by amendment of the legislation—made it tactically difficult for the MWU to find a point at which other opponents of the policy could be persuaded to confront the government. Most SACOL conservatives were reluctant to rally behind the MWU and Building Workers until after the Wiehahn Report—when it was too late.

Fourth, international pressures helped to shift the trade union leadership, particularly TUCSA and the SACOL *verligtes*. In 1964 SA was expelled from the ILO, but retained links, which they valued, with trade union organizations like the British TUC and the international secretariats of metal and garment workers. These contacts exposed them directly to the extent of international hostility to SA. In 1973, Grobbelaar returned from a stormy ILO meeting, warning that 'The world's trade union movement—east and west—is now firmly lined up against SA.' To avoid damaging boycotts, it was essential 'to remove discriminatory legislation and treat all South Africans like human beings'. Likewise, in 1980, van der Watt warned that the International Metal Federation was under 'tremendous pressure' to back sanctions against SA.[82] The need to fend off these threats was used by *verligte* unionists as an additional argument for reform.

Fifth, many white workers understood the economic arguments about the need for black advance. From the late 1960s, they were at the receiving end of an intensive campaign to persuade them of the economic and political costs of apartheid and the need for change. The main agents in this campaign were employers, the Press and the *verligte* Afrikaans intelligentsia and politicians. The Afrikaans elite effectively used the network of Afrikaner nationalist ties and organizations to cajole white labour into adopting (for them) radically new policies. Employers had an impact on attitudes at factory level, for example, by the special courses conducted by the larger companies (described by some workers as 'brain-washing' sessions).

Many of the white workers I interviewed were familiar with arguments about the high cost structure of manufacturing and the inflationary effects of the labour shortage. In a survey of white artisans in 1972/3, Feit and Stokes found that 58 per cent of them believed it was essential for further economic growth that blacks be allowed to do more skilled work. Feit and Stokes concluded that, regardless of personal prejudice, white artisans who were convinced of the economic advantages of black job advance would accept it.[83] These arguments were reinforced by white workers' own experience of the costs and inconvenience of the skill shortage—such as the decline in the telephone service, or the difficulties of getting homes and cars repaired.

Finally, as observed above, once black advance took place, the interests of white workers required that it should be recognised—if only to exert some control over it. This increasingly led white unions to insist that they must have the right to unionise blacks. This right could be misused, but it was also an essential part of the process of black advance. Whereas once the iron apartheid framework had pushed even liberal capitalists and trade unionists towards the adoption of racist policies, the dismantling of that framework generated pressures which pushed conservatives in the opposite direction—towards the adoption of less racist policies.

Social apartheid

It has been argued that social apartheid was the creation of white capital, which wanted to prevent 'social intercourse of poor white and black' as part of its attempt to divide the working class.[84] The little research available on this question suggests that there were strong pressures from white workers themselves for social separation, and an insistence that distinctions be made between themselves and blacks. In this they were supported by racial ideologists, particularly within the NP. Capitalists did not oppose most aspects of social apartheid, which (with the exception of separate facilities at the workplace) did not impose direct costs on them; but non-agricultural capitalists do not appear to have been a major pressure for it.

The Labour Party opposed 'cohabitation' of white and black and 'social commingling' (see p. 192) and the Labour majority on the Johannesburg City Council was 'notoriously rigid' in denying the use of municipal facilities to blacks.[85] Many white workers also resented any challenge to what they regarded as their superior racial status, as reflected in the decision of the Motor Mechanics Union in 1919 not to service the cars of blacks (at a time when few whites had cars).[86]

Some of these measures were functional—securing for whites superior facilities and enhancing their status. Insofar as this was so, the measures were often costly and inconvenient for capital. After 1960, the NP's insistence that employers must provide separate canteens and toilets for each race group led many employers to prefer having as racially homogeneous a labour force as possible, to avoid the duplication of facilities. This had unintended disadvantages for whites because, as the Minister of Labour complained, employers then preferred blacks, who offered a 'larger pool of labour'.[87]

But while many of these measures were intended to be functional for white workers, there were some which were not and which simply reflected a reaction against close contact with people of different habits, language and colour. A few examples: soon after Union, the Labour Party supported the Dutch Reformed Church Act, which excluded blacks from membership of the Church, except in the Cape province (this Act was opposed by the Unionist Party, which had strong links with mining capital).[88] It was the Labour–Pact government which enacted the 1927 Immorality Act, prohibiting extramarital intercourse between black and white. Simons complained that the Labour Party 'pandered to the white man's sexual prejudices' by sensationalising cases of rape of white women by blacks and demanding the death penalty for rape.[89] Tom Matthews, general secretary of the MWU, explained to an official commission in 1914 that drunkenness among white miners resulted from their having to work 'for eight hours among a crowd of dirty evil-smelling Kaffirs . . . enough to break down the moral fibre of the average man'.[90] Trade unionists like Solly Sachs, who persuaded black and white workers to combine their unions and bargain jointly, usually had to organize them into separate, parallel branches because of the 'violent prejudices' of white workers.[91]

Some of these examples reveal the effects of class differences (low-paid, ill-housed black miners less able than whites to wash and wear clean clothes); but others, such as the Immorality Act, suggest deep-rooted feelings of antipathy and hostility. Another indication of this was the physical assaults on blacks by white workers during the 1922 strike. A number of blacks were killed or wounded during these pogroms and the strike committee, fearing public reaction, issued a statement acknowledging that groups of white strikers were attacking blacks 'wantonly and without any reason or cause,' and urging them to desist. In the Cape, a mass meeting of the ICU condemned this 'murderous onslaught on defenceless, peaceful non-Europeans' and called on blacks to support the Smuts government against the strikers.[92]

Other areas in which active pressures for apartheid from white labour would seem likely are stabilization, and social and residential segregation. Apart from the fact that migrancy militated against the acquisition of skills,* restrictions on black numbers and families reduced the competition for urban resources (housing, schools, clinics, parks). *Prima facie* white labour would seem to need protection more than capitalists, who could afford to buy it for themselves. This expectation is borne out by the recent policies of capital and labour, about which we have more information.

While urban capitalists have been a major pressure for stabilization (see p. 157), white unions have been among those objecting that the government is spending too much on blacks. In 1980 SACOL unions criticized the announcement that the higher gold price would be used to improve black housing and schools, while not providing any 'relief for whites living below the breadline'.[94]

Integration in the workplace is an object of the Codes of Conduct adopted by employers' organizations (see p. 147). Resistance has come from some white unions. At the 1972 SACOL congress, resolutions were tabled urging the government to act against the increasing racial integration in industry and commerce.[95] Integration of canteens and locker rooms at the Ford Motor Company in Port Elizabeth in 1979 led to the threat of a strike by white workers.[96] Employers have found it easier to start integrating among senior staff and at head offices than among middle or lower level staff or on the factory floor.[97]

Capitalists have been in the lead in urging the easing of social apartheid—opening public facilities to blacks, permitting mixed sport etc.[98] Five-star hotels and restaurants have been opened first; the problems arise with amenities for the less well-off. However, practical considerations such as overcrowding are not the only ones; status and racist feelings remain important. Gert Beetge complained that if blacks were accepted as union members,

---

*It is not clear how aware white labour was of the connection between stabilization and skills, but they were explicit about *not* challenging the compound labour system. During the 1922 strike, the miners' Defence Committee stated: 'When Mine Negro labour is free labour it will be time enough to decide what our attitude shall be towards it, but that is not the present position or question. We are not even expressing any opinion about the compounded Native Labour system for unskilled work on the Mines, since we have no desire to encroach on it.'[93]

the wives of white workers might have to queue for sick benefits 'alongside Indian women in their saris' and that 'it affects the status and dignity of the white man to do the same work as a black.'[99]

The most sensitive areas were residential and educational segregation. Until the 1970s, capitalists did not challenge apartheid in these areas, but *prima facie* it would seem that white labour's need for it was greater than theirs. Today, it is undoubtedly the case that relaxation of these measures would be easier in wealthy suburbs like Houghton and Constantia than in Bellville or Bezuidenhout. In a recent poll, Constantia residents voted in favour of opening their suburb, and many of the wealthy private schools have opened their doors to blacks (see p. 62). The fact that the high cost of property in these areas, and private school fees, limits the impact of removing apartheid underlines the point that it is the less well-off whites for whom institutionalized social apartheid is functional; richer whites have less need of it, they can rely on class power. This does not make them morally superior but it does reduce their support for apartheid. Nor is there evidence that capitalists deliberately imposed it on white workers in order to divide the working class. It is not implausible that they might do this, but the record suggests that they did not, and that white workers were active agents pressing for it themselves, sometimes in cases where it was opposed by capital.

Changing attitudes

While opinion polls show that white labour was less in favour of change than white capital, they also show that their attitudes were changing and that they were becoming less racist; a finding with which many informed observers agreed. In 1973, TUCSA's economist, Robert Kraft, said that 'a revolution was taking place in the attitudes of white workers to their black colleagues'; whites were 'developing a respect and understanding of other racial groups; they were becoming more pragmatic and flexible.'[100] A 1977 survey into race relations in the building industry in Durban claimed there was little racial friction in those instances where whites were working under the supervision of coloureds and Indians.[101] Rising black incomes and educational standards, and hence more similar lifestyles, contributed towards these changing white attitudes.

Black workers I interviewed during fieldwork in the 1970s were overwhelmingly critical of their situation, but most of them said that the behaviour of white workers towards them was much better. There seemed to have been an improvement of which all but young workers were aware. The complaints were often of lack of equality, rather than of the abusive behaviour and even assaults which were common before.*

The erosion of apartheid is likely to be costly to white workers, not only economically but also socially and psychologically. Some of them could nevertheless benefit from the ending of the rigid system of stratification which requires all whites to keep ahead of all blacks. This imposes strains on whites trying to hold down jobs and lifestyles beyond their capacities or inclinations. Some whites have even refused to be retrained and promoted to higher jobs as the bar moved up.** In 1971, the Minister of Labour said that SA Railways had found that 'thousands' of whites were not interested in job advancement and that they constituted 'a problem'.[102] If these workers were allowed to remain where they were and ensured of job security, they could gain from the ending of the constant pressure to keep ahead which contributes to their support for apartheid.

*An example of changing relationships and problems was provided by the experience of a black worker in a small Johannesburg factory, who was promoted in 1974 to a semi-skilled job testing chemicals. His promotion was opposed by white workers who refused to train him, so this had to be done by the manager. White workers then insisted that his reports should always be countersigned by a white—any white—even one of the secretaries who did not understand the formulae. After a few weeks he insisted on signing his own reports. The whites protested but after a meeting with the manager, dropped the matter. When I interviewed him, he was pressing to be housed in an office with one of the white chemists; the others all shared, but had objected to sharing with him. The next step would be the use of their canteen and toilets. The problems had not disappeared, but they had changed. White workers were fighting a rearguard action, but acquiescing when they did not get their way.

**At Welkom, a miner told me he would not mind working alongside blacks, but that he supported the MWU's opposition to black advance because he was convinced that it would force him to move to another job. He had twice been in jobs where he had agreed to work alongside blacks and had helped to train them. But once they moved up, he was elbowed out. He did not want to be retrained and moved again, even to a better job; he wanted to remain where he was.

To sum up: white labour's support for social apartheid was *sui generis*, not contrived by capital. The reasons for this support were never purely ideological or 'irrational'; social apartheid was functional, securing for them status and privileged access to scarce urban resources, as well as gratifying their racial prejudices.

Since about 1970, capitalists have extended their campaigns against apartheid labour policies to some aspects of social apartheid, and they are more amenable to social integration than white labour. Again, apartheid is less functional for them, whereas white workers' prejudices are reinforced by their interests. White workers have reluctantly acquiesced in some erosion of social apartheid but, while their attitudes are changing and their power is declining, they remain an important constraint on further reform, particularly of residential and educational segregation.

Other strategies for white labour

Once the first major stage of black advance was accomplished, the payouts to white labour stopped. Thereafter, black wages rose faster than white; by the mid-1970s, the wage ratio had narrowed to its lowest point yet and *real* white wages were falling—for the first time since the 1930s (see Tables 9, 10 and 11). Moreover, the changes in the job structure were not limited to a 'floating bar', which could be raised or lowered at will: many jobs had disappeared and the ratchet had been broken at many points. Any attempt to unravel this process would be extremely difficult and fiercely resisted by both black labour and white capital.

This loss of control was foreseen by trade unionists like Anna Scheepers, who regarded the behaviour of white workers as 'feckless and shortsighted'.[103] The alternative strategy, advocated by the TUCSA liberals like Scheepers (and by SACTU), was to incorporate blacks in their unions and jointly to exercise more control over processes of mechanization, fragmentation and dilution, thus securing more protection for all workers and providing the basis for a better long-term relationship with black labour. Was the failure of white workers to pursue this option a sign of 'irrationality' or 'false consciousness'; or did they gain by delaying it wherever they could and extracting the highest price for it where they could not?

The argument for the *incorporation strategy*, from the point of view of white labour, rests heavily on long-term considerations—

on factors such as their age structure, how long they will want their jobs, and whether their children will want them too. The declining number of white apprentices suggests that whites will fade out of blue-collar work and that the strategy of first slowing black advance and then extracting a high price for it may have been rational economically, though this leaves open the question of whether, psychologically and politically, the whites have not missed an opportunity of working together with black labour. This consideration in turn depends on unpredictable factors, such as the likely interests and attitudes of blacks (a bird in the hand . . .). Whites are not working themselves out of white collar jobs and it will be interesting to see whether white collar unions adopt a longer-term view, either resisting black advance more doggedly, or incorporating them more thoroughly.

The broader liberal argument that removal of the job bar would be a rational policy because it would lead to a larger national product from which the whole society would benefit overlooks the point that the benefits would not necessarily accrue to white labour. They are more likely to go to black labour and white capital, and it is difficult to see how white labour could maintain its premium wages and share of social resources; indeed, these have already been reduced by the erosion of apartheid labour policies to date. But, while white workers will not voluntarily sacrifice their premium wages, they might accept a smaller *proportion* of GNP if their absolute living standards do not decline too much. This would require a fast growth rate to maintain their living standards while raising those of blacks and/or redistributing from capital to labour.

A similar objection applies to the position of white labour in a socialist society with common ownership of the means of production. The violent take-over which this would require in SA makes it likely that the national product would fall, though distribution might be more equal. Whether or not the national product falls, it seems that the only way white workers could maintain their premium wages would be by occupying a strategic role in a racially divided society, with a racially divided working class.

Initially, most white workers (like many other observers) did not foresee how far and fast black advance would go. They believed they could limit it to the floating bar and keep Africans (if not coloureds and Indians) out of skilled jobs in the white areas.

They were encouraged in this belief by politicians like Vorster and by businessmen. (Indeed this provides a much better example of their 'political disorganization' than the mistaken argument that they were tricked into supporting the job bar). There were others, including some of their trade union leaders, who warned them of the likely consequences and urged them to adopt the alternative incorporation strategy, but the trade union rank and file repeatedly rejected this, as shown by the disaffiliations prompted by the modest incorporation plans sporadically attempted by TUCSA. The SACOL unions would not even adopt this strategy in relation to coloureds and Indians, let alone Africans. There is no doubt about the repeated rejection by the overwhelming majority of white unions—whether industrial or craft—of the incorporation strategy. They only began to consider this after the Wiehahn Report made it clear that the advance of blacks into skilled jobs was inevitable and—short of a political counterrevolution—irreversible.

White workers, unlike white capital, did not have an interest in black job advance; their interests thus reinforced their prejudices. Once they could no longer stop black advance, however, their interests required the incorporation of blacks into their unions; their interests and prejudices were then in conflict. The gradual shift to the incorporation option suggests that they (like white capital) were not prepared to pay a high price for their prejudices. Even those unions still resisting black advance and unionization were often not clear-cut cases of racism over-ruling self-interest; they were usually the less skilled, whose apparently strong bargaining position could be rapidly eroded. It is therefore not inconceivable that, when they are no longer able to stop black advance, they will perform a similar *volte face*. However, incorporation is not yet far advanced; and white racism has undoubtedly been one of the factors slowing it down. Self-interest may overcome prejudice, but the adjustment takes time; blacks have meanwhile started organizing their own separate unions and the slow adaptation by white workers could have lost them an important opportunity.

The separate development option
The separate development policy offered an alternative to the closer economic integration and incorporation of blacks that most white workers rejected. But, put to the test, this policy was

rejected with remarkable unanimity by all sections of white labour.

The policy was always disliked by the mixed (white and coloured) unions, which comprised the liberal wing of TUCSA. They rejected the underlying ideology of separation, and they were generally in those labour-intensive light industries (clothing, textiles, furniture) which seemed to government planners the most suitable candidates for decentralization. Workers in these industries were consequently faced with the threat of closure of their factories in terms of the Physical Planning Act, or by 'unfair' competition from factories in the border areas or Bantustans. The danger of undercutting was serious: wages in those areas were often a half to a third lower than metropolitan wages.[104] The policy was consequently denounced in the *Garment Worker* and by trade unionists like Anna Scheepers; but these unions had little political influence.

There was also opposition from other unions in TUCSA and by the large bloc of unaffiliated unions. Their opposition was not necessarily ideological. They might not object to separation, or they might describe themselves as 'non-political', but they objected when blacks were allowed to do skilled jobs in border areas or were allowed to do these jobs at lower rates. *The Metalworker*, journal of the AEU, warned in 1970 that separate development would have a 'pronounced effect on the job structure; the decentralized areas provide a means whereby white jobs are being given to blacks. Once such jobs are given away at a lower rate, they will never be regained.'[105]

In 1972, the Typographical Union complained that some of its members had lost their jobs because firms, lured by tax and other concessions, had moved to border areas. Supporting them, TUCSA asked, 'How is the government going to reconcile its insistence that in White areas, Whites must not lose jobs to Blacks, but if a firm moves to another area, this is quite in order?'[106]

The government was more responsive to complaints from these all-white craft unions. In 1971, for example, pressures from the Motor Industry Employees Union led to the extension of job reservation to the border area of Rosslyn, in breach of assurances given to motor manufacturers (see p. 156).

In the pressures they applied on these issues, both the TUCSA liberals and conservatives acted in accordance with their usual principles. The liberals did not object to blacks doing the same jobs, but wanted the rate for the job and unionization. The conservatives, whether they supported the explicit statutory bar (Motor Union) or covert conventional bar (Typographical and AEU) wanted the extension of these policies, via the IC and Wage Acts, to these areas.

SACOL's policies, however, lacked the small-minded virtue of consistency. SACOL leaders paid lip-service to the separate development policy. In 1970, van den Berg of Yster and Staal called for a speed-up of homeland development as the answer to the labour shortage: 'We must be realistic and admit that the country cannot afford to stop industrial growth—hence our plea for an acceleration of industrial development in the homelands, to which Bantu labour-intensive industries should purposefully be moved to bring an end to integration in the White areas.' Later, he urged the government to use the IDC 'to bring about grand scale industrial development' in those areas if private capitalists would not cooperate. 'We have to choose between total integration and total separation and I would like to believe that the Government is sincere in its declared policy of separate development.'[107]

In practice, however, van den Berg's support for the policy was less than wholehearted, as was shown by his insistence that 'border areas are still white areas'[108]—because it was only in border areas that decentralization made any progress at all! The strongest challenge to the policy came from the MWU, which succeeded in maintaining job reservation on mines within the Bantustans, including Bophutatswana, even after it became 'independent' in 1977.[109]

All the trade unions then, whether liberal or conservative, English, Afrikaans or mixed, wanted the extension to the decentralized areas of SA's industrial legislation—whatever modifications they might want in that legislation. This is what one would expect of trade unions, which are always suspicious of regions, industries or groups of workers excluded from their control and liable to undercut them. They therefore opposed the suspension of SA's industrial legislation in these areas. In response to these pressures, the government agreed in 1971 that this legislation would continue to apply to *whites* working in the Bantustans, who would continue to receive the minimum wages and fringe benefits applicable to them in SA. However, this would hardly protect them from undercutting—quite the reverse! Moreover, in 1972, the Nationalists performed one of the political somersaults at which they are so adept, announcing that in future Bantustan governments would be free to make their own labour regulations; thereafter they argued that SA could not interfere in their 'internal' labour practices.[110] In the border areas, the skirmish continued, with the government granting exemptions and waiving industrial legislation wherever it could, and doing its utmost to keep the unions out.

The opposition of white labour hampered implementation of the decentralization policy. In those few cases in which capital was attracted to these areas, as a way round the job and wage colour bars, the white unions were likely—for that very reason—to oppose their going there. SACOL unions which supposedly supported separate development showed (like the AHI) that they themselves were not prepared to pay the price of implementing it. They would only support it when it applied to those sections of capital and labour which did not want it.

In 1984, there were at last signs that the MWU was prepared to negotiate the ending of job reservation in 'independent' Bophutatswana.[111] By then, this supposedly irrational and manipulated union had secured for its members almost a century of monopoly wages, as well as repeatedly demonstrating a capacity to defy both mining capital and the SA government.

8
Changing Costs and Benefits of Apartheid to the White Oligarchy

This chapter will examine: (i) the growing convergence of views among capitalists about apartheid labour policies; (ii) the rising costs of apartheid to the state; (iii) options for the oligarchy; (iv) the relationship between apartheid and economic growth.

Convergence of views among capitalists
By the early 1970s, there was a growing convergence of views among capitalists about the rising costs and inconvenience of apartheid. This was due to (i) the diversification of the interests of many capitalists, especially in mining, into the manufacturing and commercial sectors, whose interests they came to share; (ii) increasing capital-intensity and mechanization in all sectors, resulting in higher capital/labour ratios (with wages a lower proportion of costs) and the need for more skilled labour and larger markets. Further, the severe shortages of unskilled labour, which had been the major cause of the primary sectors' support for apartheid, were solved by demographic changes which (together with mechanization) led to an oversupply of unskilled labour in southern Africa. The segmented market in unskilled labour had become an inconvenience, and the costs of the segmented market in skilled labour had become very high. In both cases capitalists would have done better from the removal of barriers and a shift to a competitive, mobile labour market.

There were, however, variations among capitalists. Apartheid was less necessary for, or more costly to, those with high capital/labour ratios, a high percentage of skilled to unskilled labour, and the need for larger markets. The change was most marked for the primary sectors, which were undergoing a classic transition from a period in which elite interests required keeping down mass

227

welfare to one in which they required its growth. Technological and demographic changes, and the need for markets, were among the reasons for this transition. Another major factor was the concentration of ownership in huge capital-intensive companies like AAC, Barlow Rand, Anglovaal and Rembrandt (see p. 242), all of whom were committed to labour reform.

Growing support for socio-economic reform

These changing interests led to more support for, or reduced opposition to, the reforms progressive capital had long urged. By about 1977, these comprised a more coherent, wide-ranging reform programme. Its main elements were:

(i) a competitive, mobile market in labour—a classic demand of capitalists—including scrapping of the vertical (job and training) bars and erosion of the horizontal bars (restricting geographical movement, location of industry and stabilisation);

(ii) the removal of discrimination in employment—promotion on merit and rate for the job;

(iii) improvements in mass living standards—higher wages, improved education, health services, housing and amenities;

(iv) the extension of workers' rights, including trade unions;

(v) the removal of restrictions on black business and property rights;

(vi) the erosion of social apartheid—opening public amenities to blacks, social mixing.[1]

The reform programme did not cover residential and school segregation or political rights. The opening of private schools to blacks, and opinion polls on residential segregation, suggested that capitalists would be amenable to these reforms; but they were divided and ambivalent about political rights.

Continuing divisions over African political rights

There was strong support from businessmen for the political incorporation of coloureds and Indians; there was also a growing feeling that political concessions to Africans were necessary, but disagreement about the form these should take.

The FCI and Assocom wanted both deracialization and liberalization (see p. 179); so too did traditionally conservative Natal businessmen and farmers, who supported the Lombard and

Buthelezi reports,* which rejected the Bantustan strategy for Natal and proposed as an alternative a common society, with power shared between all races.

The leading business advocate of the liberal view was Oppenheimer, who had long argued that,

> Racial discrimination and free enterprise are basically incompatible and failure to eradicate the one will ultimately result in the destruction of the other . . . . The only economic situation compatible with apartheid is one of stagnation in which the development of the modern sector of the economy is limited to a level at which the majority of the skilled work can be handled by whites . . . . This policy is based on the belief that it is not possible for people of different race and culture to share power within a united country . . . . [The Bantustan policy] is impossible to apply. Not only has the SA government no intention of dividing SA up on an equitable basis but it would be impossible to do so . . . . Our present constitution no longer corresponds with the underlying facts of power in the country and, therefore, if it is not reformed it will become increasingly unstable . . . . The crux of the political debate is . . . are blacks to be recognised and treated as South Africans? Or is the government going to insist that their nationality and allegiance should lie solely with the independent black states . . . ? Plainly the government's policy cannot now be reversed. It is far too late for that. But could it perhaps be accommodated, as the Buthelezi Commission suggests, within a wider South African federal system, in which people of all races would enjoy an over-riding South African nationality, carry South African passports and come to feel a common South African patriotism.[3]

There was a conservative section among capitalists both on the question of political rights for Africans and on liberalization. Afrikaans capitalists—like all sections of Afrikaans society—had strong links with the NP and had received favourable treatment from the Nationalist government (see Chapter 9). They came to support the socio-economic reforms, but had reservations about African unions. Opinion polls and observation suggest that they also adhered to the NP doctrine that Africans were foreigners and should exercise their political rights via the separate development

*The Buthelezi Commission proposals were supported by representatives of the FCI and Assocom and their Natal Chambers, as well as Natal sugar farmers. The Lombard Report was commissioned by the Natal sugar industry (see p. 109).[2]

institutions. However, the distinction between English and Afrikaans capital was becoming less clearcut, with the emergence of *verligte* Afrikaners (see Addendum on p. 254).

Non-racial factors affecting political views

Among the factors reconciling capitalists to various SA governments, despite disputes over labour policy, were non-racial aspects of policy such as the maintenance of an efficient infrastructure of transport, power and telecommunications; the management of the currency; the promotion of local production and its protection from competition; and the maintenance of orderly conditions in which the economy could function and personal security be ensured.

These conditions were not intrinsically related to the race of a government, although racist propaganda, particularly during the 1950s and 1960s, suggested that they were. That belief was reinforced by disorder and economic collapse in the Congo and Uganda, and by the expulsion, or at least flight, of whites from Algeria, Mozambique and Angola. It was weakened by economic prosperity and security for whites in the Ivory Coast, Botswana and Kenya, and possibly even by the success of 'non-white' economies such as Taiwan and Japan. The fear that a black government could result in the expropriation of their business, and/or a serious deterioration in economic management, and/or a threat to their personal security, has greatly influenced the political views of businessmen (and of all whites).

The question of the amendment of SA's highly unequal distribution of income and owernship of assets is more problematical. Racial and economic factors were here inextricably linked. Any government responsive to pressures from the majority of the population would act to reduce these extreme inequalities (even more so if it tried to compensate for past discrimination); and many capitalists also accept that there must be some redistribution from high white incomes and profits (see p. 162). Thus far, concern with ownership has been secondary and limited to the creation of new opportunities in an expanding economy. Significantly, the handful of companies that own over three-quarters of the shares listed on the Johannesburg stock exchange (see p. 242) have been among the leading proponents of reform.

So far, the divisions among capitalists on political change, and the uncertainties and risks attached to it, have reduced their willingness to take initiatives in this field. However, as deracialization proceeds and black skilled and middle classes emerge (and the guerrilla challenge intensifies) they will be forced to confront this issue. Their calculations will be affected not only by their declining economic and social need for apartheid, but by increasing doubts as to whether it is an effective guarantor of political stability and security. Their perception of the alternatives will of course be crucial.

The mounting political costs of apartheid

The rising political costs of apartheid were to be seen in the radicalization of young blacks, who were turning to Marxism and particularly black consciousness, and in the alienation of the black middle class and elite, whom capitalists regarded as their potential allies. Rupert warned that unless private enterprise delivered the goods, blacks would seek 'another system'. The strategy of countering revolution by reforms and concessions was also pursued by the Urban Foundation, which argued that home ownership, better amenities and business opportunities for blacks would help 'to promote free enterprise values'.[4]

The strategy pursued by capital in response to black unrest therefore went beyond a reformist welfare programme; even when it did not explicitly embrace political reform, it envisaged a restructuring of society that involved a shift from the hierarchical racial structure to a class structure, which would be difficult to reconcile with separate political rights. The logic of the strategy required that everyone be incorporated into the same system— whether it was democratic or authoritarian.

Another factor forcing capitalists to go beyond reformism towards the logic of political incorporation was international hostility to apartheid. This was becoming a threat to security, as could be seen from the financing and training of guerrillas abroad, the arming and political radicalization of neighbouring states and the entry of the USSR into the region. This, in turn, led to SA's soaring police and defence budgets, loss of life on the border, and strained relations with its western allies.

Growing international hostility to apartheid also posed a threat to the external economic interests of capitalists, especially in Africa, where they hoped to play a leading role. Despite breaches in the OAU's trade boycott, it constituted an obstacle in the expanding African market, in which SA exporters and investors would otherwise have had natural advantages. Boycotts also created difficulties elsewhere (for example, those of SA fruit and wine in the West) and they could put SA businessmen at a disadvantage in fiercely competitive markets. Continual attempts were made to extend the trade boycott to cover investment and the supply of technology to SA. This met with some successes, notably the 1973 OPEC oil boycott, the 1977 UN Security Council embargo on the supply of arms and military technology to SA, and the restrictions imposed by the US Congress on credit facilities and loans to SA in 1978.

Businessmen took threats of boycotts and isolation seriously. Oppenheimer warned that, 'these things could move very quickly . . . [and cause] continual trouble and severe difficulties in financing companies and selling goods.'[5] After the Angolan debacle, he pointed out that Western and African states which 'secretly welcome our cooperation and help, are publicly ashamed to be seen in our company,' and that SA could only break out of this situation by internal reforms which ended race discrimination.

Leading Afrikaans businessmen shared his alarm if not, initially, his conclusion. Shortly before the Sharpeville crisis, dismay at the government's handling of SA's international relations led English and Afrikaans capital (despite the hostility that then existed between them) jointly to establish the SA Foundation to present a more 'positive' image of SA abroad. Ironically, its international concerns soon led it to act as a conduit for foreign pressures. By the late 1960s, the prominent businessmen who were its presidents (Rupert, Marais, Hersov) had joined the ranks of those calling for changes which would 'help our friends in the West to help us'.[6]

Businessmen who were most concerned about mounting external pressures were:

(i) the wide range of producers in all sectors of the economy who were dependent upon export markets;

(ii) SA companies with investments abroad, such as AAC, Barlow Rand, Gencor and Rembrandt. Investments in Africa were particularly sensitive; in 1974, the Zambian Mineworkers Union called on its government to terminate all AAC's holdings without compensation, unless the company helped in the liberation of SA. Zach de Beer, AAC's chairman in Lusaka, pointed to the company's role in the campaign to improve working conditions in SA and the rebuke its policies had earned from the SA government;[7]

(iii) multinational companies with subsidiaries in SA, such as Barclays, General Motors, Ford and RTZ. Barclays Bank, for example, was the object of a sustained international campaign and had been subjected to punitive action by the Nigerian government;

(iv) SA companies which needed foreign capital and technology, particularly important for those in oil, motors, pharmaceuticals, computers and electronics.

Another major concern of businessmen during the early to mid seventies was the shortage of investment capital, which they rated second only to labour problems as a constraint on growth. Leading businessmen argued that SA 'can generate only a small portion of the immense capital sums it needs; the balance must be attracted from overseas,' and that 'the basic reasons for the concern felt by foreign investors about SA are not financial or economic but political and they can only be removed by action in the political field . . . . SA [needs] to give proof of the ability and the will to eliminate the grievances and resentments which lie behind the rioting and the unrest in the black areas of our major cities.'[8]

Businessmen had high hopes that the reforms of the early 1970s, and Vorster's detente policy in Africa, would stabilize the political situation, open the way to economic opportunities in Africa and ease the international pressures on SA. The slowdown in reform in the mid-1970s and the collapse of detente, following the Angolan debacle in 1975/6, set back these hopes and led to the flight of foreign capital. After the Soweto riots, the situation deteriorated further and it was acknowledged by the Finance Minister, Owen Horwood, that foreign investment had been scared off.[9] Consequently, SA had to resort to bank loans at high rates of interest.

These setbacks contributed to business pressures for more far-reaching reforms, including political measures, and to their more active role in lobbying for them (see Chapter 9). They supported Botha's revival of the reform programme and pursuit of closer relations with neighbouring black states, but the Urban Foundation expressed disappointment at the slow, limited reforms, especially on black housing and education, and Oppenheimer warned that the Constellation would not succeed if it were conceived 'as a fortress or laager in a hostile world': the precondition for its success was the removal of discrimination within SA.[10]

Little is known about the impact on the interests of capital of the large armaments industry, which developed from the 1960s, in response to the threats of sanctions and armed struggle. By the early 1980s, SA was a very significant armaments producer.[11] Ownership of much of this was in the state sector—Armscor, Atlas Aircraft Corporation, the Atomic Energy Board and UCOR (Uranium Enrichment Corporation)—but there was subcontracting to the private sector. It may be that the risks of conflict are so great that the emergence of this military-industrial complex, much of it in the state sector, will not undermine the desire of private capitalists for political concessions to reduce conflict.

Further conflict and polarization could lead to more support from some capitalists for an authoritarian path of reform, or for a *kragdadige* (strong arm) policy towards neighbouring states which provided moral, and allegedly also material, support for guerrillas. But thus far capitalists have responded warily to the beating of the patriotic drum. They complained that the military call-up aggravated the skill shortage,* and the FCI expressed 'concern at the trend towards polarization and confrontation in southern Africa . . . it is in SA's interest that it be surrounded by prosperous and politically stable neighbours.'[12] Capital wanted trade and investment, not war, in southern Africa. Business organizations also warned their members against carrying the defence force logo on products supplied to the army, on the grounds that this would be counter-productive with blacks and in the export market. Multinationals in particular were nervous about involvement in defence activities: some objected to registration under the 1980 National Key Points Act, requiring security precautions at factories and offices.[13] Moreover, as seen above, most capitalists supported the extension of political rights and strengthening of democratic institutions and procedures, such as the independence of the

---

*By 1982, there was two years' compulsory military service for all male white school-leavers, followed by two months' annual training for the next twelve years.

Courts and freedom of the Press, which they saw as important for preserving their rights and ensuring their access to information both now and in the non-racial society they believed would eventually emerge.

The rising costs of apartheid to the state

The rising costs of apartheid had an impact on the government both in its capacity as employer in the state sector, and as overseer/manager of the SA economy.

Rising costs of the job bar in the state sector

The state sector was the largest employer in SA, accounting in 1980 for 34 per cent of economically-active whites (and even more Afrikaners), 16 per cent of coloureds, 12 per cent of Indians, and 14 per cent of Africans (including employment in state corporations like Iscor).[14] Although the state sector and public corporations were less constrained by considerations of profit than the private sector, they could not ignore costs, which were scrutinized by parliament and by taxpayers. With wide pay differentials, even the state sector was not immune from pressures to erode the job bar by substituting black for white labour.*

The acute skill shortage from the mid-1960s hit the state sector hard, as it had less flexibility to increase wages than the private sector. It also exposed senior officials to the reality of the skill shortage, which many officials and politicians at first denied. In 1969 a parliamentary select committee report revealed that the financial institutes division of the Treasury was 'starting to collapse because there were simply no people to do the work.' In 1970, the Johannesburg City Council's bus service for whites

---

*These pressures were evident in the action of SAR, in 1922, in replacing expensive white with cheaper black labour, which led to strikes by white workers. In 1937, similar action was taken by Iscor, despite an appeal to the Supreme Court by the white unions. The government said it accepted that the state sector had a special responsibility to white workers, but that profit considerations could not be ignored.[15]

Even the 1948 Nationalist government, in order to lower the cost of its township slum-clearance and house-building programme, used the 1951 Native Building Workers Act to train and employ skilled blacks, thereby getting round the shortage of artisans and slashing costs: black artisans were paid 2 shillings per hour compared with the white rate of 7 shillings.[16]

practically ground to a halt, when the government upheld the opposition of the Municipal Transport Workers Union to the use of coloured crews: the service was short of 30 per cent of drivers and conductors. In 1974, it was revealed that the Post Office and Railways were each short of almost 30 per cent of their skilled labour requirements, which 'could cripple vital services'. In the Post Office there was a shortage of 28 per cent of artisans and 20 per cent of telephone electricians; it was moreover losing 1,000 skilled men a year to the private sector, and the expansion of the electronics industry and imminent introduction of television would worsen the situation. The Post Office urged the private sector to stop complaining about the inefficiency of these vital services while they 'poached our skilled technicians'.[17]

As in the private sector, these shortages led to pressures from managers of the railways and Post Office for relaxation of the job bar. State sector bosses like J. G. Loubser and J. Venter of SAR, Louis Rive of the Post Office, du Toit Viljoen of Bantu Investment Corporation, and Tom Muller of Iscor added their voices to calls for labour reform, including abolition of the job bar and, later, promotion on merit. In 1971 SAR took members of the white unions to Laurenço Marques to show them how whites and blacks worked alongside on the railways.[18]

Erosion of the bar brought similar benefits—the easing of shortages and lowering of labour costs. For example, in 1971 the railways negotiated an agreement whereby 1,000 blacks, termed 'marshallers' could be employed instead of white 'shunters'. The blacks were paid R1,200 annually compared with R2,400 for whites. By 1971, 15,355 white jobs on the railways had been taken over by blacks, with similar savings and easing of labour short-ages.[19]

The defence force was also hit by labour shortages. From the early 1970s, the navy began to recruit coloureds. In 1974, in a 'new and revolutionary' step, the defence force placed adverts for African recruits in *The World* newspaper and the air force opened its ranks to blacks.[20] The public sector could no more avoid *verswarting* due to growing dependence on blacks than could private industry.

As in the private sector, the erosion of the job bar led to pressures to train and stabilize blacks. SAR were pace-setters, establishing their own large training centres and, in 1978, providing loans for family housing. The percentage of migrants was then one-third of their African workforce—lower than might be expected in view of state policy; but SAR wanted more of them stabilized.[21]

A curious example of stabilization in the state sector was provided by BAD, arch-exponent of the migrant labour policy. In 1978, a senior official, who made clear his opposition to the forthcoming Riekert concessions, confirmed in an interview that many of BAD's own African officials were stabilized. He insisted that this was 'different, because their work as civil servants often requires them to be transferred to other areas; this is not their fault, so they should be allowed to take their families with them.' He also pointed out that some of these men were well-educated, 'and you could not dream of housing a man with a university degree in a compound.'[22] So, not only did these workers have their families with them, but they could transfer their family rights to other areas even before the 1979 Riekert concessions.*

The national dimensions of the skill shortage

The costs of the job bar came home to the government (cabinet ministers and officials) in its role as overseer of the whole SA economy, with responsibility for the growth rate, inflation and the balance of payments. It was only at this national level that the true dimensions of the skill shortage could be assessed, because each firm or sector could ease its own skill shortage by raising wages to attract workers from other firms or sectors. It was only when total skill requirements and availability were examined that it became evident that the economy had outrun its traditional source of skilled labour, and that the problem would become worse with continued growth, especially as this was taking place along capital-intensive lines.

In economic jargon, the supply of (white) skilled labour was elastic (responsive to wage increases) in each sector, but in the economy as a whole the supply was inelastic, because raising wages could not increase it (except in so far as higher wages attracted

---

*I was not able to investigate the extent to which other African civil servants—teachers, policemen, nurses—exercised this exceptional right. If it was widespread, it is a telling and ironic example of the pressure to stabilize skilled workers.

immigrants to SA). It was this dimension that convinced senior politicians and officials that the job bar had to be abandoned if growth was to continue, especially as extrapolations of skill needs showed that the shortage was bound to worsen.*

These extrapolations were borne out by subsequent developments. Despite the relaxation of the bar and extension of training, there were continuing shortages even during the 1974–8 recession, and these grew worse during the rapid growth from 1978–82. This was confirmed by the National Manpower Commission and by the 1981 de Lange Report, which pointed out that for a growth rate of 4.5 per cent it was necessary to train 23,000 skilled workers and 9,500 technicians annually, but only 10,000 skilled and 2,000 technicians were then being produced.[24] The rapid expansion of the SA economy had caused it to outgrow its traditional sources of skilled labour; many years of training were required to make up the backlogs.

Manufacturing, protection and the balance of payments

The skill shortage was the most direct effect of apartheid labour policies, but there were other problems which became more evident as the bar rose. The most important were due to the horizontal bars (restrictions on mobility, stabilization, siting of industries), the wage bars and poor living conditions, and the lack

---

*For example, Wyndham calculated that, by 1980, there would be 10.4 million economically-active in SA, of whom 3.7m had to be skilled, including 0.7m with higher education to equip them for professional, technical and managerial jobs. However, in 1980, there would only be 1.7m economically-active whites. Even if they were all trained for skilled work, there would still be a shortage of 2m skilled workers. This shortage could not be filled by coloureds and Indians alone, as their total economically-active would only amount to 1.2m workers. If economic growth was to continue, at least 0.8m Africans would have to do skilled jobs. In practice the number would be far greater, as it was obviously impossible that all white, coloured and Indian workers could do skilled work. The calculation regarding the 0.67 top-level jobs produced a similar result. By 1980 there might be 350,000 whites with higher education (which would constitute *twice* the proportion of the population with higher education in the UK). This left 320,000 jobs to be filled by blacks with higher education. To attain this, the number of blacks in institutes of higher education had to increase from the 1974 figure of 10,000 to 50,000 per annum. If this target was not attained, the skill shortage would worsen and would limit growth.[23]

of adequate communications with the increasingly important African workforce. Economists claimed that this whole range of manpower problems had led to rising costs, and to uncertainty and loss of confidence among businessmen, particularly in manufacturing, and that they contributed to the decline in the profitability of manufacturing and the fall in new investment from the late 1960s.

From 1946 to 1970 the average annual growth rate in SA manufacturing was 7 per cent; but from 1969 it declined to 2.6 per cent, and by 1977 was negative.[25] The traditional cure for the problems of manufacturing was protection, which was specifically linked to the high cost of apartheid labour policies. The 1934 Customs Tariff Commission claimed that all protected industries in SA were paying higher wages than they could afford and argued that, 'The greatest competitive drawback of SA industry is the high cost of white labour, and the protection which exists is, to a large extent, a protection of the wage rates payable to whites in industry.' Likewise, the 1943 Agricultural and Industrial Requirements Commission recognised that, 'It is therefore indubitable that industrial protection is largely a protection of skilled wages at a level which had its origins in the early part of this century when the Union had to rely on imported artisans.'[26]

It was logical, therefore, that the 1924 Nationalist–Labour Pact government, proponent of the civilized labour policy, introduced systematic protection as a way of reconciling the development of manufacturing with the retention of apartheid and that it linked the granting of protection to the adoption of 'satisfactory labour policies' (see p. 19).

During World War Two there was a tremendous expansion of manufacturing behind the natural protective barriers of the war. But after the war, SA manufacturers faced intense international competition, both in their home market and in adjacent African territories, which had become an important outlet for their exports. After the Federation of Rhodesia and Nyasaland was formed in 1953, they were also faced by a tariff wall which favoured Rhodesian industry. On the recommendation of the Viljoen Commission, protection was increased in 1959 and, after Sharpeville, import controls were introduced. According to Lachmann, 'There can be no doubt that the rapid transformation of the South African economy during the 1960s . . . was stimulated by . . . substantial protection to the domestic manufacturing industry,' both by the exclusion of many foreign goods and by preferences for raw materials and capital goods.[27] Policies of domestic procurement, especially in strategic products such as armaments, energy and transport, also contributed to local expansion.

Hothouse development behind protective barriers was for some years effective in maintaining profitability, new investment and growth in manufacturing. But it *raised the cost structure of the whole economy*, as expensive SA goods had to be used in preference to cheaper imports. As the economy developed and diversified, the costs of protection became clearer, not just to consumers, but also to businessmen, because their inputs were also protected and therefore costly; for example, clothing manufacturers had to use expensive SA textiles.

The 1960s boom transformed manufacturing into the leading growth sector, accounting for 24 per cent of GDP in 1970. Its problems thus had a marked impact on the overall growth rate and especially on employment. The protection it enjoyed also became very expensive, as the deteriorating balance of payments showed. These problems led to the devaluation of the rand in 1971, the tightening of import controls, and the appointment of the Reynders Commission to enquire urgently into the problems of exports, particularly the poor performance of manufacturing.

The 1972 Reynders Report pointed out that from 1946–71, SA had almost continuous deficits on the current account of the balance of payments (imports of merchandise and services exceeded total export receipts plus net gold output by over R3,700m). Overall equilibrium was maintained by large capital inflows: during 1946–71 these equalled R3,632m (despite a net loss of R579m from 1959–64).[28] The current account deficit during this period averaged R140m annually, but was rising sharply, equalling R1,005m in 1971. The position was therefore deteriorating and by 1968 the balance of payments had become a serious constraint on growth.

According to Reynders, the basic reason for this was 'the increasingly poor competitive performance of the manufacturing sector in foreign markets'. Manufacturing exports were small: about 10 per cent of the gross value of manufacturing production and a quarter of total exports in 1970. Furthermore, the import requirements of manufacturing, particularly for capital goods, were very high. As is well-known, a protectionist, import-displacing strategy tends to worsen the balance of payments because of its heavy import requirements.[29] The fact that manufacturing had become larger than the net positive earners of foreign exchange, mining and agriculture, meant that their earnings were no longer sufficient to balance its heavy debts. Moreover, SA had a high proportion of foreign trade to GDP—53 per cent.* The poor performance of manufacturing exports thus limited growth both directly and via the balance of payments.

The Reynders Commission took a serious view of the long-term implications, in view of uncertainty surrounding the gold price and the danger of relying on inflows of foreign capital. It therefore called for an expansion of manufacturing exports to finance the balance of payments and to act, together with expansion of the internal market, as an engine to push forward the lagging growth rate. The commission accepted the view of businessmen that the organisation of the labour market lowered productivity and raised the cost structure and concluded that major 'structural changes' were required, especially in the training, motivation and access to jobs of black workers. Reynders seemed to have in mind changes affecting vertical rather than horizontal mobility; but the Commission did not regard decentralization as a solution, emphasizing the policy's high costs and damaging effects on business confidence and growth.[30]

It was at this stage that the crucial decisions were taken to relax the job and training bars—from which so much else flowed. The subsequent sharp rise in the gold price did not negate the Reynders findings, as the relief to the balance of payments was temporary: in 1975, when the gold price declined again, and the oil price rose, the current account deficit equalled R1,782m. After the Angolan debacle and the Soweto riots the situation was worsened by the flight of foreign capital. Further devaluation and deflationary policies were adopted to cope with these problems and SA experienced its worst recession since the early 1930s. The spectacular rise in the gold price from 1978 resulted in huge surpluses in 1979 and 1980, but these were converted into a deficit of almost R3bn in

---

*Compared with less than 20 per cent for the USA and Japan; 34 per cent for France; 49 per cent for the UK.

1981, when the price fell again. These volatile trends confirmed Reynders's warning about the unreliability of the gold price and the need for manufacturing to become more efficient and competitive, both to help the balance of payments and to allow growth.

Labour was not, of course, the only element in rising costs and inflation (which rose from 2.5 per cent annually in 1959/69 to 13.9 in 1974/75). Much of the rapid increase in inflation was imported; but this did not alter the fact that there were severe structural imbalances, which contributed to uncompetitiveness and inefficiency. The aggravation of internal structural problems by imported inflation increased the pressures from businessmen and public opinion to free the economy from 'self-inflicted wounds' such as job reservation, lack of training and education, constraints on the availability of labour, and skewed income distribution.

Some contradictory consequences of protection
Protection—which apartheid made necessary—thus generated contradictions which contributed to the undermining of apartheid. First, 'tariff is the mother of trusts'; by restricting competition, it encourages the emergence of large, monopolistic firms. Observers had long remarked on the tendency towards monopoly in the SA economy.[31] It was estimated in 1983 that seven companies controlled 80 per cent of the value of the R90bn shares listed on the Johannesburg stock exchange.* These large firms, in turn, have: a tendency to capital-intensity, which requires skilled labour; the need for institutionalized means of communication when faced with labour unrest (see p. 172); the need for larger markets to give them longer production runs. All these tendencies generated pressures for the erosion of apartheid.

Secondly, protection made the domestic market easier and more attractive. Hence, when searching for larger markets, manufacturers looked first to the domestic market rather than to exports, as do countries with export-led growth strategies like

---

*AAC (and its subsidiaries and affiliates) accounted for no less than 56 per cent of total shares; Barlow Rand for 7.4 per cent; Anglovaal 3.2 per cent; Rembrandt 2.1; Sanlam 9.4; Liberty Life 1.1; Old Mutual 0.8 (the latter three are life assurance companies). Their share of total national wealth (i.e. including assets not listed on the stock exchange) is of course much less—estimated at 16 per cent for the 11 biggest conglomerates in 1984.[32]

Taiwan and Hong Kong. The consequent need to raise mass consumption standards was another important pressure against apartheid. The Reynders Commission accepted the argument that SA's skewed income distribution constrained the growth of the internal market and that rising black incomes would benefit many manufacturers.[33]

Apartheid complicates international economic relations

However, the SA market was small by world standards and exports were essential in products such as chemicals to justify putting in the equipment used by the world's most efficient producers. Reynders acknowledged that growing international hostility to apartheid had adverse effects on SA's exports, especially in Africa. Apartheid thus added to SA's difficulty in expanding exports in three ways: its manpower policies made SA manufacturing costly and uncompetitive; growing international hostility endangered its export markets; and protection (which apartheid made necessary) made the domestic market easier and more attractive.

International hostility was not only damaging to trade, but also to SA's ability to attract foreign capital and technology.* This contributed to the fall in the growth rate from the late 1960s. The demand for capital was increased by the trend towards capital-intensity in all sectors and by a slower rate of domestic saving, partly due to redistribution towards blacks, whose marginal propensity to save was less than that of wealthier whites. The scarcity of capital was aggravated by the security and administrative requirements of apartheid, which meant that a high percentage of investment was absorbed by the state sector: its share of gross fixed investment rose from 35 per cent in 1950 to 53 per cent in 1979.[34]

Mechanization and unemployment

By making urban black labour scarce, as well as complicated and expensive to employ, apartheid encouraged mechanization. This was intensified by capital subsidies (such as tax allowances on investment) and by the exemption of capital goods (plant and

---

*Since World War Two about 10 per cent of gross fixed investment was financed by net capital inflows.[35]

machinery) from protective tariffs and controls: while consumer goods were protected, the effective rate of protection on capital goods was often negative.[36]

This distortion of relative factor prices (making capital artificially cheap and labour dear) led to a costly and inefficient development path. It encouraged capital-intensity, thus increasing the demand for scarce resources of capital and skill, while discouraging the use of what by the 1960s had become a surplus of unskilled labour, so contributing to growing unemployment. The problem of an unduly capital-intensive path of development leading to premature mechanization (i.e. the installation of labour-replacing machinery before the labour surplus has been mopped up) is world-wide; but apartheid intensified this tendency.

As argued above, mechanization had positive effects on the employed, raising their skill levels and wages and facilitating stabilization. But its negative effects were particularly severe in SA, where unemployed blacks were faced with the danger of banishment to the Bantustans and the loss of their SA citizenship. These political complications exacerbated the potentially explosive effects of unemployment.

Mechanization was not the only cause of growing unemployment. Other factors were the black population explosion (its average annual increase was 3.3 per cent during the 1960s); the declining capacity of the reserves to support their populations; and the slowdown in growth—to which apartheid contributed. The inter-relatedness and urgency of this cluster of problems was recognised by the Prime Minister's economic advisor, Brand, who argued that unless the unemployment rate could be brought down, 'mass unemployment', concentrated in the 16–25 age group, would eventually 'blow SA society apart'. To avoid this, he advocated 'an all-out growth strategy'. However, as he recognized, the skill and capital bottlenecks were a constraint on growth, and the distortion of relative factor prices discouraged growth along labour-intensive lines.[37] Apartheid therefore complicated the task of narrowing inequalities, particularly between urban and rural areas, and of coping with the growing unemployment problem.

Rising costs of decentralization
The decentralization policy failed to provide a way of avoiding these rising costs; rather it aggravated them. Its implementation

was limited, expensive,* and tended to be along capital-intensive lines (see p. 156). These high costs led the Reynders Commission to conclude that, 'This policy as well as the infrastructure required for its implementation will require vast sums of capital investment . . . and of imports, while making . . . no immediate contribution to exports.'[39]

The decentralization policy had, furthermore, an adverse impact on growth in the metropolitan areas, where it also aggravated capital-intensity by restricting the availability of African labour. The Reynders Commission accepted that Section 3 of the Physical Planning Act had contributed to the slowdown in growth from 1968. The Riekert Commission was more damning, concluding that Section 3 'had made no noteworthy contribution to decentralization' and was 'conducive to mechanization and automation and consequently hampered the creation of new job opportunities for the rapidly growing black population, while at the same time it places a burden on the country's balance of payments owing to the high imported content of the capital goods required for mechanization.' The Commission warned that if Section 3 was strictly applied, it would do 'incalculable harm to the country'.[40]

Growing official concern with black unemployment was in conflict with the policy of encouraging mechanization in order to reduce black numbers in white areas. This contradiction illustrates more clearly than any other the limitations of reform within the apartheid framework. The SA development path has been one of harsh extraction of surplus from the black majority, but it carried within it the seeds of long-term improvement in mass living standards because of the massive installation of extra capacity. The surplus was not frittered away on showpieces and luxuries, or funnelled into Swiss bank accounts—though there was some of this—but went overwhelmingly into productive investment. This development path is thus closer to that of industrializing countries in nineteenth-century Europe and in twentieth-century Japan, USSR and China, than to the pattern in many contemporary Latin-American and African countries, characterized by the

---

*In 1983, it was estimated to cost four to five times more to create jobs in the decentralized zones (including provision of infrastructure and services) than in the metropolitan areas.[38]

emergence of small modern enclaves and the massive transfer of surplus abroad.

Tendencies towards more broadly-based national development in SA could be seen in the redistribution of income and the extension of education, training and housing resources towards blacks. But this process could be aborted by an over-capital-intensive path of development which failed to produce jobs on the required scale. This will, in any case, be difficult because of rapid population growth and the capital-intensity inherent in much modern technology. But apartheid aggravated this problem and imposed severe constraints on the socio-economic transformation which planners like Brand recognised as essential for broader national development.

Rising political costs of apartheid to the state

The rising costs and risks posed by growing hostility to apartheid were emphasized by SA's defence chiefs, who repeatedly emphasised that the struggle against the 'total onslaught' being waged against SA could not be won by military means alone, but was 'eighty per cent political'. In 1973, Admiral Biermann, Chief of the Defence Force, warned that 'one of the aims of the communists is to disrupt cooperation between various population groups . . . . We must seize every opportunity to improve relations with our non-white countrymen.' In 1976, Major General Neil Webster said that 'failure to accommodate the rising hopes and expectations of black citizens [sic] would lead to . . . despair and frustration, the most fertile generator of the desire for political power and reform through revolution.' In 1981, General Constand Viljoen, Chief of the Defence Force, urged that SA should use its economic and military strength

> to find viable solutions to problems which could be exploited by communists and terrorist organizations. A basic principle in the revolutionary struggle was to remove the sting of the revolution by making early changes . . . from a position of strength . . . . The effort by government to accommodate the fair aspirations of all in SA was, from a security point of view, among the highest priorities.[41]

This strategy to counter revolution added to the pressures for deracialization—the erosion of apartheid—though not necessarily for liberalization.

The security threat also had high economic costs. By 1983 the defence bill reached R3bn, 14 per cent of the budget and about 4 per cent of GNP, and defence made heavy demands on scarce white manpower. The search for self-sufficiency to counter economic sanctions was also high, though less quantifiable. It resulted in the development of high-cost and heavily protected strategic sectors such as oil-from-coal, armaments, stainless steel, synthetic rubber, plastics and chemicals. Brand warned that:

> Any drive towards self-sufficiency tends to raise costs, and to harm the competitiveness of our export industries . . . . The mere threat [of sanctions] . . . has consequences; import replacement programmes get pushed ahead prematurely and at the cost of the export sectors. The result is that SA's ability to bring about the kind of constructive internal changes . . . and to contribute to the development of other countries in the sub-continent . . . would be seriously impaired.[42]

There is no clearer indication of the contradictions of apartheid than the fact that many of the problems which apartheid caused or aggravated (protection in manufacturing; high black unemployment; the expensive decentralization programme; the growing costs of defence and of strategic import-replacement) led in turn to the need for a fast growth rate. But fast growth was hampered by the skill and capital bottlenecks, and the obstacles to international trade, which apartheid itself caused.

Pressures for the retention of apartheid

Pressures for eroding apartheid were much weaker, or even absent, in labour-intensive sectors such as gold mining and parts of agriculture, except in so far as apartheid threatened their international interests. Also, the interest of white workers in apartheid had declined to a much lesser extent. Resistance was strongest among the less-skilled and in the bureaucracy, whose jobs and power often rested directly on the continuation of this costly system.[43] State sector employees, moreover, feared they could be replaced as a result of reverse discrimination by a non-white (or even non-Afrikaans) government. Socially, apartheid was still useful for many working and lower-middle-class whites, restricting entry to schools, residential areas and amenities. Politically, they were aware of the rising costs of apartheid, but fearful of the alternatives.

Options for the oligarchy

Fast growth in manufacturing (and in other capital-intensive sectors) generated pressures for the erosion of apartheid. But the oligarchy did not have to pursue this development path; it had other options, notably: (i) a rate of growth that was slower and more dependent on the labour-intensive primary sectors; or (ii) the diversion of manufacturing to the decentralized areas.

The option of slower growth geared to the availability of skilled white manpower was advocated by some white unions and by the HNP (see p. 198). This would presumably be planned to discourage capital-intensity in all sectors, constraining the growth of manufacturing and leading to more reliance on the primary sectors. It would have reduced the pressures to raise the job bar, allow permanent black urbanization and trade unions. Politically, it would not have stimulated the rising expectations (and disappointments) which contributed to the Soweto unrest. It would of course have generated another set of problems; but it was a possible and logical path of development for those whose first priority was the maintenance of apartheid.

The argument here has *not* been that 'separate development' was impossible, but that it was a costly and difficult, not a cheap, option. While expenditure was quite large—a total of R850m on decentralization from 1967–1977, plus millions more on Bantustan development—it was not on the scale required to halt, let alone reverse, the urban influx by the provision of alternative economic opportunities. The provision of additional land for the Bantustans was derisory. Although the Nationalists argued that the policy was essential for white security, they did not therefore give it the priority accorded to defence. Expenditure was markedly increased by Botha, but, paradoxically, he also made more concessions in the 'white' areas, which made it more difficult for the decentralized areas to compete.

Political factors also impeded decentralization. First, the ethnic basis of the policy required that each Bantustan must have its own growth point. Second, the subsidies, grants and concessions contained in the policy made it advantageous for areas to be declared 'growth points' and MPs pressed the government to extend this favoured treatment to their constituencies. These were the reasons for the extraordinary proliferation of growth points throughout SA to include areas such as George, Heilbron,

Cradock and de Aar, some of which were 'in the heartlands of the Cape and the Free State'—as the Minister of Planning proudly declared in parliament when he listed the 14 growth points and 44 other centres which had received assistance to promote industrial development![44]

The relatively small size of the SA economy, the high costs of new infrastructure, and economies of scale would, by economic criteria, have suggested perhaps a couple of major decentralization zones. The proliferation of growth points weakened the coherence and thrust of a policy which, as world-wide experience shows, is invariably difficult and expensive to implement; it may even have been counter-productive, reducing the possibility of a more limited decentralization and thereby resulting in the same, or even a higher, level of what its advocates termed 'over-concentration' in the metropolitan centres.

The oligarchy would not pay the high costs involved in either the separate development or the 'slow growth' options. Calls for a *faster* growth rate came from a wide range of businessmen—Waddell of AAC, Marais of Trust Bank and Len Abrahamse of Nedbank.[45] Afrikaners were prominent among them; being newly-established they needed expanding opportunities, and complained they were badly hit by the mid-1970s recession and wave of bankruptcies. The government, too, needed fast growth to finance its ambitious plans to expand SA's infrastructure, such as the huge rail/harbour developments at Richards Bay and Saldanha Bay, the oil-from-coal projects to increase self-sufficiency in oil, the nuclear enrichment programme, and the introduction of TV. It also needed fast growth to finance the defence budget and the reform programme (expenditure on black housing and education).

By the late 1960s growth had become incompatible with the maintenance of apartheid labour policies: the oligarchy was then forced to choose between limiting growth or eroding apartheid. The government tried to avoid this choice and evolved an elaborate blueprint for combining growth with apartheid. If they had succeeded, it would have confirmed the thesis that the two are compatible; but this effort failed. After the 1970 election, the Vorster/Botha governments, amidst considerable dissension in their own ranks, abandoned important aspects of their labour policies in order to sustain growth.

This is not therefore a determinist analysis: the white oligarchy had options; but these options had consequences. In particular, fast growth in manufacturing (and capital-intensive growth in other sectors) generated pressures for the erosion of apartheid, whether or not this was intended.

The 'taste for discrimination'

A striking feature of the white oligarchy's behaviour was its reluctance to pay for what Becker termed its 'taste for discrimination'. As Becker argued, discrimination is not an 'all or nothing' process, but is affected by both the degree of prejudice and the costs. People may be willing to pay something for their discriminatory preferences, but this will be influenced by the price and by their capacity to pay.[46]

Those who pressed for discriminatory policies in SA (white workers and farmers) invariably managed to shift the costs to others (black labour, mining capital). Those for whom these policies were costly (mining, manufacturing and commercial capital), opposed them, whether or not they were racists. The reason was that the costs, particularly of the job bar, were very high. Faced with paying the same wage to whites and blacks, white capital would probably have chosen white workers; but faced with a wide differential, they repeatedly attempted to substitute blacks for whites, or as white workers saw it, to 'put their selfish economic interest before the preservation of the white race'. The fact that, initially, most capitalists were English and most white workers Afrikaans, may have reinforced the reluctance to pay extra for the satisfaction of employing whites. However, white farmers, the majority of whom were Afrikaners, showed as little readiness to pay extra for a white skin as other capitalists; the only difference was their success in avoiding the job bar.

The costs of the job bar were heaviest in the mining sector, where the differential was widest, white wages a high percentage of total costs and the price of the product fixed—unlike in manufacturing and commerce, where the cost could be passed on to consumers. It was therefore logical that mining capital (though less 'liberal' than urban capital) precipitated the confrontation over the job bar.

Clearly, the 'taste for discrimination' of white capitalists was insufficient to ensure white workers of job preference at premium wage rates; hence the need for a legal job bar. In its absence, there would have been a narrowing of the wage differential and/or widespread substitution of blacks for whites.

In the absence of a wide racial wage differential, it seems likely that SA employers, like those in the USA, would have been willing to pay something for their preferences. This willingness would have reflected not only personal prejudices but also social pressures—conformity to the norms of fellow-whites (including white employees), neighbours, the chaps at the Rand Club. These social pressures—and reluctance to confront the formidable Nationalit government—must have deterred liberal (or rationalising) employers from breaking rank, until rising costs ensured they would be accompanied by a significant proportion of other employers. The fact that narrowing wage differentials during the 1970s did not stop pressures against the job bar, but were accompanied by the commitment to equal employment opportunities, indicates declining racism among employers and/or effective anti-racist pressures on them.

Apartheid and economic growth

The relationship of apartheid to economic growth is contentious. Some analysts have argued that apartheid fuelled growth; others that it was an obstacle to it. The argument in this book is that the formulation of this problem has been too crude: apartheid was functional for certain kinds of growth, notably the labour-intensive, export-oriented growth characteristic of the primary sectors until the late 1960s. It was not functional for growth in skill-intensive sectors and/or in those needing a large domestic market, such as manufacturing and, from the late 1960s, agriculture and non-gold mining.

Until the 1960s, the combined primary sectors accounted for a greater share of GDP than manufacturing, and gold mining in particular provided a sufficiently strong base for government revenue and foreign exchange to finance economic growth and permit the high costs of apartheid. Thereafter, the gold mines were no longer able to generate a surplus on the required scale.* As manufacturing overtook the combined primary sectors in terms of share of GDP, the burden of its high cost structure

---

*Though the declining role of gold as an export earner was to some extent supplemented by other minerals—platinum, chrome, uranium and coal.

became prohibitive, as could be seen from the growing balance of payments crisis.

Moreover, all sectors were becoming more capital and skill-intensive and the costs of the segmented labour market rose, as the skill bottleneck indicated. To this was added the costs of growing international hostility to apartheid—problems in acquiring foreign capital and technology and access to export markets. Apartheid had become an obstacle to continued growth—at which point the oligarchy made the crucial choice of going for growth rather than apartheid.

Many formulations of the relationship between apartheid and economic growth assume that the mere coexistence of the two meant that they must be causally related (a comparable assumption would be that the coexistence of stagnation and non-racialism meant that they must be causally related). As argued in Chapters 2 and 3, the relationship between apartheid and the *distribution* of the surplus produced by SA's rapid economic growth seems clear; but the relationship between apartheid and the *production* of that surplus is more complex. Apartheid had both costs and benefits and the net effect on economic growth is not clear. The argument that apartheid restrictions 'had depressed living standards and limited economic opportunities' was heard repeatedly this century.[47]

At the least, it is likely that apartheid was neither a necessary nor a sufficient condition for SA's impressive growth record. Other countries with lesser endowments have achieved growth without apartheid; and apartheid was not the only factor accounting for growth. Among other crucial factors were:

(i) Exceptional mineral endowments—not only the world's richest gold and diamond fields but plenty of coal to provide cheap power and, with the exception of oil, practically all other metals and minerals currently in demand—platinum, uranium, chrome, manganese, copper, vanadium, asbestos: SA is indeed the Saudi Arabia of minerals;

(ii) The availability of capital, technology and skilled labour, initially mainly foreign, later generated locally as well;

(iii) Entrepreneurship and economic management which are regarded, internationally, as being of a high standard;

(iv) Political stability.

Olson and others have argued that, in accounting for economic

growth, capital accumulation has been 'considerably less important' than technology and skill, while political stability has been
crucial.[48] These factors have been under-rated in accounting for
growth in SA.

The relationship of political stability, both to economic growth
and to apartheid, is the most problematical, both conceptually and
empirically. Defenders of white supremacy argue that it was
essential for the establishment of a political hegemony over the
diverse and warring peoples of SA, and that without this economic
development would have been impossible. Others either reject the
claim that white supremacy was essential for political stability, or
deny that it generated an acceptable form of economic growth
(measured in terms of efficiency and equity). Some would argue
that, whatever role white supremacy played initially in imposing
order and mobilising the surplus for development, the perpetuation of exclusive white power was not necessary for (or actually
harmful to) subsequent political stability and economic growth.

What was essential for economic growth was a political system
that was stable and *effective* (i.e. capable of governing). In the SA
case, this was based on an oligarchy mobilized on a racial basis,
although this could, as in most other countries, have been on a
class basis. Cultural differences and historical circumstances
would, however, have made it more difficult to construct such a
base in the short term. The *increasing* rigidities of this racial base
(demanded by less well-off sections of the oligarchy) imposed
economic costs and became an obstacle to social and political
incorporation of the new classes generated by successful economic
growth. Leading members of the oligarchy, particularly capital,
became convinced that failure to incorporate these classes by
removing the racial rigidities (which they did not regard as
intrinsic to their interests) would threaten political stability.
However, they remain worried about an alternative basis for stable
and effective government, because of the historical resentments
and fears and the lack of national cohesion.

The question arises: if sections of capital have long been
opposed to at least some major elements of apartheid, why did they
not get rid of them sooner, and why are they not getting rid of them
faster now? This poses a particular problem for those (like the
Marxists) who believe that in a capitalist society power *must* lie
with capital. It was the analysis of the political struggle that

convinced me that a Marxist framework was inadequate for explaining SA development. The economic interests of white capital (though not of white labour) can be largely explained in terms of a classic Marxist analysis of capital's need to erode obstacles to mobility and efficiency (though this is not how SA Marxists have interpreted them). But a Marxist analysis cannot account for the importance of racial/ethnic factors, nor for the power of white labour and the bureaucracy. Chapter 9 analyses the changing balance of political power and shows how this interacted with economic interests and ethnic divisions to produce first the entrenchment, and then the partial erosion, of apartheid.

Addendum

In reaction to the government's harsh handling of widespread black unrest from November 1984, business organizations (including the AHI) came out more explicitly on political rights. Their January 1985 Manifesto on reform called for common citizenship and meaningful political participation for all blacks; an end to forced removals; and the scrapping of the pass laws (this third proviso was added later).

Section C
THE POLITICAL STRUGGLE DEVELOPS

9
The Changing Balance of Political Power

The test of where power lies is whose will prevails in conflicts of interest. This study has shown that major apartheid policies (particularly the vertical and horizontal controls) reflected the interests of white agriculture and white labour and were often opposed by urban and mining capital. The obvious deduction that this reflected the balance of political power is reinforced by an examination not only of the power bases of SA governments but also of their other, non-racial policies.

From Union until the 1960s, governments mostly relied for their support on white agriculture and labour. (The two revealing exceptions were the years 1920–24 and 1939–48, when hegemony shifted temporarily to mining and urban capital respectively, resulting in the policy changes of those periods.) By 1970 the transformation of the SA economy had greatly strengthened urban capital and black labour, leading to the subsequent partial erosion of apartheid.

But the power struggle was not simply between various factions of capital and labour. It was also between national and foreign interests; between the English and Afrikaans sections of the oligarchy; and between whites and blacks, who were themselves deeply divided. This ethnic/racial/national dimension was vital in political mobilization, interacting with class, ideology and security to shape the political struggle and the balance of power.

Institutional factors were also important. The virtual exclusion of blacks from the political system hampered their mobilization, as well as alliances across colour lines. Meanwhile, the system of 'democracy for whites' not only favoured those whites (agriculture and labour) whose interests required a totally racist society, but also encouraged mobilization by the Afrikaner nationalists, who comprised a majority of the whites, by offering them the prospect of power, provided they united and prevented the extension of the black franchise. Logically, these became major goals of the nationalists.

Initially, labour and agriculture were the dominant classes in the Afrikaner alliance, but they were gradually superseded by Afrikaans urban capital and by the bureaucracy and political establishment. From the late 1960s, the diverging interests of these new classes erupted in the *verkrampte-verligte* split, which eventually tore the Afrikaner alliance apart. The combination of class and political interests accounted for the consistent tendency of Afrikaner nationalists to support more racist policies than 'the English' (although there were exceptions on both sides). The importance of class can be seen from the declining support of Afrikaners for racist policies as their class structure became more similar to that of the English.

The issues round which the power struggle revolved were the allocation of surplus (initially mainly from the mines); the size and control of the state sector; cultural and social policies (language, education, housing); and the question of 'national identity', including both SA's external (particularly imperial) links and its internal character—whether citizenship encompassed Afrikaners, whites, or people of all ethnic groups and colours.

This analysis of the shifting locus of power, and of the interaction of class, ethnic and other factors in the power struggle, will be divided into four sections: (a) White nationalism versus imperialism, 1910–48; (b) Afrikaner hegemony, 1948–78; (c) The search for a new national identity 1978–84; (d) The growing challenge to Afrikaner hegemony.

White nationalism versus imperialism, 1910–48

The policies of most governments during this period reflected the power of white agriculture and white labour, with two exceptions, when hegemony shifted to mining and later urban capital. This fluidity in the power balance, and the accompanying shifts of policy, provide revealing insights into the consistent pressures of white agriculture and white labour for more racist policies and the contrary tendency of governments based on urban capital towards some class rather than race-based policies. These latter governments had a predominantly urban English base. Support for racist policies came from Afrikaners as well as sections of 'English' society.

The struggle of white agriculture and labour, and certainly of the Afrikaner nationalists with whom they largely coincided was conducted in terms of the assertion of national against foreign interests, then incarnated in mining capital.* A brief examination of the base and policies of the five governments from 1910–48 will illustrate these propositions.

The SAP and its opponents

The electoral system was biased towards agricultural interests: at Union, almost half the whites lived in the rural areas, declining to 35 per cent by World War II; the vote was loaded in favour of rural areas** and farmers were active in politics: in 1910 over 50 per cent of MPs in the governing South African Party (SAP) were farmers.[2]

The SAP was a coalition of Transvaal's Het Volk, led by Louis Botha and Jan Smuts, and Free State's Orangia Unie, led by J. B. M. Hertzog, and it had a predominantly Afrikaans and agricultural base. The opposition Unionist Party was based on English urban seats in the Transvaal, Natal and Cape and English farmers in Natal and the Eastern Cape. Voting was therefore along English–Afrikaans ethnic lines; but class splits soon developed within both groups. The Labour Party was formed by English-speaking workers, reacting against the Unionists' close ties with mineowners. In 1914, Hertzog broke away from the SAP and formed the National Party (NP), supported by his OFS base and by Afrikaans farmers in the Cape.

The reason for Hertzog's breakaway was his rejection of the Botha/Smuts policy of conciliation between the white 'races', which aimed at healing the rifts between national and imperial interests, between English and Afrikaners, and among Afrikaners themselves.*** Hertzog believed that conciliation was being pur-

---

*In 1918, the proportion of mining dividends paid abroad was 82 per cent. This declined to 47 per cent in 1945 and 29 per cent in 1964.[1]

**Rural constituencies had a smaller number of voters, thus giving a greater value to their votes.

***Between the *bittereinders* who wanted to continue fighting the Boer War, the *hensoppers* who favoured surrender, and the National Scouts who helped the British.

sued at the expense of South African, particularly Afrikaans, interests. He wanted greater assertion of the sovereignty of SA, with the symbols of nationhood, such as its own flag and anthem. Many of his supporters wanted SA to leave the Empire and become a republic. Hertzog also wanted a greater degree of equality between English and Afrikaners in the economic and cultural spheres. He feared the younger Afrikaans culture would be swamped by English, and demanded mother tongue education in the schools and bilingualism in the civil service.[3]

But differences between 'moderate' Afrikaners in the SAP and 'militants' in the NP were not solely the outcome of national fervour; they were related to economic interests and political demography. Afrikaners comprised the majority of the electorate in the OFS and Cape (90 per cent in the OFS); but in the Transvaal, they accounted for only 32 per cent of adult males, to whom the vote was then restricted.[4] Botha and Smuts were therefore forced to take more account of English susceptibilities than Hertzog or the Cape nationalists, who could outbid them on issues such as the imperial connection and language rights.

Moreover, Herzog's agricultural base, especially in the Cape, gained less from imperial preference than sugar farmers in Natal, and they wanted freer trading policies, especially with Germany. In the Transvaal, the SAP was generally supported by wealthier maize farmers; Hertzog got some support from less well-off stock farmers in the Northern Transvaal.[5] The language issue, too, was closely related to job and career prospects, especially in the civil service, where bilingualism would be to the advantage of Afrikaners, as few of the English knew Afrikaans.

Policy towards the mining industry was another source of disagreement. The Hertzogites advocated more militant 'South Africa first' policies in relation to foreign capital, wanting a greater share of the mining surplus appropriated for national interests, particularly farming. But the difference in this regard was one of degree; Botha continued Paul Kruger's policy of milking the mines to build up the SA economy. The level of mining taxes was high: 42 per cent of profits in 1920, compared with rates of 23 per cent on gold mines in Rhodesia, 18 per cent in Australia, and 14 per cent in the USA. Railway rates were biased in favour of agriculture and against the mines. From 1918, the government, through the mining lease system, controlled the establishment of new mines, and the rate of exploitation, to prevent companies from mining the richest seams and leaving too much gold in the ground.[6]

These heavy costs on the mines were paralleled by large subsidies to agriculture: from 1911–36, South African governments raised £148m in taxes from the mining industry and spent £112m on agriculture.[7] Taken together with apartheid policies favouring white labour (the job bar) and white agriculture (preferential access to black labour), this renders untenable the view that the Botha government was a puppet of mineowners. However, the Hertzogites wanted even bigger subsidies for white farmers, a higher ratio of white to black mine workers, and policies to encourage industrialization (protective tariffs, state-sector industries), all of which would have further raised mining costs.

An alliance between white agriculture and white labour seemed logical, in terms of their class interests; but ethnic differences, exacerbated by the 1914–18 war, kept them apart. The Hertzogites opposed SA's entry into the war, which sparked off a *rebellie* among some OFS and Transvaal farmers (apparently those in the most depressed areas). English labour and capital rallied to the SAP, but its harsh handling of white strikers and rebellious Afrikaners eroded its electoral base* and led to its increasing reliance in parliament on the Unionists, with whom Smuts merged after Botha's death in 1919.

Power shifts to mining and imperial interests, 1920–24

Smuts's base and policies indicate a shift of power. He supported mineowners during the 1922 Rand rebellion over the job colour bar (see p. 113). Mining costs were cut by the reduction of mining taxes and railway rates and of import duties on food. Smuts also refused to impose duties on manufacturerd goods, and cut poor relief (financed by mining taxes).[9]

On all these issues the interests of mineowners were in conflict with local farmers, who wanted higher prices for food; manufacturers who wanted protection for the infant industries developed during World War One; and white workers who wanted strength-

---

*In the 1915 election, the SAP lost its overall majority of seats: the NP got one-third of total (and about half of Afrikaans) votes.[8] In the 1921 election, the SAP lost much of the vital Afrikaans agricultural vote.

ening of the job bar and higher levels of state aid. The costs of the depression were therefore shifted from the mines to local groups, and in 1924 mining profits reached their highest level since Union.[10] There were also the first attempts to encourage the emergence of a stable black middle and working class in the towns with some housing and business concessions to them.[11]

Among the reasons for these policies was Smuts's growing dependence on the Unionists, who brought generous contributions to party funds, the support of the English press, and English votes. Also, according to Hancock, 'Political responsibility had taught Botha and Smuts to recognise the mining industry . . . [as] South Africa's power house for economic development.' In 1920, the mines contributed 21 per cent to national income (see Table 4) and they were the major source of government revenue and foreign exchange. During the 1922 crisis many marginal mines were threatened by closure, and Smuts was convinced that, unless they were granted relief, the economic consequences for the whole country would be disastrous.

This led him to lean so far in their favour that his position became politically unsustainable. No SA government could antagonize the majority of white farmers and workers and remain in power. In the 1921 and 1924 elections, black and coloured voters in the Cape supported Smuts—to the consternation of the socialists[12]—but electorally they were not strong enough to compensate for the loss of support from white agriculture and white labour. Together these two groups were electorally unbeatable.

The political weakness of blacks

Blacks were less successful than whites, and particularly Afrikaners, at mobilizing politically. Economically blacks were dispossessed of much of their land and cattle and restricted to the role of menials in the white-dominated economy. After their defeat by the British in the Boer War, Afrikaners still had a large landed class, able to provide financial and organizational backing for the nationalist movement.

Secondly, Afrikaners had easy access to the political system—indeed were favoured by it—while blacks were largely excluded and their organization discouraged or even prevented. However, during this period, this did not require much exercise of state power. In 1938, there were only 11,100 policemen (many of them blacks) for a total population of 10m,[13] and armed force was used more frequently against white workers and Afrikaners than against blacks, still too thoroughly subdued by defeat, poverty and the network of bureaucratic controls hampering their mobility, to apply effective pressures.*

As Olson argued, political mobilization does not occur naturally but requires an investment of time, energy and money which most people make reluctantly and only when convinced it will achieve results.[14] The political system obviously offered greater incentives to mobilization to the smaller, more homogeneous Afrikaners and their political entrepreneurs than to the numerous, extremely heterogeneous blacks, for whom the prospect of power was remote.

Thirdly, Afrikaners had greater social cohesion than any other group in SA, and skilful leaders (teachers, priests, lawyers) who pressed effectively for cultural and social policies that promoted their cohesion and instilled in them a belief in their own values and culture. Blacks had never formed a nation; not only were there deep gulfs between Africans, Coloureds and Indians, but the major African tribes had different languages and political systems and had been at war with each other during the eighteenth and nineteenth centuries. During the period of white conquest some Africans, like the Mfengu in the Eastern Cape, sided with whites. The emergence of an urban proletariat and an educated, Christianised elite, which rejected the traditional leadership and was often convinced of the inferiority of black culture, added to these divisions.

Many coloureds identified with whites, whose language and religion they shared (see p. 17); their hope of incorporation into white society was encouraged by their different treatment. Indians were culturally distinct from all other groups in SA and in competition with blacks (as with whites) for jobs, land and other resources. Educational and administrative policies accentuated these differences. Ethnic differences were consequently significant among blacks—as they were among whites. In 1943 the

---

*An exception was the passive resistance campaign by the Indians under the leadership of Gandhi, which secured some concessions in the 1914 Indian Relief Act. External support, from Indian nationalists like S. K. Gokhale and from the Viceroy of India, contributed to their success.

African leader, Anton Lembede, described the goal of black unity as 'a fantastic dream which has no foundation in reality'.[15]

Class divisions were also important, particularly the rural/urban divide among Africans. This was reinforced by a widening cultural gap between the bourgeoisie and proletariat in the towns, increasingly oriented towards Western norms and incorporation into SA's emerging industrial society, and the traditionalists, based in the rural areas, who fought to retain their African traditions and the land which formed its economic base.* Their resistance contributed to the retention in African hands of significant areas of land (including an estimated 24 per cent of SA's arable land) and the maintenance of many features of African traditional society in these areas, as well as among many migrants in the towns. They were the black counterpart of whites who wished to retain their cultures and identities and reduce contact with outsiders. While their goals were often radical—sometimes aiming at the expulsion of whites and reclaiming of Africa for the Africans—their strategy to some extent dovetailed with the system of migrant labour and separate political development, and lent itself to manipulation by white segregationists.

The struggle for incorporation into white-dominated society was led by blacks based in the urban areas, though supported by some of the chiefs. The ANC, established in 1912 to organise Africans on a national scale, drew its leadership largely from the small urban elite—teachers, priests, lawyers and doctors. Its policy was termed 'moderate'—removal of discrimination, constitutional means of change, the gradual extension of a qualified franchise. The removal of the Cape African franchise in 1936 was a setback to these hopes and strengthened the radicals, both the Africanists, who rejected Western values and incorporation into white society, and those who subscribed to the goal of a non-racial society but favoured more activist means and more radical policies (universal suffrage, land redistribution, nationalization of the mines).

Among the most effective black organizations during this period were the trade unions. The membership of the Industrial and Commercial Workers Union (ICU) reached almost 100,000 before its disintegration in the 1930s. The growth of the African unions

---

*In 1936, 83 per cent of Africans were still rural (see Table 2).

in difficult circumstances (high labour turnover, low skill levels, pass laws and police harassment) were an early indication of the potential power of black labour.

Black political and labour organizations had complex relations with white liberals and communists, who brought finance and external contacts but were also a source of division and acrimony. They often advocated competing strategies: communists urged blacks to support white labour's fight for the job colour bar against the Chamber of Mines (see p. 183); liberals wanted blacks to support the English in their fight against the Afrikaners. They each wanted support on international issues: the CPSA in its opposition to SA's entry into the 'imperialist' wars in 1914 and 1939; the liberals in their support for entry into these wars. The left in SA was often preoccupied with these external ideological issues, which added to the divisions within black politics. White liberals and communists also competed with black leaders and tended, with their superior education and means, to take the decisions, thus conforming to the SA racial pattern and, unintentionally, hindering the emergence of black leadership. This was one of the complaints of the Africanists and it was a difficult problem for organizations like the ANC which were based on non-racial principles.

Nationalist–Labour Pact Government, 1924–33

In the 1924 election, the SAP was defeated by a Pact between Hertzog's National Party, representing Afrikaans farmers and workers, and the Labour Party supported by English workers.* The Pact reinforced and extended the institutional basis for apartheid policies favouring white agriculture and labour (see Chapter 2). It also adopted non-racial policies costly to mining capital, notably increased food prices, state aid for white farmers and 'poor whites',[16] and the industrialization policy to expand employment and entrepreneurial opportunities for local whites.

---

*The SAP lost over a third of its seats in Parliament (down from 79 to 52). The NP (with 63 seats) and the Labour Party (with 18) formed the Pact government. In the 1929 election, the NP was returned with an absolute majority of 78 seats out of 148 and Hertzog received about 80 per cent of the Afrikaans vote. Despite this, he retained the Pact, which remained in power until 1933.[17]

Protection for local industry was supported by the white unions, white farmers, and the small manufacturing class, but opposed by mineowners. The latter also opposed the establishment in 1928 of the first parastatal, Iscor (the iron and steel corporation), on the grounds that 'local industries would cause mining costs to soar, in that they . . . would be compelled to purchase local supplies at exorbitant prices whereas they were able to import cheaper material.' Further opposition came from commerce, which traditionally supports free trade.[18]

The fears of mineowners were realized. For some decades, SA steel prices were above international levels, and Iscor set higher prices for the inputs of the mining industry than for agriculture. The 1941 Industrial and Agricultural Requirements Commission confirmed that 'there are heavy excess costs both in agriculture and in secondary industry [which] . . . exist under present conditions only because of the surpluses artificially diverted to them (mainly from the gold mining industry) by means of taxation, price raising measures, subsidies and the like.'[19]

The changes in this range of policies shifted the costs away from white agriculture, labour and manufacturers, back to the mining industry, where the rise in costs resulted in net disinvestment.[20] Changes in government thus resulted in significant changes in policy; it was not a case of 'whoever was in office, the Whigs were in power.'

Mining capital, and the local businessmen who agreed with them on some issues, were therefore unable to prevail against white agriculture and labour, whose power rested on their industrial and political mobilization and their capacity to shake the newly-established state to its foundations. Their militancy led to the declaration of martial law in 1907, 1913, 1914 and in 1922, when Smuts needed 7,000 armed men to quell the Rand rebellion. Moreover, even when defeated industrially or militarily, white strikers and Afrikaner nationalists used their electoral power to unseat unsympathetic governments. The political system, and their effective mobilization, thus enabled local whites to defeat the economically-dominant foreign mining companies and their local allies. The political weakness of blacks meant there was insufficient pressure from them for the modest moves towards less racist policies which sections of capital periodically espoused.

However, the fact that mining capital was not able to get its way on issues on which it was in conflict with local white interests did not mean it was powerless. The functioning of the mines was crucial for the economy, and there were constraints on the policies any government could follow if it wanted them to stay in business. These constraints were illustrated when Hertzog failed to prevent Ernest Oppenheimer from closing some of de Beer's diamond mines during the 1929–33 depression. Oppenheimer said he would not bankrupt de Beers and ruin the shareholders in order to keep white workers employed.[21]

Capitalists, discouraged by low or zero profits, could refuse to produce. Hertzog could no more contemplate closure of the mines than Smuts, and nationalization was not an option to be lightly undertaken. In 1926, Hertzog experimented with state-run alluvial diamond mines,[22] but nationalized industries also had to face the problem of costs. During the depression even Iscor and the Railways were laying off whites (see p. 235).

Economic constraints on the policies of any government—English or Afrikaans, white or black, capitalist or socialist—made it impossible to solve the acute problem of high unemployment and an uncompetitive agriculture until the rapid economic growth of the 1930s and 1940s. In the meantime, what Hertzog could do—and did—was to shift the costs as much as he dared from his white agriculture/labour base to mining capital and to black labour.

Cultural and political policies cast further light on the power base and priorities of the Pact. Afrikaans replaced Dutch as one of the two official languages; bilingualism was required for state sector employees. SA's own flag and anthem were added to the union jack and 'God Save the King' and Hertzog enthusiastically supported the 1926 Balfour Declaration and 1931 Statute of Westminster, which enhanced the national sovereignty of the dominions.

However, even when he won an absolute majority in the 1929 election, Hertzog adhered to his undertaking to the Labour Party not to make SA a republic. He also retained Labour in the government because of his need for support from the English for one of the Nationalists' major objectives—the removal of Africans, though not coloureds, from the Cape franchise (see p. 17). Even so, he failed to win the required two-thirds majority for his 1926 Native Bills, which were opposed by the SAP, representing the English bourgeoisie and 'moderate' Afrikaners.

The limits on the power of Afrikaner nationalists were evident when Hertzog was forced to backtrack from his attempt to assert SA's sovereignty by refusing to follow Britain off the gold standard. The high costs, not only for the mines (denied a higher price for their gold) but also for agricultural exports (which could not compete with the products of countries which devalued) led to opposition from Hertzog's agricultural base. As on future occasions, Afrikaans voters refused to support ideologically-motivated nationalist policies which were costly to them. Instead, widespread public agitation for going off gold, and for a government of 'national unity' to deal with the economic crisis, forced Hertzog into a coalition with Smuts. The 1933 election produced an overwhelming mandate for white unity. Hertzog and Smuts won a combined total of 135 out of 150 seats, and their two parties (the NP and the SAP) 'fused' to form the United Party (UP).

White unity, 1933–9

The UP continued the racial and other economic policies demanded by white agriculture and labour, including the strategy of milking the mines—'a wasting asset'—for national development. Following the rise in the gold price, the UP imposed a high Gold Profits Surtax on the mines; while increased protection meant the mines could not gain from lower world prices for their stores and equipment. The 1937 Marketing Act, which set up producer-dominated Boards to control production and prices, systematized support for white agriculture. According to Kaplan this was supported by the FCI in return for farmers' support of protection for manufacturing.[23]

Hertzog's condition for fusion with the SAP was that it must support his 'native bills'. Smuts acquiesced in the 1936 Act removing the Cape African franchise because of his desire for white unity. But eleven of his MPs, led by Jan Hofmeyr, voted against it and began discussions about the formation of a liberal party to oppose the segregationist trend of legislation.[24] These plans were interrupted by the outbreak of World War Two, which unexpectedly increased the influence of the liberals.

The growth of Afrikaner nationalism

There was also a significant right-wing group of dissidents from Fusion. In 1934, 20 of Hertzog's 75 MPs followed D. F. Malan out of the UP and formed the *gesuiwerde* (purified) National Party. In the 1938 election, the Gesuiwerdes won 27 seats (to 111 for the UP).

As on other occasions, the dissatisfaction of the Afrikaner 'militants' had economic as well as political and ideological causes. Malan's electoral base was the rural Cape plus a few seats in the OFS and Transvaal. According to Salomon and O'Meara, Cape support came mainly from economically depressed areas: from the poorer farmers and unemployed 'poor whites' of small towns like Knysna and George. Malan also got support from some of the wealthier but discontented Cape wine, fruit and wool farmers and from SANLAM, the finance and insurance group (built up on the basis of Afrikaans agricultural savings) which owned Nasionale Pers and the Cape newspaper, *Die Burger*. Cape farmers complained that they had not benefited from imperial preference. At the NP congress that rejected Fusion, they attacked 'the threat to our wool and other markets posed by the one-sided trade with Britain and the British connection'.[25] The anti-imperialism of the NP was thus connected with the economic interests of Cape agriculture. Once again, class and ethnic interests were linked.

In the north, the Malanites received support from less well-off farmers in the OFS and Transvaal, and from the rising petty bourgeoisie in small towns and cities—teachers, clergymen, civil servants, small businessmen. This group was anti-imperialist, anti-semitic, and anti-black. They rejected Hertzog's policies of white unity and of more friendly relations with the coloureds. They wanted more social separation and tightening of pass laws and job colour bars. They organised boycotts against Indian and Jewish traders in small rural towns, and in 1936, the Malanites opposed further immigration of Jewish refugees from Nazi Germany. The xenophobia of this upwardly mobile group was both economic and ethnic in origin: resentment against English and Jews better off than themselves; fear of competition from blacks also seeking to climb the ladder. Lipset has shown that extreme racism and xenophobia are often found among rising but insecure groups who fear they may fall back.[26]

Table 13 shows that the position of Afrikaners was inferior to the English in relation to education, income, occupation, and capital ownership outside agriculture. This inferiority was intensely resented by Afrikaners, particularly by their articulate and ambitious leaders. Many have viewed Afrikaners as obsessed by a Calvinist ideology which over-ruled their 'rational' economic interests.[27] But in his seminal study, Salomon rightly stressed the central place Afrikaner nationalists gave to the economic struggle —their determination to conquer the cities and the economy, dominated by the English; a goal they termed their second Great Trek.* This meant winning for Afrikaans workers protection against 'unfair' non-white competition and for aspirant Afrikaans entrepreneurs their rightful share (control or ownership) of the economy. The principles adopted by the Afrikaner Broederbond** ** in 1933 included, 'Abolition of the exploitation by foreigners of the natural resources' of SA and 'the nationalization of finance and planned coordination of economic policy.'[28]

At the 1939 Ekonomiese Volkskongres, a movement was launched 'to penetrate the existing economic structure and gain a controlling share in the economic life of the country'. Research was published on such subjects as 'The Economy of the Afrikaner and his share in business life'. Afrikaners were urged to support Afrikaans businesses such as the insurance companies Sanlam and the bank Volkskas.

There was a division within the nationalist movement between a 'national socialist' element, supported by Transvaal trade unionists like Albert Hertzog (son of the Prime Minister) who agitated for nationalization of the gold mines and the establishment of a large state sector and those whose attacks on 'Hoggenheimer' and 'monopoly capital' did not signify opposition to capitalism *per se*, but the desire for a greater share of it for themselves. But whatever their views, economic issues—pork barrel politics—were always a prime concern of the Afrikaner nationalist movement, to the chagrin of some of its more idealistic exponents, such as Pienaar, one-time chairman of the Broederbond, who lamented the preoccupation of the Broeders with *'baantjies vir boeties'* (jobs for pals).[29]

Concern with ethnic issues and with protecting the Afrikaner's 'identity' was particularly strong among the party activists and

*The first Great Trek was the escape from British rule in the Cape Colony in the nineteenth century by trekking into the interior and establishing their own independent republics.

**'Band of Brothers'—an elite, secret society, established in 1918, which aimed at the promotion of Afrikaans interests in all areas of life and at Afrikaner 'domination in SA'.

cultural leaders, teachers and clergymen, whose *raison d'être* was tied up with the preservation of *die volk* (the Afrikaner people). This group, closely connected with the Broederbond, feared that Afrikaner identity would be swamped by the 'denationalizing' influences in the cities—the English language and institutions, and the alien ideologies of communism, liberalism, and socialism. To save their constituency from these influences, the Broederbond, especially after the breakaway by the Malanites in 1934, promoted a wide range of exclusively Afrikaans religious, cultural, social and economic organizations, such as the AHI and sports, youth and trade union bodies. These para-politicals were effectively used as instruments of socialization to bind Afrikaners together and mobilize them politically.

Among the most controversial of these efforts was the offensive launched in the trade union field by Albert Hertzog's Reform League, financed by donations from the widow of a wealthy Cape farmer. Hertzog estimated that in 1937 there were almost a quarter of a million unionized workers in SA, of whom at least half were Afrikaners. Many were in unions with English or even black workers. It was Hertzog's aim either to capture control of these unions, or to wean the Afrikaners into exclusively Afrikaans 'Christian national' unions. He also wanted to organise the many unskilled and non-unionized Afrikaans workers, who had been neglected by the English-dominated craft unions. The Reformers won control over the MWU, and fomented splits from unions such as the Garment Workers. They also established new unions, such as Spoorbond, for unskilled rail workers. By the mid-1940s, the Reformers had met with sufficient success to encourage the breakaway by a large section of Afrikaans unions to form their own exclusive federation, SACOL (see p. 194).

The attempt to 'save' the poorer, less-educated Afrikaners from denationalization was also essential for the political aims of the nationalist movement: their votes as well as their souls were wanted. Afrikaners constituted a small majority within the oligarchy; to win political control they required a high degree of solidarity. For the English the contrary was true; control depended on blurring differences.

The central planning and direction provided by the Broederbond gave the Afrikaner nationalist movement coherence and thrust. It would be a mistake, nonetheless, to see Afrikaner nationalism as primarily the outcome of the calculations of self-seeking political activists. There was tremendous grass-roots fervour among Afrikaners during the 1930s, as they began to recover from the trauma of defeat and social revolution. During the 1933 election, before Malan broke with Hertzog, he nearly lost his Calvinia seat to the Farmers and Workers Party which was opposed to Fusion; and the NP's Cape Congress rejected Fusion by 164 votes to 18. During the 1938 election, when support for Fusion was at its peak and the militants were rent by in-fighting, they still got over half the Afrikaans vote.[30]

Liberals and radicals competing with the Christian National trade unions to organise Afrikaans workers were well aware of these grass-roots attitudes, and the difficulties they led to in getting Afrikaners together with English, let alone black workers. There seems little doubt about their strong feeling of affinity for their *'eie mense'* (own people), with whom they shared language, culture and history, nor about the aversion and hostility they often felt for people of different cultures and colour, with alien languages and habits, some of whom were historical enemies with whom they had recently been at war, and with whom they were now thrust into close proximity and competition in the alien cities.

However, while Afrikaner nationalism had deep grass-roots support and was not simply drummed up by an ambitious leadership—let alone by capitalists (see below)—it was, on occasions, over-ridden by economic considerations. There were fissiparous tendencies in Afrikaans society, which were accentuated by the dissolution of their traditional bonds and by the mobility and class differentiation accompanying urbanization. These tendencies contributed to the breakaway by Malan in 1934 and to the political divisions of the next decade and a half.

The divisions within Afrikanerdom were not confined to the urban sector, as was shown by the volatile rural vote. From the mid-1930s, economic revival brought benefits to hard-pressed farmers, as well as to urban whites. Both groups proved responsive to governments which delivered these benefits; not only to the UP of Hertzog, but later to the UP of the apostate Smuts. From the time of the first split in 1914, there was a core on whom the militants (Hertzog in 1914, Malan in 1934) could rely—a core whose commitment was compounded of emotional as well as economic factors. But there were always elements who were (from the nationalist point of view) unreliable, whose economic interests prevailed over their ethnic loyalties. The tribal drum was powerful, but on its own it was not enough to provide the degree of solidarity required for political victory.

The frantic political activity of the 1930s and early 1940s was partly a defensive movement to maintain unity in the face of the attractions provided by economic revival. Moodie comments on Malan's preoccupation with social class and his anxiety that Afrikaners should not be divided on class lines.[31] There were indeed deep class divisions among Afrikaners: between wealthy and marginal farmers; between those with land and the *bywoners* who rented it from them; between the rising urban skilled and middle class and those still struggling to stay on the ladder or unemployed. Malan and the political *apparatchi* were right to see in these divisions a threat to the political solidarity they needed to win power. They had to fashion a political programme that could reconcile these differing class interests. Ethnicity alone could not hold the Afrikaner alliance together.

The failure of Fusion and the first reformist phase, 1939–48

Hertzog believed that his policies of 'South Africa first' and equality for Afrikaners would ensure a permanent partnership between the two white 'races'. But disagreement over the imperial connection split the alliance apart. Hertzog regarded SA's entry into 'England's war' as a betrayal of SA sovereignty. He broke with Smuts and was followed by 37 MPs, representing mainly rural constituencies, into an uneasy alliance with Malan. Smuts had a small majority in parliament and could rely on the support of the small Natal-based Dominion Party and handful of Labour MPs and Native Representatives (created by the 1936 Act).

In the 1943 election, Smuts increased his majority, receiving 107 seats (to 43 for the reunited Hertzog/Malan National Party*) and about one-third of the Afrikaans vote. The election results underlined the continuing importance of the rural vote: in 1943,

---

*Except for three urban seats on the Witwatersrand and Pretoria, the Nationalist seats were entirely rural/small town. They won most of the Cape rural seats (Malan's base) and practically all of the OFS seats (Hertzog's base).[32] But although they only got 29 per cent of seats, they got 36 per cent of the total vote, and an estimated two-thirds of the Afrikaans vote.

70 per cent of whites were urbanized; but 53 per cent of seats were still rural/small town.[33] The UP rump that remained with Smuts in 1939 was predominantly urban, with support from Natal and Eastern Cape farmers. It was the first government since 1920–24 that did not have a major Afrikaans agricultural component (though in 1943 Smuts won back 15 Transvaal rural constituencies from the NP). The predominantly English and urban base of the wartime UP government accounted for its reformist policies.

Given the electoral balance, and the mobilization by Afrikaner nationalists, it is surprising that Smuts won increased support, including a third of Afrikaans votes in 1943, and that he was able to carry out his more liberal race policies. One of the reasons for this was war fervour: 150,000 whites joined up, about two-thirds of them Afrikaners. They and their families resented the strident anti-war propaganda and activities (including sabotage) of the militant Afrikaner nationalists, who were moreover in disarray, with fierce infighting among Hertzogites, Malanites, and crypto-Nazi organisations like the Nuwe Orde and Greyshirts. It seems that many Afrikaners abstained from voting; some newly-arrived in the cities were not even registered. The 1943 election result therefore understated the support for an Afrikaner nationalist party.

The war also brought economic benefits to many traditional Nationalist supporters. White unemployment, endemic since Union, was practically eliminated by the manpower needs of the armed forces and war industries. White farmers gained from high food prices. For these two crucial electoral groups the jobs and high food prices resulting from 'England's war' outweighed the attractions of the Nationalists' anti-imperialist platform and their agitation against Hofmeyr's *Kaffirboetie* (pro-black) policies.

The war also increased the size and importance of the manufacturing and commercial sectors and of black labour, the classes favouring reform. In parliament, Smuts's need of the support of Native Representatives like Margaret Ballinger and of the (now more liberal) Labour Party gave an unexpected boost to their influence.[34] Increased activity by black political organizations and trade unions added to pressures for reform, particularly during the early 1940s, when there were fears of a Japanese invasion. Black leaders like Dr Xuma and Professor Z. K. Matthews, who were members of the Native Representative Council had access to leading politicians like Hofmeyr and Deneys Reitz, Minister of Native Affairs, and senior officials like Smit, whose 1942 report recommended abolition of the pass laws (see p. 20).

Whites were exposed to the anti-racist, anti-colonial ethos of the war. Many soldiers attended the adult education programmes organized by liberals like Leo Marquard and encountered ideas which challenged their traditional racial beliefs. In his analysis of the welfare legislation of wartime Britain, Anthony Crosland argued that the war ethos made it easier to persuade people to accept more egalitarian, equitable policies.[35] In SA this probably helped to persuade the conservative English to accept the more liberal wartime policies; they remained loyal, as English labour had during World War One.

All these factors contributed to the brief, unexpected reformist phase during which the influence of the manufacturing and commercial sectors and of the liberal intelligentsia temporarily eclipsed the former ruling alliance in which various combinations of conservative capital and white labour were predominant.

Reasons for the UP's defeat in 1948

The swing against the UP in 1948 took everyone by surprise; even the Nationalists did not expect to win. Their victory has been widely interpreted as resulting from the national fervour generated by the 1938 centenary celebrations of the Great Trek and from a reaction against SA's entry into 'England's war'. The importance of class interests in this watershed election has been underestimated.

By 1948 there was widespread dissatisfaction with economic policies among the white electorate, particularly white agriculture and labour. The post-war contraction and competition for jobs from demobilized soldiers intensified white labour's dissatisfaction with the erosion of apartheid labour policies (see p. 196). So too did the competition for urban resources, such as housing, due to the rapid wartime urbanization among all groups. Afrikaans workers also complained that they were excluded from the English-dominated craft unions and discriminated against in the civil service; and they were apprehensive about Smuts's plan for large-scale British immigration (as was the Nationalist leadership). These factors contributed to white industrial unrest and to the breakaway by most of the Afrikaans unions from the TUC (see p. 194).

White farmers were alarmed by the Fagan recommendations and dissatisfied with continued price controls, which eroded the benefits of the early war years and kept SA food prices below world levels. The severe 1946/7 drought sharpened their discontent.[36]

The Nationalists made full use of these discontents and fears in their *swart gevaar* (black danger) election campaign. The Fagan recommendations, erosion of the job colour bar, the black urban influx, urban slums and crime, and Hofmeyr's 'coffee-coloured budget' (i.e. increased expenditure on blacks) became major election issues.

There was also discontent among some of Smuts's traditional supporters. Urban businessmen were dissatisfied with Hofmeyr's restrictive post-war financial policies, presumably carried out in the interests of the gold mines, whose fixed price product was sensitive to inflation. They also disliked the changes in tax policy, which hit higher income earners, and the UP's conservative wing (English agriculture and labour and sections of mining capital) resented the more liberal 'native' policies.

However, as the election results showed, they did not switch their support to the Nationalists: mining capital because they feared the Nationalists' campaigns against 'monopoly capital', threats of nationalization and links with the MWU; Natal farmers because they were jingoist and anti-Afrikaans; English labour because they were engaged in a bitter fight with the Nationalists within the trade union movement. All the English resented the pro-Nazi, wartime activities of the Nationalists and feared that they would, as envisaged in the draft 1942 Republican constitution, relegate the English language to an inferior place and the English to second-class citizenship.[37] So the English conservatives remained within the UP, where they pressed for more racist policies. Already during the war, pressures from Natal conservatives had forced Smuts to enact the 1943 Pegging Act and the 1946 Asiatic Land Tenure and Indian Representation Act against Indians. Hofmeyr nearly resigned over the issue but stayed because of the war.[38]

The UP was also under growing pressure from the left. Smuts's brutal suppression of the 1946 mineworkers strike led the Native Representative Council to disband itself *sine die* on the grounds that its advice and complaints were ignored, and it was tired of speaking through a 'toy telephone'. Cautious ANC leaders were under pressure from younger activists like Nelson Mandela,

Robert Sobukwe and Walter Sisulu, who demanded universal suffrage and the removal of all race discrimination. These demands were supported by a small group of whites, and by the international anti-colonial lobbies, which prevented the incorporation of the mandated UN territory of South West Africa (and later of the High Commission territories) into SA.

Black unrest and growing international criticism of apartheid reinforced the conviction of Smuts and Hofmeyr that reform was necessary. However, these pressures were angrily rejected by the NP and led to a backlash among many whites. In retaliation against the Indian government's 1947 motion of censure at the UN, the Transvaal NP organised a boycott of Indian traders, and the Nationalists demanded tough law-and-order measures against 'agitators' and the arming of the police, which Smuts resisted.[39] But Nationalist demands struck a chord in the electorate, alarmed by urban crime and political unrest and influenced by cold war propaganda about communist subversion.

The NP did not, however, fight the election solely on a *swart gevaar* platform. They also fought it on an explicitly 'Afrikaners first' programme. The NP fielded no English candidates, it sought no English members, and the constitution of the Transvaal NP explicitly excluded Jews. They wanted domination by Afrikaners and all the symbols of that domination—pre-eminence for the Afrikaans language, a republic, and departure from the commonwealth. The defeat of Germany ended the pro-Nazi activities of the Nationalists but not their racist, xenophobic propaganda, which was not softened by the economic advances of the war years nor by the fact that most of their national/cultural demands had been met (language rights, SA sovereignty, own flag). On the contrary, their ambitions were sharpened, only to seem threatened by the post-war contraction and the more liberal UP policies.

The 'Afrikaners first' policy divided the NP from the English conservatives, who agreed with at least some aspects of their race policies. The latter remained within the UP, whose two wings were locked in conflict and united only by their fear of the Nationalists. The result was an increasingly ambiguous and contradictory policy which put the UP ideologically and politically at a disadvantage against the clear-cut, confident NP policies. The UP's vacillating policies alienated it from the liberal opposition, particularly the blacks: many coloured voters boycotted the 1948 election, contributing to the loss of some Cape seats. The liberals who remained in the UP were trapped in a losing battle against electoral pressures, which pushed the party steadily to the right until the 1970s.

While the UP was rent by conflict, the NP was pulling itself together. In the 1943 election, in which the Nationalists had won only 43 seats, Malan eliminated his rivals. In 1948 he led a united party. Its base was more prosperous, its activists enthusiastic, disciplined and convinced of the rightness of their policy. The NP had the backing of the wide range of para-politicals built up during the last couple of decades, which gave it a broad base throughout Afrikaans society. Afrikaans voters in the towns were registered and the party organization got out the vote.

For all that, the NP only won the 1948 election by five seats. Voting was along ethnic lines: the NP received 75–80 per cent of the Afrikaans vote; English constituencies voted solidly for the UP. But this division was not simply based on ethnic loyalties; it was closely related to material interests, with NP policies explicitly tailored to favour Afrikaans workers, farmers and businessmen.

White politics and the war

Stultz (and others) have argued that the reason for the nationalist victory in 1948 was SA's entry into the war. This broke the coalition between the English and moderate Afrikaners, strengthened Afrikaner nationalism, and gave the militants their chance to get into power. By entering the war, Smuts thus 'risked the policy of conciliation' and polarized whites along English/Afrikaans lines.[40] This interpretation underestimates the importance of class factors in accounting for the Nationalist victory, as well as the pressures within the oligarchy which would have pushed the English/moderate-Afrikaans coalition in a similar direction on 'native' policy.

In 1943 Smuts held an estimated 32 per cent of the Afrikaans vote, because Afrikaners were doing well (this compared with about 45 per cent which the Hertzog/Smuts alliance received in 1938). In 1948, when Afrikaners were not doing so well, Smuts's share declined from 32 to about 20 per cent.[41] Since Union, Afrikaner militants seemed able to rely on a hard core of about 55 per cent, while the SAP/UP was able to rely on a core of about 20 per cent—the *bloedsappe*, Afrikaners who fought with and remained loyal to Botha and Smuts. This left a floating Afrikaans vote of about 25 per cent (much of it in loaded rural seats) which was critical in deciding elections.

The shift in 1948 was not therefore exceptional, but close to the 1929 election result, and it did not add up to a great surge of nationalism. What changed between the early and late 1940s were: (i) economic interests—the UP's policies had become costly for white agriculture and labour; (ii) politically and organizationally the UP was in disarray and the NP had the advantage. There were also factors operating over time to the advantage of the Nationalists: (iii) political demography favoured the Afrikaners who, with their faster birthrate, increased from 56 per cent of whites in 1936 to 58 in 1960; (iv) there might have been a generational factor, with the older *bloedsappe* dying out, and the younger generation of Afrikaners, whose teachers and preachers were ardent Nationalists, becoming more militant.

Stultz gives an interesting account of this generational change among farmers in the Bethal district.[42] However, he also records that economic issues played a crucial part in their dissatisfaction with UP policy and that they were angered by an investigation into their treatment of African labourers by the UP. There were thus material reasons why they switched back from UP to NP in 1948. This example underlines the difficulty of attempting to isolate Afrikaner nationalism as a factor determining political behaviour. It was usually closely inter-related with class interest. If class and ethnicity were in conflict (as in 1943), the Nationalists could not rely on the Afrikaans floating voter; but if ethnicity and economic interests went together (as in 1948), they formed a formidable combination.

It is also unlikely that the UP would have maintained its reformist policies, even if it had won the election, because of the growing strength of the UP conservatives. If Hofmeyr had succeeded Smuts as Prime Minister and tried to continue these policies, he would probably have been replaced; another realignment with 'moderate' Afrikaners and a return to the UP's racist 1933–9 policies was then likely.

The Rhodesian analogy

There are some illuminating similarities with the course of events in Rhodesia, where the reformist experiment during the 1940s and

1950s, under Prime Ministers Todd and Whitehead, was ended by the election of the Rhodesian Front in 1962 and a reversion to racist policies.

Before World War II, Rhodesia was also basically an agricultural/mining economy with white interests requiring plenty of cheap black labour and the suppression of blacks as independent producers. Here too local whites had sufficient political power to force governments to give priority to their interests when they were in conflict with those of foreign mining companies. Consequently, tax, pricing and licencing policies ensured that a high percentage of surplus was ploughed back to develop the economy. However, Rhodesia differed from SA in not having a large and poor white working class; white workers were, from the beginning, a labour aristocracy—a situation SA reached only in the 1950s—and there was consequently less institutionalized colour bar legislation in Rhodesia to protect the bottom group of whites.

As in SA, World War Two led to the rapid growth of manufacturing. After the 1948 Nationalist victory, Rhodesian manufacturing benefited from the flight of foreign capital and of skilled English workers from SA. It also derived advantages from the larger market provided by the formation of the Central African Federation in 1953. The growth of manufacturing, with its need for more skilled, stable labour and a larger internal market accounted for the pressures for reformist measures such as rising wages, improved education, and the proposals for changes in land legislation, and for the extension of trade union and even political rights. Rhodesia began to move towards the creation and incorporation of a black middle class. These policies were supported by mining companies, which were becoming more capital-intensive, faced a less rigid colour bar than in SA, and therefore had a greater interest in skilled, stable black labour.

This reformist process, which went further than in SA during the 1940s, was aborted by the election in 1962 of the Rhodesian Front, supported by white agriculture and by the white petty bourgeoisie, consisting of skilled and white collar workers, many in the state sector, who constituted the 'centre of gravity of the white electorate'.[43]

The economic background to the white backlash in 1962 was the flagging of manufacturing and the renewed importance of agriculture, based on an expansion of tobacco exports. The switch from maize to tobacco farming was unfavourable for reformist policies, because tobacco was more labour-intensive and did not require an internal market. So in Rhodesia, too, there was a shift of power from manufacturing—a source of reformist pressures—and a reassertion of power by white agriculture and white workers, who were finding reformist policies too costly.

This analogy between the abortive reformist phases in SA and Rhodesia underlines the importance of the class dimension: NP policies were not just the outcome of Afrikaner nationalism. The interests and balance of power within the white electorate would probably have led to the success of parties espousing these colour policies even if the SA electorate had been entirely English (or Belgian). In fact, if the Afrikaner nationalist element had been absent, the more racist party would probably have got greater support because the English conservatives would have backed them.

The puzzle is not why the Smuts/Hofmeyr UP was defeated in 1948, but how it managed to carry out its mildly reformist policies during the war and get the support of the electorate in 1943. It seems to have been because of the peculiar circumstances generated by the war—very rapid growth leading to an acute skill shortage; expansion of the domestic market as SA goods replaced imports; patriotic fervour and the dislike by some Afrikaners of the extremism and infighting among the nationalists; the external threat, combined with internal black political activity; and the personalities and beliefs of individuals like Hofmeyr who, as Smuts's deputy, had unusual influence during the war. Smuts's own views underwent considerable change, influenced by the international revulsion against racism and the criticism of SA at the UN.

Far from the war ending hopes of a 'moderate native policy', it gave an unexpected filip to the pressures for such a policy. But examination of the structure of white interests suggests that reform was premature, in the sense that there was not yet within the oligarchy a large enough manufacturing and commercial class to sustain the more liberal policies against the interests that still wanted apartheid. The class base for non-racial policies within the white electorate was still too weak; so were the pressures from blacks and the international community.

The political system and ideology were also important, constraining white liberals from seeking black allies, who offered few votes or other forms of political pressure. Even those whites who advocated socio-economic reforms had a lengthy time-scale for political reform. Against the background of a colonized, poor and largely illiterate Africa the racist belief in the need for white rule was as widespread as the sexist assumption that the female half of the white race should be excluded from active participation in political life.* It was only during the 1940s that the ANC itself adopted a policy of universal black suffrage.

Nevertheless, the failure of white liberals to actively pursue the option of an alliance with the black middle and skilled classes, like the failure of English conservatives to unite with the Nationalists who were their allies on race policy, were both examples of groups not acting as their class interests suggested they should. Ethnic/racial factors at the least delayed political collaboration which was logical in class terms. Ethnicity operated both at an ideological level, constraining people's perceptions of their options, and at an institutional level: mobilization along ethnic lines was either so well established, or the ethnic gulf was so wide, that it became difficult to establish, or even conceive of, political organization across ethnic barriers. The virtual exclusion of blacks from the political system accentuated this and oriented white liberals towards participation in an electoral system where the pressures came mainly from the right.

Afrikaner hegemony, 1948–78

The key issue for our argument is whether, despite the fact that the Afrikaner nationalists were in office, power lay with capital, particularly manufacturing, the leading growth sector. It will here be contended that, as before, the political system gave the electorate real power. Consequently the Whigs were out of power as well as out of office. Political power lay with the Afrikaner nationalist alliance in which, initially, white agriculture and labour were dominant. Later, economic growth and 'Afrikaners First' policies gradually transformed white labour into a bureaucracy and created a group of Afrikaans urban and mining capitalists, who came to share the interests of other employers in eroding apartheid. These diverging class interests eventually tore apart the nationalist alliance.

*White women in SA did not get the vote until 1930.

'Afrikaners first', 1948–60

The NP's exclusive ethnic base was clear in the 1948 election results: most predominantly Afrikaans constituencies voted NP; every predominantly English constituency voted for the UP or its allies. The election also confirmed the rural base of the NP: although three-quarters of whites were then urbanized, only 22 per cent of the NP's 79 seats were urban. Its biggest gains were in the Cape and Transvaal rural areas; the Nationalists also made their first urban breakthrough, winning 13 Afrikaans working-class constituencies (miners, railwaymen, steelworkers) on the Witwatersrand and Pretoria.[44]

The UP received about 20 per cent of Afrikaans votes, but it was now primarily an English urban party: almost 90 per cent of its seats were in major urban areas. The UP also won an overall majority of *votes*—51 per cent against 41 for the NP/AP* alliance (547,000 to 443,000 votes). (The favourable loading of rural votes was among the reasons why this did not give it a majority of seats.) It was not until 1958 that the NP won a majority of votes.

In subsequent elections, the NP increased its share of seats and of votes until, in 1966, it received 75 per cent of seats and 58 per cent of votes. These gains were predominantly in urban areas: in 1966, 45 per cent of its seats (55 out of 120) were in major urban centres. But, considering that 80 per cent of Afrikaners were then urbanized, this still constituted a surprisingly low proportion of NP seats.

Rural bias in the political system was accentuated by the active political role of farmers. In 1948 almost half the Nationalist MPs were farmers (or connected with agriculture), as well as 20 per cent in the UP. Farmers were also well represented in the organizations of both parties and were major contributors to party funds.[45]

NP policies reflected its white farmer/worker and Afrikaans base: the wartime race reforms were reversed (see Chapter 2), food prices rose, expenditure on white welfare (housing and education) increased, the state sector was expanded and Afrikaners given preference in the jobs and entrepreneurial opportunities this generated. This preference was at the expense not only of blacks but also of the English, and this aspect of Nationalist policy provides a revealing indicator of where power lay.

*The Afrikaner Party under Havenga, the remnants of General Hertzog's followers.

The Nationalists and 'the English'

The 1948 election marked the exclusion of the economically-dominant English from political power. For the first time since Union, the party in power was exclusively Afrikaans. In his victory speech, Prime Minister Malan declared: 'Today South Africa belongs to us once more. For the first time since Union, South Africa is our own, and may God grant that it will always remain our own'.[46]

Afrikaner hegemony was extended over senior posts in the civil service and armed forces, from which a number of English were unceremoniously retired. Senior appointments were monopolized by Afrikaners (usually members of the Broederbond). The state sector became an Afrikaans preserve and the English were seldom appointed, even to government commissions.

Among the examples of *baantjies vir boeties* were appointments to the judiciary. From 1948, senior English members of the Bar were systematically overlooked in the appointment of judges; junior Afrikaners were rapidly promoted. When the English press complained that Afrikaners were being given preference in practically all judicial appointments, this was acknowledged and justified by *Die Transvaler*, official organ of the NP.[47]

The Nationalists used their powers of patronage to favour Afrikaans business interests. Central and local government authorities shifted their accounts from English to Afrikaans financial institutions such as Volkskas. Government contracts were steered to Afrikaans companies.[48] The IDC, state instrument for encouraging expansion of manufacturing, entered into joint enterprises with private Afrikaans companies like Federale Kunsmis. The expanded state sector, and parastatals such as Iscor, Foscor and Sasol, were used as training grounds for Afrikaans entrepreneurs.

The chairman of IDC, van Eck, acknowledged that in making appointments the state ignored 'the usual practice' of balancing the language groups; hardly any English held appointments in state corporations.[49] Andries Wassenaar, one of the leading entrepreneurs to emerge during this period, later confirmed that the IDC was used 'to strengthen Afrikaans participation in the industrial progress of the country . . . and as a bulwark against the AAC'.[50] The Afrikaans economist, Jan Sadie, commented: 'With a party in power consisting of an overwhelming majority of Afrikaners we find willingness in undertakings to seek cooperation with

Afrikaner businesses, partly because it is believed that the latter have easier access to authority . . . the government . . . has created opportunities by which the Afrikaner could obtain experience in the function of management; opportunities he would otherwise not have had.'[51]

Other measures ignored English susceptibilities. When the Nationalists withdrew support from the immigration programme, they made it clear they would prefer immigrants from Holland, and even from Germany, with which SA had recently been at war, to those from the UK. They spelt out their dislike of the Commonwealth connection and of symbols such as the shared flag, anthem, currency and the monarchy—all of which they got rid of when SA became a Republic in 1961 (on the basis of a narrow majority of 850,458 to 775,878 votes). The English also resented the attempts to segregate the two white groups by the introduction of compulsory mother-tongue education in schools, which meant that English and Afrikaans children had to be separately educated. Apart from their disapproval of such an explicitly exclusive policy, the English disliked interference with parental choice.

In the bitter parliamentary debates over these issues the Nationalists asserted that, 'The country belongs to us, in the first instance, to the people who opened it up.'[52] Together with the undermining of the constitution, erosion of the rule of law, interference with the judiciary, press, universities and churches, this made many English fear that their institutions, values and way of life, were being threatened. This contributed towards the exodus of English capital and skilled and professional workers, thousands of whom emigrated to Rhodesia and other Commonwealth countries. The point about *these policies* is that *they show where power lay* and how the government used it. If, as is alleged, power really lay with urban capital—overwhelmingly English (and foreign)—their susceptibilities would not have been over-ridden in this way.

'Afrikaners first' policies exacerbated relations between the two white groups, and much of their political energy was expended on the intra-white conflict. Many observers cannot believe that they really cared about these issues. But—as in Canada, Belgium and Ireland—they did. This had political consequences, sharpening the alienation of the English liberals, and dividing the Nationalists from the English conservatives, who often agreed with their 'native' policies.

Nevertheless, the Nationalists acted more cautiously than the English had feared. They did not enact the provisions of the 1942 draft republican constitution (which would formally relegate the English language to an inferior position) and they took no punitive measures against English, Jewish or foreign capital. Far from wrecking the economy and driving out those who knew how to operate it, the Nationalists wanted national industrial expansion and were more responsive than Jan Hofmeyr had been to pressures for increased protection. These policies, which were not specifically racial, provided the basis for a surly working relationship— rather than a state of war—between capital and government; but this did not exclude disagreements over other issues, such as labour policy and the massive expansion of the state sector, from which English capital derived less benefit than Afrikaners, and which they claimed aggravated the shortage of capital. By 1960 the IDC had invested £171m in industrial projects; some of this was in the form of loans, but most took the form of substantial holdings. Businessmen complained that the state sector was competing with them for scarce capital, which was also driven away by the Nationalists' harsh and controversial race policies and their hostility to foreign capital.

The Nationalists and foreign capital

During the Nationalists' first decade in office, there was much debate among them about the role of foreign capital. Leading Afrikaans economists like van Eck and Sadie argued for 'self-capitalization', maintaining that SA could manage a fair rate of growth without foreign capital and that this would be a preferable way of financing development. Sadie pointed to the burden of remittances and debt repayments on the balance of payments and objected that a large foreign sector 'magnifies the influence of outside forces'. Afrikaans businessmen, like M. S. Louw, attacked the extent of foreign ownership, demanding nationalization if Afrikaners did not get their 'share'.[53]

World War Two had increased SA control over foreign investment, as South Africans bought out British assets (see p. 258n). As in the post-war period, this extension of SA ownership was carried out largely under the aegis of SA English capital. The Nationalists lacked the financial strength to do this on their own, short of nationalization, which would have provoked a crisis in their foreign relations (or been very expensive if compensation was paid).

The 1948 Nationalist victory provoked a flight of foreign capital, which many Afrikaners welcomed. However, their economic managers soon realised that this had costs, such as the acute shortage of capital for investment in manufacturing, which contributed to the slowdown in growth by the late 1950s. This shortage of foreign capital meant more had to be provided from domestic sources. In 1957 local capital formation provided 97 per cent of total investment and represented reinvestment of 30 per cent of national income.[54] This intensified rate of domestic capital accumulation probably contributed to the regressive policies of the 1950s. The Minister of Labour rejected an appeal for a national minimum wage on the grounds that, 'While such an increase in wages will increase the demand for consumer goods and possibly bring about increased labour productivity . . . it could affect the profitability of our undertakings and restrict internal capital growth and expenditure.'[55]

The Nationalists also began to appreciate the need for foreign technology and international contacts. They kept up their anti-imperial rhetoric until they achieved their republic in 1961, but they were flogging a dead horse. In reality Afrikaner nationalist objectives had been met, and these preoccupations were giving way to a fear of isolation. Ironically, in view of their stance over entry into both World Wars, the 1955 Simonstown Agreement gave the UK the use of the naval base even in circumstances where SA was not a belligerent, and they were eager to send a SA contingent to Korea, to establish their credentials as a reliable Western ally.

By the late 1950s, their accession to power had modified the NP's attitude to foreign capital, as was evident from this speech by Prime Minister Verwoerd:

> There is a natural desire on the part of every country to retain control over its economic destiny . . . the encouragement of local capital formation was one of the guiding principles of our financial policies during the past decade . . . . [SA] today provides by far the greater proportion of its own capital requirements. But . . . foreign capital can still be of great assistance in the development of our resources . . . . Moreover, in many cases desirable development will not take place without the technical knowledge and business skill which accompany foreign capital . . . . [We] will continue to welcome the participation of foreign investors . . . provided this does not conflict with the general principle of a country retaining control over its economic destiny.[56]

This less hostile attitude to foreign capital was combined with continued vigilance over its activities. Foreign capital was not given a free hand, and SA's management of foreign capital—like its creation and use of the state sector to promote economic development—anticipated the actions of many newly independent countries during the 1960s and 1970s.* It was also another indicator of where power lay and of the strong sense of national identity among the whites, particularly the Afrikaners.

Apartheid policies which secured Afrikaner nationalist goals

There were three aspects of apartheid over which there was a marked and revealing division between the English and Afrikaners: institutionalized social separation, policy towards the coloureds, and the 'separate development' policy. This division reflected not only class and ideological differences, but also the political needs of Afrikaner nationalism.

Compulsory, legalized social separation was opposed by many English, particularly the bourgeoisie. Even conservatives who would not mix with blacks did not like the arrogation by the state of the power to intervene in these matters. It was a fundamental part of their creed that these decisions belonged to the individual and the family. The leading advocates of social apartheid were the NP political/ideological establishment, the 'class' with a vested interest in Afrikaner identity.** Both the Pact and the 1948 NP, which introduced legislation enforcing social and sexual segregation, had a predominantly Afrikaans base. Opinion surveys which appeared from the late 1960s confirmed a continuing sharp division between the English and the Afrikaners over this issue.[59]

In addition to the socio-economic functions which social apartheid fulfilled for less well-off whites (see p. 216), it had political functions. First, ethnic segregation strengthened Afrikaner cohe-

---

*This was acknowledged by the Zimbabwean cabinet minister, Eddison Zvobgo, when he stated in 1980 that, although he did not like the political views of Afrikaners, he admired the way they had wrenched business and political power from the British in SA.[57]

**In the debate on the 1949 Mixed Marriages Act, the Minister of the Interior, Donges, stated that the Dutch Reformed Churches had pressed for this measure. Recently, P. W. Botha (calling for a review of these laws) reminded Parliament that they had been introduced 'as a result of an approach by the Churches and certain women's organizations and after a petition to the government of the day signed by 250,000 voters'.[58]

sion. The nationalist leadership was preoccupied with this because—apart from their concern with Afrikaner identity—solidarity was essential for political power. Segregation helped to prevent some Afrikaners from fraternizing with blacks and others from becoming anglicized. The existence of the coloureds and the anglicized Afrikaners showed that not all Afrikaners felt an aversion towards outsiders—or at least not all the time. Despite the history of conflict and competition, there was a degree of ambivalence and fluidity in race relations that threatened the tight solidarity required by the Nationalist leadership and led them to resort to legal means to shore up ethnic divisions, instead of relying on conventional barriers, as the English were generally content to do.*

Second, enforced ethnic segregation divided the opposition, creating barriers between Africans, coloureds and Indians, and between them and the English, whom the Nationalists (rather flatteringly) feared would 'gang up with the non-whites against us'. Social mixing was likeliest with the growing black middle-class whom the liberals regarded as their potential political allies. Social apartheid helped to postpone increased fraternization until well into the 1970s.

Third, social distance made it easier to pursue harsh, discriminatory policies. Since the intrusion of the liberal missionaries into SA in the late eighteenth century, the liberal, humanitarian influence (especially when combined with the enlightened self-interest of employers) was a recurring irritant to advocates of racist policies. Contact highlighted the harsh effects of apartheid and intensified the conflict between discrimination and the Christian, democratic values professed by whites. Greater distance and ignorance made it easier to maintain the stereotypes and myths which rationalized discrimination.

Both the Nationalists and their liberal and black critics attached great importance to social apartheid, which became one of the most symbolic and hated aspects of their policy. Ironically, when they began to dismantle it, both denigrated its importance: the

---

*As Olson argued, in his discussion of the difficulties of political mobilization, 'The political entrepreneurs who attempt to organize collective action will be more likely to succeed if they strive to organize relatively homogeneous groups . . . and to use indoctrination and selective recruitment to increase the homogeneity of their client group'.[60]

Nationalists describing it as 'petty', their critics dismissing changes in social policy as 'marginal'. In reality, social apartheid was never marginal or petty. In addition to its recognised ideological and psychological aspects, it fulfilled important economic and political functions.

Policy towards the coloureds

Long-term political and strategic considerations suggested that, from the point of view of the oligarchy, the coloureds should be drawn into the white camp. The NP's removal of coloureds from the voters roll and systematic extension of segregation to them cast further light on its base and on the power balance.

White labour and the petty bourgeoisie did not share the liberal view of coloureds (and other sections of the black elite) as potential allies. They viewed them as competitors for jobs, education, housing and other urban amenities. The Nationalist political establishment feared that blacks were likely to vote with the English against them. An increase in the number of coloured voters (or of African representatives in parliament) could obviously upset the English/Afrikaans political balance, permanently destroying the narrow Afrikaans majority. If the main concern had been the long-term strengthening of *whites*, this would not have mattered; but as the main concern was *Afrikaner hegemony*, coloured incorporation was vetoed.

While class and political calculations were crucial in this decision, racism also played a part, particularly among the dominant Transvalers who had little contact with coloureds and regarded all 'non-whites' as being the same.* The Transvalers opposed the plea of those Cape nationalists who urged that coloureds, most of whom spoke Afrikaans and belonged to the Dutch Reformed Churches, should be recognised as *bruin* (brown) Afrikaners. All these factors—the class interests of white labour and the petty bourgeoisie, the racist attitudes of Transvaal and OFS

---

*Their racist attitudes were evident in interviews I had with senior Transvaal MPs during the early 1970s, by which time attitudes had supposedly mellowed. In rejecting a closer relationship with the coloureds, they emphasised racial, particularly physical, differences: 'Have you not seen their Hotnot features, Krissy hair, *platneuse* and thick lips?' One of them declared that he could detect the presence of coloured blood 'even over the phone—by the accent,' and that he did not want SAs to become a 'coffee-coloured race'.

nationalists, the vested interests of the political establishment, including those in the Cape, where most coloureds lived—were an obstacle to closer relations with the coloureds. Surveys confirmed the wide divergence between the English and the Afrikaners on the coloureds.[61]

During the 1960s, as apartheid evolved into separate development, the Nationalists placed increasing emphasis on cultural rather than biological differences, insisting that they did not regard other races as inferior, but different, and that this difference was not racial but cultural. This claim is contradicted by the case of the coloureds, who were culturally closer to the Afrikaners than the English. Their rejection by Afrikaners was not therefore the outcome of cultural differences, but of a range of factors, including racist feelings based on physical differences.

But if physical manifestations of race were such an important factor, why did they not over-ride the hostility towards, and lead to a closer alliance with, the English? Instead, it was precisely those Transvalers who were most adamantly against the coloureds who were also most anti-English. Race alone is not therefore the key, any more than culture, to interpreting Afrikaner nationalist political behaviour. The key is to be found in the combination of class interests and ethnic ties; what could perhaps be termed an 'ethnic class'. In this case, the 'ethnic class' was small enough to be knit together by a network of kinship ties, reinforced by a recent history of shared suffering and achievement and by intense competition and hostility, frequently erupting into warfare, with practically all other groups with whom they had been thrust into a common society. Neither the dry class categories of the Marxists, nor the tortuous race categories of the pluralists, seem able to contain the force and complexity—and yet instability—of this combination of ethnicity, class and kinship.

The separate development policy

This elaborate policy, with its separate political institutions for whites, coloureds and Indians, and independent homelands for Africans, was designed to perpetuate Afrikaner and not merely white political domination, and it drew its support overwhelmingly from Afrikaners. English conservatives regarded the Bantustans, in the words of the UP leader, de Villiers Graaff, as 'seedbeds of subversion', 'springboards for communism', and a threat to the viability of the SA economy. Liberals rejected the compulsory racial division of the population and the granting of political rights on a group rather than individual basis. They also opposed the further restrictions on the mobility of capital and labour required by the policy. Opinion polls later confirmed the marked English/Afrikaans division on the separate development policy.*

However, as the policy's economic costs became evident with its implementation from the late 1960s, the enthusiasm for it of Afrikaans capital and labour waned (see pp. 154 and 223). It then became clear that the main pressures for the policy came from the Afrikaans political and ideological establishment and the bureaucracy. The continued adherence to this policy was testimony to the growing autonomy and power of this political class.

These distinctive policies of the Afrikaner nationalists cast further light on their power base and methods of political mobilization. Like other NP policies they were tailored to secure the interests of their constituency and/or to consolidate their power base. How did the Afrikaners, comprising 12 per cent of the population, get away with this?

The failure of opposition
The failure of the economically-dominant English to stop the Nationalists led many observers to deduce that they must have wanted their race policies. Some English did support some Nationalist policies, but there was also opposition from them, as well of course as from blacks. Moreover this widespread opposition was not simply dissolved with a whiff of grapeshot. The stream of repressive legislation, arrests, detentions, trials and elaboration of the police state apparatus—all this accumulating horror was testimony to the seriousness of their opposition. But they all failed to stop the Nationalists from achieving their objectives, namely priority for the interests of Afrikaners and the establishment of a republic under exclusive Afrikaner domination; the entrenchment of the eroding apartheid structure; and the strengthening of the state as an instrument to achieve these

*In 1977, 60 per cent of Afrikaners and 22 per cent of English supported the policy, though Afrikaners were *less* willing than the English to pay for it by providing more land and development funds.[62]

objectives and to crush opposition. The reasons for the Nationalists' success included the efficiency and ruthlessness of their shock tactics, as well as the divisions, disarray and often ambivalence of their opponents.

'The English' were a composite group, including immigrants and refugees from Germany, Russia and other European countries. They all adopted the English language, and many developed an attachment to British institutions and traditions, but they lacked the social cohesion of the Afrikaners; indeed it was mainly their dislike and fear of the Afrikaners that held them together. There were also differences of economic interest and attitude among them: support for more liberal race policies came from manufacturing and commercial capital and the intelligentsia in the universities, churches and organizations like the SA Institute of Race Relations; not from English labour and agricultural capital, nor from most mining capitalists.

These differences led to deep divisions in the English-based opposition and to a vacillating, ambiguous policy. The party's two wings were agreed in opposing the undermining of the constitution, the courts, the autonomy of the universities and the Press, and the downgrading of the commonwealth connection. They often disagreed over both security and race legislation, with conservatives supporting the Suppression of Communism and Group Areas Acts, although they agreed in opposing the removal of coloureds from the voters roll and the extension of job reservation.

In an effort to maintain a united front, the UP papered over these differences, but it was shifting to the right. This was partly because the right wing had a strong grip on the party organization, reflecting the rural bias of the political system as well as the party's federal structure, which favoured the smaller, more conservative Natal and OFS provinces at the expense of the Transvaal and Cape. It was also the result of the UP's political strategy, based on the belief that they could defeat the NP at the polls by winning back 'moderate' Afrikaners. The narrowness of the NP's victory in 1948 made this seem an attainable goal until the 1953, or even 1958, elections.

However, Afrikaners were unlikely to desert the party taking such good care of their interests. The NP's electoral and constitutional jerrymandering also decreased the chances of defeating them at the polls.* Much of the UP's energy was expended in opposing measures designed to strengthen the Nationalists' initially precarious majority and to perpetuate their hold on power.

The UP provided a broadly-based opposition which had some effect in limiting the Nationalist onslaught, particularly on independent English institutions such as the universities and the Press. In this they were aided by the opposition of Afrikaans institutions such as the trade unions, Press and universities, whose dislike of interference with their *'own* rights and autonomy acted as a constraint on the NP's authoritarian tendencies,** and helped to prevent SA from becoming a fully totalitarian state.

But the UP's ineffectual opposition, geared to white electoral politics, with its inbuilt advantage for the conservatives, alienated it from blacks and dismayed its liberal supporters, who sought more effective extra-parliamentary means of opposition, using their Press, churches and other institutions and establishing new organizations such as the Black Sash and the Torch Commando. By 1952 the latter had 125,000 paid-up members and organized some of the largest mass protests and demonstrations yet seen in SA. The United South African Trust Fund, supported by English businessmen like Oppenheimer, raised large sums of money for these campaigns.[65]

Businessmen, all the same, were not ready to back the multi-racial Liberal Party, formed by Alan Paton and Margaret Ballinger after the 1953 election. Initially, the party supported a qualified

---

*For example, the removal of the coloured franchise in disregard of the special procedures laid down in the Act of Union; the creation in 1949 of six seats for the relatively small number of Nationalist-supporting voters in South West Africa, resulting in their 'spectacular over-representation' in Parliament[63] (as well as in the incorporation of the mandated territory into SA in defiance of the UN); the halting of the immigration programme to bring in (non-Afrikaans) whites; and the 1949 Citizenship Act, which made it more difficult for immigrants to qualify for the vote. In 1958 the voting age was lowered to eighteen, favouring Afrikaners with their more youthful population; in 1959 the Natives Representatives in parliament were abolished.

**Evident, for example, in the 1942 statement by Ben Schoeman, later Minister of Labour, that all trade unions were unnecessary because 'wage control and fixation should be in the hands of the state . . . self-government in industry and collective bargaining . . . should be eliminated from our economic life.'[64]

non-racial franchise; by the end of the decade, under the influence of its growing black membership, it adopted a policy of universal adult suffrage. The Liberal Party broadened its contacts with the black opposition, and played an active role in the gathering international campaign against Nationalist policies, but it made little impact on the white electorate. The Progressives, who broke away from the UP after the 1958 election, received more financial support from business, but in the 1961 election, only one of their twelve MPs, Helen Suzman, was re-elected to parliament. A major reason for the rightward trend of the electorate, despite continuing hostility between the English and Afrikaners, was fear about security.

White fears

Unrest within SA and in Africa, the attacks on SA at the UN, and cold war propaganda, fanned fears about violence and revolution. Whites were alarmed by the riots during the 1950s in the eastern Cape, Sekukuniland and Transkei, and by the Mau Mau in Kenya, vividly described in lurid press reports of whites savagely murdered by Africans. There was widespread uncertainty and fear even among liberals about the consequences of extending political rights. These fears were not just about whether Africans could manage a sophisticated economy and whether they would treat whites justly (as whites knew they had not treated them); whites were also fearful about their physical security.

The Nationalists were prone to these fears, which were part of their historical tradition. They were also skilful at stirring them up: *swart gevaar* propaganda was drummed into the white electorate over the state radio and propaganda organs. In fact, there was relatively little violence against whites, few of whom were killed or injured either in Kenya or in SA, where the government remained able to contain the unrest with a police force of less than 30,000 men in 1958 for a total population of 15m.[66] But fear and hysteria were politically useful to the government, and they stirred them up.

These psychological factors also affected white liberals, who were products of their time, influenced by its myths and prejudices. Their mental horizons were shifting, but slowly. There were not yet in Africa models of technologically advanced societies successfully run by blacks, nor of whites living securely under black rule. The upheaval which accompanied the emergence of independent African states temporarily exacerbated white fears that they would not be safe under black rule. Because of these security fears, the pressure for major political changes had to come from blacks, who were still too weak and unorganized to apply it.

The gulf between white liberals and blacks was deepened by class and cultural differences, and by enforced segregation. The importance of these factors can be seen by comparing the situation in the 1950s with that in the 1970s, when the emergence of substantial numbers of blacks with similar education and life-styles made cooperation easier, despite their greater militancy.

Even those whites who did not like Nationalist race policies, or believed they would in the long run prove unworkable, wanted strong government, and fears over security inhibited their willingness to rock the boat. And—whether or not they liked it—they were in the same boat. They might want to change the way in which the boat was managed, or the direction in which it was headed, but they did not want to overturn it, remembering Hilaire Belloc's adage: 'Always keep a hold of nurse, for fear of finding something worse.' The fear of finding something worse was a potent factor influencing the political behaviour of many of the Nationalists' opponents—a fear fed by the very radicalization of black politics which Nationalist policies, and black despair of finding influential white allies, helped to cause.

The black opposition

During the 1950s, there was a great deal of opposition from blacks. The ANC's cautious policies were challenged by younger members, whose 1949 Programme of Action recommended passive resistance and strikes. Closer links were established with the Communist Party, whose influence was evident in the drafting of the 1956 Freedom Charter.* In 1959, partly in reaction against the growth of (mainly white) communist influence, the Africanists broke away and formed the Pan Africanist Congress (PAC).

As Gerhart has pointed out, PAC policy is more in the tradition of the orthodox, Black Power nationalists found in the rest of

---

*For example, in the proposal that 'the mineral wealth of our country, the banks and monopoly industry shall be transferred to the ownership of the people as a whole.'

Africa than is the non-racial doctrine of the ANC. PAC's social base was more middle-class, younger, and more educated than that of the ANC; teachers and high school students were prominent in its ranks. Another component of its support were the *tsotsis*—young, unemployed, urban blacks, more educated than the proletariat, but unable to break into the ranks of the petty bourgeoisie: they comprised a 'politically volatile element . . . frustrated and prone to violence'.[67]

The black opposition, too, was rent by divisions and failures of political strategy. Luthuli, the ANC president, remarked on the leadership's remoteness from the masses.[67a] This gulf seemed evident in the lack of support for its major campaigns to boycott Bantu education schools and resist the Western Areas removal scheme. Most people were unwilling to sacrifice the education of their children, or to turn down improved housing. Even during the regressive 1950s, their material needs constrained the willingness of many blacks to support a boycott strategy which often focussed on issues of symbolic significance to the elite, but costly to the masses.

Ethnic divisions among the opposition remained deep. The congress movement, despite its commitment to non-racialism, found it expedient to retain separate organizations for Africans, coloureds, Indians and whites, which coordinated their activities at leadership level. The 1949 anti-Indian riots by Africans in Durban were an indication of grass-roots hostilities which their leaders could not always control and which the government could manipulate.

Another instance of the difficulties of working across race lines was the lack of cooperation between the English and the coloureds, despite the fact that much of the political energy of both groups was centred on the campaign to defend the coloured vote. The class and cultural gap between them was even greater than between coloureds and Afrikaners. The racism of the conservative English (and their concern to win support from 'moderate' Afrikaners) even led them to oppose the inclusion of coloureds in the Torch Commando. The non-racialism of the liberals precluded them from 'ganging up' with the coloureds against Afrikaners or Africans.

There were also obstacles to cooperation from the coloured side. Rejected, frustrated and alienated, the well-educated, articulate coloured leadership was often more vigorous in condemning the weak, half-hearted defence of their rights by the equivocal UP than the overtly discriminatory policies of the Nationalists. Some of them claimed they preferred 'the straightforwardness of the Nationalists to the hypocrisy of the English'. (As Dahrendorf remarked, when people who are antipathetic to one another have to live together, hypocrisy can be a 'public virtue'.[68])

There was continued bitter in-fighting between liberals and communists, much of it, as before, over seemingly remote international issues. The members of the opposition often fought each other with greater ferocity than they attacked the government; it seemed a symptom of their growing demoralization and despair—and it was safer.

The cohesion and solidarity of the Nationalists, by contrast, was reinforced by their powers of patronage and by educational and cultural policies which welded Afrikaners together. The Nationalists were also skilful in wielding and consolidating their power. They approached their objectives cautiously, observing some of the legalities, picking off their opponents one by one, while trying to win over the doubters in their own ranks and to neutralize the opposition of the English conservatives. For example, they did not, in stormtrooper fashion, immediately throw the coloureds off the voters' roll. They first fought it through parliament, then through the Courts, and finally resorted to a complicated legalistic device which bored most people, whose attention was by then absorbed by other issues. There seemed no point during the long-drawn-out process at which the government's opponents could agree to rally their forces and confront them.

In 1948 SA was an oligarchic democracy which seemed on the verge of gradually incorporating the black vanguard into its ranks. By 1960 this process had been unambiguously reversed and the Nationalists had transformed their precarious hold on power into an iron grip. In defiance of world trends, they pushed back the black elite and reinforced the hierarchical race structure. SA was also losing its democratic features and acquiring many of the characteristics of a police state. There were three main mechanisms whereby this transformation was effected:

(i) *Direct coercion*: While the Nationalists were cautious and preferred to observe the legalities, they did not conceal the jackboot. Black activists, and whites who supported them or promoted inter-racial cooperation which undermined the divide-and-rule policy, were subjected to political intimidation and physical violence. Savage penalties, including banning, house arrest, heavy fines and whipping, were imposed for non-violent, passive resistance to apartheid measures. Opponents were subjected to police surveillance and harassment, to possible loss of jobs and, for Africans, endorsement out of the urban areas. As demonstrators got beaten up, and activists tortured, their numbers shrank. The fear of physical violence had a major effect on the black and radical opposition (as it did on the white electorate). The government knew this; hence its willingness to display the jackboot, despite the ignominy this brought it in western circles.

(ii) *Indirect coercion* : One of the hallmarks of Nationalist rule was the vast network of bureaucratic controls, which bore heaviest on Africans but affected other groups as well. The most important controls were the pass laws, governing not only African mobility but also access to jobs, housing and the right to have their families live with them, thus giving officials immense power over the basic requirements of existence. A large network of informers ensured that they could be used against the government's opponents. These controls intimidated, exhausted and demoralised people and deterred them from stepping out of line. Another deterrent was the prospect of lengthy and costly Court cases, such as the four-year treason trial, involving 156 leading opposition members (including whites). The expansion of the role and powers of the state gave officials a subtler range of pressures which could be used on coloureds, Indians and whites. Coloureds and Indians needed official approval for housing, business, and even advanced educational opportunities. Whites needed licences and permits for imports, labour, the siting of factories, government contracts, foreign exchange and travel abroad. The use of these ever-expanding powers ensured the compliance of most blacks and whites. The police and armed forces were seldom required, and did not during this period grow as fast as the bureaucracy. Indirect bureaucratic coercion was the Nationalists' major control mechanism.[69]

(iii) *Psychological and ideological controls* : The astute use of their propaganda organs, and censorship of opposing views, enabled the Nationalists to stir up fear and racism, thus consolidating their own base, neutralizing much English opposition, and deepening the divisions among their opponents. This process was aided by institutionalized social and political separation, which made it difficult for blacks and whites to establish working political relationships, or even to get to know one another.

The whole opposition was taken aback by the Nationalists' shock tactics and demoralized by the daunting problem of confronting an efficient and ruthless government, equipped with the full range of modern methods of coercion and propaganda, and with little respect for constitutional rights, legal procedures, and 'the rules of the game'. How should the Johannesburg City Council react when the government rode roughshod over their opposition to the Western Areas removals? What should the universities do when apartheid was forced on them despite their protests? It was against their traditions and beliefs to act illegally— let alone to resort to violence. Even the ANC remained reluctant to resort to such methods; there were growing doubts about this among its supporters, but the commitment to constitutionalism, the rule of law and non-violence was still deep. They had, moreover, good practical reasons for keeping down the level of violence when they were unarmed and likely to be the main sufferers from it. But the inability of the white and black opposition to halt the brutal Nationalist offensive hastened their decline and led to increased support for, or at least acquiescence in, government policies.

The opposition were also at a disadvantage ideologically. They had predicted that Nationalist policies would be unworkable—but they *were* working. Their alternative policies meanwhile were experimental and uncertain, and there were not yet relevant models of success to which they could point. In time this would change: many Nationalist policies would prove unworkable, while the uncertainties and risks of opposition policies would seem to offer at least the prospect of a long-term solution; but that time had not yet come.

In the meantime, the Nationalists could ridicule opposition policies and point confidently to their own success and achievements—and there were some achievements to point to. The Nationalists were not only brutal policemen; they were also efficient administrators and innovative managers and entrepreneurs. They were committed to the country and, unlike the Europe-oriented elites of Latin-America with their Swiss bank accounts, they reinvested their profits (and forced others to do likewise) to develop what was Africa's leading economy. These achievements were not, as they claimed, theirs alone: blacks and the English contributed massively to them, while Nationalist policies set back the country's social and political development. But the growth and modernization of the SA economy continued under their aegis; its effects were valued not only by themselves but also by many English and blacks, and this reduced their willingness to overturn the boat.

The argument that failure to stop the Nationalists from implementing apartheid labour policies demonstrates that manufacturing (the leading growth sector) *must* have wanted these policies, is based on a mistaken assessment of both the interests and power of manufacturing capital, and an over-simple view of how politics works. It overlooks the importance of fear, uncertainty and risk on behaviour, and the effect of failure in demoralising and discouraging people (white as well as black) from trying to achieve what they want; and, conversely, the importance of success in persuading them to acquiesce in policies they do not like.

This argument also mistakenly assumes that those opposed to a government will resist it tenaciously all the time, and on all issues. In SA, neither the English nor the blacks opposed the government all the time, or on all issues—except for a tiny minority totally committed to the political struggle. Most people functioned within the system in which they found themselves, even if they would have preferred to change at least parts of it. Their failure to secure changes was not necessarily because they did not want them, but because they lacked the power to achieve them and/or found the costs and risks too high. This sounds obvious, but it is the opposite assumption of political behaviour which underlies the analyses contested here. Moreover, while English manufacturing capital opposed Nationalist labour policies during the 1950s and 1960s, there were other Nationalist policies to which they were not opposed, such as industrial protection. They therefore operated within a system, parts of which they tried (unsuccessfully) to change, but other parts of which they accepted.

The contradictory effects of the Sharpeville crisis, 1960–68
The widespread internal unrest and international outcry to which the 1960 Sharpeville shootings gave rise (see p. 29) caused alarm

within the oligarchy. For the first time, appeals by liberals and business organizations to 'redress grievances' of blacks received support from sections of the Afrikaner Nationalist establishment, notably the AHI, SABRA (Afrikaans equivalent of the Institute of Race Relations), and *Die Burger*. Senior Cape ministers like Donges and Sauer called for concessions to the coloureds and more evidence of the 'positive' aspects of separate development.[70]

It even seemed that concessions similar to those of the 1940s might be made: the pass laws were suspended and black wages raised. But when Verwoerd recovered from the assassination attempt on his life by a white liberal, he opposed concessions, accused businessmen of 'paving the way for black domination' (see p. 151) and dealt peremptorily with the SABRA reformists, whose leader, Nick Olivier, was driven out of the NP and Broederbond. Verwoerd forced the Dutch Reformed Churches to dissociate themselves from the resolutions taken at their 1960 Cottesloe conference condemning the migrant labour system, and to purge themselves of dissidents like Beyers Naude. The NP's Federal Council backed him in opposing concessions to coloureds.

The black and non-racial opposition was smashed: the 1960 Unlawful Organizations Act enabled the government to ban the ANC and PAC; the African trade unions were decimated by bannings and intimidation. Henceforth, any form of African organization (even cultural and sporting) was discouraged. African townships observing the stay-at-home, like Langa near Cape Town, were ringed by police and army, who moved into them, beating up people indiscriminately. This show of force frightened people and helped to break the stay-at-home strike. Hundreds of people were detained, including white liberals and communists, and the first big wave of political exiles left. The government was glad to see them go, but they played a leading role in organizing the international anti-apartheid campaign which later caused the government so much trouble. However, their departure, and the imprisonment of Congress and liberal leaders after Rivonia and other trials, weakened the opposition.

The government skilfully exploited white fears of violence. Against the background of unrest in the Congo, and the threat of international sanctions against SA, whites were alarmed by the mass march of blacks from Langa to Cape Town. These events increased their fear of rocking the boat. Faced with the failure of pressures for reform, and the government's success in re-establishing law and order, businessmen rallied round to stabilize the economy.*

So, while Sharpeville confirmed the existence of pressures for reform, it also illustrated the government's strength and the weakness of the opposition. Blacks were unable to sustain mass action; progressive capital was unable to make the Nationalists change course. Instead of Sharpeville generating a new wave of resistance, it marked the peak of twelve years of opposition, which collapsed soon after, giving the government little trouble for another dozen years.

However, the Nationalists were alarmed by the wide-ranging hostility, particularly by the sharp business reaction and the flight of foreign capital. They responded with a contradictory package of policies, which made some concessions to their critics, while increasing their capacity to withstand opposition.

There was an enormous accretion in the power of the state. The standing army of under 8,000 men and defence budget of R44m in 1961 were increased to almost 44,000 men and a budget of R257m in 1971; while the fear of sanctions led to the strengthening of the heavy industrial and (mainly nationalized) armaments sectors and state stockpiling of oil. By 1980 SA was a very significant armaments producer and had attained a high degree of self-sufficiency in energy (see p. 246). The scale of these efforts—far in excess of the requirements of the local situation—partly reflected the impact of international pressures, including the threat of economic sanctions (imposed on Rhodesia in 1966) as well as promised international support for the armed struggle, to which the exiled ANC and PAC were now committed. These threats also intensified the trend towards authoritarianism, evident, for example, in the 1962 General Law Amendment and 1967 Terrorism Acts, which extended the power of the police and executive at the expense of

---

*A leading businessman later wrote that businessmen were 'torn between loyalty to SA, hostility towards the government and concern over internal security' and that in conflicts with government they felt they had to 'work within the framework of the law . . . [and could not] move beyond the subtle and undefined boundary of public or political acceptability'.[71] Until the significant increase in black bargaining power from the mid-1970s, these political pressures came largely from the right.

the judiciary, by the power to detain suspects indefinitely without trial.

Economically, the Nationalists acted swiftly to stem the flood of capital 'deserting' SA in its hour of need. In 1961 import controls prevented SA residents from remitting funds abroad and prohibited the repatriation of foreign capital, although not of dividends. Expansionary economic policies were adopted to encourage manufacturing and build up a capital goods sector. Manufacturing replaced agriculture as the favoured sector: in addition to protection, domestic procurement, and cheap raw materials and capital goods, steel and food prices, previously above world levels, were now kept below international levels.[72]

But these developments do not support the argument that the Nationalists were 'saved' by foreign and English capital and that they, in turn, adopted the labour policies these groups really wanted. Foreign capital deserted them in their hour of need; the boom which began at the end of 1961 was achieved without foreign capital, which only began to return on a significant scale in 1965.[73] Many English capitalists also tried to get their money out before exchange controls were clamped down, but most of them were trapped. The collapse of share and property prices meant they were stuck with their assets—in the same boat as the Nationalists. Moreover, while they did not like the government's labour policies, these were not their sole concern: they also wanted the restoration of political stability. Against the background of events in the Congo, this was a high priority for practically all whites, whatever their disagreements with other NP policies.

The government, for its part, did not adopt a policy of priority for manufacturing in response to pressures from English and foreign capital, but in order to increase economic self-sufficiency and to provide jobs and entrepreneurial opportunities for its own supporters. It was determined, moreover, that the development of industry should not undermine, but fit in with, the apartheid framework, and that Afrikaners should have a major share of the benefits of expansion. In this latter aim they were successful. Afrikaans businessmen, and financial institutions like SANLAM, bought shares at rock-bottom prices after Sharpeville. By the end of the 1960s boom, Afrikaners owned a bigger share of the economy (see Table 13). They also increased the share they controlled via the state sector, with the expansion of state enterprises such as SASOL and Iscor, and the establishment of new state corporations such as Armscor, Soekor and Alusaf. The Afrikaners thus emerged from the Sharpeville crisis owning or controlling a larger share of the economy and with a greatly expanded state apparatus.

Moreover, while businessmen were relieved by the restoration of political stability and the expansionary economic policies, *they were not converted to support for apartheid labour policies*. On the contrary, the economic boom intensified the costs of apartheid and increased their pressures against it (see Chapters 6 and 8). Relations between government and capital were therefore complex: there were areas of common interest (economic growth, political stability) and areas of conflict (labour policy, expansion of the state sector).

White unity?

Some NP leaders argued that, in view of internal unrest and external pressures, more conciliatory policies should be adopted towards foreign capital and the English. Henceforth, foreign capital was actively courted as a source of investment and technology for manufacturing, and as a shield against international isolation.[74] A couple of English political appointments were made to the Cabinet and Senate. White immigrants, including those from Britain, were again sought to strengthen the white group and ease the skill shortage (see p. 34).

These more conciliatory policies towards the English (and foreign capital) were opposed by the smaller Afrikaans capitalists and by *verkrampte* ideologists and politicians.[75] *Volkshandel*, journal of the AHI, periodically railed against the stronghold of foreign companies on the SA economy, complaining that they did not use their own money but raised it locally and were pushing out smaller firms.[76]

The militants also disliked the gestures to the English and the immigration policy. Albert Hertzog, Minister of Health and Communications, and Piet Meyer, head of the SA Broadcasting Corporation (SABC) and chairman of the Broederbond, argued that Afrikaners were the only true South Africans, and that the English must be Afrikanerised before they could be accepted as equals.[77]

The reasons for continuing militancy were not simply emotional and ideological, although these were important elements in the attitudes of intellectuals like Hertzog and Meyer. There was still a long queue of *boeties* wanting *baantjies*—seats in parliament and the cabinet, ambassadorships, government licences and contracts, which they did not want to share with the English. The gulf between English and Afrikaners had also been widened by the bitter disputes of the last decade and by the NP's systematic segregation of the two groups in their separate schools and organizations. The leadership, uncertain and divided over this issue, found it difficult to change this quickly; conciliation of the English remained at the level of tokenism.

However, the security threat ensured the begrudging acquiescence of most English in Nationalist rule; so did the growing international campaign against SA, which alienated the English from their British connections, especially after the United Kingdom imposed sanctions on Rhodesia. In the 1966 election, the Nationalists got an estimated 16 per cent of English votes.[78] But their support remained limited and most English resented the tokenism; the few who joined the Nationalists were unrepresentative and were cold-shouldered.

The fact that the English, despite their stated dislike of many Nationalist policies, prospered under their rule, led the Nationalists (and others) to accuse them of hypocrisy, and to taunt them with their irrelevance and carping, unconstructive criticism. *Die Burger* joked that the English 'joined the Progressives, voted for the UP, and thanked God for the Nationalists'. This view underestimated the resentment and alienation of many English. Its effects were the political apathy and cynicism that powerlessness, guilt and loss of self-respect breed. Alienation also drove some of them into exile, where they became activists in the international campaign against apartheid.

Despite the urgent security situation, it was not therefore a state of 'white unity' that prevailed within the oligarchy, but rather what Weber termed government by 'minimum consent', with the opposition conducting 'negative politics' and playing a spoiling role as 'impotent fault-finders'.[79]

Negative politics, the result of exclusion from power and responsibility, affected the whole opposition, whose militant rhetoric and infighting rose in proportion to their declining organization and influence. An extreme example was the 'non-collaboration' policy of the Trotskyites (mainly teachers, lawyers, students) who dominated coloured politics, and whose influence inhibited the strategically placed coloureds from cooperating either with white liberals or with the Congresses.

The material concessions to blacks after Sharpeville (see p. 36) contributed to declining unrest. But Verwoerd also became convinced of the need for political concessions, arguing that 'one cannot govern without taking into account world trends and also trends in Africa.' This led him to set up the separate development institutions and, in 1963, to launch Transkei on its path to independence. He explained: 'In the light of the pressures being exerted on SA, there is no doubt that eventually this will have to be done, thereby buying for the white man his freedom and right to govern himself.'[80] This was hardly the 'concession' his critics had in mind, but it was an indication that external pressures had an impact, though their effects could be unintended.

The expansion of the state machinery greatly strengthened the Nationalists, while the opposition was further weakened by the brutal government assault and by their own divisions. In the face of this huge disparity in power, particular significance attached to the growing dissension within the NP over the post-Sharpeville changes in policy, which led to splits in the party under Verwoerd's successor, B. J. Vorster.

The *verkrampte–verligte* struggle, 1968–78

Rapid economic growth and 'Afrikaners first' policies reshaped Afrikaans society, leading to the emergence of a class of urban and mining capitalists and transforming Afrikaans labour into a bureaucracy. The origins of the *verligte/verkrampte* split lay in the diverging interests of these classes. The reforms of the 1970s were a sign of the growing influence of the *verligtes*; but their limited nature, and the difficulties in implementing them, indicated the continuing power of *verkramptes*. These conflicts, and the growing difficulties of party management, accounted for the contradictions of NP policy and the indecision and paralysis that characterised Vorster's last years in office. They provide a further instance of the threat that diverging class interests posed to Afrikaner solidarity. Being in office, the NP was able to use the resources of state to delay, though not prevent, a split.

Growing class divisions among Afrikaners

By 1970 Afrikaners were no longer a nation of farmers and workers with a small petty bourgeoisie. Only 8 per cent were still economically active in agriculture, while 88 per cent were urbanized. 27 per cent of Afrikaners were still in blue-collar work, while those in white-collar jobs (albeit many at a low level) increased to 65 per cent (see Table 13).

The Afrikaans share of ownership of the private sector rose from 3 per cent of manufacturing and construction before World War Two to 15 per cent in 1975; from 5 to 21 per cent of finance; and from 1 to 30 per cent of mining. It was estimated that the total Afrikaans share of the private sector outside agriculture (which they already dominated) rose from less than 10 per cent in 1948 to 25 per cent in 1978. Afrikaans incomes increased much faster than those of the English, narrowing the Afrikaans–English per capita income ratio from 100 to 211 in 1946 to 100 to 141 in 1976. (This continuing gap was partly due to larger Afrikaans families).[81] The class structure of Afrikaners had therefore become more similar to that of the English. One of the differences was the high proportion of Afrikaners employed in the state sector: 36 per cent, compared with 14 per cent of English.

These changes in class structure were soon accompanied by changes in attitude. Opinion surveys showed increasing support among Afrikaners for more *verligte* policies. The proportion favouring mixed sport rose from 4 per cent in 1970 to 76 in 1978; of those who would accept blacks in the same jobs as whites, from 38 to 62 per cent. However, the polls also showed that, while the gap between English and Afrikaans attitudes was narrowing, the English were still more liberal: in 1977, Schlemmer found that 78 per cent of Afrikaners still supported 'a consistent policy of apartheid' compared to only 25 per cent of English.[82]

The narrowing of the gap in English–Afrikaans views on race as their economic interests became more similar, shows that class was an important factor shaping attitudes. But the continued differences, holding class and education constant, show that class was not the only factor. Other factors were the more systematic indoctrination of separatist views among Afrikaners; their embodiment in a system of separate cultural and social institutions; the time lags before attitudes adjust to changing circumstances;

and continuing class differences between Afrikaners and the English, who still dominated the private sector outside agriculture, despite the striking Afrikaans gains.

Research surveys also confirmed the observation that support for reforms came from the more educated, higher-income Afrikaners, while those with less education and lower incomes tended to be more racist.[83] *Verligtes* included a wide cross-section of the Afrikaans elite: professionals, a section of the intelligentsia, some of the top echelons of the civil service (particularly economists, diplomats, the military) and leading businessmen like Rupert, Wim and Dawie de Villiers, Wassenaar, Hupkes and Jan Marais, many associated with Cape-based firms, which had expanded throughout SA.

Cape capital had close links with Nasionale Pers, publishers of *Die Burger*, which later established *Rapport* and *Beeld* newspapers in the Transvaal, where its intrusion was resented by the provincial NP hierarchy. The Afrikaans press also had close links with the NP: cabinet ministers sat on the Boards of Nasionale and of its northern rival, Perskor. But from the late 1960s, Afrikaans newspapers became more independent and critical, stimulated by the circulation battle developing between the two groups.[84]

While the *verligtes* were Afrikaners who had made it and no longer needed protection against blacks, English or foreigners, *verkramptes* still wanted the retention of 'Afrikaners first' policies. They tended to be the less well-off and less educated, although they also got support from those with a vested interest in nationalism (teachers, clergy) and in continued Afrikaner hegemony (the political and bureaucratic establishment).

The *verkramptes* were not confined to the small group of purists who broke away with Albert Hertzog to form the HNP in 1969. A larger rump remained within the NP and its parapoliticals, including Piet Meyer, head of the SABC, and Andries Treurnicht, leader of the Transvaal NP, both of whom served as chairmen of the Broederbond. The HNP established its own weekly newspaper, *Die Afrikaner*, with funds controlled by Albert Hertzog, and sought support from smaller farmers and from trade unions: Gert Beetge of the Building Workers and Arrie Paulus of the MWU were leading members.

The NP *verkramptes* were strongly represented in the party organization and caucus and in the parapoliticals, and drew their support from white workers and the lower-middle levels of the bureaucracy. In departments like BAD and Community Relations, their strength went right to the top. They were supported by the Pretoria newspaper, *Hoofstad*, and the Perskor group, published by Marius Jooste. They also had their intelligentsia in the universities and particularly the Church.[85]

Vorster's policies reflect the changing power balance

The declining power of white agriculture was evident in changes in labour policy (see p. 96), as well as in the movement of prices against agriculture and in the reduction of concessional freight rates and of support for marginal farmers. Farmers complained that industrial protection raised their costs, for example of trucks and fertilizers.[86] The industry–agriculture protection deal came under attack from both sides as its costs to both parties rose.

The erosion of apartheid labour policies was evidence of the declining influence of white labour, as was their declining share of the wage bill. Vorster handled white labour skilfully, avoiding a confrontation with the MWU, which openly defied government policy by their refusal to relax the job bar in Bantustan mines (see p. 118). Among the reasons for Vorster's caution was the concern expressed by mining MPs, such as Cas Greyling, in the caucus and the growing support for the HNP among white miners, who shouted down Nationalist MPs at by-election meetings. The government condemned the MWU's stance, but did not force the issue, concentrating instead on isolating the MWU from other unions and from white public opinion, which had been so important in 1922. Indicative of changing public opinion were the attacks on the MWU by the *verligte* Afrikaans press, which accused it (on the issue of skilled work in Bantustan mines) of attacking the 'whole being' of NP policy and urged the government to 'call its bluff'.[87]

It is doubtful whether a non-Afrikaans government could have secured such a peaceful adaptation by white labour. However, the Wiehahn recommendations were a shock to SACOL, which claimed it had been misled by the government (see p. 205); thereafter relations between the NP and SACOL deteriorated.

Parri passu with the declining influence of white agriculture and labour, there was an improvement in government relations with urban and mining capital. By the late 1960s, the government shared mineowners' anxiety about high skilled labour costs: many marginal mines were heavily subsidised and closure would have had serious consequences for SA's deteriorating balance of payments (see pp. 117 and 240). Relations between mining capital and government had also improved; the mines were by now largely SA-owned and had diversified into other sectors of the economy and therefore become less hostile to the industrialization policy.* Moreover, Afrikaners had acquired a stake in the mining industry. In 1964, Federale Mynbou took over General Mining, increasing the Afrikaans share of gold mining from 1 to 9 per cent and giving them interests in uranium, coal and asbestos. Federale were assisted in this takeover by AAC, because Oppenheimer believed that greater Afrikaans involvement would lead to more sympathy for business problems in government circles.[89] In 1968, Tom Muller, chairman of Federale and brother of the Minister of Foreign Affairs, became the first Afrikaans President of the Chamber of Mines. The superior access of Afrikaners to officials and cabinet ministers also contributed to the appointment of Desmond Krogh and, later, Hennie Reynders as Directors of the (predominantly English) FCI.

The growing influence of urban and mining capital was evident not only in changes in labour policy but also in non-racial policies, for example concerning the state sector. Afrikaans capitalists like Wassenaar, Wessels and Coetzer of Federale Mynbou, added their voice to the complaints that English businessmen had long made about 'creeping socialism'.[90] The government set up a committee to enquire into state sector 'encroachments' and IDC and Iscor announced they would sell off some of their interests to the private sector.[91]

Social policy illuminates the changing power balance

Social policy was a revealing indicator of the changing power balance within the oligarchy and of the growing impact of external pressures. Opinion polls bear out the expectation that whites were *more* conservative about social, than about economic and political

---

*In its evidence to the Viljoen Commission, the Chamber of Mines conceded that the mining industry had ultimately derived benefits from the establishment of state industries like Iscor, which kept the price of SA steel below international levels in the post-war period.[88]

policies. In 1969–72, when the relaxation of social apartheid began, only 4 per cent of Afrikaners (the crucial electoral group) favoured mixed sport, 90 per cent were against mixed marriages and 85 per cent against mixed social gatherings. Even in 1977, only 19 per cent of Afrikaners favoured the use by blacks of white recreation areas, compared with 62 per cent who accepted the admission of blacks to the same jobs and at the same salaries as whites, and 47 per cent who favoured recognition of African unions.[92]

However, most whites adapted more readily than expected once changes were made, as shown by the big increase in the proportion accepting mixed sport (see p. 307). Opinion polls therefore give a useful picture of attitudes and pressures which politicians must cope with at a particular moment, but they are not necessarily good predictors of behaviour; for this an analysis of interests is required.

The crucial factor in the relaxation of 'petty' apartheid was international pressure, interacting with a particularly effective internal pressure group, the Afrikaans *verligtes*. A wide spectrum of the rising Afrikaans elite—sportsmen, academics, journalists, doctors, businessmen, diplomats—found themselves shunned by their peers abroad. Vorster was more responsive to their needs than Verwoerd. He was also persuaded by their argument that social discrimination constituted a barrier to more friendly relations with black elites in Africa, and that the separate development policy would be more defensible if shorn of 'unnecessary discrimination'.

Social apartheid became a major bone of contention between *verligtes* and *verkramptes* because this was the first area in which policy was officially relaxed. The concessions on sport and petty apartheid from 1968 (and the detente policy in Africa) were the first signs of the growing influence of the *verligtes*. Their victory was aided by the lack of organised vested interests opposed to social change; opposition was diffuse and the agitation of the HNP made NP *verkramptes* like Mulder and Treurnicht reluctant to express their distaste too openly. Overt opposition was mainly confined to the local level, which reduced the political costs of social changes. Initially, too, social changes were largely restricted to upper-class whites, to whom they were more acceptable; by 1978, 8 out of 10 five-star hotels were opened to blacks, but only 7 out of 1,112 one-star hotels.[93] Low costs were also a factor from the point of view of the external lobbies; boycotts in this area involving lower costs for SA's friends and enemies alike.

The slow decline of 'Afrikaners first' policies

Policies towards the English and foreign capital were, as before, illuminating in identifying the NP's base and the strength of Afrikaner nationalism. Despite the friendlier rhetoric, there was continuing ambiguity towards foreign capital. Anxiety to attract it led to the award (resented by local mining companies) of generous coal export allocations to foreign oil companies like Shell.[94] But the Nationalists remained determined to control and limit the activities of foreign companies. In 1973, the government announced that it would act on the recommendation of the 1970 Franszen Commission into Fiscal and Monetary Reform by restricting foreign shareholdings in banks and insurance companies to 50 per cent. This stirred up the Afrikaners-versus-English-and-foreigners debate. The Afrikaans press hailed the announcement as the culmination of General Hertzog's 'SA first' policy and a means of countering foreign meddling in SA affairs. The London *Financial Times* and the Johannesburg *Financial Mail* denounced it as a 'nationalistic' banking policy.[95] (This measure was not enforced and was overtaken by Botha's easing of controls on foreign capital, reflecting the *verligtes*' desire to reduce SA's isolation and their willingness to open it to external influences.)

Despite an improvement in Afrikaans–English relations, the English were still excluded from any share in government. They were not consulted over the drafting of the 1977 constitution, which was designed to retain power in Afrikaans, and not simply white, hands. Its tricameral legislature was intended to prevent an alliance between the English and the coloureds and Indians, and to ensure that the English would exercise little leverage as the minority group within the white chamber, where the right to elect the powerful executive President lay with the majority party. Therefore, unless there were further splits within the NP, the country's most powerful economic group (like its most numerous group) would still be excluded from government.

There were continuing attempts to limit the growth of English economic power. In 1977, Iscor announced it would sell Samancor, the West's largest manganese producer. But it drew back when the highest bidder was AAC, refusing to let the leading English corporation expand into another strategic sector. The government also blocked the attempted merger between the English publishing houses Argus and Saan on the grounds that this would lead to a monopoly. Meanwhile, the Afrikaans press received lucrative government printing contracts, for example of telephone directories, enviously described by the much-harassed English press as a 'licence to print money'.

The political struggle

The limited reforms, and continuation of 'Afrikaners first' policies, show that the shift of power was incomplete. Dissatisfaction was sharpened by the disappointment of expectations fuelled by promises of reform. This resulted both in outbursts of anger by blacks (1973 Durban strikes; 1976 Soweto riots) and in the growing barrage of criticism from businessmen and their more effective political mobilization.

The 1970 election marked the first check to the NP's steady increase in votes and seats since 1948. For the first time there was a modest swing to the left (i.e. towards less racist policies). Most HNP candidates lost their deposits; the UP/Progressives gained. In the 1974 and 1977 elections, the Progressives began to displace the UP as a smaller but more liberal opposition. The ethnic divide within the oligarchy also began to break down, as the English conservatives moved towards the Nationalists, who won an estimated third of the English vote in 1977.

After the defeat of the HNP in the 1970 election, Afrikaans businessmen and press became less inhibited about criticising the government and supporting the demands for reform that came from English capital. In 1971/72, leading Afrikaans businessmen, including Wassenaar, C. H. J. van Aswegen, Marais and Rupert, were reported to be urging support for a 'reform-minded' coalition more sympathetic to business interests. The Nationalists reacted sharply to these manoeuvres: Trust Bank lost millions of rands of official third-party insurance investment funds, which the parliamentary opposition claimed were withdrawn to punish its chairman, Jan Marais.[96] Theo Gerdener, leading *verligte* in the cabinet, was frozen out of the NP and established the Democratic Party, with financial backing from Rupert. Nevertheless, the government did also make its first concessions, including the adoption of Gerdener's policy of narrowing the wage gap and the crucial 1973 reforms on the job and training bars (see p. 59).

Despite its huge majority, the government was extremely nervous about the first public changes, such as the introduction in 1971 of black bank tellers at Barclays working alongside whites and the 'multi-national' banquet given by Hastings Banda, President of Malawi, during his state visit to SA, which were headlined in the press and fiercely attacked by the *verkramptes*.* History had taught the Nationalist leadership to fear challenges from the right. The *verkramptes* were strongly represented in the party organisation and parliamentary caucus and were given an inbuilt advantage by the political system.

Vorster argued that SA's interests (economic growth and security) required changes. He possessed impeccable nationalist credentials (he was an ex-Greyshirt, had been interned as a German sympathiser during the war, and had subsequently been the feared Minister of Justice who introduced detention without trial). This, and the discipline and loyalty of party members, enabled him to secure the acquiescence of many doubters to these first steps, and to limit the *verkrampte* breakaway. But he did not rely on appeals to reason and loyalty alone. In the fierce infighting that took place within Afrikanerdom, he acted ruthlessly against the right-wing dissidents, driving Hertzog and his supporters out of the NP, the Broederbond and most of the parapoliticals, and using against them the security police he had controlled as Minister of Justice.[97] The resort to authoritarian measures against right-wing dissidents increased as the reaction against reform built up.

Among the reasons for the reaction were the severe 1974–8 recession, which weakened the pressures for reform and increased white labour's resistance (see p. 209); Vorster's concern to maintain Afrikaner unity and hence his power base; and the collapse of detente with Africa and growing international pressures, which

---

Die Afrikaner frequently carried the photo of Vorster sitting at Banda's banquet between two Malawian women, and at by-elections the HNP plastered this on billboards. Confronted with the deed, Vorster stolidly (if ungallantly) replied, 'I did it in the interests of SA and, if it was necessary for the interests of SA, I would even do it again.'

were a set-back to the *verligtes'* strategy and prestige. The reason for the growth of external pressures was the changing regional and international balance of power, but the fact that pressures increased apace with reforms engendered resentment and undercut the argument that changes would help to reconcile SA with the outside world. Finally, the 1976 Soweto riots and the Angolan debacle earlier that year initially led to a closing of ranks and intensified the backlash.

The *verligtes* were, however, shaken by the riots, with their stark revelation of black hatred of 'separate development,' and by the Angolan debacle and the outcry over the death in detention of Steve Biko, which revealed the extent of SA's isolation internationally. As after Sharpeville, there were pressures for reform rather than reaction, particularly from businessmen, who felt they 'could no longer sit on the sidelines, leaving the process of social change in the hands of politicians'.[98] English and Afrikaans capitalists were now more effectively mobilized in joint organizations like SACCOLA and the Urban Foundation (see p. 160). Their complaints encompassed labour policy, the coloureds and urban blacks, the size of the state sector, SA's international isolation, and Finance Minister Diederichs's costly miscalculations over the gold price. Their barrage of criticism provoked a sharp reaction from Vorster, who denounced in parliament Andries Wassenaar's book, *The Assault on Private Enterprise* (an attack on the state sector)[99] and told English businessmen to stay out of politics (see p. 179). During Muldergate, Afrikaans capitalists were actively involved in the lobbying over Vorster's successor which led to Mulder's narrow defeat by the *verligtes'* candidate P. W. Botha.[100] This paved the way for their closer relationship with him.

Muldergate, the NP and the state

'Politics is the clash of interests masquerading as the strife of principles; or the conduct of public affairs for private advantage.' Ambrose Bierce, *The Devil's Dictionary*.

As Verwoerd used to say, the NP was not merely a political party but a nationalist movement. This, and its long period in office, led its supporters to identify the party with the state, and in their eyes legitimized the exclusion of other groups from government and the concentration of power in the hands of the party/state.*

Throughout the Nationalists' period in office, the executive concentrated power in its own hands at the expense of parliament, the courts and other independent centres of power. Increasingly, ministers were empowered to act by decree, without reference to parliament. Laws could be suspended and exemptions granted; people could be banned, arrested and detained without recourse to the courts; the National Supplies Procurement Act allowed the government huge powers over production and manpower. Growing dissidence within the NP and the difficulties of party management led to increasing authoritariansim within the party itself.

However, the struggle wracking the NP was not only a conflict between the representatives of diverging class interests and ideologies. It was also a power struggle between rival factions or cliques, mostly regionally based, fighting for control of the NP and hence of the state, which the Nationalists increasingly treated as their own private fiefdom. The Cape Nationalists, led by P. W. Botha, the Defence Minister, had close connections with Cape capital and its press, and with the army. The Transvalers, led by Connie Mulder, Minister of Information, were close to the security service BOSS, and to the weaker and less *verligte* Transvaal capitalists (Marius Jooste, Louis Luyt), with whom Mulder's circle was involved in the business deals out of which the Mulder-gate scandal arose.**

*This feature, together with the high level of grass-roots activism, and the strong leadership and strict party discipline (issues were widely discussed, but once the decision was taken, obedience was expected) suggest the NP has much in common with the 'democratic centralist' parties of one-party states like Tanzania and the USSR. The NP shared their intolerance towards opposition and would probably have liked SA to become a one-party state. But with its narrow base it was restrained by the resistance this would have provoked from the English, who were attached to their independent institutions. Curiously, both the NP's grass-roots activism and the strict party discipline and authority of the leadership declined simultaneously.

**The 1978 Erasmus Commission confirmed press revelations that R64m of public funds were illegally appropriated for surreptitious attempts to buy, or set up, English newspapers in SA and abroad; that much of this money could not be accounted for; and that Mulder lied to parliament about these funds.

The exposure of Muldergate by the SA press confirmed that SA was not yet a totalitarian state. There still existed independent institutions, resting heavily on the financial strength of English capital, and commanding sufficient loyalty (from some Afrikaners* as well as English), to enable them to defy the governing NP. Moreover, declining cohesion among Afrikaners was widening their scope for action.

The Nationalists' identification of their interests with those of the state resulted, inevitably, in the blurring of public and private interests and increasing corruption. Initially this was, allegedly, confined to lower-level officials dealing with blacks (passes, permits, etc.); but with the expansion of state power, it seeped to higher levels of the bureaucracy and infected the whole society. Some argue that corruption is functional, oiling the wheels of state and overcoming bureaucratic obstacles.[101] But in SA, it operated as a corrosive rather than a lubricant, undermining the loyalty to the party and state both of those who did not indulge in it (and therefore resented it) and of those who were involved, and whose main concern became the protection of their private rather than of the public interest.

The revelations of corruption also had an impact on rank-and-file supporters, particularly as the NP was a nationalist movement, embodying many of the deepest beliefs of Afrikaners, and with a leadership whose authority was enhanced by the qualities of idealism with which their followers invested them. Muldergate shattered this image. Even amongst the Afrikaans majority who continued to vote Nationalist disillusionment set in, eroding the trust on which the Nationalist leadership had been able to rely and adding to the problems of discipline and party management. Public opinion polls showed a drop in the NP share of the vote from 67 to 58 per cent at the time of Muldergate.[102] This disillusionment coincided with growing doubts about the workability and morality of separate development among Afrikaans intellectuals, which deepened the confusion and disarray in the Nationalist movement and undermined the cohesion essential for Afrikaner hegemony.

*For example, Judge Anton Mostert, who was shocked by the irregularities he was asked to investigate by Vorster and insisted on public disclosure.

The search for a new national identity, 1978–84

'There is nothing more difficult to arrange, more doubtful of success, and more dangerous to carry through, than to initiate a new order.' Niccolo Machiavelli, *The Prince*.

By the late 1970s, there was growing conflict between capital and the bureaucratic/political adherents of apartheid. Capital was now more united by capital-intensity in all sectors and by the emergence of large oligopolistic companies committed to deracialization. The bureaucratic/political class was demonstrating a Weberian autonomy and ability to impose its will, intervening directly in the production process, exerting controls over the movement of both capital and labour, and appropriating 'surplus value' for social purposes as well as for its own enrichment and consolidation of power. Capital was both spurred and strengthened by growing pressures from black labour and the emerging black middle class, encouraged by international support.

Botha's election as party leader and Prime Minister was not a true reflection of the power balance within the NP. If Muldergate had not thrown the *verkramptes* into disarray, Botha's supporters would not have defeated the heir-apparent, Mulder, whose Transvaal base accounted for almost half of Nationalist MPs and had provided all the prime ministers since Malan. Despite Muldergate, Botha was elected by the caucus by only 98 votes to 74 for the disgraced Mulder.

Botha's vulnerability was soon demonstrated by his difficulty in imposing his authority on the party, the caucus and the bureaucracy,* and by the strong electoral swing to the HNP at by-elections. In the 1981 general election, the HNP and Mulder's National Conservative Party together won 17 per cent of the total vote (compared with 3 per cent for the HNP in 1977) and an estimated third of Afrikaans votes. They did not win any seats, but in almost two dozen constituencies reduced the NP majority to less

---

*For example, Botha was forced to drop his 1979 suggestion for reform of the sex laws, while the bureaucracy blocked implementation of concessions to Section 10s (see pp. 72 and 323). Cabinet ministers publicly criticised government decisions: Treurnicht, for instance, condemned the decision to allow coloureds to play in the 1980 Craven rugby school championships, and Botha was unable to prevent Treurnicht's election as Transvaal party leader in 1979/80.

than 2,000 votes. There was also a strong *verkrampte* offensive in the parapoliticals—always an important touchstone of Afrikaner political trends—where the struggle between *verligtes* and *verkramptes* was finely balanced, with the latter well entrenched in the Dutch Reformed Churches.

In 1982, a further *verkrampte* breakaway was precipitated by the proposed new constitution. Treurnicht denounced the government as 'integrationists, power-sharers and sell-outs of the white man's heritage'.[103] Followed by seventeen MPs, he established the Conservative Party (CP) which became the leading party of the right, with its own newspaper, *Die Patriot*. It was estimated that the support of the right-wing parties was 22 per cent of total (and 40 per cent of Afrikaans) voters.[104] The NP's support was down to less than 50 per cent. However, on issues on which Botha was opposed by the right, he could usually rely on support from the NRP and even the PFP.

These political realignments reduced the English/Afrikaans divide. In the 1981 election, the NP won an estimated third of the English vote. The PFP won 60 per cent of the English and 5 per cent of the Afrikaans vote. In the referendum, this inter-ethnic trend was strengthened: Botha received an estimated two-thirds of English votes, including a third of PFP supporters (despite the PFP's opposition to the new constitution, on the grounds that it did not go far enough).

Despite the undoubted shortcomings of the 1983 constitution, opinion polls confirmed that the result was a vote for reform and that, within the white electorate, there was growing support for more *verligte* policies and for 'power sharing' with blacks, including Africans.*

To counter the *verkrampte* threat, Botha resorted to a variety of stratagems, for example the introduction of twelve nominated members of parliament, and the referral of controversial issues to extra-parliamentary committees staffed by his appointees. These manoeuvres culminated in the introduction of the 1983 constitution, whose tortuous design reflected his attempt to retain as much as possible of his Afrikaans base, reinforced by recruits from

---

*In a 1983 survey, Schlemmer found that 58 per cent of NP supporters, and 89 per cent of Progressives, supported power sharing 'with elected leaders of all groups', provided there were 'safeguards against domination'.[105]

among the English, coloureds and Indians, and to strengthen executive powers against challenges from both left and right.

Botha's elaborate 'rationalization' of the civil service was largely undertaken (as such exercises usually are*) in order to place his own men in key positions and to bypass immovable opponents. It also had at least one more substantial effect—the diminishing of Verwoerd's Bantu Affairs empire. Some of its functions were reduced (controls over Section 10s); some were hived off to other departments (labour to the Department of Manpower). This process is obviously a precondition (though not a sufficient condition) for incorporating Africans into a common administrative system.

Unlike Vorster, Botha was prepared to sacrifice Afrikaner unity for broader national objectives, and he began to redefine SA nationalism more broadly. His 'Twelve-point programme' contained no reference to Afrikaners and he urged that people should 'not become so emotional about Afrikaner unity that they lose touch with reality' (see p. 51). His problem was to secure new sources of support quickly enough to compensate for the loss of Afrikaners. Many of his intended supporters were still subject to discrimination. Social and cultural divisions, and the lack of shared political organizations, made it difficult to construct an alliance quickly. Moreover, apart from historical resentments, the leaders of formerly excluded groups had reservations about Botha's limited reform programme, particularly the exclusion of Africans. In a fluid situation, they wanted to keep their options open.

The security threat and growing military influence

When Botha became Prime Minister, he was confronted by widespread internal unrest—the post-Wiehahn wave of strikes and riots and boycotts by black schoolchildren and students. There was also increased external pressure. The 1977 Security Council arms embargo seemed likely to be followed by more boycotts and sanctions; the wars in Namibia and Rhodesia escalated, and were followed by the election of Mugabe in newly-independent Zimbabwe.

*Compare Gerschenkron's account of Khrushchev's administrative rationalization in the USSR.[106]

Botha gave the *verkramptes* no chance to outflank him on security issues,* which he used to rally support. The *rooi gevaar* (red threat) replaced the *swart gevaar* as a rallying cry, and all South Africans were urged to unite against the 'total onslaught' being waged against the country by international communism. The security threat was advanced both as a reason for supporting reform (to counter communist subversion by spreading the benefits of 'free enterprise') and to justify measures to strengthen the executive against challenges from both the left and right.

However, the increasing prominence of the military in areas outside their usual sphere was due not only to the security situation but also to the need of Botha, who had been Minister of Defence since 1966, for dependable supporters in his struggle to assert his authority over the NP and the state. Consequently, there was strong representation of defence personnel on the State Security Council (which some observers believed was more powerful than the cabinet), and on the new interdepartmental cabinet committees created by Botha to bypass the bureaucracy.[108] The influence of the military was also evident in growing defence expenditure (see p. 247) and in their control over information. The SA press had been prevented from reporting the 1975 Angolan invasion, which South Africans first heard of from the foreign press. This tight censorship was resented by Afrikaans as well as English newspapers. The military, for their part, were angered by press disclosures about the involvement of defence force officers in the abortive 1983 Seychelles coup and by criticism of the 1983 strike against Maseru, in Lesotho. General Magnus Malan, brought into the cabinet as Minister of Defence, demanded that the Defence Act be tightened to prevent 'lies and blatant propaganda', and the military urged tighter press curbs in their evidence to the 1980 Steyn Commission.[109]

Capitalists too opposed increasing authoritarianism, as well as heavy military demands on scarce resources such as skilled man-

---

*The HNP urged the use of 'the full might of the military to wipe out' ANC and SWAPO bases in neighbouring countries, and warned that if Namibia became independent, the HNP would 'retake South West Africa for the whites'. Opinion polls showed that the electorate supported a hard line on security: 80 per cent of whites supported military attacks on guerrilla bases in neighbouring states, while 72 per cent believed that SA should stop food exports to states aiding guerrillas.[107]

power (see p. 234). They were also concerned about hawkish foreign and regional policies, wanting trade and investment, not polarization and confrontation. The Chamber of Mines, for example, was alarmed by Botha's threat that SA would react to sanctions by withholding mineral supplies.[110]

There were thus constraints on the expansion of military power from important sections of the oligarchy (including of course the bureaucracy on whose territory they were encroaching). The tradition of civilian control, and the fact that the army was mainly a citizen force,* also tended to constrain the growth of military power. Factors tending to increase that power in the future could include an enlargement of the professional core of the army; the further erosion of SA's political and judicial structures which might occur if the new constitution proved unworkable; a deteriorating security situation; and the seemingly inexorable tendency of bureaucracies to expand.

Botha's relations with capital
Unlike previous Nationalist leaders, Botha courted capitalists. At the 1979 Carlton and 1981 Good Hope conferences, he urged them to participate in politics,[112] and he appointed them to government commissions and committees. Botha introduced some of the racial reforms they wanted (see Chapter 3), as well as non-racial measures such as the reduction in the size of the state sector,** the lowering of high marginal tax rates, and the easing of monetary and foreign exchange controls, both for non-residents and for SAs wishing to invest abroad.

There were, however, continuing disagreements between Botha and capital over the horizontal controls (mobility, stabilization, decentralization) and the related question of black citizenship and political rights, as well as over the authoritarian trends.

The breach with white labour
The Wiehahn reforms were a shock to the white unions supporting the Nationalists, and led to a breach not only with militants like the

---

*In 1982, armed forces totalled 81,400, of whom 53,100 were conscripts (total mobilizable strength was 404,500).[111]
**The share of real public spending in GDP fell from 30 per cent in 1976 to 27 per cent in 1982.[113]

MWU and the Building Workers, but with SACOL's president Nieuwoudt, who felt he had been misled by the NP, particularly by the Minister of Labour, Fanie Botha. White labour's dissatisfaction soon fed into the political arena. In parliament, Nationalist MPs like J. H. B. Ungerer and J. G. Swiegers, representing the industrial areas of Sasolburg and Uitenhage, condemned the labour reforms and black unions.[114] The government's anxiety could be seen from advertisements it placed in *Die Transvaler* before the August 1979 by-elections explaining the new labour reforms and the measures to protect white workers. This did not halt the strong swing in working class constituencies to the HNP, and later the CP.

The NP lost a substantial proportion of the white labour vote; but while relations deteriorated with SACOL, they improved with TUCSA, which *verligte* SACOL unions like the Railway Artisans joined. In 1979 the Minister of Labour opened the annual TUCSA conference for the first time since the NP assumed office. There were still potential problems, as shown by TUCSA's dislike of the progressive amendment of trade union legislation (see p. 206), but the political risks to Botha will be diminished by the impending change in the political system, which will constitute the final step in the detoothing of white labour.

The bureaucracy's power to obstruct reform

The bureaucracy and the *verkrampte* political establishment were more effective in limiting reform, as was illustrated by a number of cases, including the removal of squatters from the townships around Cape Town. Pressures for this came from local BAAB officials and from Nationalist MPs who urged the implementation of congress decisions to 'hasten the removal of black people from the Western Cape'.[115] Senior BAD officials made no secret of their opposition to the concessions for Section 10s. In his evidence to the Grosskopf Committee, J. H. T. Mills, former head of BAD, urged the strengthening of influx control and objected to the granting of property rights to Africans on the grounds that 'private property is not indigenous to Bantu law and customs.'[116]

The bureaucracy's capacity to limit and obstruct reforms on mobility and stabilization was testified to not only by the Black Sash, the Urban Foundation, and other observers, but also by the ex-Postmaster-General, Louis Rive, appointed to oversee the improvements to Soweto, and the Minister of BAD, Piet Koornhof, who likened the bureaucracy to a tortoise, which might move very slowly, but was likely to prove completely immobile if pressured.[117]

One of the most significant examples of its power was the retention of the decentralization policy, opposed by both white capital and labour (see pp. 154 and 223). However, it had more success in imposing negative measures (restrictions on black mobility, stabilization, and expansion of factories), than in promoting decentralization. Neither the bureaucracy nor its opponents had the power to enforce their options. The result was a stalemate, with decentralization neither meaningfully enforced nor abandoned.

The bureaucracy fought to maintain these controls for various reasons:

(i) They depended on them for their jobs, their power and those extra gains to be made from the corruption inherent in any system of excessive controls, licences and permits.* The corruption that this bred was testified to not only by researchers, but by the official Commission on the 1962 Paarl Riots[118] and by evidence in cases which occasionally reached the courts.**

(ii) They acted as a social control mechanism to reduce crime and overcrowding in the cities. South African officials were not unique in arguing for this; influx control was widely favoured by many colonial regimes in Africa.[120]

(iii) The controls provided the essential demographic and physical preconditions for the separate development policy, designed to secure continued Afrikaner—and not just white—political hegemony. This mattered most to the officials and politicians whose jobs and power were directly tied up with Afrikaner hegemony.

---

*Hence that South African music-hall figure, the policeman, demanding of anyone performing any activity: 'Did you get a licence?'

**For example, in 1978, an official of the West Rand Administration Board was convicted of accepting bribes from 691 people over a five-month period. The bribes were surprisingly small—R5 a time, totalling R3,455.[119] In Soweto the 'going rate' was then said to be R25, which would produce over R17,000 on this number of cases. The Report of the 1981 Parliamentary Select Committee on Public Accounts expressed concern about maladministration and misapplication of administration board funds.

In his study of modernization, Huntington argued that reform was more difficult in societies in which an effective bureaucracy already existed, such as the Russian, Chinese and Ottoman empires, than in feudal societies lacking a central administration; and that bureaucratic obstruction had frequently led reforming governments to turn to the army for support—which of course created another set of problems.[121]

A verkrampte *counter-revolution?*

If the 1983 constitution proves unworkable, could the 1970s reforms, like those of the 1940s, be reversed by a *verkrampte* counter-revolution? Changes in the structure of SA society—the decline of forces favouring apartheid and the strengthening of those against—make it unlikely that the socio-economic reforms would be reversed, unless economic contraction or technological developments eliminated the skill shortage. However, a backlash could lead to rescinding of the trade union reforms and the halting of further reform.

A counter-revolution would require the further tightening of authoritarian controls; but this could also accompany an attempt to force through the social and political incorporation of blacks. There is not thus a straightforward correlation between authoritarianism and racism. However, it seems unlikely that the present 'political class' would initiate the incorporation of Africans—even if they would operate such a system once it was in place. A more authoritarian path of reform is therefore likely to fall short of full deracialization. The strong tendency towards authoritarianism will be constrained by well-articulated pressure groups within the oligarchy, including some of Botha's supporters, who see this route as a cul-de-sac and a threat to their own rights. But the option of military rule remains in reserve if the 1983 constitution fails.

It is also possible that, even if the new constitution proves in some respects inoperable (the coloured and Indian houses cease to function; there are constant deadlocks), the underlying strength of the SA economy and administration and the weakness of its opponents—will enable it to survive the intensification of conflict and periods of political paralysis, while continuing the confused, incremental process of reform.

Timing

Timing is an important key to understanding political developments. Time lags prolonged the power of the classes with a vested interest in apartheid, despite their declining economic and electoral importance, because they were strongly entrenched in the NP and the state. Meanwhile, it took the opponents of apartheid longer to mobilize and deploy their power than was anticipated by those who predicted that their growing economic importance would lead to the erosion of apartheid. This delayed effect was partly due to the government's ability to shift the costs of apartheid by protection, etc. It was also partly due to the system of democracy for whites, which favoured Afrikaner nationalists (and their major classes, white agriculture and white labour) while capital was fragmented and lacked leverage on the NP until the emergence of a larger group of Afrikaans urban capitalists.

Policies of verligtes and verkramptes

By 1984, policies advocated by leading *verligtes* like the economist, Jan Lombard, were in many respects similar to the policies of liberals in the 1940s. The main elements of *verligte* policy were the promotion of 'free enterprise', involving the removal of apartheid restrictions on economic activity, reduction in the size and role of the state sector, and the removal of legally enforced discrimination (the 'separateness of groups' should express itself 'spontaneously').[122] However, many *verligtes* were evasive about separate residential areas and schools and ambivalent about full black mobility, because of its connection with political rights. The permanence of urban blacks and the impossibility of creating a credible geographic and economic base for separate development were now officially accepted, for example, by the van der Walt and Riekert Commissions (see p. 79). *Verligtes* were beginning to draw the political consequences, arguing that urban blacks could not be represented via the Bantustans and that 'the traditional leaders are not the . . . true leaders.'[123] But most of them still stopped short of publicly accepting the Lombard Report's conclusion that the only alternative was power sharing (though not one man one vote) in a multiracial society (see p. 109).

Verkramptes believed this would be the inevitable outcome of *verligte* policies. Treurnicht broke from the NP over the 1983 constitution which, he said, downgraded the white parliament to a 'little chamber' which could be over-ruled by the multiracial President's Council and would be the first step to 'one man, one vote'. Treurnicht also opposed the shift to 'free market' forces and the removal of legalized discrimination, arguing that 'an open market and social integration would make apartheid unworkable.'[124] The HNP viewed 'free market' policies as representing an unholy alliance between international capitalism and communism, and it denounced Botha's government as 'not only the biggest *Kaffirboetie* government, but also the biggest Hoggenheimer government. It looks after the blacks and the rich people [and serves the interests of] the new colonialist powers, Russia and America.'[125]

Verkramptes continued to stress the importance of Afrikaner identity, viewed in racial, not cultural, terms. Treurnicht argued that, 'Every people has the right to be exclusive . . . the Afrikaner must be maintained as a unique nation; and the Afrikaner Volk must be a closed community because openness means losing identity.' He regarded the Mixed Marriages, Immorality and Group Areas Acts, and separate educational systems, as essential for safeguarding group identities.[126] Jaap Marais, Hertzog's successor as HNP leader, believed that, 'Every nation has its distinctive features—language, culture, religion; but these may be changed or exchanged. The one permanent feature is the racial identity. This is at the heart of nationhood . . . . There can be no black Englishmen, just as there can be no white Zulus.'[127]

Racism, including 'Afrikaners first' policies, was therefore a continuing element of *verkrampte* thinking. But, as this study has repeatedly found, this did not simply reflect 'irrational' ideological factors; racist policies served the interests of the *verkramptes'* constituency, as well as their calculations about the risks of change. They did not believe that reform would forestall revolution, but that it would raise 'false expectations' and cause confusion and upheaval. The CP wanted a return to the status quo ante-Botha (both Vorster and Mulder denounced the Wiehahn reforms and Botha's willingness to review the Land Act and sex laws).[128] The HNP wanted a return to the status quo ante Vorster.

On foreign policy, there was no clear-cut division, with some *verligtes*, especially the military, as hawkish as the *verkramptes*. However, the *verligtes* were less parochial and isolationist, wel-

coming external contacts and willing to open up SA to outside
influences. On political liberty and democracy, the *verligtes* were
divided: the military tended to the view that the reshaping of SA
society would require authoritarian measures against both left and
right; while the *verligte* press and intelligentsia opposed the curbs
in the 1982 Newspaper Act and expressed disquiet at the powers
envisaged for the State President in the new constitution,
described by *Rapport* as 'virtually unlimited powers, without
proper . . . checks'.[129] The *verkramptes* became unexpectedly
ambivalent on authoritarian measures, fearing the restriction of
their own rights and liberties.

The views of most NP politicians were spread between the
verligte and *verkrampte* poles, with the cabinet leaning towards
the *verligtes* and the caucus towards the *verkramptes*.[130] The
views of the caucus and party were more *verkramp* than those of
the electorate* and of the Afrikaans elite, hence Botha's attempts
to reduce the power of both party and caucus.

Growing opposition to Afrikaner hegemony

From the early 1970s, opposition pressures had an increasing
impact on government policy. Amongst the reasons for this were
socio-economic changes which strengthened the bargaining power
of white capital and the black middle and working classes and
transformed attitudes and expectations, especially those of the
younger, more educated blacks in the towns. External support for
black demands was another important factor, although its effects
were complex and, in some cases, unintended. But, despite the
growth in opposition of all kinds—industrial, political, the armed
struggle—divisions among the opposition remained deep, the
level of mobilization low and, by 1984, there was no credible
alternative government in sight.

Realignments within the white opposition

Vorster's reforms precipitated the long-averted split between the
UP conservatives and liberals. After the 1977 election the Progressive Federal Party (PFP) became the largest opposition party with
17 seats to 135 for the NP.** For the first time SA had an official

---

*Compare Lipset's finding that the views of political activists, whether of the left
  or the right, are generally more militant than those of the rank and file.[131]

**The PFP was established in 1977 between the Progressive Party and the UP
  Reformists led by Jappie Basson and Harry Schwarz.

opposition committed to the removal of race discrimination, including extension of the franchise to all blacks. It was an indication of the leftwards shift of the whole political spectrum (i.e. towards less racist policies).

The PFP was a (sometimes uneasy) alliance between the liberal intelligentsia and English capital and professionals. Its founders and supporters included the Oppenheimers, the Menells and Hersovs of Anglovaal and Max Borkum, chairman of the Johannesburg stock exchange.* It won seats in SA's wealthiest English constituencies (Houghton in Johannesburg, Sea Point and Constantia in Cape Town). As it was joined by the UP remnants it broadened its base to include more average middle-class constituencies like Edenvale and Bezuidenhout. However, after the 1981 election it still had only 26 seats to 131 for the NP.

Until 1974, when the Progressives had only Helen Suzman in parliament, their strategy was to use it as a public platform to attack the stream of racist and authoritarian legislation. The expansion of the party's organization and parliamentary representation led to the elaboration of an alternative blueprint for SA, based on their principles of the rule of law, democracy and multiracialism. A significant feature of their 1978 constitution was the shift away from the Westminster model (majority rule in a unitary state) towards a rigid federal constitution with 'consociational' devices providing for power sharing and protection of minorities.** These reflected the conviction of PFP intellectuals (especially Stellenbosch University academics like van Zyl Slabbert and Andre du Toit) that SA's multiethnic society and turbulent history required safeguards for minorities and that the white electorate would never agree to 'simple majoritarianism'.[132]

The PFP's base bears similarities to that of the *haute bourgeoisie* described by Glazer and Moynihan in their study of ethnic politics in New York. During the 1960s this class led the campaign for the removal of discrimination against Negroes and Puerto Ricans,

---

*During the 1970s, no less than four of the PFP's handful of MPs (Zach de Beer, Alex Boraine, Rene de Villiers, Gordon Waddell) were prominent members of AAC.

**Consociational policies provide ethnic and other minorities with substantial control over their own affairs, representation in the government, and protection against being overwhelmed by the majority by devices such as minority vetos. The PFP constitution provided for a veto on most new legislation by a 15 per cent minority.

whom they were 'better able to empathise with', than less well-off whites.[133] This greater empathy (both in New York and SA) was connected with an interest in, and less competitive relationship with, the blacks whose advance they supported.

Racial divisions in SA obscure the sharp class divisions within white (including English) society, particularly in relation to the ownership of assets. McGrath estimated that the top 5 per cent of whites owned over 50 per cent of the wealth,[134] so that intra-white class divisions are almost as sharp as class divisions in the UK, with an enormous concentration of wealth in the hands of those leading families of the *haute bourgeoisie* who established the PFP.

The resulting differences in interests and views were reflected in divisions within the PFP. The ex-UP Reformists like Schwarz, representing average middle-class constituencies, favoured 'local option', permitting white neighbourhoods to retain segregated schools and residential areas if they wished. The Suzman wing wanted the outlawing of racial discrimination in public institutions and policies of affirmative action favouring blacks. But on economic and welfare policies, the Friedmanite line of big business supporters like Waddell was opposed by Schwarz, who favoured higher levels of state activity, both to provide public welfare (pensions, etc.) and to intervene in economic management by protecting consumers and small businessmen against 'monopolistic abuse'.[135]

Defence was another divisive issue, with disputes at party congresses over conscientious objectors, and conflicting reactions to the 1981 raid against alleged ANC bases in Mozambique, applauded by the representatives of 'Middletown SA', who had sons fighting on the border, but condemned by the liberal intelligentsia. The PFP leader, van Zyl Slabbert, tried to overcome these divisions by the formula that military service was justifiable provided it 'created a shield behind which we can pursue the goal of peaceful constitutional change'.[136]

Whatever the disagreements, the elaboration of these policies was a sign of growing confidence and of a feeling that the Party could move from the politics of protest to seeking power—or at least more influence. The sharpening of the *verligte-verkrampte* split after Botha's accession led to the expectation of a political polarization from which both the PFP and the *verkramptes* would gain at Botha's expense. The PFP would then play a 'balancing' role, supporting Botha in return for bolder reforms.[137] However, even after Treurnicht's breakaway in 1982, Botha still had a large majority.* In the 1983 referendum on the constitution, he held his ground against Treurnicht's CP and gained at the expense of the PFP.

In the 1981 election the PFP made its first breakthrough among Afrikaners, winning an estimated 5 per cent of the Afrikaans vote (concentrated among the young, highly educated and wealthy). But Afrikaans capital and the *verligte* intelligentsia mostly remained in the NP, held by Botha's reforms and that potent mixture of historical, material, institutional and kinship links termed 'ethnic ties'. Political and ideological factors were also important: *verligtes* believed they could achieve more by remaining within the party in power, and they continued to give priority to group rather than individual rights, although this ideological divide was reduced as the PFP shifted towards consociational policies.

Botha's reforms (and the fear that he might be defeated by Treurnicht) also limited the PFP's advance among the English middle class. Although the PFP won 60 per cent of English votes in the 1981 election, two-thirds of the English voted for Botha's 1983 constitution, including a third of PFP supporters, who would not vote with Treurnicht against a constitution which they perceived as taking a 'first step in the right direction' by bringing coloureds and Indians into parliament.

The PFP disliked the extensive powers which the 1983 constitution gave to the State President and the demotion of the role of parliament and of the opposition.** The PFP's strenuous campaign against the constitution also reflected their growing sensitivity to black views and the conviction of the liberal intelligentsia that, by excluding Africans, it failed to confront SA's central political problem and would exacerbate racial tensions.

*In 1983 the state of the parties in parliament was as follows: 126 seats for the NP, 27 for the PFP, 17 for the CP, 8 for the NRP (a UP remnant, based in Natal).

**The majority party in each Chamber would elect members of the key electoral college and President's Council, while much of the debate would be transferred from parliament to standing committees attempting to reach consensus behind closed doors, thus reducing the value of the public platform provided by parliament.

The PFP's relations with the left were problematical. The 1968 Political Interference Act prohibited the PFP from having black members and was an obstacle to political cooperation. During the 1970s, the Act was increasingly ignored as the Nationalists themselves sought contact not only with the officially sanctioned Bantustan leaders, but with the Soweto Committee of Ten, many of whose members were banned. The PFP cooperated with Buthelezi, the coloured Labour Party and other blacks using the separate development institutions to press for reform. But the PFP was usually spurned by black organizations operating outside the official system and also by the small group of white radicals and Marxists (based on the universities and churches). They disliked the PFP's big business connections and consociational devices, and suspected that its affluent supporters wanted the best of both worlds. Moreover, the fact that there was little prospect of power for the PFP reduced its attraction as an ally, while the energy, education and wealth of its activists meant they would intensify the competition for leadership roles among the crowded ranks of the opposition's aspiring political entrepreneurs.

Despite its cautious policies and devices to limit majority rule, the PFP has not deviated from its opposition to authoritarianism (including measures like detention without trial) nor from its commitment to a common citizenship for all South Africans. This led to its opposition to Bantustan independence and the proposed cession of Ingwavuma to Swaziland (on the grounds that these measures deprived Africans of their SA citizenship) and to its rejection of the Nationalist strategy of incorporating coloureds and Indians politically, while making only economic concessions to urban Africans. Van Zyl Slabbert argued that 'it is a fallacy to believe that an urban black middle class in itself will be a stabilizing factor . . . . To ignore their political aspirations . . . while improving their socio-economic position is to contribute to a revolutionary situation.'[138] The PFP's adherence to these principles, and its opposition to the 1983 constitution, might in time improve its relations with black political organizations.

It is fashionable to dismiss white liberals as 'irrelevant'. Yet they represent important interests and helped to keep alive ideas, institutions and multiracial contacts that could serve as a bridge to a less racist and more democratic society. Robert Birley, the British educationist who helped redesign German education after the war, remarked that SA liberals, unlike those in Nazi Germany, did not collapse before the Nationalist onslaught. The key factors in their survival, and limited but useful role, were the vigour of the English press, universities, and organizations such as the Black Sash and Institute of Race Relations; the financial strength of English capital; and their external contacts and support.

Coloureds and Indians: black vanguard or white reinforcements?
The 1948 Nationalist government inflicted a severe setback on the emerging coloured and Indian elites (businessmen, professionals, intelligentsia, skilled workers). Nor were the effects of apartheid confined to them: roughly a quarter of all coloureds and Indians were uprooted by removals under the Group Areas Act. Coloureds lost their century-old vote, suffered the humiliation of compulsory racial classification and social segregation, and were rejected by people with whom they had ties of blood, language and religion (see pp. 23 and 32). These policies aggravated the upheaval and disorientation resulting from rapid postwar urbanization. The effects were evident in severe social and health problems (levels of alcoholism, malnutrition and infant mortality rivalled those of Africans*) and in political alienation. Mostly this took the form of despair and apathy, but the elite was antagonised and radicalized.

The articulate coloured intelligentsia (mainly teachers and priests in the schools and colleges) denied that coloureds were a group—or indeed that the concept of an ethnic or racial group had any validity. They were the foremost exponents of the policy of nonracialism, rejecting not only the Nationalists' 'multinational' policy, but also the multiracial policy of the liberals and of the ANC. Their political strategy was based on a Trotskyite analysis conceived in wholly class terms, with capital the enemy against which all sections of labour (including white labour) must unite.[140]

This strategy rejected 'opportunistic' alliances with the (white or black) bourgeoisie and would make no concessions to demands for the protection of racial minorities—insisting that their security lay in the abolition of all racial distinctions. They adopted a policy of 'non-collaboration' towards separate racial institutions such as

*Some studies found higher levels of infant mortality among coloureds in urban areas than among Africans.[139]

the Bantustans and the Coloured Council set up by Vorster in 1968 (see p. 32), which they boycotted.

The Trotskyites were a small group, but their ideas had considerable influence among the younger, more educated coloureds, many of whom now identified themselves as blacks. After the Soweto riots, unrest spread to coloured schools and colleges. In 1980, thirty-two people died in rioting in Cape Town.

The coloured Labour Party (led by Sonny Leon and, later, by Alan Hendrickse and David Curry) was prepared to use the Coloured Council as a means of securing socio-economic concessions and as a platform for political mobilization and voicing of their demand for full social and political incorporation for all blacks. Their 1977 du Preez constitution advocated universal suffrage in a unitary SA.

The proportion of coloureds participating in elections for the Council declined from 38 per cent in 1969 to 28 per cent in 1975. These low polls partly reflected political apathy, particularly in relation to a Council with such limited powers. The continued presence of most coloured unions in TUCSA was a significant indication of continued coloured cooperation with whites. However, political radicalization, particularly in the Cape peninsula, where almost 40 per cent of coloureds live, contributed to the Labour Party's increasingly militant stance, for example, in calling for disinvestment and overseas boycotts of SA. The party became so uncooperative that the Council was disbanded in 1980.

Faced with Botha's offer of a House of Representatives in the new tricameral parliament, the Labour Party, amidst considerable dissension, decided to participate, while reiterating its commitment to work for the inclusion of Africans. The 30 per cent turnout in the 1984 election was widely regarded as a setback for Labour and a victory for the UDF and National Forum, who opposed participation.*

---

*As a proportion of those eligible to vote the turnout was 20 per cent. The United Democratic Front (UDF), which subscribed to the ANC's Freedom Charter, was formed to campaign against the 1983 constitution. It was an umbrella organization to which hundreds of community organizations (claiming membership of over 2m people) were affiliated. The smaller National Forum was an alliance of Trotskyite and Black Consciousness groups.

The separate development institutions provoked a similar polarization in the smaller Indian community. The level of participation in the SA Indian Council was lower: only 8 per cent in its 1981 election. Indians had less bargaining power than the more numerous coloureds, with their close ties of blood and culture with the ruling Afrikaners. The Indians were, moreover, potential scapegoats for both Africans and whites (surveys revealed strong anti-Indian feeling[141]). The 1949 Durban riots and the expulsion of Asians from East Africa probably left Indians feeling more scared of Africans than of whites. Inkatha's denunciation of the Labour Party's decision to participate in the 1983 constitution as 'a treacherous betrayal of black liberation' caused apprehension among Indians. Surveys showed that they wanted Africans included; but they also wanted protection for minority rights.[142] Nevertheless, the Indian Council decided to 'give it a try'; but the 18 per cent poll for the Indian House of Delegates was an even clearer victory for the boycotters.

However, the 1983 constitution provided only a limited political incorporation against a background of continuing social and economic segregation. If coloureds and Indians were offered more substantial reforms and fuller incorporation in the near future, non-collaboration principles would be tested against a range of class and security interests, racial feelings and resentments, and longer-term calculations about the relative strength of whites and Africans.

There has been a strong revulsion against racism among many coloureds. The identification by younger, more educated coloureds of themselves as blacks seems to have given Lembede's dream of black unity more foundation in reality (see p. 263). If the rising, but still small, coloured middle class encounters competition or resistance from whites, then its class interests could reinforce its desire for an alliance with Africans.

The interests and attitudes of coloured labour could be different. From the 1960s, rapid growth and 'coloured labour preference' policies ensured to coloureds substantial gains in wages, occupations, education and even housing. The relatively strict application of influx control in the Western Cape, where most coloureds live, kept down African numbers in this area and hence African competition for jobs and urban resources. However, coloured politicians, including those in the Labour Party, supported demands for the relaxation of this policy. This was recently conceded by Botha (see p. 83n), and it will obviously increase African numbers and competition in the area (though it might also stimulate economic growth).

Coloured workers will then be in a position relative to Africans that Afrikaners once were in relation to blacks (and white workers in New York in relation to Negroes and Puerto Ricans). It is a situation that often sharpens racial awareness and hostility. If it had this effect on sections of coloured labour, African labour would need the support of capitalist employers in opposing policies of exclusion (whether or not they were explicitly racist). This would replicate that pattern, so familiar in SA and elsewhere, in which the racial policies of the *haute bourgeoisie* are often more progressive than those of the lower-middle and working class. The implication here is not that coloured labour is more racist than white capital, but that its interests might push it towards more racist policies. Political trends among coloureds and Indians therefore still seem fluid and uncertain.

African politics: Collaboration, reform or revolution?

There were deep divisions among Africans over the separate development institutions, not only between opponents and supporters of their use, but also between those (like Matanzima and Mangope) who accepted them as part of a long-term solution and those (like Buthelezi and Ntsantwisi) who would only use them as a step towards securing full political rights.

Divisions over the homelands policy partly reflected the long-established rural/urban traditional/modern divide amongst Africans. Such support as there was for the policy came exclusively from within the homelands.* Urban Africans were adamantly opposed, not just for ideological reasons, but because they feared the policy would be used as a justification for removing their tenuous urban rights. Their fears were acknowledged by the

---

*The 1979 Quail Commission found 42 per cent of those living within Ciskei would accept independence, but the preference of 90 per cent of Ciskeians was for a unitary, multiracial SA with a common franchise for all races. Other more acceptable options were a confederation, or independence on more favourable terms.[144]

official Cellie Commission into the Soweto riots, which considered that this policy contributed to 'the general mood of resistance and revolt.'[143]

The argument of Chief Kaiser Matanzima of Transkei (and the other three Bantustan leaders who accepted 'independence' and loss of SA citizenship) was that partition in their own separate states was the only way Africans could win political rights, and that the history and cultural identity of Transkei (which Matanzima envisaged as incorporating the historical Xhosa lands down to the Fish River) made it as well-qualified for independence as neighbouring Lesotho (see map).

Active support for the policy came from what Stultz and Southall termed its 'beneficiaries'. These bore a striking resemblance to the policy's white advocates, and largely consisted of the Bantustans' political establishments, including many nominated chiefs, and their burgeoning bureaucracies (by 1979 there were 170,260 employees in the homeland administrations).[145] The Matanzima brothers, for example, were rewarded by the Transkei Assembly for their 'faithful service in the development of their country' by the grant of valuable farms in the land transferred by SA to Transkei, as well as by their participation in numerous business deals involving the Transkei Development Corporation. These benefits were frankly acknowledged by George Matanzima who said that 'of course, the Prime Minister [Kaiser] who worked so hard to acquire the land, will be among the beneficiaries, and so will his brother George.'[146]

Independence rid the homelands of white rule and apartheid, but not of political repression. Transkei's 1977 Public Security Act tightened SA's draconian security laws, making it a treasonable offence, punishable by death, to criticise Transkei's independence or suggest its reunification with SA. Furthermore, the Bantustans failed to secure the additional land and consolidation crucial to their strategy. Frustration, and the ambivalence which had always characterized Matanzima's attitude to white SA, led to his breach of diplomatic relations with SA in 1978 and his offer to Nigeria and the exiled ANC to provide a base for the 'armed struggle'. But the failure to secure international recognition forced Matanzima to resume relations with the only state which recognised him and on which he remained completely dependent economically. However, in 1983 he openly expressed his disillusionment with independence and (the Public Security Act not-withstanding) his desire to rejoin a federal SA[147] and to escape from the cul-de-sac in which independence had landed him.

Buthelezi's strategy

Other homelands leaders, notably Chief Gatsha Buthelezi of Kwa-Zulu, refused independence, but tried to use the Bantustan institutions as instruments of political mobilization and pressure. Buthelezi argued that the number, strength and long-established presence of the whites meant that any settlement would have to take more account of their interests and fears than had been the case in Kenya or Zimbabwe. He opposed violence because black political and military weakness meant that, in an armed conflict, they would become 'cannon fodder'. Instead, blacks must use every means available to build up their political organization and their economic power as workers and consumers.

As the basis for a settlement Buthelezi proposed a rigid federal constitution, with guarantees for minorities (including consocia-tional devices such as representation for all groups in the cabinet) and an initial experiment in multiracial power sharing in Natal/ Kwa-zulu.[148] He reassured businessmen that their investments would be safe and opposed disinvestment and boycotts on the grounds that economic growth and external contacts helped to erode apartheid. However, he was adamant that he would never accept independence, warning that, 'If ever the SA government forces me and my people to become independent at the point of a gun, I would reply with a gun.'[149]

Buthelezi established Inkatha, ostensibly a Zulu cultural organ-ization but with the colours of the ANC and open to all Africans. By 1984 it claimed membership of three-quarters of a million, although few non-Zulus joined. Buthelezi cultivated alliances with coloureds and Indians (with whom he established the SA black Alliance) and with white liberals, both within SA and abroad. His popular base among the Zulus, and wide range of allies, enabled him to resist the government's attempts to replace him with the compliant Zulu King, Goodwill, and strengthened his bargaining power.

Buthelezi succeeded in resisting independence and in blocking the proposed cession of land to Swaziland (see p. 55)—both important aspects of the grand apartheid design. However, he failed to secure African inclusion in the 1983 constitution; nor could he allay the opposition of urban Africans to his use of the Bantustans. On the contrary, they claimed his effective use of these institutions lent them such credibility as they possessed. Their hostility was sharpened, and his ambivalent relations with the exiled ANC deteriorated, with the political radicalization following Transkei independence and the Soweto riots. The decline in his popular support outside Natal* was not redressed by his opposition to the 1983 constitution. Rather the polarization it generated intensified resentment against all blacks who worked within the system.

In a political vacuum, Buthelezi's strategy contributed to the change in white attitudes and the revival of black opposition; but it failed to secure political concessions or to serve as a base for national black mobilization. The reaction against 'independence', and the government's unresponsiveness to reformists like Buthelezi, undermined their credibility and alienated them from their potential allies, the urban black middle class. This weakened the base for a broader 'moderate' black coalition by alienating and radicalizing urban blacks.

It is sometimes argued that the Bantustans are too well-established to be reversed. But their fragmented and backward state, and their mostly authoritarian and unpopular regimes, seem more likely to have alienated their inhabitants than to have created the interests and loyalties that might sustain them. They failed to achieve legitimacy or even credibility, either within SA or internationally. Instead, they became ridiculed Casinostans—sources of cheap labour and places like Sin City,** where white South Africans went to indulge in the gambling, mixed sex and blue films forbidden them in puritan SA. However, while the Bantustans are hopelessly weak vis-à-vis SA, it is conceivable that, faced with a weak successor government, they could become a focus for regional centres of power. But these regional/ethnic tendencies existed anyway, and policies of partition or even confederalism may have been weakened by their association with the Bantustans.

---

*Opinion polls showed a decline in Buthelezi's support on the Witwatersrand from 42 per cent in 1977 to 17 per cent in 1981 and a owing to the ANC, whose increasingly daring sabotage he condemned. His Natal base, however, remained strong at 59 per cent.[150]

**Sun City, the gambling capital of Bophutatswana.

African industrial power

All politicians concerned with liberating Africans from their disabilities, from Buthelezi to the ANC, were interested in the potential power of African labour. From the late 1960s, there was a slow revival of African unions, which grew from two unions with 16,000 members in 1969 to 25 unions with about 70,000 members in 1977. After the Wiehahn reforms, they grew more rapidly: by 1984 there were 35 unions with over 400,000 members. However, this still accounted for less than 10 per cent of the African workforce, though a much higher proportion in sectors such as motor cars, metals, stevedoring, textiles and food processing.

The unions encompassed a wide range of interests, views and strategies. The African unions affiliated to TUCSA* generally confined themselves to workplace activities and avoided political commitments. The CUSA and FOSATU unions gave priority to industrial issues and to establishing well-run unions with a strong shop floor presence, but they saw the interest of African workers as bound up with their economic and political disabilities and declared their commitment to 'wide-ranging political change and a society in which workers could control their own destiny'.[151] The third category, which included the unaffiliated Black Consciousness unions in the Eastern Cape, were loosely organized unions which gave primacy to 'community' rather than industrial issues and wished to be more directly involved in the political struggle.

Ironically, the in-plant committees set up by the 1973 Act as a substitute for unions (see p. 67), probably contributed to the unions' growth. Over 2,000 committees involving 600,000 workers were set up. Some unions encouraged workers to use them and to opt for the elected works committees, which the union was able to take over itself. These gave them experience and popularized the idea of negotiation among both workers and management.

*In 1983, about a quarter of unionised Africans were in TUCSA, another quarter in the Federation of SA Trade Unions (FOSATU) and the Council of Unions of SA (CUSA), the rest were in unaffiliated unions. The relatively large number in white-dominated TUCSA was partly because of the extension to Africans of closed shop agreements signed with the longer-established TUCSA unions; partly because of historical and institutional links and the attractions of an established federation which took care of workers' pensions and sickness funds and was less vulnerable to police surveillance.

The refusal of the unions to accept the committees as an alternative to trade union rights was a crucial factor leading to the appointment of the Wiehahn Commission; but it was not the only factor. In 1977, despite the growing importance of African labour, the unions had less than 100,000 members and they lacked the capacity to compel the appointment of Wiehahn and acceptance of its major reforms. In securing this they were greatly aided by support from progressive capital, the liberal press and lobbies, and international pressures (discussed below).

After the Wiehahn reforms the question of whether to register and use the official Industrial Council negotiating machinery became a contentious issue. The TUCSA unions were the first to register. The CUSA and FOSATU unions did so only after the system was amended to meet their demands that unions should be open to all Africans, including migrants (and in the case of FOSATU to all races). Most of the unaffiliated unions refused to register, even after the system was amended but, by 1984, they were beginning to make use of the new Industrial Court, which gave some judgments in favour of workers in cases of unfair dismissal.

The racial composition of the unions was another divisive issue—whether they should be exclusively African, open to all blacks, or to whites as well. The CUSA unions were almost exclusively African; the FOSATU unions were nonracial. In TUCSA Africans were either in multiracial unions or in 'parallels' affiliated to white or coloured unions. Most of the unaffiliated unions were, in theory, open to all blacks. In fact, the independent black unions were mainly African, with a minority of coloureds and Indians and a few whites. In the early stages an important, though not dominant, role was played in the organization of many black unions by whites like Alec Erwin (FOSATU), Loet Douwes Dekker and Eric Tyacke (CUSA) and Neil Aggett of the Food and Canning Workers, who died while in detention for his trade union activities. But whites were not admitted to and played no role in organizing Black Consciousness unions like SA Allied Workers Union (SAAWU) and the Motor Assemblers and Component Workers' Union (MACWUSA), based in the Eastern Cape motor industry.

The difficulties over race were evident even before the Wiehahn Reforms. In 1977 the white SA Society of Journalists deregistered (foregoing its advantages under the IC Act) in order that Africans could join. But they were rebuffed by black journalists, who wanted their own separate organization. When the Boilermakers opened its doors to Africans in 1980, more coloured than white members left in protest. In 1983, the black Insurance and Assurance Workers Union of SA (IAWUSA) called for a boycott of the Liberty Life Company which was prepared to recognise a non-racial, but not a blacks only, union. But there were some successes for the supporters of multi- (or non)racial unions, such as FOSATU's National Union of Motor Assembly and Rubber Workers and the Boilermakers (see p. 206).[152]

Unions committed to nonracialism were faced not only with prejudice and cultural differences, but also with practical problems such as skill differences, and by differences in interest imposed by apartheid, which forced Africans, whites and coloureds to live in different areas and subjected Africans to special housing and mobility problems, which did not affect other workers. This led van der Watt of the Boilermakers to argue (as had the Congress movement) that white, African and coloured workers should initially be organized into separate branches of the same multiracial union, sharing the same secretariat and bargaining together, until they could evolve into a more closely integrated nonracial union.[153]

The Wiehahn reforms were followed by the rapid growth of the more 'militant' unions, especially in the Eastern Cape, and by a wave of strikes, as well as by consumer boycotts against firms like Fattis & Monis which refused to recognise African unions. The causes of labour unrest included wages, unfair dismissals, union recognition and broader issues such as the proposed 1981 pensions legislation (which made it more difficult for workers to withdraw their pensions early). On many of these issues workers won major concessions from employers and/or government. But the community oriented unions in particular were under heavy pressure from the police (and from Chief Sebe's thuggish Bantustan administration in the Eastern Cape) and were badly hit by repeated detention and imprisonment of their leaders like Thozamile Gqweta.

The post-Wiehahn wave of strikes had its origins partly in rivalry between unions, as they outbid each other in the competition for members. It also resulted from grass-roots pressures which union organizers were often unable to control. Among the reasons for this was the urgent need of African workers for the speedy settlement of grievances. With insecure urban rights, they could not move to another job or hang around waiting for lengthy bureaucratic investigations.

The unions were affected by the growing political radicalization and they all objected to the Orderly Movement bill and the exclusion of Africans from the 1983 Constitution.[154] From 1981, attempts were made to establish a working alliance among the black unions, 'in view of the intensifying state attacks on the trade union movement'.[155] At the same time, the Boilermakers led a breakaway from TUCSA in order to establish a closer relationship with the independent black unions (see Chapter 7). Major realignments within the trade union movement, with the emergence of a nonracial (or multiracial) bloc, therefore seemed possible. However, both the Black Consciousness unions and the bulk of the white (and many coloured and Indian) unions seemed likely to stay out.

The responsiveness of many (though not all) of the black unions to the amendment of the industrial relations system wrought by their pressures, gives some support to the view that, as in many modernizing societies, the industrial labour force wants reform rather than revolution.[156] However, there were also signs of a reservoir of militancy, particularly among younger more skilled workers,[157] deriving from special features of the SA situation, namely the 'social dissonance' (discussed below) caused by continuing discrimination outside the workplace and the lack of political means of redress. It seems inevitable that at least sections of African labour will periodically add their weight to attempts to change this. Their actions will be influenced by their material needs, their feelings of resentment and nationalism, and by the evident desire of many of them to survive in the 'East European' situation in which they have to operate.

Rise and destruction of the Black Consciousness movement

Black Consciousness represented a revival of the Africanist tradition, modified (at least in theory) to include coloureds and Indians. From the late 1960s, there was a rapid growth of organizations reflecting this philosophy, such as the Black Peoples Convention and the SA Students Association (SASO), a breakaway from the liberal, multiracial National Union of SA Students.

Black Consciousness asserted a belief in black values and leadership, rejecting cooperation with white liberals and radicals, whom they regarded as playing 'a confusing and diversionary role' in black politics; their proper role should be to educate whites. For blacks, the main task was psychological liberation, as a prelude to social and political advance. This meant developing their own ideas and identity, instead of adopting the (liberal or Marxist) ideas of whites. Black Consciousness, said Steve Biko, was 'the realization by blacks that, in order to feature well in this game of power politics, they have to use the concept of group power'. Biko denied that they were anti-white racists, arguing (like General Hertzog after Union) that only after blacks had established themselves in their own organizations, under their own leadership, could they cooperate with whites on equal terms.[158]

Their stress on black identity and hostility to white liberals led the government initially to tolerate them, thus enabling the movement to get established. But its rejection of the Bantustans, promotion of unity among Africans, coloureds and Indians, and advocacy of overseas boycotts of SA, soon led to persecution. This reached its zenith during the 1976 Soweto riots, when hundreds of young blacks, who hurled themselves at armed police, were killed or wounded; many more were detained or put on trial. This time these *kragdadige* tactics did not have their usual effect; opposition was not crushed, but inflamed. The official reaction was to increase the repression—more arrests, trials, torture and deaths in detention, including Steve Biko. In reaction to the outcry following his death, all seventeen Black Consciousness organizations and the Soweto newspaper, *The World*, were banned. Unrest continued and spread to African and coloured schools and colleges throughout the country, followed by strikes and sabotage. For the first time, the government was faced with an opposition prepared to fight back against it with its own violent and ruthless methods.[159]

The savage reprisals turned the Soweto riots into the funeral pyre of black consciousness, destroying its organizational base. The student activists were weakened by their strained relations with the best organized sections of black society—Inkatha, which they spurned, and black labour, with which they failed to establish a working relationship. According to Gerhart, a couple of brief sympathy strikes on behalf of those killed at Soweto were 'well supported' by black workers; but the call for a longer strike led to serious clashes between students and migrant workers in Soweto and Cape Town.[160] These may have been encouraged by *agents provocateurs*, but there were differences of interest and attitude between the students, often from lower-middle-class families, with some tenuous rights in towns, and the migrants, who were working class, their rural-based families entirely dependent on their incomes; the latter were scared of losing their jobs at a time of high unemployment and did not share the immediate concern with loss of urban tenure from which they were anyway excluded.

Although support for Black Consciousness was limited to the youth and intelligentsia,* the students' courageous defiance had an enormous impact, radicalizing the whole political scene and increasing the risks of collaboration with the government. Suspected police informers were killed; houses of policemen and officials were burnt; the entire Soweto Urban Bantu Council resigned in 1977 in response to pressure from the Soweto Students Representative Council. In the 1983 elections for the new Community Councils for urban Africans there was a low 21 per cent poll (10 per cent in Soweto). Student unrest also contributed to the educational reforms and broader concessions to the urban blacks (see Chapter 3), as was clear from the Riekert Report's repeated references to the need to defuse the explosiveness of urban blacks, and from the acknowledgement by senior Nationalists like Heunis that the 'impatience . . . frustration . . . rising expectations and aspirations' of blacks had to be taken into account in policy-making.[162] The government did not, however, permit institutionalized outlets for their growing militancy; there were thus an increasing number of recruits for the armed struggle.

The revolutionary option
After they were outlawed, the ANC and PAC adopted revolutionary strategies which, in the words of Alfred Nzo, the ANC's secretary-general, 'totally reject the notion that . . . the struggle of our people is aiming at reform within the apartheid system . . . our objective is the seizure of power, which our people will use to bring

---

*A 1977 survey revealed support among Africans of only 4 per cent.[161] African labour in particular seemed unsympathetic to school boycotts, regarding the students as lucky to get an education and wary of their belief in the power of spontaneous mass action to prevail over bullets and tanks.

about the radical political, economic, social and cultural transformation of SA.'[163]

The efficiency and ruthlessness of the security police soon led to the smashing of their organizations and the imprisonment of Nelson Mandela, Govan Mbeki, Robert Sobukwe and other leaders. The remnants fled abroad, establishing offices in London, Lusaka and other capitals from which, together with the anti-apartheid lobbies, they mounted campaigns which secured the sports boycott, the 1977 arms embargo, and the exclusion of SA from the UN, ILO and other international organizations.

ANC and PAC recruits were also trained in various African and communist countries for the armed struggle. The Soweto riots swelled their numbers: it was estimated that by 1978, 4,000 students had fled the country to join the underground,[164] particularly the ANC. Their radicalizing effect was evident in the rising incidence and boldness of acts of sabotage, including the bombing at the Koeberg nuclear power station in 1982 and the 1983 Pretoria bombing, in which eighteen people were killed and many wounded. Opinion polls showed that within SA the ANC gained in the wake of the brutal destruction of the Black Consciousness movement (see p. 339n). ANC flags and salutes were defiantly displayed at the trials and funerals of political activists and the UDF openly subscribed to its Freedom Charter (see p. 334n).

The Charter proclaimed that, 'SA belongs to all who live in it, black and white, and no government can justly claim authority unless it is based on the will of all the people.' But the ANC's non-racialism was a recurrent source of dispute within the nationalist movement, leading to the PAC breakaway in 1959 and to a further breach in 1969, when the ANC's Morogoro conference opened membership to whites, coloureds and Indians, previously organised in their own separate congresses. Africans were thus conducting their own debates about who was a South African and about the place of whites (and others) in the society—whether they should be incorporated as full members, or whether they were colonists, who should be expelled or only allowed to remain on sufferance.

Another source of dissension was the ANC's links with the SA Communist Party, whose influence was reflected in the number of Communists reportedly on its National Executive Committee and in the Marxist-Leninist and anti-Western rhetoric of its journal, *Sechaba*. ANC spokesmen pointed out that, while it received support from the Soviet bloc, it also had close ties with Western countries like Sweden.* The ANC seemed to encompass a broad range of views: social democrats who favoured a mixed economy and non-racialism; Marxists who agreed with the non-racialism, but wanted nationalization of the means of production; and Africanists, who might be capitalist or socialist, but whose prime objective was African rule.

The more successful sabotage attacks of the 1980s provoked a devastating SA retaliation against neighbouring countries which permitted an ANC or PAC presence; and P. W. Botha warned that SA 'has not come anywhere near to using the weaponry it could well utilize in the event of greater pressure against us'.[166] By 1984 the rising costs and risks forced neighbouring states into reducing such facilities as they afforded the ANC, and even into non-aggression pacts such as the Mozambique–SA Nkomati Accord. SA began to look almost as dominant in the region as the USSR in Eastern Europe.[167]

Even if the Nkomati Accord sticks, however, it is unlikely to halt the activities of the ANC and PAC, which will increasingly attempt to operate from within SA. This outcome would reduce the possibility of that combination of internal unrest and external attack which SA's military planners dread—and which would evoke a fearsome retaliation from them.

Despite the increase in opposition of all kinds, SA's military and economic power meant that, for the proponents of armed struggle, no less than for those using political or industrial means, there were still narrow limits to what they could achieve, on issues (such as political rights) touching white security.

Reasons for the revival of opposition
Dissidence within the oligarchy from the late 1960s widened the area of public debate. The acknowledgement that reform was needed stimulated opposition, while the contacts of businessmen with black unions, and of the Urban Foundation with black

---

*It was estimated that in 1983 the ANC received $8m from the USSR and $5m from Sweden, and that ANC and PAC together received well over $10m from the UN and its specialised agencies.[165]

community organizations like the Soweto Committee of Ten, set precedents for cooperation across colour lines, which it had been a major aim of Nationalist policy to prevent. The government's own multinational policy sanctioned breaches of sacred taboos and provided platforms which were used to attack apartheid and mobilize blacks.

During the early 1970s, and again under Botha, more opposition was tolerated, perhaps partly because of official recognition that pressures were necessary for the reforms they now wanted. This enabled the black consciousness organizations and trade unions to get established and facilitated contact across racial lines. Later, it proved difficult to stop inter-racial fraternization and to draw clear lines between the 'licenced' critics and those whom the government still wanted to exclude. White liberal lobbies like the Black Sash and the student activists were more deeply involved than hitherto with the growing number of black community organizations. These developments made it more difficult to run in harness the fairly democratic system for whites with the repressive system for the rest of the population.

The changing climate of opinion was also an encouragement to opposition, which became more widespread and diffuse, much of it surfacing in parapolitical and professional organizations, and penetrating more deeply into the English and even Afrikaans establishments. A handful of clergymen had long denounced apartheid, but the churches now began to talk seriously of defying the state. The 1980 Anglican Synod decided that it would no longer apply for permits for multiracial church gatherings, which should be 'a right and not a concession in Christian countries'. Methodist synods endorsed proposals in support of people who broke laws restricting inter-racial contact, and there was growing church support for civil disobedience, defiance of unChristian laws such as the Mixed Marriages Act and the Orderly Movement Bill, and for conscientious objectors who did not want to serve in the SA Defence Force.[168]

Professional groups, such as teachers, nurses and judges, protested against official policies and bureaucratic arrogance. In his evidence to the 1980 Hoexter Commission into the legal system, Judge John Didcott denounced the undermining of the Courts by the executive as part of a deliberate strategy to weaken the judiciary by ensuring 'less power for the Supreme Court . . . its infiltration by civil servants, and the growing suzerainty over it of the Department of Justice'. The 'seething discontent' of which Didcott warned was not limited to English judges, as shown by Judge Mostert's insistence on making public his findings on Muldergate.[169]

The anger and resentment of the judges was symptomatic of frustration and alienation among many highly-qualified people, who felt that an 'anachronistic' system was hindering them from fulfilling their professional roles and threatening the welfare and security of the whole society. Many of them were highly skilled specialists and technocrats; discretion and authority had to be delegated to them, and their cooperation was essential for the efficient functioning of the economic and social infrastructure. As some observers had predicted, the values and rationalizations justifying a hierarchical, immobile and authoritarian society, with promotion and position determined by rigidly ascriptive criteria, conflicted with their rationalist training and their more egalitarian, or at least more meritocratic, and therefore colour-blind, values. These developments (perhaps analogous to the wish of capital for race-free markets), and the diffusion of power that takes place in a complex, high-technology society, made it more difficult for the government to manipulate public opinion and intimidate its opponents in the old way, and created a climate of opinion more favourable to reform and to opposition, even though it had not yet found effective expression in political organization.

Demographic factors were generally regarded as strengthening the relative long-term position of blacks. However, their effects were complex. The decline in the proportion of whites from 21 per cent of the population in 1911 to 17 per cent in 1970 and a projected 14 per cent by 2000 convinced many that the days of white rule were numbered and that history was 'on the side' of black liberation. This belief contributed to the decision to incorporate coloureds and Indians into the oligarchy, which might serve as a wedge for African advance, but might also delay it. Rapid black population growth also increased the burden on black wage-earners, reduced per capita incomes and aggravated unemployment. The net effect on black, particularly African, bargaining power is therefore problematical.

The impact of rapid economic growth seems more positive (though some would demur), strengthening the classes which were the major pressures for change, that is, capital-intensive employers and black workers, especially those with skills. By 1970 blacks accounted for almost 80 per cent of the workforce, and their educational and skill levels and real incomes had risen markedly (see Chapter 3). This strengthened their bargaining power as producers and consumers. The press provides an example: in 1962 blacks accounted for 19 per cent of the readership of all newspapers; by 1979 this had risen to 36 per cent—60 per cent in the case of the *Rand Daily Mail*, which consequently employed more black journalists and gave wider coverage to the activities of black unions, the Soweto Committee of Ten and even the exiled movements.[170] Likewise, the coloureds came to account for a growing share of the readership of the Afrikaans press.

Many social scientists believe that industrialization sharpens aspirations to equality. Gellner argued that occupational mobility made people resistant to the idea of themselves as permanently inferior ('modern society is not mobile because it is egalitarian; it is egalitarian because it is mobile') and that it was more difficult to secure toleration of profound inequalities in a society in which, because of the need for a literate, educated workforce, socialization was standardized. Affluence and enhanced welfare also made workers less vulnerable to economic pressure.[171]

In SA, the economic advance of the 1960s and 1970s did not placate the black vanguard, and certainly not their children. Instead, the promise of reform—and then its limitations—sharpened their sensitivity to the pervasive discrimination which remained, intensifying what Isaiah Berlin called social dissonance (and others have termed status inconsistency)—a disjunction caused by advances in some areas and lack of progress in others.[172] The social system no longer possessed the coherence and stability which, however painful, provided a feeling of inevitability; uncertainty led to tension and explosiveness.*

The Soweto rioters, children of relatively well-off blacks, seem to present a classic case of expectations first raised by the talk of reform and then disappointed—among other things by the severe

---

*Compare de Tocqueville's well-known passage: 'The most perilous moment for a bad government is when it seeks to mend its ways . . . . Patiently endured so long as it seemed beyond redress, a grievance comes to appear intolerable once the possibility of removing it crosses men's minds . . . .'[173]

mid-1970s recession, which aggravated unemployment among young blacks with some schooling but without the skills to fill the vacancies for skilled jobs, and by the insistence of BAD on the citizenship issue and the use of Afrikaans as a medium of instruction in schools (which precipitated the riots).

As with Afrikaner nationalism, political militancy acquired mass support when political principles fused with issues directly affecting peoples' interests. Compulsory Bantustan citizenship undermined tenuous black rights in the towns; few teachers and pupils in Soweto were proficient in Afrikaans and its compulsory use as a medium of instruction created severe problems. There was much less unrest in Natal, where most black schools were sited in areas under Kwa-zulu control and language and citizenship were not issues, because Kwa-zulu refused to take independence or enforce the Afrikaans medium in schools.

Perhaps the best example of the effect of social dissonance was provided by rising labour militancy. The 1973 Durban strikes and subsequent mine riots took place at a time of rising wages, while the post-Wiehahn wave of strikes occurred at a time of unprecedented improvements in wages, job prospects and workers' rights.

In my interviews with black workers during the 1970s, they often denied they were better off, or even said they were worse off, though they would then confirm the facts about their occupational advance and higher incomes.* However, other aspects of their lives—migrancy, restrictions on mobility and on urban and political rights—remained unchanged. Even at the workplace, there were sometimes sources of increased tension due to the manner in which black advance took place. The floating bar, which facilitated the earlier stages of advance, often led to the downgrading of jobs taken over by blacks. Management believed that blacks must surely be grateful for the battle being waged on their behalf; but on the shop floor the view was different. Workers complained that employers were only advancing them because they could not find

---

*In their study of ethnic politics in New York, Glazer and Moynihan recorded similar findings: 'The 1960s have seen an enormous increase in the number of Negroes in stable jobs; it has simultaneously seen an enormous increase in militancy. It is quite common for spokesmen . . . to insist that nothing has changed, indeed that blacks are worse off than before.'[174]

suitable whites and that they were 'exploiting us' by downgrading the pay and status of the jobs opened up. These factors, plus the strains imposed by upward mobility, contributed to the intensified discontent expressed by many black workers whose occupations, real incomes and prospects were improving.

The tensions generated by economic advance, rising expectations, and the contradictory and frustrating combination of real reform in some areas and 'no change' in others, resulted in the most explosive outburst of mass feeling since Union, and in the capacity to sustain strikes and riots longer, despite repression. But the severe 1982/3 drought did not provoke similar demonstrations among the least well-off blacks in the rural areas and resettlement camps.

Research confirmed that dissatisfaction was increasing and was most pronounced among better-off, more educated and younger blacks.[175] 'It's the door that squeaks that gets the grease,' said Malcolm X.[176] The government's concessions showed its concern with rioting students, restless workers, and alienation among the urban black middle classes; but there were few concessions for the rural and poorest blacks.

International pressures

External pressures and influences also contributed to the revival of opposition. Despite boycotts and threats of isolation, SA was more closely integrated into the world economy (see p. 241). After the independence of Mozambique and Angola in the mid-1970s and of Zimbabwe in 1980, it was in more direct contact with Africa than hitherto. This made it more difficult for the Nationalists to turn their backs on external pressures as Malan and Strijdom had done.

The clearest examples of the contribution of international pressures to reform were the changes in social policy, especially sport (see p. 56), and labour policy. In regard to labour, the combination of leverage on multinational companies, threats of economic boycotts, and the parallel pressures for change coming from white capital within SA, produced the most significant reforms yet. On job advance, education and training and wages, the liberal lobbies were pushing at an open door: Gerdener's policy of narrowing the wage gap was already being implemented in 1972 (see p. 65)—before the 1973 Durban strikes. Revelations in the *Guardian* about 'poverty wages' paid by British companies, and a subsequent House of Commons enquiry strengthened and accelerated the wage increases and ensured that they continued during the mid-1970s recession. (It is interesting that external pressures gained momentum in areas in which changes were already occurring, perhaps because the lobbies were encouraged by the possibility of success.)

However, in relation to trade unions, the prospects for reform were more finely balanced and external pressures more decisive. The 1976 EEC and Sullivan Codes of Conduct for foreign companies operating in SA attached central importance to the recognition of representative black unions, and the 1974–9 British Labour government and the Carter administration in the USA appointed Labour Attachés in Pretoria to monitor the policies of their companies towards the unions. During the 1979 Ford strike, US diplomats were present in Port Elizabeth and acted as intermediaries between the company and the unions.[177] British pressures helped to ensure that Smith & Nephew renewed its pioneering recognition agreement with the National Union of Textile Workers in 1977, despite intense contrary pressure from the SA government. Recognition agreements with unregistered African unions were also signed by other multinationals under pressure (Kelloggs, Colgate-Palmolive, Johnson & Johnson). They helped to persuade the SA government first to appoint the Wiehahn Commission and later to ease registration procedures in order to avoid the emergence of an unofficial system of bargaining (see p. 169).

The international trade union movement was also closely involved in the struggle for black trade union rights. The International Metal Federation, British TUC, the International Confederation of Trade Unions and national unions like the German IG Metall provided funds and technical support for the unions and for their training organizations,* most of which received substantial funding from abroad.[178]

In 1975 the International Metal Federation established a regional council for SA, on which conservative white unions served, alongside Jane Hlongwane of the (black) Allied and Engineering

---

*During the early 1970s The Urban Training Project in Johannesburg and Trade Union Advisory Council in Durban were set up to inform African workers of their rights and to provide training and legal aid for their unions.

Workers Union. In 1982, two white unions (the Amalgamated Engineering Union and SA Electrical Workers Association) were expelled from the regional Council because of complaints from black unions about their racist and unhelpful attitudes.[179] In disputes involving metal unions, the Federation sent out observers and put pressure on the head offices of multinational companies like Volkswagen during their 1980 Port Elizabeth strike and Alfa Romeo during their 1983 recognition dispute.[180] The Metal Federation also exerted pressure directly on the SA government, making representations (combined with warnings of boycotts) over the banning of trade unionists and over the initial, limited reforms contained in the Wiehahn White Paper. This helped to push the government towards the subsequent amendments of the 1979 legislation, which were even discussed in advance with international trade unionists by some of the businessmen engaged in lobbying.[181]

The Minister of Labour, Fanie Botha, acknowledged that pressure from the international trade union movement 'had become far too great to be ignored'.[182] This close international involvement in the struggle for black trade union rights was the most successful example of the policy of 'constructive engagement'*—reinforced by the threat of sanctions.

The Reagan administration's 'constructive engagement' policy (and the Thatcher government's similar policy) seemed to rely mainly on inducements, particularly the prospect of ending SA's diplomatic isolation. Botha's desire to respond to this friendlier stance contributed to the withholding of the draconian 1982 press law, the reduction of banning orders in 1983, and to Botha's significant 1984 concessions to Africans in the Western Cape (see p. 83). In announcing the latter, Botha specifically stated that 'the free Western world is extremely sensitive to large-scale removals of people . . . . We simply cannot go on as if we had no need to heed them.'[184] However, external pressures have not yet secured the

---

*The term was, I think, first used in my 1976 article 'British investment in SA: is constructive engagement possible?' Subsequently, it was invoked, and attacked, as justification for a 'business as usual' policy towards SA. But the article stressed the need for both carrots and sticks and for close scrutiny of business practices, particularly in the area of trade union recognition, which would enable blacks to take care of their own interests.[183]

political incorporation of Africans, nor a Namibian settlement. There were clearly limits to the concessions which either the 'hard' Carter or 'soft' Reagan strategies could secure, particularly on matters perceived as affecting white security.[185]

Some of the successes achieved by international pressures complicated the anti-apartheid campaigns. In 1983 the International Federation of Mining and Power Workers proposed a boycott of SA coal. The black National Union of Mineworkers (NUM) deplored the apartheid policies which provoked the proposed boycott, but pointed out that pit closures threatened their jobs. The NUM wanted continued international support, for example in its court case against mining companies over safety regulations, and it sought links with other mine unions in African countries which shared the same employers and provided labour for SA mines. But it did not want economic boycotts which threatened its members' improving wages and job prospects.[186] Likewise in sport, the Transvaal Cricket Council, which had fought for integrated sport down to club level—and not just tokenism as in rugby—were angered by their continued exclusion from world cricket,[187] which was cited by *verkramptes* as evidence that the outside world wished to destroy, not reform, white South Africans.

The significant impact of international pressures on SA has been noted throughout this study. This was acknowledged both by P. W. Botha and Fanie Botha and by Chris Heunis, Minister of the Interior, who stated that 'the Southern African problem had been internationalized and the opinion of the international community could no longer be disregarded in the context of domestic reforms.'[188] Heunis was the architect of the ambiguous 1983 constitution, and this illustrates the point that the effects of external pressures were complex and sometimes unintended.

The most successful pressures were those which aimed at specific, limited goals (improved wages, trade union rights, mixed sport) and reinforced internal pressures for change (business and sports lobbies, black unions, community groups resisting population removals). External pressures with broader goals which affected the security of the SA state or questioned its legitimacy (economic or military sanctions aimed at changing the whole system or overthrowing the government) could have unintended effects, contributing to the white backlash of the mid-1970s,* strengthening authoritarianism and militarization, and feeding the paranoia and resentment that led to massive retaliation against neighbouring African states. However, militarization, in turn, also had some unexpected effects, drawing blacks into the armed forces which, as social scientists have noted, often opens the way to citizenship.[190] In SA, P. W. Botha argued that, 'People could not be expected to give their lives for their country if they did not have a say in the way it was run.'[191]

The sensitivity of SA to external pressures was linked to its close cultural ties with the West, and its deep involvement in the world economy—Asian and African as well as Western. Political scientists like Huntington cite many instances in which 'the pressure of the international struggle' led to reform, to 'defensive modernization', and often to militarization and hence on to foreign conquests.[192] Huntington also noted that the principal threat to the stability of rigidly-ordered societies came not from external military threats but from 'the invasion by foreign ideas'—which the cultural boycott (preventing academics and artists from going to SA or having their work performed there) seems calculated to forestall.

The impact of international pressures on the SA government's opponents was also complex, providing material and moral support and some protection, but also fostering illusions about their strength. The sponsors of the unending stream of UN resolutions and rhetoric encouraging neighbouring African states to adopt confrontationist postures towards SA did not put their money where they put their mouths when the fragile, newly-established states bore the brunt of SA retaliation. A realistic strategy would have to take account both of the constructive role which international pressures can play and of their limitations and dangers.

---

*This is illustrated by the swings in public opinion before and after the death of Biko and subsequent bannings and detentions of October 1977. Initially, these events led to a drop in the Nationalists' share of the vote from 51 per cent (70 per cent of Afrikaners, 32 English) to 46 per cent (64 per cent Afrikaners, 29 English). As international pressures built up, culminating in the November 1977 Security Council arms embargo, public opinion rallied behind the Nationalists, whose support rose to 55 per cent (75 per cent Afrikaners, 34 English), *exceeding* what they had before.[189]

Black political mobilization: possibilities and problems

The history of the Afrikaners (and of other societies) suggests that material improvements alone do not dissolve historical resentments: when accompanied by the insecurity and strain bred by rapid mobility and status inconsistency (or social dissonance) they are more likely to intensify political extremism and conflict. SA seems to provide a classic case of this explosive mixture, particularly in the case of the black elite (including coloureds and Indians). The election of the Nationalists in 1948 set back the development of this elite, which is consequently small, weak and resentful, and more likely to regard whites as competitors than as allies, and to conform to the prediction that 'while a large middle class . . . can be a moderating force in politics, the creation of a middle class . . . is often highly destabilizing . . . the true revolutionary class in most modernizing societies is the middle class' rather than the industrial labour force.[193]

A volatile and readily mobilized constituency is now provided by unemployed younger blacks. Their expectations are high, but their education was severely disrupted by the upheavals of the last decade, and the severe post-1982 recession has made it more difficult to provide jobs for them.

The shared interests of black labour and white capital have enabled them to develop institutionalized means of negotiation, but African workers seem likely to be more militant than other proletariats because of the disabilities to which they are still subjected. Reformers like Buthelezi have been damaged by their association with the limited and ambiguous reform programme and branded as sellouts.

Intensified racial polarization and conflict therefore seem likely— at least for a transitional period. However, there are also obstacles to successful mobilization based on an anti-white alliance, as well as some possibilities for alliances across race lines. The white oligarchy is a more formidable opponent than the white regimes elsewhere in Africa. It is more numerous and more committed to the country, and has no alternative 'home' to return to. It is self-governing, with no metropolitan power to prevail over it, and it is economically strong, well armed and well organized. Coloureds and Indians comprise a significant mestizo group, some of whom might side with the whites if there was a sharp racial polarization (and if they were offered full incorporation).

There might also be some Africans (minority tribes* and even one of the major groups, say, a section of the Zulus or Tswanas) for whom intra-African rivalries loom larger than anti-white feeling. Unless the whites adopt a CP/HNP policy uniting all blacks against them, any political split would be unlikely to reflect the simple 80–20 per cent division of the population along the colour line.

Changing African attitudes

There are furthermore shared interests and ties between whites and blacks, including Africans. Recent research bears out the observation of Feit, in his study of the ANC, that many Africans see their welfare as bound up with that of whites, who are perceived, not just as exploiters and oppressors, but as making a crucial contribution to the economy.[195] (Respondents made statements such as, 'Without the whites our economy would collapse', and said they did not want to follow in the footsteps of Zaire and Uganda).

But research also revealed declining tolerance towards whites ** and growing black discontent, militancy, and preparedness to assert their rights, by force if necessary. The Buthelezi Commission found 'a growing climate of revolutionary ideology', with violence becoming a 'respectable option', particularly among the educated. However, militancy was not necessarily correlated with racist or undemocratic views. Many of the militants were democrats who favoured minority rights. Hanf concluded that 'the more democratic a black South African is, the stronger his demands for political rights, and the readier he is to adopt non-peaceful means to attain them.' Conversely, the most racist were the least educated and well-off, who were also less prepared to assert themselves politically. As with whites, support for racism came from the less well-off and less educated, supplemented (as both PAC and Black Consciousness showed) by support from sections of the intel-

---

*Research has shown that minority tribes like the Venda, Shangaans and Pedi, are apprehensive about the possibilities of change and the likely outcome for themselves.[194]

**In 1977 only 64 per cent of Africans under 35 years of age would have accorded whites political rights under an African government, compared with 82 per cent of those over 35 years.

ligentsia—teachers, priests, political activists—whose jobs and roles could be enhanced by racially exclusive policies.

Growing militancy did not necessarily lead to support for completely confrontationist or revolutionary policies. In 1983 only 35 per cent of Africans supported the sports boycott (less than the 43 per cent of coloureds and 53 per cent of Indians); and only 36 per cent supported disinvestment by foreign companies in SA.[196] Africans also showed a preference for private ownership of property and business over state or communal ownership (65 per cent to 32 in a 1977 survey). They wanted a chance to share in the fruits of capitalism but, except for land, did not reject white ownership. However, Marxism had become influential among younger blacks, and surveys showed a growing hostility to capitalism, though this may have been mainly to white capitalism.

Mayer and other researchers confirm the impression of observers that the official emphasis on ethnic differences has been counter-productive, provoking a reaction against 'tribalism', particularly among urban Africans.[197] However, while ethnic differences do not appear to have sharpened with industrialization and urbanization, as they did among the Afrikaners and ethnic groups in many other parts of the world, they have not disappeared. The two most successful examples of African political mobilization were the Zulus in Inkatha (using the Bantustan institutions) and the Ovambos in SWAPO (rejecting the Bantustans). Ethnicity thus remained a powerful force which could not simply be manipulated by the SA government nor ignored by black nationalists.

The same caveat applies to African attitudes as to those of whites: while surveys may accurately reflect the state of opinion at a particular moment, they are not necessarily good predictors of behaviour (for which an analysis of interests and power is required). The 1968–71 surveys of white attitudes towards sport, social change and job reservation gave little hint of how rapidly they would adapt to the changes which were soon introduced (see p. 311). As the options of Africans change, these attitudes are likely to shift, as they did in Zimbabwe, where support for Muzorewa and his policies evaporated when the voters had Mugabe and Nkomo as alternative candidates. Support for moderates or for 'second-best' consociational policies may likewise decline when SA Africans have a wider range of options.

While surveys bear out the impression of hardening attitudes, particularly among the young, they do not show Africans as solidly anti-white, but as highly differentiated in their views, reflecting the complexities of class, education and ethnic/regional factors. Moreover, while there was overwhelming opposition to apartheid, support for a *revolutionary* strategy 'to overthrow the whole system' was inhibited by the material interests, links with whites, and the fear of disorder and instability of many blacks.

The most important link with whites was the workplace, where relations were often quite good, and there was mutual recognition of interdependence and of the gains for substantial numbers of blacks from rising incomes and from expanding education and health services, housing and pensions. Other ties were religion (in 1978 about 50 per cent of Africans were members of Christian churches, including one million in the Dutch Reformed Churches[198]) and language (many spoke English; Afrikaans was widespread in the OFS, Transvaal, Namibia and even Botswana).

There clearly were blacks, particularly among the intelligentsia and youth, who were available for revolutionary mobilization. But many blacks seemed less available for this than their undoubted hostility to apartheid and the government suggested. Their interests oriented them towards reform rather than revolution. They did not want a violent upheaval and the destruction of the economy. This no doubt contributed to the ANC's moderation, evident in its reluctance to resort to violence and its subsequent attempts to avoid civilian deaths.

However, the greater incomes, education and integration into the common society which created shared interests also intensified the social dissonance arising from the incompleteness of the process, particularly the lack of social and political structures to 'match' the more complex and highly differentiated economy.

Beyond negative politics
These intangible but compelling pressures not only pushed the government towards reform, but also had implications for the opposition, particularly for the revolutionary strategy (counterpart of the government's crude policies of coercion and manipulation) which threatened to disrupt the functioning of this increasingly differentiated society, with its complex and overlapping interests, and more ambivalent and sophisticated attitudes.

Exile and exclusion from power encouraged uncompromising attitudes and policies, remote from political reality (that is, what interests and the power balance made feasible). This not only made the opposition unresponsive to the limited opportunities for change that emerged but also inhibited black political mobilization, because most people are discouraged, if not alarmed, by ambitious schemes and strategies ('overthrowing the whole system') which seem unobtainable or, if attained, risky and possibly unworkable.

Ethnic complexity, overlapping class structures, and shared interests make possible alliances across colour lines. Minorities of coloureds, Indians and English have a strong interest in avoiding a replay of the period of Afrikaner hegemony by an African group, especially as the opposition from a section of the oligarchy and its allies would be likely to guarantee a civil war.

Among both blacks and whites there are thus forces converging towards political and social incorporation and the emergence of a new national identity to complement the integration wrought by the economy. There are also forces pushing in the opposite direction. As before, these have their origins not only in 'irrational' ideological and ethnic factors, but are closely bound up with both class interests and security concerns—the anxiety (often unspoken) about political order, which is the precondition for the functioning of any society.

The habit of 'negative politics' into which discrimination and exclusion from power drove the opposition is not conducive to negotiation and compromise. Furthermore, the contemporary *mentalité* is averse to compromises on 'race' (as it once was on religion) and antipathetic to devices for gradual change such as loaded or qualified franchises. Yet the balance of forces, resentments and fears, and the continuing divisions in SA, are such that anything short of a destructive full-scale revolution will require substantial concessions on all sides.

An important key to the white oligarchy's likely political behaviour is their perception of themselves as a national class, committed to the country. Even 'enlightened' ruling classes do not, in their home base, voluntarily abdicate power. Under pressure, they make concessions and incorporate other classes into the social and political system, thereby diluting their own ranks while strengthening the state, as Gibbon described (see p. 49).

The test of whether the white oligarchy performs this classic reforming role—or whether it merely modernizes apartheid—will be its willingness (i) to recognize those South Africans termed black as citizens; and to accept that they should have (ii) political representation and (iii) participation in government.

However, in SA it will be exceptionally difficult to implement this classic reform process in a reasonable time, because the salience of racial/ethnic divisions will hinder the construction of those cross-cutting alliances which prevent polarization and provide stability. Instead, political mobilization is likely to take place along racial lines—a tendency which the Nationalists' segregationist policies strengthened. This leads the white elite to fear that the introduction of majority rule will have revolutionary consequences—that it will rapidly lead to the total replacement of the whole power structure, which they now dominate.

In the UK, for example, the broadening of political participation did not mean the exclusion of the ruling group from power. During the lengthy period of successive extensions of the franchise (see p. 82n) the ruling elite were able to compete in constructing political packages which introduced many changes in response to mass pressures, but also ensured continuity and stability. The prospect of sudden and total exclusion from power, and of a complete changeover with its unforeseen consequences, is feared— and will be opposed—by many whites who now support not only deracialization and economic redistribution, but also African political representation and participation in government.

These fears (and the rejection of a gradual extension of the franchise) have led to amendments to the classic Western model. The PFP liberals propose the grafting on to it of consociational devices which will guarantee white political participation and slow down the rate of change by minority vetos. A positive interpretation of Botha's ambiguous policy suggests that he might gradually incorporate Africans politically (by extending to them citizenship, representation, and participation in government) but that power would remain in white hands for the foreseeable future. He would also retain the option of falling back on separate political entities if 'power sharing' did not work. The *verkramptes* oppose all power sharing. They believe it will be unworkable; if political rights must be extended to blacks, they want this to be done on a separate basis, leaving whites in control of their own destiny.

The African model of political change is of a complete 'take over' from the departing colonial power and the rapid extension of the franchise, exemplified in Nkrumah's slogan 'Seek ye first the political kingdom'. The difficulties of coping with this rapid transition led to the establishment of one-party states, with even less provision for minorities than in the classic Western model. This rapid change in the power structure did not, however, lead to comparable socio-economic changes, except for a small elite. Instead, it proved extremely difficult for the incoming governments—whether reformist or revolutionary—to effect profound social changes rapidly. Attempts to force the pace could lead to a breakdown in government, or even to sessionist attempts to break away from the state.

In SA, the expectation of Africans that their turn had come to take over has been intensified by the post-1970 socio-economic advances and reforms; by the SA government's own acknowledgement that discrimination was wrong and that blacks were entitled to political rights; and by international support. But, instead of these expectations being satisfied, they were then faced with the prospect of being permanently frozen out politically.

These fears and resentments were compounded by SA's recent progress in securing international respectability (the Nkomati Accord, Botha's 1984 tour of Western Europe). The feeling that they had their backs to the wall, and could lose out, did not lead to greater willingness to compromise but (as has often been the case with whites) to a backlash and hardening of attitudes. Hence the increased unrest and polarization accompanying the introduction in 1984 of the new constitution.

Black bargaining power is growing, but for the foreseeable future it seems unlikely that they will be able to impose by force straightforward majority rule on an undivided SA. However, they seem likely to have the capacity to prevent meaningful African (and probably black) participation in carrying out the Nationalist design of separate African political representation and to inflict on the SA government heavy costs and risks—acts of sabotage, recurrent strikes and unrest, the withholding of international legitimacy, the continued threat of sanctions and isolation.

It is difficult to foresee the effects of these growing pressures. They could lead to further concessions, such as fuller incorporation and the willingness to talk rather than to shoot and detain.

They could also lead to a backlash and to the halting of reform. The third alternative is that they could lead to a more authoritarian path of reform, that is further deracialization and economic redistribution, but the curbing of all political activity—white conservative as well as black radical. This further postponement of the fundamental political issue would be more fiercely resisted than hitherto, because of the expectations that have been raised and the more broadly-based organizations that have been established. If this led to a backlash against SA internationally it might also be accompanied by an isolationist strategy—as happened after Sharpeville—with the SA government retreating from the more outgoing economic, cultural and diplomatic policies that it has pursued since about 1970.

On both sides there is some recognition of the difficulties and costs of imposing their preferred option and of the consequences— 'too ghastly to contemplate' as Vorster said[199]—of deepening polarization and violence. These realistic assessments (and the shared interests and ties of whites and blacks) provide the main hope—though it is a slender one—of a willingness to search for formulae that will provide a rate of change the social system can tolerate and that will help SA to get through the long and difficult transitional period required for forging a broader national identity.

It might help to narrow the gulf between the two sides if they clarified their divergent, but largely implicit, assumptions about the manner and pace at which social change usually occurs. History suggests this seldom happens quickly, even under revolutionary governments (though it happens unevenly and cataclysmic events may accelerate—or retard—the process). Moreover, the incremental socio-economic changes, which some dismiss as marginal or even functional for the status quo, can over the longterm add up to profound social change and the shift in the balance of power that accompanies it.

10
The Debate About South Africa: Some Conclusions

Apartheid cannot simply be explained as the outcome of capitalism or of racism. Its origins lie in a complex interaction between class interests (of white labour as well as of sections of capital) and racism/ethnicity, reinforced by ideological and security factors.

The dominance of white agriculture and white labour until the mid-1960s was based on political, not economic power. The system of 'democracy for whites' gave these highly mobilized classes the power to defeat at the polls governments pursuing policies contrary to their interests, as happened during 1920–24, when foreign-owned mining companies secured political dominance, and again during 1939–48, when hegemony shifted to manufacturing and commercial capital.

The 1924 election ensured priority not only for the alliance of white agriculture and labour against the black vanguard, but also for national against foreign interests. The 1948 election secured priority for Afrikaners, the less well-off whites. By the mid-1960s these preferential policies, and the rapid industrialization nurtured by the Afrikaner Nationalists, generated their own contradictions, leading to the emergence of Afrikaans capitalists who came to share the interest of other employers in eroding apartheid. Their conflict with white labour, transformed into a bureaucracy, tore apart the Afrikaner alliance.

However, the strength of ethnic ties, the institutionalization of apartheid, and time lags before changes in interests fed into the political system—as well as deep divisions among the opposition—enabled the Afrikaner political establishment to maintain its power base and hegemony. The unexpected election of P. W. Botha in 1978 marked a further lurch in the power balance towards capital. The subsequent reforms (labour and social policy; concessions to Section 10s; political incorporation of coloureds and Indians) split the NP. The conservatives were not routed, however, as the difficulties in implementing reform showed. The 1983 constitution reduced the threat from the right and seems likely to provide the framework for a continuing process of limited deracialization, without much broadening of participation in government. But while the authoritarian grip remained strong, it did not become total—reflecting the resistance of important elements within the oligarchy, including capital. These democratic remnants enabled sections of the opposition to survive, and may yet serve as a bridge for broadening the system.

The origins of authoritarianism did not lie solely in attempts to impose apartheid on the black majority (or 'Afrikaners First' policies on the English). As the record of other industrializing societies shows, authoritarianism is frequently intensified by the strains of modernization. In addition to their racist policies, SA governments pursued many centralizing and modernizing policies likely to be adopted by any government wishing to unify and develop the country and to establish a national identity. This latter aspect was obscured by their insistence on separate nations—even while their actions welded the inhabitants into the same industrial culture and society.

Underdevelopment theories and the SA case

The 1924 election settled not only the struggle over the job colour bar and civilized labour policy, but also the questions of protection and subsidy for white agriculture and manufacturing. It was a major victory for (white) national interests against foreign capital, ensuring that a high proportion of the surplus generated by the gold mines would be ploughed into the development of the SA economy, rather than repatriated abroad, despite the fact that foreigners then held 80 per cent of gold mining shares (see p. 258).

SA did not therefore conform to Gundar Frank's model of a peripheral, colonial economy 'underdeveloped' by metropolitan, imperial capital.[1] Yet SA appeared to have all the ingredients that should have made it an ideal examplar of these theories. First, the dominant role of foreign mining capital, the major generator of surplus. Second, the defeat by imperial forces of blacks and of Afrikaner nationalists, who resisted the hegemony of this capital. Third, the presence of a substantial English group, hostile to the

Afrikaners and ideal candidates for the role of *comprador bourgeoisie* (agents of imperial capital). A Frankian scenario would lead one to expect that, 'independence' and 'self-government' notwithstanding, SA development would be subordinated to imperial interests, particularly those of mining capital; that it would remain an exporter of primary products required by the metropolitan power and an open market for its products; and that its economic policies (fiscal, monetary, transport, labour) would be geared to a high rate of surplus extraction for foreign capital and minimal reinvestment for local development, as happened in Liberia, Zaire, and Zambia.

Why this did not happen in SA, with its far higher levels of foreign investment and commitment of imperial military forces, is a large and fascinating question. Two likely answers can be eliminated. First, the SA case cannot simply be cast in terms of a successful 'national bourgeoisie versus imperialism' struggle, because of the key role of white labour. Nor can the objections to this be met by recasting white labour as a 'petty bourgeoisie' or even labour aristocracy. The question of whether they would become first a labour aristocracy and then a petty bourgeoisie was precisely what was at issue in the early decades of this century. At that time, white workers were a true proletariat, separated from the means of production, wholly and often precariously dependent upon the sale of their labour. They fought for the right to organize themselves and then used their workers' organizations, votes, and even guns, to insist, in the teeth of resistance from mining capital, that they become a labour aristocracy. The concession of this right was a major element in the victory of 'national' against foreign forces.

Second, their struggle against the British led Afrikaners to claim that the victory was due to them—Africa's first successful nationalists. But Afrikaners lacked the economic strength and financial know-how to prevail over metropolitan capital on their own. A crucial role was played by English labour (then more skilled and organized than Afrikaans labour) and by local English capital—manufacturers who began to compete with British imports, and SA mining houses* which by 1945 had ensured that

---

*AAC was established in 1917, Angloval in 1933.

50 per cent of mining capital was in South African hands. Without the financial strength and skill of this local English/Jewish capital, it is doubtful whether this level of national control could have been attained. Whatever their cultural affinities with Britain, the South African 'English' (like the American colonists in the eighteenth century) were no less assiduous than Afrikaners in pursuing their own economic interests, not those of the imperial power.

National capital in turn was aided in its struggle with metropolitan capital by the support it received from the expanding SA state and by the retreat of imperial power—trends that were accelerated by the two world wars. The SA state did not then emerge solely as an instrument to mobilize and discipline the labour force, but also as a weapon for national against imperial interests, then very assertive in the region. This external factor contributed substantially to the expansion of the SA state, as it did again from the 1960s, with growing international (and regional) hostility to apartheid. Curiously, though SA had by then become less dependent on foreign capital (generating more of its own investment), it had become more open to foreign influences, partly because of its more thorough integration into the world economy, partly because of the oligarchy's desire to retain its close cultural ties with the west.

The need for extra-economic coercion

Locally, the expanding state apparatus served primarily the interests of the politically dominant white farmers and workers. As argued in Chapters 4–8, their interests could not be secured by the operation of 'free market' forces, but required the extra-economic coercion and institutionalized racism that were the distinctive features of apartheid.

The interests of mining capital were more complex. Once blacks were conquered and partly dispossessed of their land, mineowners could probably have coped with a free labour market, which would have reduced their high skilled labour costs. This in turn would have reduced the pressures for their repressive policies towards unskilled labour, which were also connected with restrictions on stabilization, on recruitment in rural areas, on the terms of entry for foreign labour, and the high level of mining tax (to subsidize white agriculture and the large state sector).*

Manufacturing and commercial capital did not need extra-economic coercion and preferred to rely on market mechanisms and class power—as in other capitalist societies. Manufacturing was compensated by protection, but without the costs of apartheid labour policies it could have managed without protection, or at least with less.

However, even progressive capital shared the belief that white hegemony was necessary for political stability, the precondition for both economic growth and personal security. This belief was reinforced by the racist norms of the time, as well as by the difficulties of creating political and administrative structures that could accommodate the disparate (and recently warring) peoples of what was becoming South Africa.

Racist norms and security fears militated against any extension of political rights perceived as likely to threaten white hegemony, but they did not require extra-economic coercion. The decisive factor here was the dire need of white agriculture and white labour—the decisive electoral groups—for controls over unskilled black labour and for the suppression of black producers and skilled classes. *Their needs required the structuring of a totally racist society*; hence their constant pressures not only for economic apartheid, but also for social and political apartheid, including measures which were often opposed by urban (and even mining) capital.

The enormous task of structuring a totally racist society was facilitated by the administrative and military capacity which had emerged, partly in the process of conquest, partly in response to external pressures.

---

*The fixed price of gold complicates the problem of identifying the beneficiaries of the mining surplus. Fogel and Engerman argued that the main gainers from slavery in the USA were UK buyers of cheap cotton textiles.[2] Likewise, it could be argued that among the beneficiaries of apartheid were the (mainly foreign) purchasers of gold, who received their product at a fixed price for almost half a century, despite rising costs.

Capital, the state and Afrikaner nationalism
SA development since Union does not support the thesis that the
state was the instrument of capital. The interests of the economically dominant mining and urban capitalists were often over-
ridden when they were in conflict with those of white labour or the
bureaucracy or of economically weaker agricultural capital. The
key to this lay partly in the political system, partly in the nature of
political mobilization, which was along ethnic, not class, lines.
Afrikaner nationalism is the most striking example of this, and it
poses severe problems for a Marxist analysis.

Most Marxists (and liberals) treated Afrikaner nationalism as an
aberration, or ignored it. O'Meara was one of the few who
confronted the problem; he treated it, like white racism, as
functional for the interests of capital: 'The ideology of Afrikaner
nationalism developed as the ideology of a particular form of
capital accumulation . . . . The *volk* displayed little interest [in
ideological debates] . . . Afrikaans workers were weaned away
from ideologies of class . . . [their trade unions] were initiated,
inspired, led, financed and maintained by the petty bourgeoisie
and Afrikaans bourgeoisie and eschewed any concept of class
struggle'; the NP failed to win the support of unions with 'a
militant history of struggle'. Often O'Meara seemed to deny the
existence of a white working class, referring to it as a 'petty
bourgeoisie'.[3]

But, at least until the 1950s, there *was* a white working class,
which was active and militant, particularly when fighting for the
job colour bar. Their fight over this issue was against capital and,
on occasions, against governments responsive to capital. The most
militant union was the MWU; after its capture by the Hertzogites
in the 1930s, it ardently supported the NP, to which it remained
loyal until the 1970s, when the NP began to support the efforts of
capitalists to undermine the job colour bar. The MWU then
became a key backer of the HNP.

White workers (like businessmen) indeed showed little interest
in tortuous ideological debates over Afrikaner identity (or Marxism); but they nevertheless had strong views about what they
wanted. Alternatives to white racism and to Afrikaner nationalism
were put to them; the Afrikaner 'petty bourgeoisie' were not alone
in propagandizing among them. Within the trade union movement, liberals, Marxists and the Chamber of Mines itself, com-

peted against Hertzog's Reform League for influence. Faced with these alternatives, most white workers chose to support the job bar, exclusive Afrikaans unions, and the Afrikaner nationalist party.

White workers 'eschewed class struggle' only after they got what they wanted. They achieved this after a militant struggle during which many of them died, or were injured, exiled and lost their jobs. After 1924, they had no need to resort to such desperate measures, having easier, more effective legal and institutionalized means of achieving their aims. If black workers become as active under the banner of black nationalism, Marxists will not refuse to accord them autonomy and importance; yet they too will have members of the petty bourgeoisie—teachers, intellectuals, white collar workers—among their leaders and organizers.

Many Marxists recognise 'conflict of capitals' as a key to the development process, but (racial) conflict of labour seems harder for them to swallow. Marxists therefore reduce white workers in SA to the status of puppets, manipulated by capitalists and petty bourgeois ideologists, because of the awkward problem posed for Marxism by their reactionary role in SA and by the phenomenon of white racism—and particularly Afrikaner nationalism—which served as a more effective basis for political mobilization than class interests. It is not implausible that capitalists would attempt to cream off a section of labour by stirring up racism and nationalism; but in this case the argument is unsustainable. The costs of apartheid to capitalists were too high, leading them to oppose major aspects of it; while the prejudices of white labour were reinforced by their interests.

Moreover, during the 1930s and 1940s, when Afrikaner nationalists were mobilizing, the dominant capitalists in SA were overwhelmingly English, Jewish and foreign, and they did not like the anti-English, anti-semitic and anti-capitalist rhetoric of the Nationalists, their support for Germany, and the crypto-Nazi movements like Ossewabrandwag and Greyshirts, which were part of the Afrikaner nationalist scene. They were alarmed by the activities of the Reform League in the trade union movement and apprehensive about the draft 1942 Republican constitution which relegated the English language and people to an inferior place in the proposed Afrikaner republic.

When the Nationalists got into power in 1948, they gradually modified their policies towards (non-Afrikaans) capital. But the fact that capitalists then coexisted with the Nationalists and came to regard them less unfavourably, is not evidence that they really supported them all the time. This view ignores their continued opposition to many apartheid labour policies, and is based on a *post hoc ergo propter hoc* fallacy (similar to arguing that if Western capitalists reach an accommodation with Mozambique, Cuba or China, this must mean that they were never opposed to them).

The dominant capitals in SA did not support Afrikaner nationalism; it thrived despite them. The new myth that Afrikaner nationalism was the creation of capital ignores their opposition to it, as well as the support it received from Afrikaans labour. Likewise, the insistence that capital, as the hegemonic class, must have wanted apartheid labour policies, overlooks the power of non-capitalist classes, first white labour and later the bureaucracy and political establishment, whose interests required not only continued white rule but Afrikaner hegemony.

Today, as during the 1920s, Marxists are mistaken in identifying the interests of capital with the maintenance of a streamlined or 'restructured' apartheid and failing to see that capitalists— despite some reservations and ambivalence—are among the pressures for its erosion; while white labour and the bureaucracy, despite some changes in attitude, remain its major sources of support. The refusal to nurture the feasible alliances across racial lines (such as that between sections of white capital and black labour) and, instead, pursuing the chimera of total non-racialism or proletarian solidarity, will simply intensify racial polarization.

The fact that self-interest played a major role in the pressures from within the oligarchy for less racist policies has led some people to dismiss the value of these pressures and of the reforms that flowed from them. This raises the question of what their behavioural theory is.

The assumption in this study is that the attempt to act in what they perceive to be their self-interest is a major component of human behaviour—of capital as well as labour, of blacks as well as whites. Second, that this does not preclude moral considerations, nor emotional and aesthetic preferences. Third, that when self-interest is enlightened, that is leads to morally desirable actions (reducing discrimination or inequality), then it should be encouraged not only because of its positive effects but also because the element of self-interest is likely to make 'good' behaviour more durable. Fourth, there could, however, be a politically significant distinction between the self-interest which searches for long term 'non-zero-sum' game solutions to reconcile conflicts and the narrower self-interest which only makes limited concessions to defuse opposition. Even the latter, however, can have unintended consequences, and can in time become transformed into the former.

Class and ethnicity: a reformulation

From this analysis of how changing interests and power interacted to shape the political struggle in SA since Union, the following reformulation of the relationship between class and ethnicity is suggested:

(i) It was *easier* to forge alliances based on ethnic rather than on class ties. Ethnicity acted as a more effective cement, binding people together. The existence of ethnic organizations, even if these were cultural rather than political, made it difficult to establish class-based organizations which cut across them. As Nairn found in his study of nationalism in Britain, social and political divisions tended to take place along the lines of ethnic rather than class cleavages.* This led Nairn, a Marxist himself, to identify the Marxist/Leninist theory of nationalism as Marxism's 'great historical failure'. (Although the belief that capitalism would break down racial and ethnic barriers was not exclusive to Marxists but was shared by Weber and by modernization theorists like Apter.[5])

(ii) *But ethnicity did not provide an inevitable, nor sufficient, basis for political alliances*. On a number of occasions, a significant section of the Afrikaners, most cohesive of the ethnic groups, formed alliances with outsiders against other Afrikaners; and the same has been true of the English and of blacks. Ethnicity was not therefore so 'natural' and strong a tie as to prevail over all other interests; class conflicts within the group were not simply over-ridden by ethnic ties. National leaders had to construct a package (at the expense of outsiders) enabling their constituents to avoid

---

*'As capitalism spread and smashed the ancient social formations, they always tended to fall apart along the fault-lines contained within them . . . these lines were nearly always ones of nationality (although . . . religious divisions could perform the same function) they were never ones of class.'[4]

choosing between ethnic and material interests. It was of course easier for them to align ethnic and class interests (thus consolidating their base) when they were in power. But even then, the alliance was not immune from the fissiparous effects of class conflicts, as the fragmentation of the Afrikaner alliance in the 1930s—and again in the 1970s—demonstrated.

(iii) The splintering of the alliance showed that, *when people were forced to choose* between ethnic and class interests, ethnicity did not invariably prevail (as Nairn now believes). Indeed, SA during this period provided no important instances of groups acting against their perceived economic interests (with one proviso, discussed below). Examination of those cases in which white workers or farmers were believed to have acted in an economically 'irrational' manner (slowing the growth rate, raising the cost structure) shows that they invariably managed to shift the costs of these actions to others (mining capital, black labour). As Becker argued (see p. 250) discrimination is not an all-or-nothing process; the willingness to indulge in racial/ethnic preferences is related to how much it costs. SA governments showed great ingenuity in shifting the costs of racism away from their white or Afrikaans constituency. When they were unable to do this, whites (including Afrikaners) showed a marked reluctance to pay for their racial/ethnic preferences.*

(iv) Economic or class interests were thus a necessary condition for understanding political behaviour, but they were not sufficient; in particular, *class could not explain the particular alliances and policy packages that were constructed*. It is impossible to understand the alliance between the sections of labour, agricultural capital, and petty bourgeoisie which comprised the victorious NP in 1948 without recognising that the force which drew and bound them together was Afrikaner nationalism. The agents in the political struggle could not be comprehended purely in class terms, for class issues assumed an ethnic form; both class and ethnic factors are essential for an understanding of political behaviour.

*Those who continually cite Glazer and Moynihan on the power of ethnicity overlook the significance of their conclusion on voting patterns in New York: 'class interests and geographical location are the dominant influences in voting behaviour, whatever the ethnic group involved.'[6]

(v) The proviso referred to under (iii) above was *security*. People were willing to sacrifice their economic interests and ethnic preferences if their security (the safety of themselves, their families and their property, and of institutions which safeguarded them) was perceived as threatened. Risks are more difficult to quantify than gains, but people were prepared to bear heavy costs for defence and greater self-sufficiency. Security threats tended to intensify group feeling, but they could also lead to the blurring of ethnic lines in order to enlarge and strengthen the group (General Hertzog's policies towards the English and coloureds in the 1930s; Botha's policies towards these groups today). Security threats could lead to economic and social concessions but also to authoritarianism and militarization. Their impact on political behaviour was therefore complex and unpredictable.

(vi) What proved unexpectedly weak was a second proviso I had expected to find: that if people were rich enough they would be prepared to pay for their ethnic preferences—to pay a price *themselves*, as distinct from shifting the costs to others. But mining capital did not use the rising gold price of the 1970s to pay for the perpetuation of the job bar; and the NP's supporters did not use their growing prosperity to pay for 'separate development', which was implemented only to the extent that its high costs could be shifted to others. However, this issue is complicated by the need to distinguish between (a) the greater ability of people to pay for their 'taste for discrimination' as they got richer, but (b) the association of higher incomes with less racist attitudes (due to education, foreign travel, etc.). It may be that, over time, rich people, or their children, shift from (a) to (b), and that this is what had happened in SA by the time these choices became feasible in the 1970s.

The depth and persistence of ethnic/racial feelings, both in 'modernizing' and in developed societies, is now widely recognized.[7] Today, few scholars would argue that SA's virulent racism is unique or due to any inherent characteristics of the white oligarchy; rather it is an extreme case of a world-wide phenomenon, generated by a peculiar combination of historical and structural features.

Moreover, a deeper historical analysis reveals that, even in SA, ethnicity has never been fixed and immutable, but fluid, adaptable, and constantly interacting with class, ideological and other factors. This interpretation is reinforced by the partial erosion since about 1970 of racial structures and attitudes that once seemed immutable.

If Gellner is right in arguing that 'it is the need for homogeneity which generates nationalism' and not vice versa[8] then, the economic forces welding together the people of South (and even southern) Africa could—given time—generate a broader, more inclusive South Africanism.

History, however, suggests that the evolution of new relationships, attitudes and institutions will require a long and difficult transitional period, which most observers would judge was not available to SA. The possibilities that this evolution will be effected are therefore slender. However, fifteen years ago few would have dared to hope for even this much.

Epilogue—January 1986

How have the analysis and predictions of *Capitalism and Apartheid* stood up during the eventful and terrible two years since 1984?[1] There has been an intensification of the main trends it identified, viz: the ambiguous process of authoritarian reform; black radicalization; and the impact of international pressures on internal South African developments.

However, these processes have also been critically affected by those unforeseen 'events' which Harold Macmillan once identified as the chief obstacle to the best-laid plans of politicians. These events were: the continued fall in the price of gold and other minerals, on which SA relies heavily for foreign exchange earnings, as well as a severe and prolonged drought which hit SA's agricultural production and exports. The economic setback, particularly to the balance of payments, coincided with the adoption of 'free market' policies; but the consequent relaxation of foreign exchange controls did not, as was hoped, lead to increased foreign investment. Instead, the shortage of capital (and resultant high interest rates in SA) led to virtually uncontrolled borrowing abroad by both the state and private sectors from foreign banks, much of this in the form of uncovered short-term loans. This rendered the SA economy extremely vulnerable to unfavourable international developments.

These soon followed, with an exponential increase in international pressures against apartheid. This was partly the result of domestic politics within the USA; partly a reaction to developments within SA, particularly the scenes of violence and police brutality beamed nightly over American television screens. The resulting wave of revulsion forced the Reagan administration to impose a package of economic sanctions on SA in September 1985.

These measures, though mild, were of symbolic importance, leading to the adoption of similar steps by the EEC and Japan, and strengthening the lobby for trade embargos and 'disinvestment'.

The increased calls for sanctions—and growing violence within SA, which the July 1985 State of Emergency failed to quell—contributed to the flight of foreign capital and the refusal by American (and later other) banks to renew SA's short-term loans of $14bn, due in 1985. The subsequent foreign debt crisis led to a drastic fall in the rand, the closure of the Johannesburg stock exchange, and the declaration by SA in September 1985 of a moratorium on many of its foreign debts.

As after Sharpeville and Soweto (see Chapter 9 above), the interaction of external and internal pressures generated a complex chain-reaction of effects, intensifying both reformist and authoritarian pressures, and raising the political temperature and the level of violence—by blacks, by the police, and by the SA army in the region. The withdrawal of foreign contacts also seemed likely to herald that retreat into a beleaguered siege economy, which was anticipated above as one of the more sombre possibilities if Botha's difficulties of political management increased (see p. 364).

Optimists believed that the fever was approaching its climax: the disease had to get worse before it could get better. Pessimists feared that the slender possibilities offered by the ambiguous post-1970 reforms were diminishing and that their disappearance would herald, not a rosy dawn, but a long darkness, which might leave no victors in southern Africa.

The Epilogue will briefly analyse the intensification—and close interaction—of authoritarian reform, black radicalization, and international pressures on SA.

Intensification of authoritarian reform[2]

The inauguration of the tricameral parliament in September 1984 reduced the right-wing threat to President Botha, and accelerated the changes in race policy. According to the criteria for 'real reform' set out above (pp. 14 and 81), these were, as before, a mixture of genuine reforms and of ambivalent changes which had the potential to modernize or to destroy apartheid.

Genuine reforms included the abolition of the Mixed Marriages Act and Section 16 of the Immorality Act, restricting sex across the colour line, and of the Prohibition of Political Interference Act, restricting political cooperation among the races (on these Acts see pp. 28 and 32). There was continued progress on the job colour bar. The government was now committed to removing the last remaining statutory job bar on the mines, and issued new policy guidelines to remove race discrimination in the civil service.[3] If adequately implemented, these will increase the number of blacks in senior posts and help to reduce bureaucratic obstruction of reform.

There were further inroads into the horizontal controls (restricting African mobility and stabilization in the towns). Statutory amendments and judicial decisions extended African property rights and mobility in urban areas.[4] Gerrit Viljoen, Minister of Cooperation and Development, announced that influx control and the traditional policy of impeding African urbanization were being reviewed and would be replaced by a policy of 'orderly urbanization'. This was accompanied by a moratorium on forced removals and, in September 1985, by the President's Council recommendation that the pass laws be abolished, which would remove restrictions on the right of Africans to seek work freely and live with their families.

However, it is not yet clear what action the government will take on this recommendation. The deteriorating security situation makes it unlikely that the pass laws will be totally abolished in the near future. Moreover, the extension of urban and property rights is still taking place within the segregated framework imposed by the Group Areas Act, except in the case of 'open' central business districts.

This pattern of concessions within a segregated ethnic framework was also evident in areas such as education. There has been an enormous effort to improve black education. Since 1982/83, there have been further big increases in expenditure,* and the huge Black-White differentials have narrowed (see p. 62). But the state schools remain segregated—though the recent establishment of a single coordinating education department may be the first step away from this.

The reduction of inequality and discrimination within a segregated framework suggested that the SA government was moving

---

*In 1985/6, the education budget was R5bn, compared with R4.3bn for defence.

to the 'separate but equal' principle that, in theory, existed in the USA before the 1954 Supreme Court judgment in the Brown case.[5] But many black students angrily rejected this principle, boycotted the schools, and took to the streets.

Their objections to the principle of segregated education and residential areas were reinforced by practical difficulties and blunders in implementing these concessions. The rapid expansion of black education created enormous problems. The lack of qualified teachers, of classrooms and of equipment, plus the boycotting and disruption of the classes of those attending school, caused a drop in educational standards, evident in deteriorating exam results—despite the huge increase in expenditure.

The cost of upgrading township services, housing, transport and health, especially during the recession, made it convenient for the government to proclaim as a 'free market' principle the policy that subsidies should be phased out and the costs shifted to consumers (of all races). Consequently, the Botha reforms were accompanied by steep increases in rents, taxes and transport costs—at a time of deepening recession and unemployment. These increased charges were, moreover, imposed by the unpopular new Community Councils, elected in low polls and staffed by politicians and officials who lacked legitimacy and were widely regarded as collaborators and profiteers.

The problem of concessions (i.e. reduction of inequality; extension of property rights and mobility) within a segregated framework was most contentious in the area of political rights. After September 1984, Botha made significant concessions of principle, accepting that there should be a 'united South Africa, one citizenship and a universal suffrage'. This would include SA citizenship forAfricans in the 'independent' homelands (if they so wished), and African representation in the central government. Botha also offered to release Nelson Mandela and to negotiate with representative black leaders, including the ANC, provided they abjured violence.[6]

But Botha insisted that African political rights would have to be exercised within ethnic structures (such as the tricameral parliament with its separate white, coloured and Indian chambers). However, some signs of a possible modification of this policy were already evident in the Regional Services Councils (on which representatives of separate racial authorities served together for the first time) and in the interest the government now showed in the Buthelezi proposals for an experimental multi-racial government in Natal, which they had previously vetoed (see p. 338).

The aversion of blacks (and of many white liberals) to the segregated ethnic principle, as well as the practical problems of implementation, led to a widespread denial by blacks that there had been any improvement in their situation; many insisted it had worsened. Negative attitudes towards the reforms were undoubtedly reinforced by the authoritarian context in which policies were still unilaterally made.

During Botha's first five years in office, particularly while the new constitution was being debated, there was some relaxation of constraints on political activity. Banning orders were lifted; the number of trade unions and community organizations multiplied; the establishment of national organizations like the UDF and National Forum was tolerated. The government itself participated in placing the question of African political rights, including contacts with the ANC, at the centre of the political debate. The NP *verligtes* and press seemed to be preparing public opinion for a shift of policy towards the banned political organizations.

It is still unclear what the Government's intentions were and why this process went awry. Objections within the NP and the security forces were probably one reason; another was the growing rejection of ethnic institutions by blacks, including coloureds and Indians, as their low polls in the tricameral parliamentary elections showed (see p. 334).

This rejection of the NP's new political dispensation—even as a transitional arrangement—took place against a background of mounting political unrest and violence; school boycotts, strikes (including the big November 1984 'stayaway' on the Reef); consumer boycotts; acts of sabotage, and an increasing number of attacks on black officials, policemen, alleged informers and their families.

In responding to the unrest, the security forces conformed to the old *kragdadige* patterns: trade unionists and community leaders were detained and often tortured;* there was a mounting toll of deaths and injuries arising from police action; there were

---

*At the same time as the Industrial Court was entrenching and extending the rights of black unions!

frightening allegations that right-wing death squads (with alleged police connections) were responsible for the unsolved murders of Victoria Mxenge, the lawyer defending treason trialists in Natal, and of Matthew Goniwe, the Eastern Cape community leader. The Kannemeyer Commission investigating the shooting of twenty unarmed blacks by police during a funeral procession at Uitenhage confirmed complaints of police indiscipline, as well as inadequate equipment for less brutal methods of riot control. Racist attitudes, and the relatively small size of the police force,* were other factors accounting for their lethal tendency to resort rapidly to arms when under pressure. In the fifteen months from the tricameral elections in August 1984, almost nine hundred people were killed (the majority by police action; but many by 'Black-on-Black' action), and hundreds more injured.

The extension of police powers by the State of Emergency, and the reinforcement of the police by the army, did not halt the violence, but rather inflamed it, and also outraged international opinion, thus contributing to the debt crisis and the calls for further sanctions. In reaction to this, press censorship was tightened, especially over foreign correspondents and television coverage.

These measures, especially if combined with the retreat into a siege economy, seem likely to lead to a reversion to the tighter authoritarianism of the 1960s. It was argued in Chapters 3 and 9, that 'authoritarian reform' might, in quieter times, be a deliberate Nationalist strategy (à la de Gaulle) for eroding apartheid from above, while repressing both black radical and white racist pressures. However, in the present turbulent conditions, with enhanced police and military power—plus internal violence and external threats—tighter authoritarianism seems more likely to weaken the pressures for reform, and also the flexibility which the political system was developing since 1970, and which created the possibility for evolutionary adaptation.

It is an inherent inconsistency of 'authoritarian reform' that the chief instrument for implementing the process is the bureaucracy, including the police; that is, those sections of the oligarchy who are least in favour of, or even hostile to, reform. However, the serious problem of maintaining law and order in the transition to a

*In 1985, there were 45,600 men, of whom almost half were blacks.

new system was not simply the result of police 'indiscipline' and racist attitudes—important though these were. The main problem stemmed from the misuse of the police to enforce racist laws (passes, Group Areas, population removals) that had nothing to do with their proper functions of maintaining order and preventing crime. Indeed, many observers deny that the police normally bothered much about crime in black areas. They therefore performed no services valued by the community and had no legitimacy in their eyes. Clearly, they will not be able to reverse this and prevent a further descent into anarchy until they are shorn of these racist functions and of the attitudes accompanying them.

Within the oligarchy, the major pressures for reform continued to come from capital and the liberal lobbies and press. As anticipated, the logic of the reforms pushed all the major employers' organizations into confronting the question of African political rights, as Assocom and the FCI were already doing (see pp. 179 and 254).

They made a strong demarche to the government over the detention of trade unionists after the November 1984 stayaway. This was followed by their 1985 Manifesto on Reform calling for 'a universal citizenship' and 'meaningful political participation'* for all blacks.[7]

In September 1985, some leading businessmen held discussions with an ANC delegation, headed by Oliver Tambo, in Lusaka, although Afrikaans businessmen withdrew from the meeting under pressure from the SA government. However, businessmen remain concerned about the restoration of law and order (though in the context of reform and negotiations with representative black leaders).[9]

Businessmen were also opposed to mandatory economic sanctions, which threatened their interests, but not necessarily to other pressures on the SA goverment.[10] Indeed, as in 1948, 1960 and 1976 (see Chapters 8 and 9), capitalists in 1985 demonstrated their own (damaging) judgment on the viability of apartheid as capital fled the country in alarm and foreign banks refused to renew loans. In doing this they were, once again, acting in terms of their own

---

*In his evidence to the UN panel on transnational corporations in SA, the Director of FCI, van Zyl, stated that this meant one-man, one-vote in a federal system.[8]

interests, prompted by: (a) the rising costs and risks engendered by political unrest in SA; (b) low returns due to the severe recession in SA; (c) the 'hassle factor' for foreign companies due to the growing reaction against apartheid in the West.

Foreign bankers were alarmed by SA's precipitate action in unilaterally declaring a moratorium on its debts, instead of renegotiating them. They feared this would set a precedent for the many other debtor nations. Pretoria miscalculated in believing its action would guarantee a favourable renegotiation although it is not without some leverage over its creditors.

So capitalists, instead of 'propping up' apartheid, dealt it a savage blow, through their 'market' sanctions. The complex effects of this whole train of events were neither intended nor controllable by any of the parties concerned. They may yet prove damaging to SA, its creditors and, possibly, the whole international monetary system.

Most SA businessmen cannot, of course, get out. If SA retreats into a beleaguered siege economy they will—like most SAs with jobs and homes to protect—continue to operate within the system in which they find themselves, even though they increasingly want to change it. Some, of course, may gain from buying up foreign assets cheaply and replacing imports.[11] But most businessmen disliked and feared this prospect and hoped to forestall it by a programme of reform.

To sum up: the ethnic and authoritarian form of many (but not all) the changes has been widely interpreted as evidence that Nationalist policies will modernize, not erode, apartheid. This belief was reinforced by the 1979 Riekert proposals (now being abandoned); but it is not consistent with the genuine reforms (job bar, trade unions, sport), nor with the measures which remove disabilities and reduce inequality (abolition of Masters and Servants Laws; narrowing of differentials in wages and in state expenditure on education and health). Moreover, even ambiguous changes within a segregated framework involve concessions of principle (property rights; the right to uniform standards),* and it seems likely that—as with the 'floating job bar' and sport (see Chapter 3)—they will pave the way for further changes, and that they are part of a long-term process which will erode apartheid.

---

*This had been explicitly denied by the Separate Amenities and Bantu Education Acts (see pp. 24 and 28).

But, while the logic and momentum of policy points in this direction, there is opposition and disagreement within the NP, accounting for the contradictions of policy and problems of implementation. There are also uncertainties and fears about the risks and consequences of reform and about the likely black reaction. Hence the tentative, experimental nature, particularly of the political reforms, which Botha himself acknowledged when pointing to the likely transitional nature of the 1983 Constitution (see p. 53).

These uncertainties and fears account for the characteristic 'two-track' policy of the Nationalists: striking out on a new route, but keeping in reserve remnants of the old, so that if it does not work, they will have a line of retreat. The problem is not just racism and the fear of possible black vengeance. It is a deeper, more general fear aroused by the disorder and insecurity prevalent throughout much of Africa. Racists allege this disorder is peculiar to Africans; most liberals and radicals deny that it has any political relevance to events in SA.

It is, unfortunately, all too relevant; but there is no evidence that it is connected with racial/genetic factors. The emergence of 'nations' from arbitrary boundaries in Europe was often associated with disorder, including clan and intergroup violence. The issues are too complex to explore here, but there are likely to be many analogies with different parts of Africa. This political turmoil in Africa has moreover been accompanied by immense economic and cultural changes, such as industrialization and the introduction of Western science. The enormity and rapidity of this transformation; the fragility of the institutions and boundaries established by the relatively short-lived colonial powers; and the subsequent power vacuum and lack of trained people left by their abrupt departure—these structural factors are the sources of the disorder and upheaval, not the personal capacities or inclinations of Africans.

In SA, where the colonial power did not depart, but became indigenized, the transformation went much further and the power and institutions became more firmly rooted. The issue is not just white rule, but the preservation of institutions, rules and processes. The declared aim of 'smashing the system' rather than reforming or amending it (or of implementing very rapid and largely unspecified changes) raises substantial fears which are not only racist (though they are usually expressed in racial terms by both sides in this debate). They also reflect the universal fear that violence and disorder could destroy those fragile rules and structures that—however flawed—are the barrier against the ever-threatening Hobbesian state in which it is common to starve to death, a luxury to have roads, schools and clinics, and in which all life is 'solitary, poor, nasty, brutish and short'. As this study has shown, there are an increasing number of whites in SA today who could live in a non-racial society. The problem is the transition—how to get there safely.

The political difficulties of reform in SA are compounded by the relative speed at which immense social changes now have to take place. In the USA and India, for example, dismantling of the deep barriers of race or caste takes decades. In SA, this process was delayed by the advent of the Nationalists and now has to occur at a relatively rapid rate.

Moreover, there is an unusual psychological and political difficulty in SA. The oligarchy is receiving little of the credit and applause which usually accompanies—and encourages—the removal of disabilities and discrimination. Nor (because they will not give blacks votes) will reform help white politicians win political support from the beneficiaries of reform, who might otherwise provide an alternative constituency to compensate for the loss of disgruntled conservative voters. This is partly because white politicians cannot seek black support too overtly, for fear of a white backlash; but mainly because race discrimination has become anachronistic, that is, widely regarded as unthinkable, although (or perhaps because) the rest of the world was so recently practising it. They therefore refuse to give any credit for the (rather slow) removal of something which, they now maintain, should never have existed in the first place.

If consistently applied, this stance would mean that there should never be any welcome or credit for the removal of any disability or injustice (slavery, child labour, sexual inequality) because these too should never have existed in the first place.

This purist attitude by yesterday's sinners (perhaps connected with their very recent ascent to a state of grace) ignores the fact that huge social changes are no less painful because belated; and that they are especially difficult when entailing high risks and sacrifices of privilege. All this increases the political difficulties of managing a process which is invariably messy, muddled, littered with appalling blunders and errors, and lacking the coherence, consistency and nobility that we feel it should have and that, in retrospect, historians often impose on it.

Black radicalization

The black reaction to the Botha dispensation was one of widespread (though not total) rejection, in the 'negative politics' tradition (see p. 305), now spilling over into violence, which had become a respectable option among younger blacks. The school boycotts of late 1983 did not abate, but became part of a much wider tide of protest, violence and anarchy. This spread not only to black townships in the major urban/industrial centres—PWV, the Durban complex, Cape Peninsula, Eastern Cape—but also to smaller *platteland* towns and rural areas, which had hitherto been free of unrest.

There were manifold reasons why the newly-emerging possibilities for reform on the white side met with rejection and growing radicalization among blacks. Outbursts of pent-up resentment and rage were to be expected as, from 1970, the constraints on black organization and political activity were somewhat eased. The subsequent 'stop-go' policy—recurrent repression, expectations raised and then disappointed by ambiguous reforms and unfulfilled promises—was a recipe for frustration, stress and explosion.

Second, SA's severest recession in half a century aggravated the enormous socio-economic problems common in rapidly urbanizing societies and accentuated here by apartheid and the contrast with white affluence. The relaxation of influx controls, and the long-term effects of rapid population growth, raised to yet higher levels of intensity and pain the problems in the townships—overcrowding, inadequate transport, services and amenities, and crime.

Third, the spark for an explosion was provided by the imposition of increased taxes and fares, at a time of recession, by unpopular local councils—and by police handling of the subsequent unrest. These were the *coup de grâce* in provoking rebellions that often seemed inspired by the police and the bureaucracy.

Fourth, the segregated ethnic form of the institutions that the government was beginning to provide as institutionalized outlets for these pressures was anathema to many blacks, especially in the volatile urban areas. The Bantustan policy left a heritage of distrust and suspicion among blacks, including many who were opposed to violence and wanted negotiated change. Their aversion to the ethnic principle was strengthened by the action of the four Bantustan leaders who accepted 'independence', thus depriving Africans of their South African citizenship—while securing material benefits for themselves and 'brother George' (see p. 337). Black aversion also extended to those who rejected independence and the tricameral constitution, like Buthelezi, from whom urban blacks became increasingly alienated.

To *verligte* Nationalists, the Bantustan institutions (notwithstanding their original intentions) and the 'multi-national' policy became a way round apartheid (p. 49). But ethnic institutions were unacceptable to blacks, especially the intelligentsia and youth. The 1983 constitution intensified their hostility; they saw it, not as a transitional device, but as a permanent means of dividing Africans from coloureds and Indians.

Fifth, was the growing belief, particularly among the young, in a quicker, more radical alternative to the slow, difficult process of negotiated reform and compromise, even in the more liberal and far-reaching version offered by, say, the PFP. Their attitude was summed up in the cry 'We want it all and we want it now'. This belief (much encouraged by growing international support) inspired the students who boycotted school and tried to force others to do likewise, disrupting the classes and exams of those who attended* with the slogan: 'Liberation now—education later'. Observers commented on the mood of 'political exhileration' among the youth, and both the government and black politicians referred to a 'revolutionary climate of opinion'. This is not, however, the same thing as a revolutionary situation, in which the institutions of state control can be overthrown. There was not yet any sign that the SA Police or the SA Defence Force would be taken over or defeated. The result was an enormous and widening gulf between what the government was prepared to do and the

---

*The 1985 exams were written under appalling conditions by many black pupils—caught between conflicting pressures from the authorities (to make them write) and the boycotters (to prevent them from writing).[12]

expectations and demands of the radicals, whose ranks were swollen by the unoccupied school boycotters and the unemployed.

Radicalization led to the erosion of the middle ground and weakening of the mediators and bridge-builders essential for negotiation and compromise. This political polarization and weakening of the 'moderates' (which became a label to be avoided) was partly the result of the Nationalists' own policies.

As shown above, they had long hampered the emergence of a black middle class and stable urban proletariat and of black farmers—the classes likely to have an interest in political stability and orderly change. There was thus a weak social base for political moderation.

The black business, professional and skilled classes now emerging in the 'white' areas (the largely bureaucratic elite in the Bantustans was a rather special case) were still subject to severe restrictions. They were cooped up in their ghettos, their mobility hampered by pass laws, Group Areas and educational and social segregation. Only a few very rich blacks (including coloureds and Indians) could buy their way out of this. Social dissonance was consequently sharp among this class, and especially their children (see p. 350). The adults did not like the violence; nor did they like the police reaction; their attitudes seemed extremely ambivalent.

The members of the black vanguard had long been prevented from organizing politically, or even from fulfilling their role as community leaders. Instead, the government set up its own alternative leadership, mainly based in the Bantustans. Their failure to deliver results, and the blunder of Bantustan 'independence', proved counterproductive. Black leaders who use official institutions, welcome government reforms, or even hold discussions with them are now in danger of being branded as collaborators or stooges. Black officials, policemen and alleged informers and their families have become targets of assassins and of mob violence.

'Moderate' has become a dreaded label. Politicians who argue, against an emotional tide, for policies of reason, realism and compromise, need a secure base and the confidence that they can deliver results. Black politicians have neither this secure constituency nor an opponent who is sensitive to their political needs.

Significantly, the major exception to the lack of institutionalized negotiating power was the black trade unions. They had won the right to determine their racial composition and to become non-ethnic (see p. 340). They had an independent power-base and kept their distance from the government. They had developed a mostly cold, but effective, working relationship with many employers.

The unions were affected by the political radicalization, refusing to confine themselves to work-place issues and using their economic muscle in a disciplined and impressive way during the November 1984 stayaway, and in organizing or supporting a number of effective consumer boycotts. However, they resisted attempts to pull them out on constant strikes and stayaways (particularly during the recession) and disliked the anarchic violence that disrupted township life.[13] But the position of the unions in a polarizing situation was precarious. They were in danger of being squeezed between the pressures of the revolutionaries and the security police, who arrested and detained their leaders.

Escalating international sanctions were also problematical for the unions, increasing both the opportunities and the dangers facing them. International attention continued to be an important source of support and protection, supplying funds and training and putting some pressure on firms like BTR Sarmcol, Goldfields, and Gencor, which still refused to recognize black unions and/or sacked striking workers. But the prospect of extensive economic sanctions, including disinvestment, faced them with a painful dilemma, reflected in the dismay of workers at the closure of the Alfa Romeo factory, and in the contradictory FOSATU statement on disinvestment.*

This represented a hardening of the earlier position of the black unions (see p. 355), but its contradictions reflected the ambiva-

---

*The General Secretary of FOSATU, Joe Foster, said: 'We have no mandate from our members there [Port Elizabeth] to say they [foreign investors] must withdraw, and it would make no sense to advocate their withdrawal at this stage.' Mr Foster added that FOSATU supported the disinvestment campaign and might call for the withdrawal of foreign investments in future if this was in workers' interests. Mr Alec Erwin, FOSATU's National Education Secretary, said that foreign multinational companies in South Africa should not be allowed to withdraw their investments. These had become part of the social structure and should remain.[14]

In December 1985, FOSATU became part of the Congress of SA Trade Unions (COSATU). Its President, Elijah Barayi, declared his support for nationalization of the mines and disinvestment by foreign companies.[15]

lence of workers with jobs and homes who wanted genuine, far-reaching reform which destroyed apartheid, but did not want the economy on which their livelihood depended smashed up.

There was much greater, and more effective, black political organization outside the official system, particularly by the UDF. Its strength rested on the rapid growth of the numerous community organizations affiliated to it. The UDF encompassed a wide spectrum of views. Its leading members included prominent advocates of non-violence like Bishop Desmond Tutu and the Rev. Allan Boesak. It was also sympathetic to the ANC and some of its leaders supported the ANC aim of making the townships ungovernable. The effects of radicalization were evident in its negative attitude to the PFP's attempt to mobilize a broad alliance to press for a National Convention.

As anticipated (p. 347), the Nkomati Accord did not reduce the ANC's role within SA. On the contrary, ANC colours, and Mandela's portrait, were increasingly displayed at demonstrations and at the funerals, which became important political gatherings. But it is difficult to assess how extensive and effective their organization was and how much they were in control of the unrest.

Some observers believe the hardening of ANC policy, particularly the declaration of 'People's War', was simply the belated endorsement by the exiled movement of growing militancy in the townships, where the pace was set by the young radicals, and the ANC was in competition with AZAPO (linked to the reviving PAC), which denounced ANC's growing contacts with white liberals and businessmen and with Western leaders. It was also unclear just how 'ungovernable' the ANC wanted the townships to be and what their reactions were to the shocking scenes of brutality and anarchy—with justice dispensed by the mob, people hacked and burnt to death, and widespread looting and thuggery. There were growing strains within the ANC as it was torn between the pressures of grassroots militancy and the desire to retain its image of moderation, and its increasing respectability, in the West.[16]

The effects of radicalization were evident in the ANC's harder line on violence, with the decision at the 1985 Consultative Conference at Kabwe in Zambia to extend the armed struggle to 'soft' targets and to proclaim a 'People's War'. Mandela refused the offer of conditional release, saying that he could not abjure violence unless the ANC was unbanned and all its imprisoned members released. At the Kabwe Conference, ANC reiterated its rejection of a National Convention, on the grounds that the only issue for negotiation was the mechanics for establishing majority rule. It also insisted that new institutional and constitutional structures could take no account of the multi-ethnic composition of the population.[17]

But there were doves as well as hawks in the ANC, and the white businessmen and PFP politicians who sought discussions with ANC leaders found more common ground than they expected and believed they might prove flexible over transitional arrangements and guarantees to reassure whites.

Growing radicalization did not necessarily mean growing anti-white feeling. Few whites were killed or injured during the unrest (though segregated residential areas were probably the main reason for this). There has moreover been increasing inter-racial cooperation: between Inkatha and the PFP and the Afrikaner *verligtes*; within the UDF, which was open to all races and had white, coloured and Indian members. At Kabwe, the ANC opened its ranks to all races and elected whites, coloureds and Indians to its National Executive Committee. Local black and white community organizations, even in traditionally conservative small towns like Cradock and Port Alfred, got together to try and settle the problems caused by strikes, riots and boycotts, thus attempting to fill the vacuum left by the paralysis at the centre, which seemed able to respond only by the crude resort to force.[18]

But these hopeful contacts and efforts could quickly be swept away by increasing violence and bloodshed—and/or by tightening authoritarianism— if the situation worsens. This could pose a threat not only to black-white relations, but could also, as recent events in Durban showed, lead to fighting between Africans and Indians, as well as to intra-African conflicts, with growing violence among ANC/UDF, Inkatha and AZAPO/PAC.

Growing impact of international pressures
The acceleration of international pressures during the past fifteen months* intensified their mixed, often contradictory effects noted

---

*This is not the place to explore the reasons for this acceleration, but I hope to do so elsewhere, in a study of the interaction between international pressures and domestic developments.

above (p. 352), and pushed forward the complex process of 'change' in SA.

On the positive side, these pressures jolted whites and strengthened the arguments of those appealing for reform, not only businessmen and sportsmen, but President Botha himself cited external pressure as one of the reasons for reform (see p. 354). The black and non-racial opposition were greatly encouraged and, in many cases, aided and protected by the external support they received.

But the rapidly escalating external pressures also fed opposition illusions about their strength, contributing to the belief that victory was so imminent as to justify such extreme (but supposedly temporary) measures as the cessation of schooling and making the townships 'ungovernable'—with all this meant for the daily lives and future prospects of their inhabitants. It strengthened the tendency towards 'negative politics' and the rejection of everything the government did, including reform. External pressures thus raised unrealistic expectations, remote from both the realities of power and the difficulties of securing a settlement, and reduced the readiness to negotiate and compromise—at least among the township militants, though not necessarily among the exiled leadership, concerned about their increased Western support.

External pressures also had some negative effects on whites. Any government takes seriously threats of armed struggle, trade sanctions, oil boycotts, diplomatic isolation, etc. In SA, these threats stirred up white fears and even paranoia, and were used as arguments for harsh security measures. The beleaguered atmosphere stimulated aggressive regional policies as SA over-reacted to the hostile rhetoric of weak, neighbouring black states and engaged in preemptive destabilization to ensure its military domination of the region. These factors strengthened the hawks and contributed to the authoritarianism and militarization that have, in turn, extended the cycle of violence throughout southern Africa.

The escalating pressures for sanctions also created political problems for reformers because of the lack of response to the reforms—indeed even a *disincentive* as, in some cases, the reforms stimulated demands for further sanctions.

This was most evident in cases which 'raised the ante'. When SA met certain requirements, for example, by deracializing cricket, soccer and athletics, the stakes were raised, and it was contended that it was impossible to play non-racial sport in a racist society. The sports boycott, instead of being lifted, was actually tightened, on the grounds that, as the medicine had worked, heavier doses should be administered.

This deprived reformers of those rewards and responses that they could point to as an argument for further changes. Instead, a chorus of voices abroad began to claim the credit for all the reforms (which they also often denied were taking place!).

For example, it was widely claimed that the 1985 abolition of the Immorality and Mixed Marriages Acts was due to overseas pressure.[19] In fact, these laws had long been a key issue for *verligtes*, and Botha had expressed his wish to amend them in 1979 (see p. 51). The timing was determined mainly by the inauguration of the Indian and Coloured Chambers of the tricameral constitution. This was one of the reforms they could 'deliver' to their constituency. The claim that this was due to external pressure was a misunderstanding of the dynamics of SA politics.

As shown throughout this book, the main engine of reform has been internal, particularly the need of capitalists for skilled, stable labour and for larger markets—needs which derive from the long-term processes of industrialization, urbanization and rapid black population growth. These pressures led directly to the major reforms in labour and urban policy (in which external pressures generally played a very secondary role).

There has, in fact, been least progress on those issues to which foreigners gave priority, viz. political rights and pass laws. This was mainly because they impinged on white security. There was, consequently, less pressure for these reforms from within the oligarchy. Sport was an exception: this was an area in which the costs and risks of reform were low (though not negligible, leading to a split in the NP). Moreover, there was an influential group within the oligarchy which willingly acted as mediators in pushing for this relatively low-cost change.

The socio-economic reforms (including sport) have, logically, increased the momentum for full deracialization, including political rights. But this remains constrained by white fears and by the NP's wish to retain power. Currently, external pressures contribute to the growing white realization that they must move on this issue; but they also stir up security fears. This illustrates the deeply contradictory effect these pressures have on whites (who still make the political decisions). On issues affecting vital white interests, there seems to be a *threshold*, beyond which the (initially often positive) effects of external pressures tend to become negative or even counterproductive.

The fear that reform was being viewed as a sign of weakness, and was even stimulating the imposition of further sanctions ('more of the same medicine'), contributed to a white backlash. Botha was accused of being 'America's lackey'[20] and there was a swing towards the *verkramptes* in by-elections: in October 1985, the ultra-right-wing HNP won its first parliamentary seat (though external pressures and reform were not the only reasons for this).

Predictably, this evoked a *kragdadige* reaction from Botha, with tough security measures (detentions, treason trials, tightening of press and television censorship), and sabre-rattling in the region (Cabinda and Gaborone raids; threats against Zimbabwe). In his disastrous 'Rubicon' speech of 15 August, Botha's concern to 'warn off' the advocates of pressure obscured the fact that this speech was a further small step towards the acceptance of African citizenship and political participation.

The course of events was a setback not only for Botha's policy, but also for the emergence of the political processes essential for negotiation and compromise. The political ferment and unrest released by the 'lifting of the lid' was something SA needed to learn to live with and to provide institutionalized outlets for. Initially, this process was bound to be messy, turbulent and even bloody. But the addition to this stormy process of external pressures and threats (of trade embargoes etc) raised the political temperature, and increased the difficulties of political management, to that threshold point at which a backlash was triggered. The besieged atmosphere was inimical to the (thin but growing) toleration of non-violent actions such as boycotts and strikes, and it strengthened the hard-liners who wanted to suppress all political activity.

The impeding of political processes was also evident in the case of Namibia. Here the besieged atmosphere, and the lack of incentives for good behaviour, added to the formidable difficulties of achieving a settlement. As the Defence Minister, Magnus Malan, argued, a settlement would not bring any rewards to SA. On the contrary, instead of 'buying time' for further reform, it would merely 'reduce the timescale for further action against

SA'.[21] For example, the offer of an international guarantee of the removal of some diplomatic (or the non-imposition of economic) sanctions would have strengthened the hands of the 'doves' who favoured a settlement. But, even if they had wished to, the Contact Group would probably have been unable to deliver this carrot. The consequent lack of incentives strengthened those who argued that SA's interest lay in hanging on and prolonging the negotiations.*

Likewise, in the nuclear field, the USA cannot offer the usual *quid pro quo* (supplies of enriched uranium) in return for SA's adhesion to the Nuclear Nonproliferation Treaty. It thus lacks an important source of leverage in its attempt to persuade SA to sign. Indeed there are now pressures to expel SA from the International Atomic Energy Agency.[22] This will remove from SA the constraints that bind all members. It will not stop SA from developing nuclear weapons. If it raises the costs, then SA—like practically all governments— will divert resources from other projects in order to give priority to what it perceives as its security needs. The risk of development of nuclear weapons in southern Africa will thus probably be increased for the sake of scoring one more paper victory against the SA government.

It will be argued that SA should not be in Namibia, nor should it have nuclear weapons; and that it therefore deserves no incentives for concessions on these issues. But SA *is* in Namibia, and it *has* a nuclear capacity. The world is full of things that should be otherwise. This is no reason to acquiesce in them; but the political problem is how to deal with them in a way that involves the least risk and damage to all parties, especially in a case where the costs to the whole region could be so high.

Some argue that the problem is the lack, not of incentives, but of *penalties* which, they maintain, have been symbolic and ineffective, except for mandatory measures like the arms embargo. But while this raised SA's defence costs, it had unintended consequences, such as the growth of a substantial arms industry.

The informal and voluntary sanctions imposed by capital as it periodically fled the country have been among the more effective pressures. These 'market' sanctions worked better because they

---

*I am assuming that the presence of Cuban soldiers was primarily an American, and not a SA, concern; though SA was willing to pick up, and play, this card.

interacted effectively with a crucial mediating group within the oligarchy. Secondly, they were not seen as punitive and interventionist and therefore involved less loss of face for Botha than formal demands from other governments. Third, they were more flexible both to impose and to remove. Finally, they were consistent in applying to SA the same principles as to other countries, for example, the IMF and bankers' view that SA needs political reforms that will establish free markets for both capital and labour. However, the ability of capital to influence government policy has also been limited and has also had some unintended effects. It might yet precipitate SA's retreat into a siege economy.

Clearly, there are enormous difficulties for the international community in applying effective pressures to SA, especially as there is disagreement about their aims. The wide variety of aims, strategies, values and interests of the many states concerned accounts for the confusing and often conflicting signals sent to SA, and for the lack of clear incentives and penalties—not that these would necessarily secure their intended aims, as the arms embargo and bankers' sanctions show.

A respite from further sanctions might facilitate reform by lowering the political temperature, reducing security fears and enabling the various parties to give internal reform their full attention. But it seems unlikely that the dynamics of international politics will permit this. The anti-apartheid campaign has become an international moral crusade with its own momentum, although events within SA (particularly the conduct of the police and army) are still the main determinant of the pace and intensity of this campaign.

Perhaps the experience of the last few years will lead to more awareness of the limits and dangers, as well as of the possibilities, of external pressures, particularly of the need to gear them more closely to internal developments, and to use them to strengthen the 'soft-liners' and negotiators among both blacks and whites.

This would require a more differentiated policy, which sends clear, consistent signals that respond to good, and react against bad, behaviour. For this policy to be acceptable, positive responses must be restricted to genuine reforms (i.e. deracialization, including, but not only, the extension of political participation) not to ambivalent changes such as the tricameral constitution or the Nkomati Accord (largely the outcome of *force majeure*). Yet, the welcome these received by some Western governments led to the suspicion that they were colluding in the imposition of neo-apartheid solutions and SA military domination of the regime. The backlash against this in the West strengthened the pro-sanctions lobby.

External pressures have the capacity to make the situation worse as well as better. They are not a simple, straightforward alternative to violence. In some circumstances, they harden attitudes, complicate or impede negotiations, and even intensify violence. Nor should this be rationalized by the dangerous fallacy that, because the situation in SA is so bad, it can get no worse. SA has a functioning economy that feeds, clothes and educates millions of its citizens. Moreover, it cannot surely be doubted that both sides—black and white—still have an enormous potential capacity to unleash much greater violence, so that deaths will not, as at present, be counted in their hundreds, but in their tens of thousands.

It is this prospect—'too ghastly to contemplate'—that provides the incentive, indeed the moral duty, to pursue the difficult, and now often unpopular, role of nurturing the diminishing possibilities of reform and negotiated change that still remain.

Tables

Note on tables

SA statistics are dogged not only by the usual problems of incompleteness and inconsistency, but by uncertainty surrounding the position in the society of Africans, who were often left out of the industrial censuses before World War Two, and of the unemployment statistics for much of the period thereafter. The heavy dependence of agriculture on African labour contributed to the paucity and unreliability of data on agricultural labour (see pp. 45 and 92). Recently, inhabitants of 'independent' Bantustans have been excluded from official statistics; however, they have, whenever possible, been added to the tables here. Furthermore, official restrictions on African numbers in 'white' areas, and on the jobs they could perform there, meant that the official statistics invariably underestimated the number of Africans present and working there and excluded the incomes earned by illegal workers (see pp. 46, 73f and 78).

The selection of material, particularly on occupations and wages, has been determined partly by the data available (very poor on the period before World War Two) and partly by what was needed to illustrate arguments in the text (hence the fuller coverage of wages during the 1940s and 1970s).

TABLE 1: POPULATION OF SA, 1911–80
Number (in millions) followed (in brackets) by percentage of total.

Census Year	1911	1936	1960	1980
*Whites**	1.3(21)	2.0(21)	3.1(19)	4.5(16)
Africans	4.0(67)	6.6(69)	10.9(68)	20.8(72)**
Coloureds	0.5(9)	0.8(8)	1.5(9)	2.6(9)
Indians	0.2(3)	0.2(2)	0.5(3)	0.8(3)
Total	5.9(100)	9.6(100)	16.0(100)	28.7(100)

* Of whom about 60% are Afrikaners.

** Including 3.9m in the 'independent' homelands of Transkei, Bophutatswana and Venda. In 1980, Africans were classified into the following 'national' groups and homelands:

Zulu	(5.5m)	Kwazulu
Xhosa	(5.2m)	Transkei and Ciskei (of whom about 80% were classified as Transkeians)
North Sotho	(2.4m)	Lebowa
Tswana	(2.1m)	Bophutatswana
South Sotho	(1.9m)	Qwa Qwa
Shangaan/Tsonga	(0.9m)	Gazankulu
Swazi	(0.7m)	Kangwane
Ndebele	(0.7m)	Kwandebele
Vhavenda	(0.5m)	Venda

Source: *SA Statistics 1982* and *Statistical Survey of Black Development 1980* (Benso).

TABLE 2: URBANIZATION

Number (in millions) and percentage of each group urbanized.*

Census Year	1911		1936		1951		1960		1970		1980	
	No	%	No	%	No	%	No	%	No	%	No	%
Whites	0.7	51.6	1.3	65.2	2.1	78.4	2.6	83.6	3.3	86.8	4.0	88.3
Africans	0.5	12.6	1.1	17.3	2.3	27.2	3.5	31.8	5.1	33.1	6.9	32.9
Coloureds	0.3	46.7	0.4	53.9	0.7	64.7	1.0	68.3	1.5	74.1	2.0	74.6
Indians	0.07	43.2	0.2	66.3	0.3	77.5	0.4	83.2	0.6	86.7	0.7	90.6
Total	1.5	24.7	3.0	31.4	5.4	42.6	7.5	46.7	10.4	47.8	13.6	47.1

* Estimates of African urbanization for the year 2000 range disconcertingly between 46 and 75 per cent, depending on trends in government policy, as well as economic and demographic factors (Cilliers and Groenewald, p. 33 ff).

Source: *SA Statistics 1982*, except for 1980, which is from S. P. Cilliers and C. J. Groenewald, *Urban Growth in South Africa 1936–2000* (Dept. of Sociology, Stellenbosch University, 1982), whose estimates include Africans in the 'independent' homelands. This accounts for the fact that their proportion of Africans urbanized is lower than the 38.3% in the official statistics (and overall level of 53.2 for all groups), because the homelands' unbanization level is lower.

TABLE 3: DISTRIBUTION OF THE AFRICAN POPULATION, 1946–80

Number (in millions) and percentage of total.

	1946		1960		1970		1980	
	No	%	No	%	No	%	No	%
In homelands	3.1	40	4.0	37	7.4	47	10.7	53
In 'white' SA	4.7	60	6.8	63	8.5	53	9.5	47
Total	7.8	100	10.8	100	15.9	100	20.2	100

Source: *Fagan Report*, p. 14; *Statistical Survey of Black Development, 1980;* M. Lipton, 'The SA Census and the Bantustan Policy', in *World Today*, June 1972.

TABLE 4: SECTORAL CONTRIBUTIONS TO GDP* (PERCENTAGES), 1911–80

	1911	1936	1951	1960	1970	1980
Agriculture	21	15	19	11	8	7
Mining	28	19	13	14	10	23
*Manufacturing and Construction***	5	13	22	24	27	26
Services	46	53	46	51	55	44

* At factor cost and current prices.
** Construction usually accounted for between one-sixth and one-seventh of this total.
Source: *SA Statistics 1982*.

TABLE 5: ECONOMICALLY ACTIVE (THOUSANDS) BY RACE AND SECTOR, 1951 AND 1980

Sector	Year	Whites	Africans	Coloureds	Indians	Total	% active in sector
Agriculture	1951	145	1,252	98	13	1,509	33
	1980	102	1,673	149	7	1,931	20
Mining	1951	57	449	4	1	510	11
	1980	90	768	13	2	873	9
Manufacturing and Construction	1951	250	360	109	24	742	16
	1980	463	1,103	307	108	2,011	21
Services	1951	503	932	152	44	1,629	34
	1980	1,202	2,229	375	124	3,930	41
Unemployed and Unspecified	1951	28	118	42	14	202	6
	1980	41	735	84	15	291	9
Total Economically Active	1951	984	3,111	404	94	4,592	
	1980	1,928	6,523	928	256	9,635	

Sources: 1951 figures from H. Houghton, *The South African Economy*. 1980 figures from *SA Statistics 1982*; and *1982 Statistical Survey of Black Development*, Part 2, for information on Transkei, Bophutatswana and Venda.

TABLE 6: RACIAL OCCUPATIONAL STRUCTURE (THOUSANDS), 1960 AND 1980

Occupation	Year	Whites	Coloureds	Indians	Africans*	Total
Professional/Technical	1960	138	14	5	48	206
	1980	371	51	23	205	650
Administrative/Managerial	1960	59	1	2	6	68
	1980	126	3	4	5	138
Clerical Worker	1960	276	9	8	19	313
	1980	505	70	53	211	839
Sales Worker	1960	97	10	23	29	160
	1980	196	38	37	180	451
Service Worker	1960	59	118	15	711	902
	1980	156	153	17	1,174	1,499
Agricultural Worker	1960	117	128	12	1,475	1,731
	1980	89	155	6	1,734	1,992
*Production and Related Worker and Labourer***	1960	376	214	43	1,316	1,949
	1980	434	387	104	2,304	3,230
*Unclassified and Unemployed****	1960	28	59	17	286	391
	1980	28	71	12	702	813
Total Economically Active	1960	1,150	554	126	3,890	5,720
	1980	1,905	928	226	6,524	9,613

* Includes 'independent' homelands.

** The Department of Labour's more detailed *Manpower Surveys* show that within this category the number and proportion of blacks in semi-skilled, skilled and supervisory jobs increased: for example, as a proportion of artisans and apprentices, coloureds and Indians increased from 15 per cent in 1971 to 24 per cent in 1983, and Africans from 3 to 8 per cent (Source: *Manpower Survey* No. 9 of 1971 and No. 15 of 1983).

*** On the unreliability of statistics on African unemployment and agriculture see p. 377 above.

Sources: *SA Statistics, 1972 and 1982;* and *1982 Statistical Review of Black Development,* Part 2, for data on Transkei, Bophutatswana and Venda.

TABLE 7: RACIAL CONTRIBUTION (PERCENTAGES) TO
OCCUPATIONS, 1960 AND 1980

Occupation	Year	Whites	Coloureds	Indians	Africans
Professional/	1960	67	7	2	23
Technical	1980	57	8	4	31
Managerial/	1960	87	1	3	9
Administrative	1980	91	2	3	4
Clerical	1960	88	3	3	6
	1980	60	8	6	25
Sales	1960	61	6	14	18
	1980	44	8	8	40
Service	1960	7	13	2	78
	1980	11	10	1	78
Agriculture	1960	7	7	1	85
	1980	5	8	—	87
Production/	1960	19	11	2	68
Labourer	1980	16	13	3	69

Source: Calculated from Table 6.

TABLE 8: SOURCES OF LABOUR ON GOLD MINES, 11–82

Year	South* Africans	FOREIGN MIGRANTS						Grand Total	% Foreign Migrants
		Lesotho	Botswana	Swaziland	Mozambique	Others**	Total Foreign Migrants		
1911	69,000	—	—	—	—	—	104,000	174,000	60
1931	113,000	—	—	—	—	—	113,000	226,000	50
1951	113,092	31,448	12,246	6,322	91,978	31,602	173,596	286,688	61
1961	146,605	49,050	20,216	6,784	100,678	65,012	241,740	388,345	62
1971	86,868	64,056	20,498	5,640	95,430	98,055	283,679	370,547	77
1973	81,375	76,403	20,352	4,826	83,390	112,480	297,451	378,826	79
1975	101,553	75,397	17,440	7,356	91,369	28,731	220,293	321,846	69
1978	204,318	91,278	17,647	8,269	35,234	32,048	184,476	388,794	48
1982	257,954	99,034	18,148	9,422	47,150	16,262	190,016	448,170	42

* Including 'independent' Bantustans.

** Mainly Malawians.

Source: M. Lipton, 'Men of Two Worlds' *Optima*, Vol. 29, No. 2/3, 1980, Table 11.

TABLE 9: RACIAL SHARES OF TOTAL PERSONAL INCOME
(PERCENTAGES)

	1924/5	1946/7	1960	1970	1980
Whites	75	71.3	71.2	71.9	59.9
Africans	18	22.2	21.4	19.3	29.1
Coloureds	5	4.5	5.5	6.5	7.6
Indians	2	2	1.9	2.3	3.4

Source: M. McGrath, *Racial Income Distribution in SA* (Dept of Economics, Natal University, 1977); and Bureau of Market Research of the University of South Africa, cited by N. Bromberger, 'Government policies affecting the distribution of income' in R. Schrire (ed) *South Africa – Public Policy Perspectives* (Juta, 1982).

TABLE 10: AVERAGE ANNUAL WAGES (RANDS) IN PRIVATE
MANUFACTURING AND CONSTRUCTION, 1915–82

Year	Whites		Africans		Ratio of White to African Wages (African = 1)
	Current Prices	'Real' Wage (1970 Prices)*	Current Prices	'Real' Wage (1970 Prices)*	
1915/16**	341	1,168	65	223	5.3
1929/30	453	1,258	89	247	5.1
1935/6	452	1,413	84	263	5.4
1939/40	512	1,418	96	278	5.3
1944/5	768	1,726	184	414	4.2
1947/8	918	1,889	210	432	4.4
1949/50	1,034	1,951	222	419	4.7
1952/3	1,348	2,106	266	416	5.1
1954/5	1,526	2,278	288	430	5.3
1959/60	1,872	2,463	348	458	5.4
1965	2,325	2,735	437	514	5.3
1970	3,633	3,633	609	609	6.0
1972	4,355	3,854	733	649	5.9
1975	6,119	3,893	1,265	805	4.8
1980	9,761	3,514	2,148	773	4.5
1982	15,802	4,305	3.590	978	4.4

*   Deflated by the cost of living index for all groups to approximate 1970
   purchasing power.
** This Table is based on data that have been stitched together from a variety of
   sources which are not strictly comparable. In particular, the years 1915/16
   and 1929/30 include some workers in government undertakings, and in 1955/6
   changes were made in industrial classifications. However, the figures seem
   sufficiently comparable to indicate the trend.
Sources: Wages at current prices derived from *Union Statistics for Fifty Years,
   1910–60*; and W. F. J. Steenkamp, 'Bantu Wages in South Africa, *SA
   Journal of Economics*, June 1962; and *SA Statistics 1972* and *1982*.

TABLE 11: AVERAGE ANNUAL WAGES (RANDS) ON GOLD MINES, 1911–1982

Year	Whites		Africans*		Ratio of White to African Wages (African = 1)
	Current Prices	'Real' Wage (1970 Prices)**	Current Prices	'Real' Wage (1970 Prices)**	
1911	660	2,632	57	225	11,7
1921	992	—	66	—	15,0
1931	753	2,214	66	186	11,3
1941	848	2,312	70	191	12,1
1951	1,609	2,745	110	188	14,6
1961	2,477	3,184	146	188	16,9
1971	4,633	4,379	221	209	20,9
1972	4,936	4,368	257	227	19,2
1975	7,929	5,035	948	602	8,4
1982	16,524	4,501	3,024	824	5,5

* Cash wages only, excluding payment in kind, which formed a high proportion of African remuneration (48% in 1977). Changes in this may obviously affect total remuneration and therefore also changes in the ratio.

** Deflated by the cost of living index for all groups to approximate 1970 purchasing power.

Source: M. Lipton, 'Men of Two Worlds', *Optima*, Vol. 29, No. 2/3, 1980.

TABLE 12: SECTORAL WAGE COMPARISONS (RANDS)

	Whites			Africans*		
	1952/3	1969/70	1975/6	1952/3	1969/70	1975/6
Manufacturing and Construction	1,348	3,633	6,119	266	609	1,265
Gold Mines	1,736	4,329	7.929	113	208	947
White Agriculture	—	1,845	4,008	72	135	491

* The agricultural wage includes payment in kind, the mining wage does not (see note to Table 11).

Sources: Tables 10 and 11 above; agricultural wages from M. Lipton, 'South Africa: Two agricultures?' in F. Wilson (ed) *Farm Labour in SA* (Philip, 1977) Table 3; and *1976 Agricultural Census*.

TABLE 13: ENGLISH/AFRIKAANS DIFFERENTIALS

Percentage Urbanized

	1911	1936	1960	1974
All whites	52	65	84	90
English	n.a.*	88	94	95
Afrikaners	25	48	77	88

Occupations (percentages)

Type of Work	1936		1960		1974	
	Eng	Afrik	Eng	Afrik	Eng	Afrik
White collar	n.a.	28	69	43	72	65
Blue collar	n.a.	32	26	41	27	27
Agriculture	n.a.	41	3	16		8
		100	100	100	100	100

Afrikaans Percentage Share of Ownership of Private Sector

	1938/9	1954/5	1975
Agriculture	87	84	82
Mining	1	1	18**
Manufacturing and Construction	3	6	15
Commerce	8	26	16
Transportation	n.a.	14	15
Liquor and Catering	n.a.	30	35
Finance	5	10	25

* Not available.

** The takeover in 1976 of Union Corporation by General Mining was estimated to increase this share to 30%.

Sources: H. L. Watts, *A social and demographic portrait of English-speaking white South Africans* (roneo, Natal University, 1976); H. Adam and II. Giliomee, *The Rise and Crisis of Afrikaner Power*, Chapter 6.

TABLE 14: GOVERNMENTS AND PRIME MINISTERS, 1910–84

1910–1919: South African Party (SAP), Louis Botha

1919–1924: South African Party (SAP), J. C. Smuts

1924–1933: Nationalist-Labour Pact, J. B. M. Hertzog

1933–1939: United Party (UP), J. B. M. Hertzog

1939–1948: United Party (UP), J. C. Smuts

1948–1954: National Party (NP), D. F. Malan

1954–1958: National Party (NP), J. G. Strijdom

1958–1966: National Party (NP), H. F. Verwoerd

1966–1978: National Party (NP), B. J. Vorster

1978–   : National Party (NP), P. W. Botha

Sources

This study has drawn on a wide range of both primary and secondary material – Hansards and official statistics and reports, as well as the South African press which, despite censorship, has continued to provide a great deal of information and critical comment. The post-1970 explosion of research and polemic, across the whole ideological spectrum, has added enormously to the stock of secondary work.

The single most valuable source was my interviews, at regular intervals since 1970 (for this and other projects), with a wide range of South Africans, particularly with businessmen, workers and trade unionists, and with officials and politicians concerned with labour policy. These interviews were mostly off-the-record and therefore unattributable, but it has usually been possible to quote from published statements of the people concerned, or to illustrate the points they made from other sources.

Guide to abbreviated references

Benso	Bureau of Economic Research, Pretoria.
Ballinger, *Union to Apartheid*	M. Ballinger, *From Union to Apartheid* (Bailey Bros & Swinfen, 1969).
Clack, 'Industrial Relations'	G. Clack, 'The changing structure of industrial relations in South Africa with special references to racial factors and social movements' (PhD, London School of Economics, 1962).
Davies, 'Capital, the State'	R. Davies, 'Capital, the State and White Wage Earners. An Historical Materialist Analysis of class formation and class relations in South Africa' (PhD, Sussex University, 1977).
Fagan Report	Union of SA, *Report of the Native Laws Commission 1946–48* (Chairman: Fagan) U.G. 28–1948.
Farm Labour	F. Wilson, A. Kooy and D. Hendrie (eds), *Farm Labour in South Africa* (Philip, 1977).
F.M.	*Financial Mail* (Johannesburg).
Frankel, *Capital Investment*	S. H. Frankel, *Capital Investment in Africa* (OUP, 1938).

413

HAD	House of Assembly Debates.
Hart, *African Entrepreneurship*	G. Hart, *African Entrepreneurship* (Rhodes University, 1972).
Horwitz, *Political Economy*	R. Horwitz, *The Political Economy of South Africa* (Weidenfeld & Nicholson, 1967).
H.S.R.C.	Human Sciences Research Council.
Industrial Legislation Commission	*Report of the Industrial Legislation Commission* (Chairman: Botha), U.G. 62/1951.
Leftwich, *South Africa*	A. Leftwich (ed), *South Africa: Economic Growth and Political Change* (Allison & Busby, 1974).
Lipton, *Optima*	M. Lipton, 'Men of Two Worlds', in *Optima* Vol. 29, Nos. 2/3, 1980.
N.M.C.	*Report of The National Manpower Commission for 1982* RP 45 – 1983.
OUP	Oxford University Press.
Oxford History	M. Wilson and L. Thompson (eds) *The Oxford History of South Africa*, Vol. 11 (OUP, 1971).
Price and Rosberg	R. Price and C. Rosberg, *The Apartheid Regime* (University of California, 1980).
RDM	*Rand Daily Mail* (Johannesburg).
Reynders Report	*Report of the Commission of Inquiry into the Export Trade of South Africa* (Chairman: Reynders) RP 69/1972.
Riekert Report	*Report of the Commission of Inquiry into Legislation affecting the Utilization of Manpower (excluding the legislation administered by the Departments of Labour and Mines)* (Chairman: Riekert) RP 32/1979.
SA Digest	*South African Digest* (Pretoria).
SAF	South Africa Foundation.
SAIRR	South African Institute of Race Relations.
SAJE	*South African Journal of Economics*.
Salomon, 'Afrikaner Nationalism'	L. Salomon, 'The Economic Background to the Revival of Afrikaner Nationalism', in J. Butler (ed), *Boston University Papers in African History*, Vol. 1 (Boston, 1964).
Simons, *Class and Colour*	H. J. and R. E. Simons, *Class and Colour in South Africa, 1850–1950* (Penguin, 1969).
S.T.	*Sunday Times* (Johannesburg).

Star (W)   *Star* (Johannesburg), weekly airmail edition.

Survey (and relevant year)   Annual *Survey of Race Relations*, published
                                     by SAIRR.

Thompson and Butler   L. M. Thompson and J. Butler (eds)
                                     Change in Contemporary South Africa
                                     (University of Southern California, 1975).

van der Horst, *Native Labour*   S. T. van der Horst, *Native Labour in South
                                     Africa* (OUP, 1942, and Cass, 1971).

Verwoerd Speaks   Pelzer (ed) *Verwoerd Speaks. Speeches
                                     1948–66* (APB, 1966).

Viljoen Report   *Report of the Commission of Inquiry into
                                     Policy relating to the Protection of Industry*
                                     (Chairman: Viljoen) UG 36/1958.

Wiehahn Report   *Report of the Commission of Inquiry into
                                     Labour Legislation, Part I* (Chairman:
                                     Wiehahn) RP 47/1979.

Notes

CHAPTER 1

1 M. C. O'Dowd (mimeo, 1964), later published in Leftwich, *South Africa*.

2 R. Horwitz, *Political Economy* ; and *Expand or Explode: Apartheid's Threat to Industry* (Business Bookman, 1957). W. H. Hutt, *The Economics of the Colour Bar* (Deutsch, 1964).

3 N. Bromberger, 'Economic growth and political change in South Africa' in Leftwich, *South Africa* ; and 'Government policies affecting the distribution of income' in R. Schrire (ed), *South Africa: Public Policy Perspectives* (Juta, 1982). M. Lipton, 'White Farming: a case-study of change in South Africa' in *Journal of Commonwealth and Comparative Politics*, March 1974; 'South Africa: Authoritarian Reform?' in *World Today*, June 1974; 'British investment in South Africa: Is constructive engagement possible?' in *South African Labour Bulletin*, October 1976; 'The Debate about South Africa: Neo-Marxists and neo-Liberals' in *African Affairs*, 1979, Vol. 78; and 'Men of Two Worlds', a monograph published in *Optima*, Vol. 29, Nos. 2/3, 1980.

4 K. Marx and F. Engels, *Selected Works* (Lawrence & Wishart, 1950), Vol. I, pp. 312–24.

5 F. A. Johnstone, 'White prosperity and White supremacy in South Africa today' in *African Affairs*, 1970, Vol. 69. M. Legassick, 'South Africa: Forced labour, industrialization and racial differentiation' in R. Harris (ed) *The Political Economy of Africa* (Boston, 1973). See also H. Wolpe, 'Industrialization and Race in South Africa' in S. Zubaida (ed) *Race and Racism* (London, 1970). S. Trapido, 'South Africa in a comparative study of Industrialization' in *Journal of Development Studies*, 1971, Vol. 7.

6 M. Legassick and D. Innes, 'Capital restructuring and Apartheid: a critique of constructive engagement' in *African Affairs*, 1977, Vol. 76. D. Kaplan, 'Class Conflict, Capital Accumulation and the State' (PhD Thesis, Sussex University, 1977). Davies, 'Capital, the State'.

7 H. Adam, *Modernizing Racial Domination* (University of California, 1971).

8 H. Blumer in G. Hunter (ed) *Industralization and Race Relations* (OUP, 1965). S. Greenberg, *Race and State in Capitalist Development* (Yale, 1980).

9 J. Slovo, 'South Africa: no middle road' in Davidson, Slovo and Wilkinson, *The New Politics of Revolution* (Penguin, 1976). No Sizwe (pseudonym), *One Azania, one nation: the national question in South Africa* (Zed, 1979).

10 M. Weber, *Economy and Society* (Bedminster, 1968).

11 Simons, *Class and Colour*. B. Bunting, *The Rise of the South African Reich* (Penguin, 1964). Slovo, *op cit.*

12 O'Dowd, *op cit*. M. Lipton, *op cit*. Salomon, 'Afrikaner Nationalism'.

13 Among proponents of this view are: L. Kuper, *Race, Class and Power* (Duckworth, 1974). H. Adam and H. Giliomee, *The Rise and Crisis of Afrikaner Power* (Philip, 1979). D. Welsh, *South Africa: Power, Process and Prospect* (Inaugural lecture, University of Cape Town, 1982).

14 Others who have been searching for new ways of defining the relationship between class and ethnicity include H. Giliomee and R. Elphick (eds) in *The Shaping of South African Society 1652–1820* (Longmans, 1979); and K. Hughes in his review of their book in *Social Dynamics*, Vol. 5, 1979.

15 As in footnote 7 of Chapter 10 below.

16 For example, I. D. Macrone, *Race Attitudes in South Africa* (OUP, 1937). S. Patterson, *The Last Trek* (Routledge, 1957).

17 On these issues see A. de Toit, 'Ideological Change, Afrikaner Nationalism and Pragmatic Racial Domination in South Africa' in Thompson and Butler. K. Danziger, 'Modernization and the Legitimation of Social Power' in H. Adam (ed) *South Africa: Sociological Perspectives* (OUP, 1971). F. Van Zyl Slabbert and D. Welsh, *South Africa's Options (Philip, 1979).*

18 On the debate see H. Wright, *The Burden of the Present: Liberal Radical Controversy over South African History* (Philip, 1977). M. Lipton, 'The Debate about South Africa' (cited in footnote 3 above), and 'The Engelse Pers and the Geldmag' in H. Giliomee, *The Parting of the Ways* (Philip, 1982), p. 94. S. Marks, 'Liberalism, Social Realism and South African History' in *Journal of Commonwealth Political Studies*, Vol. X of 1972. B. D. Kantor and H. F. Kenny, 'The Poverty of Neo-Marxism: the South African Case' in *Journal of Southern African Studies*, Vol. 3, 1976.

19 K. Hughes, 'Challenges from the past', *Social Dynamics*, Vol. 13 (1), 1977.

CHAPTER 2

1 Johnstone, 'White Prosperity' (see footnote 5 of Chapter 1 above).

2 A. Sachs, 'The instruments of Domination' in Thompson and Butler.

3 On the history of SA before Union see C. W. de Kiewiet, *A History of South Africa: Social and Economic* (OUP, 1941). *Oxford History*, Vols. 1 and 2. T. R. H. Davenport, *South Africa: a modern history* (Macmillan, 1977). R. Elphink and H. Giliomee, *Shaping* (see footnote 14 of Chapter 1 above). S. Marks and A. Atmore (eds), *Economy and Society in Pre-Industrial South Africa* (Longmans, 1980).

4 T. D. Moodie, *The Rise of Afrikanerdom* (University of California, 1975), p. 262.

5 On policy and legislation see van der Horst, *Native Labour*. G. Hart, *African Entrepreneurship*. Horwitz, *Political Economy*. E. Hellman (ed), *Handbook of Race Relations in South Africa* (OUP, 1949). M. Horrell, *Legislation and Race Relations* (SAIRR, 1971). The annual *Surveys*.

6 M. Banton, *Race Relations* (Tavistock, 1967).

7 *Fagan Report*. Union of SA, *Third (Interim) Report of the Agricultural and Industrial Requirements Commission* (Chairman: van Eck), U.G. 40–1941. Union of SA, *Report of the Interdepartmental Committee on the Social, Health and Economic Conditions of the Urban Natives* (Chairman: Smit) 1942.

8 Cited in D. Welsh, 'The Growth of Towns' in *Oxford History*.

9 J. C. Smuts, *The Basis of Trusteeship* (SAIRR, 1942).

10 A. Paton, *Hofmeyr* (OUP, 1964), Chapter 13.

11 G. Hart, *African Entrepreneurship*, p. 102. M. Ballinger, *Union to Apartheid*, pp. 95ff.

12 *Fagan Report*, pp. 46–50.

13 D. W. Krüger (ed), *South African Parties and Policies, 1910–60* (Human and Rousseau, 1960), pp. 402ff.

14 R. de Villiers, 'Afrikaner Nationalism' in *Oxford History*, p. 408.

15 G. Hart, *African Entrepreneurship*, pp. 103–4.

16 *Survey 1981*, p. 220.

17 On Nationalist policies and legislation see Ballinger, *Union to Apartheid*. Horwitz, *Political Economy*. *Oxford History*. G. Hart, *African Entrepreneurship*. G. V. Doxey, *The Industrial Colour Bar in South Africa* (OUP, 1961). The annual *Surveys*.

18 *Viljoen Report*, pp. 32f.

19 *Verwoerd Speaks*, pp 83–4.

20 The relevant measures were the Natives (Abolition of Passes and Co-ordination of Documents) Act of 1952, the Native Laws Amendment Acts of 1952 and 1957, and the amendments to the Natives (Urban Areas) Act in 1952, 1955 and 1957.

21 *Verwoerd Speaks*, p. 50.

22 Statements by A. H. Vosloo, Deputy Minister of BAD, at meetings of the Transvaal Agricultural Union, 25 April and 27 August 1968, kindly made available from his collection of press cuttings by K. Gottschalk of the African Studies Department, Cape Town University.

23 Lipton, *Optima*. Verwoerd's 1955 speech in Parliament, *Verwoerd Speaks*, p. 168.

24 W. M. M. Eiselen, 'Harmonious Multi-Community Development' in *Optima*, March 1959.

25 *Verwoerd Speaks*, p. 49.

26 *Ibid*, p. 42.

27 *Survey 1955/6*, p. 131.

28 *Industrial Legislation Commission*, pp. 224ff.

29 Bunting, *South African Reich* (see footnote 11 of Chapter 1 above), p. 353. On policy towards African trade unions see also M. Horrell, *South Africa's Workers* (SAIRR, 1969). Simons, *Class and Colour*. P. Bonner, 'Black trade unions in South Africa since World War II' in Price and Rosberg. W. H. Thomas (ed), *Labour Perspectives on South Africa* (Philip, 1974).

30 In terms of the 1956 and 1959 Amendments to the IC Act.

31 Cited in R. Schrire. 'South Africa's policy of racial separation: a case-study of the Transkei' (PhD thesis, University of California, 1972).

32 By the 1949 Mixed Marriages Act and 1950 amendment to the Immorality Act.

33 Estimate by G. Findlay, cited in I. Goldin, 'The Coloured Labour Preference Policy' (roneo, Institute of Commonwealth Studies, London, 1982).

34 The 1960 Amendment to the Factories, Machinery and Building Workers Act.

35 *Survey 1955/6*, pp. 199 and 214.

36 H. Pollak, cited in S. van der Horst, *Progress and Retrogression in South Africa* (SAIRR, 1971).

37 *Summary of the Report of the Commission for the Socio-Economic Development of the Bantu Areas within the Union of South Africa* (Chairman: Tomlinson) UG 61/1955 (henceforth Tomlinson Report). On this policy see also J. Lombard, J. Stadler and P. J. van der Merve, *The Concept of Economic Co-operation in Southern Africa* (Econburo, 1968). M. Horrell, *The African Reserves of South Africa* (SAIRR, 1969). C. Hill, *Bantustans: the Fragmentation of South Africa* (OUP, 1964). M. Lipton, 'Independent Bantustans' in *International Affairs*, January 1972, and 'The South African Census and the Bantustan policy' in *World Today*, June 1972. G. Maasdorp, 'Economic Development Strategy in the African homelands' (roneo, SAIRR, 1974), and 'Industrial Decentralization and the economic development of the homelands' in R. Schrire (ed), *South Africa: Public Policy Perspectives* (Juta, 1982). J. Butler, R. Rotberg and J. Adams, *The Black Homelands of South Africa* (University of California, 1977). G. Carter, T. Karis and N. Stultz, *South Africa's Transkei: The Politics of Domestic Colonialism* (Northwestern University, 1967). N. M. Stultz, *Transkei's Half Loaf* (Yale, 1979). P. Lawrence, *The Transkei: South Africa's Politics of Partition* (Ravan, 1976). R. J. Southall, 'The Beneficiaries of Transkeian Independence' in *Journal of Modern African Studies* 1977, Vol. 15; and *South Africa's Transkei: the political economy of an 'independent' Bantustan* (Heinemann, 1982). B. Streek and R. Wicksteed, *Render Unto Kaiser: A Transkei Dossier* (Rowan, 1981). The periodic *Statistical Review of Black Development* (Benso).

38 Cited in Schrire (see footnote 31 above).

39 In his 1959 speech in parliament, *Verwoerd Speaks*, pp. 271ff.

40 *Ibid*, pp. 53 and 283 (my italic).

41 Bromberger, 'Government policies' (see footnote 3 of Chapter 1).

42 As in footnote 39.

43 Eiselen, as in footnote 24 above.

44 Verwoerd's 1959 speech (cited in footnote 39 above). Interview with Gerrit Viljoen in A. Starcke, *Survival: Taped Interviews with South Africa's Power Elite* (Tafelberg, 1978), p. 172. My interviews in South Africa.

45 In his 1956 speech in parliament, *Verwoerd Speaks*, pp. 102ff. *White Paper* on the Tomlinson Report (WPF, 1956).

46 G. Hart, *African Entrepreneurship*, pp. 98 and 105.

47 These conditions were frequently spelt out by the Minister of Labour, for example, in *HAD*, Vol. 23 of 1968, cols. 3453–4, Vol. 29 of 1970, col. 2068, and Vol. 24 of 1968, col. 6490.

48 *HAD*, Vol. 19 of 1967, col. 1682.

49 Lipton, 'South African Census' (see footnote 37 above).

50 Republic of South Africa, *White Paper on the Report by the Interdepartmental Committee on the decentralization of Industries* (Department of Industries, 1971).

51 See, for example, R. First, J. Steele and C. Gurney, *The South African Connection* (Temple Smith, 1972), Chapter 4.

52 *HAD*, Vol. 30 of 1970, col. 3312. See also speech by Jan Haak, Minister of Economic Affairs, *RDM*, 25 March 1970.

53 This preoccupation was evident in many official reports and pronouncements, for example, the 1958 *Viljoen Report*.

54 *Survey 1969*, p. 93.

55 *HAD*, Vol. 28 of 1970, col. 1941. Speech by Helen Suzman, cited in *Survey 1968*, p. 168. Van der Horst, 'Progress and Retrogression' (see footnote 36 above).

56 Lipton, *Optima*, section 1. *Survey 1967*, pp. 168f. *Survey 1968*, pp. 166f.

57 *Survey 1970*, p. 164.

58 The Labour Bureaux were provided for in the Native Labour Regulations Act and were activated by the 1964 Bantu Labour Act and the Bantu Labour Regulations of 1964, 1965 and 1968. On the legal and administrative framework for this system see the *Riekert Report*, Chapter 3.

59 *Verwoerd Speaks*, pp. 27 and 50f.

60 See *Report of the Commission of Inquiry into European Occupancy of Rural Areas* (Chairman: de Toit), 1960.

61 *HAD*, Vol. 30 of 1970, col. 3919.

62 Van der Horst, *Native Labour*, pp. 251 and 264.

63 *Ibid*.

64 *Industrial Legislation Commission*, pp. 22–3 and 159.

65 *Ibid*, p. 22. Salomon, 'Afrikaner Nationalism', p. 236.

66 Department of Labour, *Work Reservation* (1961, my italic).

67 The term used by R. Kraft in 'Labour: South Africa's Challenge of the 1970s' in *Optima*, Vol. 21, No. 1, of 1970.

68 2.9 per cent of the total workforce of 7.5m in 1970; *South African Statistics 1982*.

69 Van der Horst, *Native Labour*, pp. 244–5.

70 L. Kuper, *An African Bourgeoisie* (Yale, 1965), p. 262.

71 *Work Reservation* (see footnote 66 above).

72 Interview with Anna Scheepers, President of the Garment Workers Union, and other trade unionists and employers in the Transvaal clothing industry. See also *S.T.*, 2 and 7 February 1971.

73 For example, H. Chenery *et al, Redistribution with Growth* (OUP, 1974). S. Archer, 'Perverse Growth and Income Distribution in South Africa' (roneo, 1973). J. Knight and M. McGrath, 'An Analysis of racial wage distribution in South Africa', *Oxford Bulletin of Economics and Statistics*, November 1977.

74 S. Kuznets, *Economic Growth of Nations* (Harvard, 1971).

75 On the wages debate see M. Lipton, 'Neo-Marxists' and 'The Engelse Pers' (cited in footnotes 3 and 18 of Chapter 1 above).

76 On problems regarding statistical data on Africans see Note to the Tables (p. 377).

77 1921 figures from *Union Statistics for Fifty Years* (1960); 1970 figures from *South African Statistics 1982*.

78 W. F. J. Steenkamp, 'Bantu Wages in South Africa' in *SAJE*, Vol. 30 of 1962. D. Pursell, 'Bantu Real Wages and Employment Opportuniuties in South Africa' in *SAJE*, Vol. 36 of 1968. Van der Boegarde, 'Occupational Wage Differentials in the South African Metal Industry' in *SAJE*, Vol. 30 of 1962.

79 Lipton, 'White Farming' (cited in footnote 3 of Chapter 1 above).

80 'South Africa: two agricultures?' in *Farm Labour*.

81 J. Nattrass, *The South African Economy* (OUP 1981), Table 9.4. C. Simkins, 'What has been happening to income distribution and poverty in the homelands?', Carnegie Conference Paper in *Development Southern Africa*, Vol. 1, No. 2, of 1984.

82 V. Zaslavsky, *The Neo-Stalinist State* (Harvester, 1982), Chapter 6.

83 See K. I. Vaughn, *John Locke: Economist, Social Scientist* (Athlone, 1980), Chapters 3 and 4.

84 S. P. Cilliers and C. J. Groenewald, *Urban Growth in South Africa 1936–2000* (Department of Sociology, Stellenbosch University, 1982).

85 1946 figures calculated from *Fagan Report*, pp. 10 and 19; 1970 from the *Riekert Report*, Table 2.12.

86 Lipton, *Optima*, p. 165.

87 J. Connell, B. Dasgupta, R. Laishley and Michael Lipton, *Migration from Rural Areas* (OUP, 1976).

88 *Riekert Report*, p. 241.

89 Lipton, 'The South African Census' (cited in footnote 37 above).

90 *Op cit.*

91 The abolition of labour tenancy was provided for in the 1913 and 1936 Land Acts and in the 1932 Native Service Contract Act and 1964 Bantu Laws Amendment Act.

92 W. A. Lewis, 'Economic Development with Unlimited Supplies of Labour' in A. N. Agarwala and S. P. Singh, *The Economics of Underdevelopment* (Galaxy, 1963).

93 The report was not published, but see K. Owen, *Foreign Africans: Summary of the Report of the Froneman Committee* (SAIRR, 1964).

CHAPTER 3

1 This argument was set out in my 1974 paper 'Authoritarian Reform' (cited in footnote 3 of Chapter 1 above).

2 *HAD*, Vol. 30 of 1970, col. 4209, and Vol. 42 of 1973, col. 346. See also Vorster's speeches in *RDM*, 23 August 1973, and in F. R. Metrowich (ed), *Towards Dialogue and Detente* (Valiant, 1975).

3 In an interview in *Die Transvaler*, 7 August 1979; and in speeches in his George constituency, *RDM*, 10 November 1980; at the Transvaal Congress of the NP, *RDM*, 3 September 1980; and at Springbok, *SA Digest*, 21 May 1982.

4 From an interview in *Die Transvaler*, quoted by Andries Treurnicht in *HAD*, Vol. 100 of 1980, col. 3854; and in Botha's speeches to NP Congresses in the Cape and Transvaal, *RDM*, 26 September 1979 and 3 September 1980; and in a SABC interview, cited in *SA Digest*, 19 March 1982.

5 As in footnote 3; see also Chris Heunis, Minister of the Interior, responsible for the 1983 constitution, *The Times* (London), 2 June 1982.

6 *HAD*, Vol. 85 of 1980, cols. 214 and 246ff. See also Botha's '12 point programme', expounded to the 1979 Natal Congress of the NP (published as SAF briefing paper No. 25).

7 In terms of the 1970 Bantu Homelands Citizenship Act and the 1976 Status of Transkei Act (and subsequent Status Acts of the other Bantustans which became independent). Section 6 of the Status Act laid down that anyone classified as a citizen of the homeland concerned 'shall cease to be a South African citizen'. See the article by Black Sash's president, Sheena Duncan, 'Reform: Quo Vadis', in *South Africa International*, October 1982.

8 *HAD*, Vol. 72 of 1978, col. 579.

9 *HAD*, Vol. 85 of 1980, cols. 249ff; and statement by Botha following discussions with leaders of non-independent Bantustans, *SA Digest*, 22 February 1980.

10 Heunis in *SA Digest*, 20 May 1983; and in *HAD*, Vol. 85 of 1980, cols. 249ff.

11 *Washington Post*, 25 February 1982.

12 See his speech 'South Africa's outward policy' in *South Africa in the World* (Suid Afrikaanse Akademie vir Wetenskap en Kuns, 1970); and *HAD*, Vol. 29 of 1970, col. 51.

13 See his speech at the 1979 Carlton Conference, and in *HAD*, Vol. 1 of 1980, cols. 248ff. Also speech by Koornhof, Minister of Co-operation and Development, at Plettenberg Bay on 22 March 1980 (roneo, Department of Co-operation and Development).

14 *Ibid*, and see point 8 of the '12 point programme', and Botha's speech to the 1979 Transvaal NP Congress, *RDM*, 19 September 1979.

15 In an interview in *RDM*, 5 November 1979.

16 M. Horrell (ed), *Laws Affecting Race Relations in South Africa* (SAIRR, 1976), pp. 377ff.

17 *RDM*, 11 August 1977. Reaffirmed in a letter by Koornhof to the International Tennis Federation, *RDM*, 23 February 1978.

18 Interview with Viljoen, *The Times* (London), 24 November 1981. *Survey 1979*, pp. 583f.

19 *Survey 1983*, p. 220. See sections on social segregation in earlier *Surveys*.

20 *Die Vaderland*, 17 March 1975.

21 See, for example, *RDM*, 31 August 1970, 4 April 1973, 9 August and 6 December 1974, 7 and 30 January 1975, 9 January 1978, 27 August 1979, 4 November and 30 December 1980. *Beeld*, 27 November 1974. *SA Digest*, 5 December 1980. *Southern Africa Report*, 2 and 9 September 1983.

22 *RDM*, 26 September 1979 and 3 September 1980.

23 *Survey 1981*, p. 55.

24 S. Brand in *RDM*, 5 November 1979.

25 By the 1973 Coloured Farmers Assistance Law and 1980 Agricultural Amendment Act. See also *HAD*, Vol. 56 of 1975, col. 5231. *F.M.*, 18 February 1977. *White Paper* on the Riekert Report (1979).

26 Diederich's budget speech, *HAD*, Vol. 43 of 1973, cols. 3533f. Vorster's speech to the Motor Industries Federation on 3 October 1973 (roneo, Pretoria, 1973).

27 *Wiehahn Report* and *White Paper* on the Wiehahn Report.

28 *Star (w)*, 16 April 1975.

29 See, for example, Speech by Cape Nationalist, F. Conradie, in *Beeld*, 18 November 1974.

30 Connie Mulder, Minister of Information, *Survey 1977*, p. 190.

31 *RDM*, 25 April 1981.

32 *Survey 1972*, p. 259.

33 As in footnote 26 above.

34 In terms of the 1976 Black Employees Inservice Training Act.

35 *Survey 1972*, p. 268. *HAD*, Vol. 44 of 1973, cols. 7961–3.

36 *RDM*, 25 and 28 April 1980.

37 *NMC*, Table 3.2.3.

38 Horrell, *African Reserves* (SAIRR, 1969), p. 89.

39 By the 1972 Education Account Abolition Act.

40 Statement by M. C. Botha (roneo issued by BAD, Pretoria, 30 December 1976).

41 *RDM*, 6 May 1980.

42 In 1980, at the government's request, the HSRC appointed a Committee under J. P. de Lange to investigate and make recommendations on education policy. Its main report, *Provision of education in the RSA*, was published in 1981 and the government's White Paper in 1983. For a discussion of this see K. Hartshorne, *Can Separate Mean Equal?* (*Indicator*, University of Natal, 1984).

43 *Survey 1981*, p. 335.

44 *South African Statistics 1982*. *Survey 1972*, p. 344; *1976*, p. 324; and *1983*, pp. 417ff.

45 NMC, Table 3.1.1; L. Kuper, *An African Bourgeoisie* (Yale, 1965), p. 149. *Statistical Survey of Black Development 1982*. J. Butler, 'South Africa's role in Southern Africa: an historical view' (roneo, Wesleyan University, 1981).

46 Based on my fieldwork in SA factories, and on interviews with officials and politicians, in 1970 and 1974. The objective of maintaining the ratchet was also set out in official statements and publications such as the *White Paper on the Report of the Interdepartmental Committee* (Dept of Industries, 1971). See also pp. 33f above.

47 A survey of 200 companies employing 0.5m workers, cited *Survey 1979*, p. 273.

48 See the survey of signatories to the Sullivan Code for U.S. Companies, *Survey 1978*, p. 257 and *1981*, p. 214.

49 *Manpower Survey No. 15* (Department of Manpower, 1983) Vol. 1, Section B.

50 *Ibid.*

51 Based on an examination of the Industrial Council Agreements for the relevant years, clarified by discussions with trade unionists and Seifsa officials.

52 *HAD*, Vol. 29 of 1970, col. 975.

53 *RDM*, 12 November 1971. *S.T.*, 28 November 1971.

54 Calculated from *NMC*, Table 5.1.

55 The Fifth Report of the House of Commons Expenditure Committee on *Wages and Conditions of African Workers employed by British Firms in South Africa* (HMSO, 1974). The inquiry was prompted by Adam Raphael's articles in *The Guardian*, March–May 1973.

56 *Volkskas Economic Spotlight*, June 1983.

57 M. McGrath, 'Distribution of Personal Wealth in South Africa', *Indicator* (University of Natal), Vol. 1, no. 2, of 1983.

58 *NMC*, p. 227. See papers by L. Loots and C. Simkins in *Mannekragbenutting: Manpower Utilization* (HSRC, 1979).

59 Nattrass and Simkins (see footnote 81 of Chapter 2 above).

60 *Statistical Survey of Black Development 1982*.

61 C. Simkins, 'Some Aspects of the Carnegie Conference' in *Development Southern Africa* Vol. 1, No. 2, of 1984.

62 H. Pollak in *Race Relations News* (SAIRR), June 1976.

63 See speech by Gerrit Viljoen, Minister of Education, *Star (w)* 9 October 1982.

64 *HAD*, Vol. 56 of 1975, col. 4955.

65 For example, the Court's decision in the case of Fodens (SA) against the United African Motor and Allied Workers Union, *F.M.*, 22 July 1983.

66 *HAD*, Vol. 30 of 1970, col. 4090.

67 *HAD*, Vol. 56 of 1975, cols. 5230f. Lipton, *Optima*, Section 1. *Star*, 29 October 1975. *RDM*, 21 August 1976 and 25 May 1978. *Survey 1972*, p. 143 and *1976*, pp. 186ff.

68 *Southern Africa Report*, 19 August 1983.

69 This was made clear in the *Riekert Report* and subsequent *White Paper*. This section on the Riekert concessions is based on my analysis in *Optima*.

70 *RDM*, 8 May 1979. *Survey 1981*, p. 242.

71 Lipton, *Optima*, p. 89.

72 *N.M.C.*, Table 7.4.

73 The discussion of migrancy based on Lipton, *Optima*.

74 See, for example, *RDM*, 22 June 1983.

75 *White Paper* on the Riekert Report, pp. 5 and 9.

76 *Survey 1983*, p. 262.

77 Study by L. Loots, cited *RDM*, 18 May 1978. On complaints by officials about bypassing of the Bureaux, see Lipton, *Optima*; and *Survey 1981*, p. 119.

78 See papers by G. Mare and C. Simkins in *Resettlement* (SAIRR, 1981). *A Land Divided* (Black Sash, 1982). The Surplus Peoples Project, *Forced Removals in South Africa* (1983). Official figures from the BAD cited in *Survey 1980*, p. 452.

79 *Op cit.*

80 *White Paper on the Report by the Inter-departmental Committee* (Department of Industries, 1971), p. 7. P. J. Riekert, 'The economy of the Republic with special reference to the homelands and border industrial development' (roneo, SAIRR, 1970). See also W. F. J. Steenkamp, 'Labour Policies for Growth during the Seventies in the established industrial areas' in *SAJE*, June 1971. T. Bell, *Industrial Decentralization in South Africa* (OUP, 1973).

81 By the 1974 Amendment to the Bantu Laws Amendment Act.

82 *HAD*, Vol. 76 of 1978, cols. 210f.

83 *RDM*, 26 March 1976. My interviews with employers and trade unionists in the garment industry.

84 *Riekert Report*, p. 227.

85 *Riekert White Paper*, pp. 14f.

86 *Statistical Survey of Black Development 1978*, Table 47.

87 Lower estimates are given by Bell, *Decentralization* (see footnote 80 above).

88 Riekert (then economic advisor to the Prime Minister), 'Homelands' (cited in footnote 80 above).

89 For example, by H. Reynders of Pretoria University in *Survey 1971*, p. 215.

90 Bell, 'Some Aspects of Industrial Decentralization in South Africa', in *SAJE*, Vol. 41, No. 4, of 1973. J. Lombard and P. J. van der Merve, 'Central Problems of the Economic Development of Bantu Homelands' in *Finance and Trade Review*, Vol. 10, No. 1, 1972. Maasdorp (cited in footnote 37 of Chapter 2 above).

91 In his speech to businessmen at the 1980 Good Hope Conference (published by the Department of Foreign Affairs, 1981).

92 Speech in parliament by van Zyl Slabbert, Leader of the Opposition, quoted in the PFP newsletter *Deurbraak*, July 1984. On Bantustan expenditure see also Benso statistical reviews.

93 On the potential and failure of agricultural development see Lipton, 'Two Agricultures' in *Farm Labour*.

94 Lipton, *Optima*, p. 92.

95 *Ibid*.

96 *HAD*, Vol. 38 of 1972, col. 5277.

97 *RDM*, 2 April 1981.

98 J. A. Lombard (ed), *Alternatives to the Consolidation of Kwazulu* (Benso). The 'Benso Report' in *Development Studies Southern Africa*, Vol. 2, No. 4, of 1980.

99 See 'The Promotion of Industrial Development: An Element of a Co-ordinated Regional Strategy for Southern Africa', Supplement to *SA Digest*, 2 April 1982.

100 *HAD*, Vol. 9 of 1964, col. 68.

101 V. Cromwell, 'The Nature of British Parliamentary Reform' in K. Bosl (ed) *Der Moderne Parlamentarismus und seine Grundlagen in der Standischen Reprasentation* (Berlin, 1977).

102 *SA Digest*, 7 September 1984. *The Times* (London), 27 September 1984.

CHAPTER 4

1 This argument, with both its positive and negative features, was set out in my 1974 paper 'White Farming' (cited in footnote 3 of Chapter 1 above). For the argument that the shift to more fully capitalist farming intensified apartheid see papers by Trapido and Legassick cited in footnote 5 of Chapter 1.

2 *SA Statistics 1982*. S. Brand, 'The contributions of agriculture to the economic development of South Africa' (PhD thesis, Pretoria University, 1969).

3 Lipton, 'White Farming'.

4 As in footnote 60 of Chapter 2, pp. 19–20.

5 Lipton, 'White Farming'.

6 G. M. E. Leistner, 'Foreign Bantu Workers in South Africa', *SAJE*, March 1967.

7 Van der Horst, *Native Labour*, pp. 114, 146 and 290.

8 M. Wilson in *Oxford History*, p. 65.

9 K. Marx, *Capital*, Vol. 1, section 8.

10 Van der Horst, *Native Labour*, p. 293. P. Rich, 'African Farming and the 1913 Natives' Land Act' (roneo, Saldru conference, Cape Town University, 1976).

11 Van der Horst, *Native Labour*, p. 294.

12 T. Muil, 'The Tenant Labourer System in Natal' (roneo, Saldru, 1976).

13 My interviews with farmers in 1978. See also *Riekert Report*, pp. 183ff.

14 Van der Horst, *Native Labour*, p. 297. H. Houghton, The South African Economy (OUP, 1964), p. 151.

15 Van der Horst, *Native Labour*, pp. 285, 289 and 296. F. Wilson in *Oxford History*, p. 142.

16 S. Siebert and A. Guelke, *Is State Control of Labour in South Africa Effective?* (Mandrake Trust, London, 1973).

17 Brand (see footnote 2 above).

18 M. Morris, 'The Development of Capitalism in South African Agriculture', *Economy and Society*, Vol. 5, No. 3, of 1976.

19 *Survey 1958/9*, pp. 311ff, and *1959/60*, pp. 266ff.

20 *Verwoerd Speaks*, p. 50.

21 Horwitz, *Political Economy*, p. 208.

22 N. Bromberger and E. van der Vliet, 'Farm Labour in the Albany District' in *Farm Labour*. In the same book see also J. B. Knight's seminal paper on the problem of agricultural statistics, 'Is South Africa running out of unskilled labour?'

23 This argument, first set out in my 'White Farming' paper, now seems generally accepted.

24 *SAAU Survey* (mimeo, Pretoria, 1972).

25 *Second Report of the Commission of Inquiry into Agriculture* (Chairmen: du Plessis/Marais), R.P. 84 of 1970, pp. 158 and 174–5.

26 *F.M.*, 13 and 20 September 1974.

27 From my interviews in the mining industry.

28 *RDM*, 5 September 1974. *HAD*, Vol. 57 of 1975, col. 7811. *Star*, 11 June 1975. *F.M.*, 4 April 1975.

29 *RDM*, 20 November 1971, 22 November 1974 and 9 September 1976.

30 See, example, *RDM*, 3 September 1970, 8 December 1972 and 10 May 1973. Also Natal Agricultural Union memo on labour policy (roneo, 1973).

31 *RDM*, 4 July 1974.

32 A. J. Petersen, 'Changes in Farm Labour in the Elgin District' (roneo, Saldru, 1976).

33 As in footnote 25 above.

34 *RDM*, 3 September 1970.

35 See A. W. Stadler, 'Agricultural Policy and Agrarian Politics' (roneo, Saldru, 1976). M. Lipton, 'South Africa: Two Agricultures?' in *Farm Labour*, and my subsequent exchanges with Professor F. R. Tomlinson in *Social Dynamics*, Vol. 5, no. 2, and Vol. 6, Nos. 1 and 2.

36 Evidence to the Riekert Commission by the Sugar Industry Labour Organization, SILO (roneo, Durban, November 1977), and by the SA Cane Growers Association (roneo, Durban, undated). Dissatisfaction with the bureaucracy, particularly the BAABs, was reiterated at the 1982 SAAU congress; this information is from interviews with SAAU officials in Pretoria in 1983.

37 Silo evidence to Riekert Commission cited in footnote 36.

38 *Ibid.*

39 *Riekert Report*, pp. 133ff and 186f; and Riekert, *White Paper*, p. 9.

40 See Trapido (cited footnote 5 of Chapter 1).

41 *Farmers Weekly*, 30 June 1976.

42 As in footnote 37.

43 *RDM*, 10 May 1973.

44 Lipton, 'White Farming', Table 2.

45 F. Wilson in *Oxford History*, p. 146.

46 In their evidence to the Viljoen Commission; see *Viljoen Report*, p. 18.

47 T. Ardington, 'Factors affecting wages and employment in sugar farming' in *Farm Labour*, Table 3.

48 In speeches at Congresses of SAAU and the Transvaal Agricultural Union, *RDM*, 3 September 1970, 8 December 1972 and 10 May 1973. See also Report by the Natal Agricultural Union on *Service Conditions of Bantu on farms in Natal* (NAU, mimeo, C20/1973).

49 Lipton, 'White Farming'.

50 For example, *Rapport*, 11 and 25 August 1974, and *Die Transvaler*, 12 August 1974. The SABC programmes sparked protests at the annual SAAU congresses, *RDM*, 21 August 1974, and at the OFS Congress of the NP, *RDM*, 22 November 1974.

51 *Farmers Weekly*, 23 October 1974.

52 *F.M.*, 21 March 1975. *RDM*, 12 July 1980.

53 Simons, *Class and Colour*, p. 362.

54 A. Gerschenkron, *Continuity in History* (Harvard, 1968), Chapter 7.

55 See the following papers in *Farm Labour:* A. Kooy, 'Farm labour in the Karoo'; G. Young, 'Labour in Transvaal Agribusiness'; J. Maree, 'Farm labour in the Dealesville District, OFS'.

56 Maree, *op. cit*, p. 135.

57 K. Marx and F. Engels, *Selected Works* (Lawrence & Wishart, 1950) Vol. 1, p. 35.

58 A leading exponent of this view was F. R. Tomlinson, Chairman of the Tomlinson Commission. See my exchange with him on these issues, cited in footnote 35 above.

59 Van der Horst, *Native Labour*, pp. 104ff.

60 See, for example, M. Wilson, in *Oxford History*. C. Murray, *Families Divided: the impact of migrant labour on Lesotho* (Cambridge, 1981). G. Arrighi, *The Political Economy of Rhodesia* (Mouton, 1967). C. Bundy, 'The emergence and decline of a South African peasantry', *African Affairs*, Vol. 71, 1972. W. Beinart, 'Peasant Production, Underdevelopment and the Traditionalist Response in Pondoland' (MA Thesis, University of London).

61 The argument here is based on my 'South Africa: Two Agricultures' in *Farm Labour*.

62 Van der Horst, *Native Labour*, p. 315.

63 *Op cit*, p. 310.

64 M. Ballinger, *Union to Apartheid*, p. 67.

65 *Verwoerd Speaks*, p. 36.

66 'South Africa: Two Agricultures' in *Farm Labour*. See also Michael Lipton, *Why Poor People Stay Poor* (Temple Smith, 1977).

67 *Survey 1980*, p. 121. A. L. Schaffer, 'The Development of Small Cane Growers in the South African Sugar Industry' (roneo, SA Sugar Association, Durban, 1976).

68 *Daily News*, 21 August 1980. My interviews with officials and farmers in Natal in 1978.

69 *RDM*, 14 August 1980. *Sunday Express*, 16 March 1980.

70 *RDM*, 1 September 1973, and Barry Streek in *RDM*, 27 April 1981.

71 Lombard, *Alternatives* (cited in footnote 98 of Chapter 3).

CHAPTER 5

1 F. A. Johnstone, *Class, Race and Gold* (Routledge & Kegan Paul, 1976). Davies, 'Capital, The State'.

2 Chamber of Mines, *Eighth Annual Report for 1896*, pp. 61ff. Simons, *Class and Colour*, p. 55.

3 Simons, *Class and Colour*, pp. 55 and 83. D. Denoon, 'The Transvaal Labour Crisis', *Journal of African History*, Vol. 7, No. 3, of 1967.

4 F. Wilson, *Labour in the South African Gold Mines* (Cambridge, 1972), p. 8.

5 Simons, *Class and Colour*, pp. 90ff.

6 Van der Horst, *Native Labour*, pp. 181f.

7 *Ibid*. K. Hancock, *Smuts* (Cambridge, 1968), Vol. 2, p. 63.

8 Hancock, *Smuts*, pp. 65ff.

9 For an account of the Rand rebellion see Simons, *Class and Colour*, Chapter 13. Hancock, *Smuts*, Chapter 4. E. Roux, *Time Longer Than Rope* (Gollancz, 1948), Chapter XIV.

10 M. Legassick, 'The Rise of Modern South African Liberalism: Its assumptions and social base' (Institute of Commonwealth Studies, roneo, 1973), p. 17.

11 Wilson, *Gold Mines*, pp. 10 and 157.

12 *Ibid*.

13 Cited van der Horst, *Native Labour*, p. 184. Simons, *Class and Colour*, p. 301.

14 Frankel, cited in Horwitz, *Political Economy*, p. 240. See also Frankel, *Capital Investment*, pp. 94ff.

15 C. van Onselen, *Chibaro: African Mine Labour in Southern Rhodesia 1900–33* (Pluto, 1976).

16 Salomon, 'Afrikaner Nationalism'.

17 Horwitz, *Political Economy*, p. 217.

18 S. F. Frankel, *Investment and the Return to Equity Capital in the South African Goldmining Industry, 1887–1965* (Blackwell, 1967), pp. 7–9 and 45.

19 Estimate by A. J. Norval, former chairman of the Board of Trade, cited in Wilson, *Gold Mines*, p. 117.

20 *Op cit*, p. 114.

21 *AAC Annual Report 1970*.

22 Wilson, *Gold Mines*, p. 118. *Star*, 21 June 1966.

23 In terms of the 1964 Mines and Works Act regulation permitting the Government Mining Engineer to issue blasting certificates of competence to miners of any race in the Bantustans, or to allow them to do these jobs without the certificates.

24 *HAD*, Vol. 30 of 1970, col. 3636. *RDM*, 8 October 1970.

25 Statement by A. W. S. Schumann, President of the Chamber of Mines, in *Mining Survey*, No. 76 of 1975.

26 *RDM*, 15 August 1974.

27 *RDM*, 2 July 1973.

28 *AAC Chairman's Review 1983*.

29 *Financial Times* (London), 23 February 1972.

30 Van der Horst, *Native Labour*, pp. 149, 111 and 117.

31 Johnstone, *Class, Race and Gold*, p. 27.

32 Van der Horst, *Native Labour*, p. 133.

33 *Ibid*.

34 On wages and recruitment see van der Horst, pp. 191ff. Wilson, Chapters 3 and 4. W. J. Breytenbach, *Migratory Labour Arrangements in Southern Africa* (African Institute, Pretoria, 1972).

35 M. Williams, 'An Analysis of South African Capitalism', *Bulletin of the Conference of Socialist Economists*, February 1974.

36 Michael Lipton, *Why Poor People Stay Poor* (Temple-Smith, 1977). E. Dean, *The Supply Responses of African Farmers: Theory and Measurement in Malawi* (North Holland, 1966).

37 Johnstone, *Class, Race and Gold*, p. 44.

38 Wilson, *Gold Mines*, p. 107.

39 *F.M.*, 6 June 1975 and 21 October 1977. Goldfields own *Annual Report* and *Chairman's Review* for 1973 and 1974, urging 'caution with regard to increases in minimum wages'. My interviews in the mining industry and with trade unionists. See also R. Stares, *Consolidated Goldfields Limited* (Christian Concern for Southern Africa, London, 1975), and *Consolidated Goldfields Limited: Anti-Report* (Counter Information Services, London), and footnote 61 below.

40 Lipton, *Optima*, p. 110.

41 *RDM*, 9 December 1974.

42 *Star*, 24 June 1975 and *Star (w)*, 13 September 1975. *RDM*, 20 November 1974. *F.M.*, 6 December 1974.

43 *Influx Control and Economic Growth* (Address to the Free Market Foundation in Cape Town, 1983).

44 Statement by A. W. S. Schumann, *RDM*, 20 November 1974.

45 Statement by A. C. Fleischer, Director of Labour at Chamber of Mines, *RDM*, 16 February 1982.

46 Salomon, 'Afrikaner Nationalism', p. 231.

47 Cited in Lipton, *Optima*, Section 3.

48 The ensuing analysis from my monograph on migrant labour, based on fieldwork in the mining industry during 1978, published in *Optima*. See also footnote 61 below.

49 T. Gregory, *Ernest Oppenheimer and the Economic Development of Southern Africa* (OUP, 1962), pp. 573–81.

50 *RDM*, 15 August 1975.

51 In a speech to the 1979 Assocom Conference in Bloemfontein (roneo, 1979).

52 See, for example, Morris D. Morris, *The Emergence of an Industrial Labour Force in India* (Berkeley, 1955).

53 Van der Horst, *Native Labour*, p. 178.

54 Wilson, pp. 78–9. G. Clack, 'Industrial Relations', p. 222.

55 As in footnote 48.

56 In an interview in *The Times* (London), 14 April 1980. On disagreements within the Chamber see *F.M.*, 21 October 1977.

57 *F.M.*, 28 September 1984.

58 L. M. Thompson in *Oxford History*, p. 355.

59 M. Wilson in *Oxford History*, p. 66.

60 *RDM*, 2 September 1972. For similar arguments by senior AAC directors see Zach de Beer, 'Industrial Relations in free enterprise societies and Guidelines for South Africa' in *Optima*, Vol. 26, No. 4.

61 Goldfields denied the suggestion in my article on migrant labour, published in *Optima*, Vol. 29 of 1980, that, as a largely foreign-owned company, they might take a shorter-term view than SA-based companies, preferring to maximize their profits now. They threatened an injunction to stop publication, unless a disclaimer was inserted into the article, alleging that it contained 'untrue statements' about this and about their labour policies. *Optima* (house journal of AAC and de Beers) inserted the disclaimer, without allowing me the right of reply, though they subsequently compensated me for this unwarranted allegation and issued a statement making it clear that they did not doubt my integrity or competence.

CHAPTER 6

1 As in footnotes 1, 2 and 3 of Chapter 1. Also H. Houghton, *The South African Economy* (OUP, 1964).

2 As in footnotes 5 and 6 of Chapter 1. Also M. Legassick, 'The Making of South African Native Policy, 1903–23: The Origins of Segregation' (mimeo, Institute of Commonwealth Studies, London, 1973); and 'Legislation, Ideology and Economy in Post-1948 South Africa' in *Journal of Southern African Studies*, Vol. 1, No. 1 of 1974.

3 B. Bozzoli, 'The Roots of Hegemony: Ideologies, Interests and the Legitimation of South African Capitalism' (PhD thesis, Sussex University, 1975), pp. 298ff.

4 *Op. cit*, pp. 246 and 310f.

5 Van der Horst, *Native Labour*, pp. 246 and 252.

6 *Industrial and Agricultural Requirements Commission* (cited in footnote 7 of Chapter 2), pp. 35 and 56ff.

7 Simons, *Class and Colour*, p. 561. Seifsa, *Organization and Structure of the Metal and Engineering Industries in the Republic of South Africa* (Seifsa, undated).

8 Davies, 'Capital, the State', p. 305. Suzman's speech in *HAD*, Vol. 86 of 1954, col, 5971. On the opposition to extension of the job bar from the FCI, Assocom, Seifsa, and others see also *Survey 1953/4*, p. 128 and *1955/6*, p. 184; and M. Horrell, *South Africa's Workers* (SAIRR, 1969), p. 91.

9 *Viljoen Report*, pp. 32–4.

10 Horwitz, 'Expand or Explode' (see footnote 2 of Chapter 1), pp. 10f, citing Schoeman, the Minister of Transport, and *Die Burger*.

11 FCI, 'Survey of Manpower' (roneo, 1970). Cape Chamber of Industries, 'Report of the Committee on the Labour Shortage in the Western Cape' (roneo, 1970). W. W. van Breda and H. P. Langenhoven, *The Utilization of Non-White Labour* (University of the OFS, 1972). HSRC, *Die Vraag na en aanbod van blanke mannekrag* (1973). Manpower Surveys of the Department of Labour and the *Economic Development Programmes* of the Department of Planning. And speeches acknowledging the severity of the skill shortage by Prime Minister Vorster, *RDM*, 24 October 1975, and the Minister of Labour in *Survey 1971*, p. 232.

12 *RDM*, 10 December 1970. *F.M.* supplement, 23 July 1971 and *F.M.*, 9 August 1974.

13 See discussion on this in *Reynders Report*, pp. 36 and 380ff.

14 For example, June 1970 issue of *Volkshandel*, Journal of the AHI, and statement by the AHI's president, B. P. Marais, cited in *RDM*, 21 August 1970.

15 For example, *RDM*, 15 and 18 May 1971. *RDM*, 22 March 1973.

16 *Survey 1975*, p. 191.

17 *F.M.*, 1 September 1978.

18 UAL Survey, cited in *Survey 1974*, p. 236.

19 'Aide Memoire: A Labour Policy for the 1970s' (roneo, FCI, Pretoria, 1975).

20 The various 'Codes of Employment' were published in *Race Relations News*, March 1978.

21 For example, *RDM*, 4 May 1972, 4 April 1974 and 8 May 1980. *Survey 1971*, p. 192 and *1972*, p. 264. Wim de Villiers, *The Effective Utilization of Human Resources in South Africa* (General Mining Corporation, 1974).

22 For example, by Polaroid, British Petroleum, Pepsi-Cola, Mobil and others.

23 *RDM*, 6 April 1981.

24 *Fagan Report*, p. 42 (Seifsa was then known as Safema).

25 *Viljoen Report*, p. 32.

26 My interviews with Assocom officials. De Villiers Graaff, Leader of the Opposition, in *HAD*, Vol. 105 of 1960, cols. 8110ff. H. Hartmann, *Enterprise and Politics in South Africa* (Princeton, 1962), p. 90. Ballinger, *Union to Apartheid*, p. 435. Greenberg, *Race and State* (cited footnote 8 of Chapter 1) pp. 202f.

27 *Riekert Report*, pp. 135, 145, 153ff, 191, 197–8.

28 *Op cit*, p. 191.

29 *Op cit*, pp. 154, 167, 191, 198, 245–6.

30 *Op cit*, p. 166.

31 *Op cit*, pp. 154–6 and 251.

32 *Op cit*, p. 229.

33 Cited C. Diamond, *SAJE*, Vol. 40 of 1972, p. 50.

34 My interviews with officials of the Chambers of Industry and Commerce. See also 'The Western Cape – Coloured and White Labour Preference Area' (Black Sash Fact Paper for the 1980 National Conference).

35 *Cape Times*, 22 April 1970.

36 *Cape Times*, 25 March 1970.

37 *Survey 1970*, p. 95.

38 Mr. Greyling of the AHI, reported in *Race Relations News*, August 1973.

39 *RDM*, 4 July 1980.

40 *Riekert Report*, p. 227.

41 In a speech to the *Financial Mail*'s annual international conference (roneo, November 1982).

42 *F.M.*, 20 June 1975.

43 *Survey 1970*, p. 106.

44 'Aide Memoire' (cited in footnote 19 above).

45 *Riekert Report*, p. 229.

46 My interviews with a wide range of businessmen.

47 *Fagan Report*, Section 3.

48 For example, to the Viljoen Commission and in their representations to the Prime Minister after Sharpeville (see footnote 26 above).

49 'Aide Memoire'. See also statement by FCI Director, Hennie Reynders, on the effects of migrancy on stability and productivity, *Star*, 29 May 1975.

50 *Star (w)*, 23 October 1976, and in its journal *Volkshandel*, cited in *RDM*, 12 March and 15 July 1976.

51 *RDM*, 6 October 1972.

52 'Statement of policy and strategy' and 'Guidelines for activities in the field of housing' (roneos, Urban Foundation, 1977); also their *Annual Reports*.

53 For example, *RDM*, 2 September 1980 and 3 and 24 June 1983.

54 Bozzoli, 'Roots of Hegemony', pp. 300ff and 314ff.

55 Houghton, *South African Economy*, p. 163.

56 D. O'Meara, 'Class, Capital and Ideology in the Development of Afrikaner Nationalism' (PhD Thesis, Sussex University, 1979; published in 1983 by Cambridge, but references here are to the thesis), pp. 159 and 203.

57 Ballinger, *Union to Apartheid*, pp. 435–6. Clack, 'Industrial Relations', p. 223.

58 For example, *Survey 1971*, p. 184 and *1972*, p. 243. Also publications of Christian Concern for Southern Africa (CCSA) in London.

59 D. Etheredge, 'Wages, Productivity and Opportunity' (SAIRR, 1973).

60 *F.M.*, 4 April 1975. See also Merton Dagut, *Star*, 26 June 1975.

61 *RDM*, 4 April 1974.

62 *RDM*, 8 May 1973.

63 *RDM*, 17 September 1971 and 9 October 1973.

64 *Star (W)*, 25 June 1977. See *Reynders Report* on the importance of the internal market.

65 *Star*, 10 April 1972. *RDM*, 11 November 1975. *F.M.*, 3 December 1976.

66 This was proposed at the 1970 and 1973 conferences of the Institute of Administrators of Non-European Affairs, *RDM*, 8 June 1970 and 15 November 1973.

67 E. S. Sachs, *Rebel Daughters* (MacGibbon & Kee, 1957), p. 63.

68 *Industrial Legislation Commission*, pp. 211ff.

69 Interviews with trade unionists and businessmen. Horrell, *South Africa's Workers*, pp. 67 and 78.

70 As in footnote 57.

71 'Bantu participation in labour negotiations' (FCI roneo).

72 For example, Seifsa's memorandum to its members on the 1973 Bantu Labour Relations Regulation Amendment Act (roneo, August 1973). Paper by Natal businessman, Chris Saunders, on 'Black labour and the development of the South African economy' (roneo, presented at a meeting at Fleur du Cap in September 1974). *Star*, 6 September 1975. *Survey 1976*, p. 319. Wim de Villiers in *F.M.*, 4 April 1975.

73 See FCI's 'Aide Memoire' (cited footnote 19 above). *RDM*, 26 April 1973. *Star*, 22 May 1975.

74 In a speech to the Institute of Personnel Management (roneo, 1974). *RDM*, 9 October 1973.

75 *Star*, 13, 14 and 15 August 1974.

76 W. D. Wilson, 'Commitment to growth in South Africa' in *Optima*, Vol. 25, No. 2, of 1975.

77 For example, report on the 1979 Assocom Conference in *Post*, 19 October 1979. *Survey 1983*, p. 204, on the dispute between the Liberty Life Company and the black Insurance and Assurance Workers' Union of South Africa (IAWUSA) over the Company's insistence that it would only recognize a union open to all races.

78 *Industrial Legislation Commission*, pp. 147ff.

79 As in footnote 74.

80 Survey by Market Research Africa cited in *Survey 1974*, p. 317. J. Nattrass and I. Duncan, *A Study of Employers' Attitudes towards African Worker Representation* (Natal University).

81 *F.M.*, 21 December 1973.

82 *F.M.*, 6 June 1975. *Star (w)*, 1 November 1975.

83 *RDM*, 1 December 1976.

84 My interviews with businessmen. *RDM*, 25 May 1978. *F.M.*, 24 March 1978. Also *Wiehahn Report*, Part 1, pp. 30–31.

85 See Seifsa's 1979 Guidelines to its members and the attack on these by FOSATU in *RDM*, 7 December 1979.

86 On FCI policy, *RDM*, 25 September 1980 and 14 April 1981; and *Survey*

1982, 163. On Assocom, *RDM*, 30 October 1980. On AHI and Seifsa, *RDM*, 14 May 1980; *F.M.*, 4 April 1980; and *Survey 1981*, p. 191.

87 For example, *RDM*, 10 October 1980. *Financial Times* (London), 7 November 1980. *F.M.*, 16 September 1983, supplement on 'The Chloride Story'. On the opposition of white unions see Chapter 7.

88 Including agreements signed by leading companies such as Barlow Rand, Colgate, Johnson & Johnson, Chloride.

89 See *New York Times*, 10 August 1981, on a leaked security police memorandum to East London employers on union-busting tactics. Also *RDM*, 31 October 1980.

90 'Is freedom of association being derailed?' (Information Bulletin issued by Midlands Chamber of Industry, 23 August 1982; reprinted in Press Cuttings Service of AAC Industrial Relations Dept). *RDM*, 19 June 1980 and 14 April 1981.

91 *F.M.*, 9 September 1983.

92 In Barlow Rand's *Annual Report 1983*.

93 M. Olson, *Rise and Decline of Nations* (Yale, 1982), p. 22.

94 Ross and Hartman, *Changing Patterns of Industrial Conflict*, cited in Clack, 'Industrial Relations', p. 245.

95 Simons, *Class and Colour*, Chapter 25. E. Feit, *Workers without Weapons* (Archon Books 1975). T. Lodge, *Black Politics in South Africa since 1945* (Longmans, 1983), Chapter 8.

96 *Industrial Legislation Commission*, p. 211.

97 Comments by spokesmen of strike-hit eastern Cape motor companies, *RDM*, 19 June 1980.

98 *RDM*, 6 November 1980.

99 Clack, 'Industrial Relations', p. 220.

100 *AAC Industrial Relations Review 1982*.

101 *Survey 1972*, p. 338.

102 See Wim de Villiers and Chris Saunders, cited in footnote 72 above.

103 Trades Union Council (UK), 'Visit of the General Council Delegation to South Africa' (roneo, December 1973).

104 Hart, *African Entrepreneurship*, p. 100.

105 *Op cit*, p. 102.

106 Kuper (cited in footnote 70 of Chapter 2), pp. 271ff. Hart, p. 104.

107 Hart, p. 106.

108 *Star (w)*, 14 May 1977.

109 *Survey 1975*, p. 194.

110 *RDM*, 17 April 1980. On the change in AHI policy see *RDM*, 28 April 1978.

111 *RDM*, 22 August 1979.

112 For example, *RDM*, 7 December 1979. *Survey 1981*, pp. 162–3.

113 Speech to 1976 Assocom Convention, *Star (w)*, 23 October 1976.

114 'Views on the Republic of South Africa Constitution Bill' (roneo, Assocom, Johannesburg, 1983).

115 *F.M.*, 19 September 1980.

116 *F.M.*, 20 August 1976.

117 As in footnote 114. *SA Digest*, 27 May 1983.

118 *RDM*, 6 October 1982. *SA Digest*, 27 May 1983. Also Assocom's 'Views on the Constitution'.

CHAPTER 7

1 Simons, *Class and Colour*, pp. 276 and 297. E. Roux, *Time Longer than Rope* (Gollancz, 1948), p. 156.

2 F. A. Johnstone, *Class, Race and Gold* (Routledge, 1976), p. 72. Davies, 'Capital, the State', pp. 142, 157–60, 208–9, 371.

3. Salomon, 'Afrikaner Nationalism'. Van der Horst, *Native Labour*, Chapter 11 and p. 238.

4 Simons, *Class and Colour*, p. 53.

5 *Op cit*, p. 159. Salomon, 'Afrikaner Nationalism'.

6 Simons, p. 508.

7 *Op cit*, p. 128.

8 *Op cit*, p. 226.

9 *Op cit*, pp. 174 and 561.

10 *Op cit*, p. 52.

11 *Op cit*, p. 53.

12 *Op cit*, pp. 96 and 130.

13 *Op cit*, p. 338.

14 *Op cit*, pp. 227–8.

15 Clack, 'Industrial Relations', pp. 213 and 216.

16 S. Greenberg, 'Trade Unionism in a bounded Working Class' (roneo, Yale, undated), p. 17.

17 Horrell, *South Africa's Workers* (SAIRR, 1969), pp. 5ff.

18 Simons, *Class and Colour*, pp. 174–5.

19 Doxey, *The Industrial Colour Bar in South Africa* (OUP, 1961), p. 117.

20 Roux, *Time Longer than Rope*, pp. 135ff. Simons, pp. 128–30 and 162. Doxey, pp. 35 and 119.

21 Simons, pp. 162 and 176. Roux, p. 135.

22 Roux, pp. 137 and 266. Simons, pp. 155, 173 and 193–4.

23 N. Glazer and D. Moynihan, *Beyond the Melting Pot* (M.I.T. 1970, 2nd edition), p. xxiii.

24 Simons, p. 558.

25 *Industrial Legislation Commission*, p. 214.

26 Roux, pp. 344ff. Simons, pp. 513 and 573ff.

27 *Industrial Legislation Commission*, pp. 214f.

28 Cited Clack, 'Industrial Relations', p. 213.

29 Horrell, p. 22.

30 Doxey, p. 111. Welsh in *Oxford History*, p. 183.

31 Cited Clack, 'Industrial Relations', p. 213.

32 W. F. J. Steenkamp, 'Labour Policies for growth during the 'seventies', in *SAJE*, Vol. 39 (1971).

33 *'Union Statistics for 50 years'*, A-30; and see Table 13 above.

34 Horrell, *South Africa's Workers*, pp. 98ff.

35 *South African Statistics 1972*, A23 and A27.

36 My interviews with trade unionists. *RDM*, 13 October 1970, 14 February, 10 March and 5 November 1971.

37 *RDM*, 1 June and 27 August 1970. 1 May 1971 and 20 July 1973.

38 For example, the speech by J. van Wyk, *RDM*, 28 August 1972.

39 *RDM*, 14 February 1971. *S.T.*, 6 December 1970.

40 *RDM*, 3 and 16 September 1971.

41 *RDM*, 5 October 1972.

42 *RDM*, 22 March 1972.

43 My interview with Mr. Paulus in 1978. Greenberg (as in footnote 16 above), p. 37–8.

44 *RDM*, 2 May 1978.

45 *RDM*, 29 September 1980. *Survey 1981*, p. 151.

46 Greenberg, *op cit*, p. 43.

47 *RDM*, 22 March 1972 and 7 March 1973.

48 *Star*, 20 June 1975.

49 My interviews. Horrell, *South Africa's Workers*, pp. 28–36.

50 *RDM*, 30 July 1970. *F.M.*, 11 August 1972. *Press Digest* (roneo, Jewish Board of Deputies), 31 August 1972.

51 Cited in *South African Labour Bulletin*, July 1976.

52 *RDM*, 25 and 26 October 1973.

53 *RDM*, 3 January, 26 April, 23 May and 3 August 1973, and 15 and 26 March and 17 May 1974.

54 *RDM*, 17 October 1974.

55 *Star*, 4 April 1975.

56 *F.M.*, 24 September and 22 October 1976.

57 *Wiehahn Report*, pp. 20, 30, 42–5, 54–5 and 61.

58 *RDM*, 17 May and 26 September 1979, and 30 January and 5 March 1980.

59 *RDM*, 13 August 1980 and 17 February 1981.

60 From The Paulus Report, cited in *Star*, 31 January 1980.

61 My interviews. *RDM*, 18 March 1981.

62 *RDM*, 23 April 1981, and 13 June and 30 September 1983. *F.M.*, 8 October 1982 and 9 September 1983.

63 My interviews. *F.M.*, 15 February 1980, 22 July, 9, 16 and 30 September and 14 October 1983.

64 *RDM*, 25 April and 12 June 1980.

65 Horrell, *South Africa's Workers*, pp. 93ff. Wilson, *Gold Mines*, p. 116. *RDM*, 24 October 1970.

66 *HAD*, Vol. 30 of 1970, col. 3636. *RDM*, 8 October 1970. *S.T.*, 18 October 1970.

67 *RDM*, 6, 9, 13, 25 January and 2, 9, 13 February 1973.

68 *RDM*, 9 March 1979 and 28 January 1981. *Survey 1981*, p. 184.

69 *RDM*, 7 November 1979.

70 Statement by the Durban Master Builders Association, *RDM*, 27 August 1977.

71 *Ibid. RDM*, 10 and 19 February 1971.

72 *F.M.*, 12 October 1973. *Survey 1975*, p. 171.

73 *RDM*, 9 June 1971.

74 *RDM*, 12 August 1971. *F.M.*, 20 August 1971. Greenberg, *op cit*, p. 34.

75 *RDM*, 15 and 17 May 1978. *Star*, 14 April 1975. *Star (w)*, 7 February 1976. *F.M.*, 1 September 1978. *Survey 1976*, pp. 315–16.

76 *Survey 1977*, pp. 225 and 267. *Survey 1978* , p. 217.

77 *Manpower Survey No 9* of 1971 (Department of Labour, Pretoria).

78 My interviews, especially with officials of BAD. See also H. Adam, 'The South African Power Elite' in *South Africa: Sociological Perspectives* (OUP, 1971).

79 Horrell, *South Africa's Workers*, pp. 18 and 95–6.

80 *RDM*, 15 May 1978. Prohibitions on striking were tucked away in various obscure acts, for example, the 1978 Medical, Dental and Supplementary Health Service Professions Amendment Act.

81 *Die Mynwerker*, 15 March 1978.

82 Grobbelaar in *RDM*, 3 July 1973. Van der Watt in *Survey 1980*, p. 168.

83 E. Feit and R. Stokes, 'Racial Prejudice and Economic Pragmatism: a South African case-study' in *Journal of Modern African Studies*, 1976, Vol. 14, No. 3. This is based on their longer 'Prejudice under pressure: White South African artisans and the labor shortage' (roneo, University of Massachusetts, Amherst).

84 Davies, 'Capital, the State', p. 145.

85 Simons, *Class and Colour*, p. 174.

86 *Op cit*, p. 226.

87 *Job Reservation* (cited in footnote 66 of Chapter 2).

88 Simons, p. 128.

89 *Op cit*, p. 129.

90 Doxey, p. 117.

91 E. S. Sachs, *Rebel Daughters* (MacGibbon & Kee, 1957), p. 119.

92 Roux, *Time Longer than Rope*, pp. 158–9.

93 Simons, p. 279.

94 *RDM*, 30 January 1980.

95 *RDM*, 8 June 1972.

96 *RDM*, 10 November 1979.

97 My interviews. Other reports on integration of facilities in *Financial Times* (London), 20 March 1981. *RDM*, 5 March 1981.

98 One of the numerous examples was Jan Marais of Trust Bank in *RDM*, 4 June 1970.

99 *RDM*, 19 February 1971 and 28 May 1973.

100 *RDM*, 6 April 1973.

101 *RDM*, 27 August 1977.

102 *Survey 1971*, p. 196.

103 My interviews.

104 T. Bell, 'Some aspects of Industrial Decentralization in South Africa', *SAJE*, Vol. 41, No. 4, of 1973.

105 Cited in *RDM*, 19 May 1970.

106 *RDM*, 16 October 1970 and 19 December 1972.

107 *S.T.*, 6 December 1972. *Daily Despatch*, 4 January 1972.

108 *RDM*, 26 November 1970.

109 See Paulus' defiant statement in *S.T.*, 26 March 1978.

110 *Survey 1970*, p. 155. *Survey 1971*, pp. 224–5. *Survey 1972*, pp. 202–3.

111 *Star*, 15 and 29 March 1984.

CHAPTER 8

1 For further examples of support for socio-economic reform (in addition to those given in Chapters 4–6) see speeches by Chris Saunders of Tongaat in *Urban Foundation Annual Review for 1982*; Mike Rosholt's speech to Nafcoc in *SAF News*, July 1982; speech by Albert Robinson, Chairman of JCI, *RDM*, 31 October 1980.

2 *The Buthelezi Commission*, Vols. 1 and 2 (H & H, 1982). *RDM*, 1 August 1980.

3 Condensed from AAC *Chairman's Statement* for 1980 and 1982; speeches in *Cape Times*, 24 March 1970; *RDM*, 23 May 1978 and 22 October 1981; and *SA Digest*, 30 October 1981.

4 *Star*, 1 May 1974. *RDM*, 1 December 1976.

5 *RDM*, 30 June 1970.

6 On the Foundation see the book by its Director, L. Gerber, *Friends and Influence: the Diplomacy of Private Enterprise* (Purnell, 1973). R. First *et al*, *The South African Connection* (Temple Smith, 1972), pp. 221ff.

7 *RDM*, 2 September 1974.

8 *RDM*, 11 June 1976. AAC *Chairman's Statement 1977*.

9 *Financial Times* (London), 3 December 1976.

10 *RDM*, 3 April 1980 and 6 February 1981. *Urban Foundation Annual Review 1983*.

11 *Jane's Defence Review*, cited in *Survey 1983*, p. 581.

12 Federated Chamber of Industries, *Annual Report* (cited in AAC press cuttings service, October 1983).

13 *Business International SA: A fresh look at South Africa* (1982, ABI Research Report).

14 *South African Statistics 1982*, 1–34. For numbers in government service in 'independent' Bantustans see p. 337 above.

15 Davies, 'Capital, the State', p. 139. D. Kaplan and M. Morris, *South African Labour Bulletin*, Vol. 2, No. 6.

16 Doxey, *The Industrial Colour Bar In South Africa* (OUP, 1961), p. 183.

17 *RDM*, 10 and 27 September 1974. *Survey 1969*, pp. 109f. *Survey 1970*, p. 85.

18 *Star*, 20 August 1975. *RDM*, 17 May 1978. *S.T.*, 2 January 1972.

19 *Survey 1972*, p. 319.

20 *RDM*, 6 December 1974 and 15 June 1976.

21 My interviews. Lipton, *Optima*.

22 My interviews with officials at BAD in 1978.

23 C. H. Wyndham of the Human Sciences Laboratory of the Chamber of Mines in a paper delivered at the 1974 Conference of the Institute of Personnel Management. Number of Coloureds and Indians from D. J. M. Vorster, 'Labour Requirements for the 1970s: How can they be met?' (roneo, 9th Conference of National Development and Management Foundation). See also *Vraag en Aanbod* (cited in footnote 11 of Chapter 6).

24 *N.M.C. 1981. Survey 1981*, p. 341.

25 Statement by Reynders, Director of the FCI, *RDM*, 15 March 1978. *S.T.* Business News, 12 February 1978.

26 Horwitz, *Political Economy*, pp. 251–2 and 476.

27 D. Lachman, 'Import restrictions and exchange rates' in *SAJE*, 1974, Vol. 42. *Viljoen Report*, p. 24.

28 *Reynders Report*, pp. 10ff. See also SA Reserve Bank, *Quarterly Bulletins*.

29 For example, I. Little, Skitovsky, and Scott, *Industry and Trade in Some Developing Countries* (OUP, 1970).

30 *Reynders Report*, pp. 21ff, 137ff, 247ff, 396f, and 623f.

31 W. F. J. Steenkamp, 'Monopoly & Competition in South Africa', in E. H. Chamberlin (ed), *Monopoly and Competition and their Regulation* (Macmillan, 1954).

32 *Financial Times* (London), 11 August 1983 and 20 February 1984. Mercabank, *Focus on Key Economic Issues*, No. 34.

33 I am indebted to Jerry Helleiner and Michael Lipton for a useful general discussion of protection, monopolies and markets. They are not, however, responsible for my analysis of the South African case.

34 Calculated from Reserve Bank *Quarterly Bulletins*.

35 S. S. Brand, 'Opportunities for the 1980s' (roneo, School for Business Leadership, Unisa, 1983).

36 S. P. J. du Plessis, 'Effective Tariff Protection in South Africa', *SAJE*, Vol. 44 of 1976.

37 *RDM*, 21 February 1979. See also Prime Minister Vorster on the gravity of the unemployment problem in *HAD*, Vol. 30 of 1970, col. 4085.

38 *S.T.* Business News, 22 May 1983.

39 *Reynders Report*, p. 37.

40 *Op cit*, pp. 34, 111 and 139. *Riekert Report*, pp. 232f.

41 *Race Relations News*, April 1973. *Cape Argus*, 17 January 1976. *SA Digest*, 28 August 1981.

42 In a speech to the 1978 Assocom conference, *RDM*, 19 October 1978. *Financial Times* (London), 31 January 1983.

43 An attempt to calculate the administrative costs of apartheid has been made by M. Savage, 'The Challenge of Change and Some Arithmetic of Apartheid' (SAIRR, 1977).

44 *HAD*, Vol. 55 of 1975, cols. 1675ff.

45 *RDM*, 30 October 1971. *S.T.* Business News, 19 February 1978. For other examples of business pressure see *RDM*, 21 August. AAC *Chairman's Statement 1971*.

46 G. Becker, *The Economics of Discrimination* (University of Chicago, 1957 and 1971).

47 For a summary of some of these arguments see Frankel, *Capital Investment*, pp. 128ff.

48 M. Olson, *Rise and Decline of Nations* (Yale, 1982).

CHAPTER 9

1 J. C. du Plessis, 'Foreign Investment in South Africa' in Litvak and Maule, *Foreign Investment: the Experience of Host Countries* (Praeger, 1970). Houghton, *The South African Economy*, p. 111.

2 A. Stadler, 'The South African Party System, 1910–48' (PhD, Witwatersrand University, 1971), p. 235. On the political system see also L. M. Thompson, *The Republic of South Africa* (Little Brown, 1966). G. Carter, *The Politics of Inequality* (Thames and Hudson, 1958). On the loading of the rural vote see K. Heard, *General Elections in South Africa, 1943–70* (OUP, 1974). N. M. Stultz, *Afrikaner Politics in South Africa, 1934–48* (University of California, 1974), p. 146.

3 See his 1912 de Wildt speech in D. W. Krüger, *South African Parties and Policies* (Human & Rousseau, 1960), p. 65.

4 Hancock, *Smuts* (Cambridge, 1968), Vol. 2, p. 23.

5 O'Meara, 'Class, Capital and Ideology' (cited footnote 56 of Chapter 6 above), p. 13.

6 Frankel, *Capital Investment*, Chapter 4. de Kiewiet, *History of South Africa* (OUP, 1941), pp. 162ff. G. Lanning and M. Mueller, *Africa Undermined* (Penguin, 1979), Chapters 6 and 7.

7 Frankel, *op cit*. Lipton, 'Two Agricultures' in *Farm Labour*. Brand, 'Contribution of Agriculture' (cited in footnote 2 of Chapter 4 above).

8 Hancock, *Smuts*, p. 25.

9 Kaplan, 'Class Conflict' (cited footnote 6 of Chapter 1 above), pp. 71f.

10 Horwitz, *Political Economy*, p. 183.

11 On these aspects of the 1920 Native Housing and 1923 Native (Urban Areas) Acts see T. Lodge, *Black Politics in South Africa Since 1945* (Longmans, 1983), pp. 4f.

12 Simons, *Class and Colour*, Chapter 12.

13 A. Sachs in Thompson and Butler, p. 233.

14 Olson, *Rise and Decline*, Chapter 2.

15 G. Gerhart, *Black Power in South Africa* (University of California, 1978), p. 76. On black political developments see also R. Stanbridge, 'Contemporary African Political Organizations and Movements' in Price and Rosberg. P. Walshe, *The Rise of African Nationalism in South Africa* (University of California, 1971). T. Karis and G. Carter (eds), *From Protest to Challenge: A documentary history of African Policies in South Africa* (Hoover 1972), 3 vols.

16 As in footnotes 6, 7, 9 and 10 above.

17 Heard, *General Elections*, p. xii.

18 E. Rousseau, quoted in Williams (see footnote 35 of Chapter 5 above).

19 Horwitz, *Political Economy*, Chapter 15. On protection see also Frankel, *Capital Investment*. Bozzoli, 'Roots of Hegemony'. Kaplan, 'Class Conflict'. *Report of the Agricultural and Industrial Requirements Commission* (cited in footnote 7 of Chapter 2); *Reynders Report*.

20 As in footnote 14 of Chapter 5.

21 T. Gregory, *Ernest Oppenheimer and the Economic Development of Southern Africa* (OUP, 1962), pp. 250 and 277.

22 Lanning, *Africa Undermined*, p. 133.

23 Kaplan, 'Class Conflict', p. 239.

24 Paton, *Hofmeyr* (OUP, 1971), Chapter 7. Hancock, *Smuts*, Chapter 14. Ballinger, *Union to Apartheid*, p. 96.

25 Salomon, 'Afrikaner Nationalism'. O'Meara, 'Class, Capital and Ideology', pp. 44ff. On the growth of Afrikaner nationalism see also M. Roberts and A. Trollip, *The South African Opposition 1935–45* (Longmans Green, 1947). B. Bunting, *The Rise of the South African Reich* (Penguin, 1964). T. D. Moodie,

The Rise of Afrikanerdom (University of California, 1975). Adam and Giliomee (cited in footnote 13 of Chapter 1). Du Toit in Thompson and Butler. Stultz, *Afrikaner Politics*.

26 S. M. Lipset, *Political Man* (Mercury, 1963), pp. 68ff and Chapter 4.

27 Salomon, 'Afrikaner Nationalism'.

28 Moodie, *Afrikanerdom*, p. 113. I, Wilkins and H. Strydom, *The Broederbond* (Paddington Press, 1951; Jonathan Ball, 1978).

29 Moodie, p. 102.

30 Hancock, *Smuts*, p. 252. Stultz, *Afrikaner Politics*, p. 93.

31 Moodie, p. 133.

32 Heard, *General Elections* (see footnote 2 above), Chapter 2.

33 Calculated from Heard.

34 Ballinger, *Union to Apartheid*, Chapters 8 and 9.

35 C. A. R. Crosland, *The Future of Socialism* (Jonathan Cape, 1956), p. 45.

36 Stultz, *Afrikaner Politics*, pp. 126–7.

37 *Op cit*, p. 81. Moodie, *Afrikanerdom*, p. 220.

38 Paton, *Hofmeyr*, pp. 290f.

39 Ballinger, *Union to Apartheid*, p. 88.

40 Stultz, *Afrikaner Politics*, p. 66.

41 *Op cit*, pp. 88 and 93. Carter, *Politics of Inequality*.

42 Stultz, pp. 148–9 and 117.

43 See the seminal essay by G. Arrighi, *The Political Economy of Rhodesia* (Mouton, 1967). C. Leys, *European Politics in Southern Rhodesia* (OUP, 1959). M. Faber, *Towards Economic Independence* (Cambridge, 1971).

44 Simons, *Class and Colour*, p. 589. Heard, *General Elections*, Chapter 3; Heard is the source for the analysis of election results until 1971.

45 My interviews. See also Stadler (cited in footnote 2 above), p. 234. Carter, *Politics of Inequality*, p. 175.

46 J. Robertson, *Liberalism in South Africa 1948–63* (OUP, 1971), p. 40.

47 See the article by Joel Mervis, former *Sunday Times* editor, in *RDM*, 18 October 1980.

48 Bunting, *South African Reich*, pp. 378ff. Adam and Giliomee, *Rise and Crisis*, Chapter 6. Welsh in Leftwich, *South Africa*.

49 Bunting, *South African Reich*, p. 384.

50 A, Wassenaar, *The Assault on Private Enterprise* (Tafelberg, 1977), p. 123.

51 Bunting, p. 380.

52 Carter, pp. 54ff. J. Stone, *Colonist or Uitlander? A study of the British Immigrant in South Africa* (OUP, 1973).

53 Hartmann, *Politics and Enterprise*, pp. 25ff and 37.

54 *Op cit.*

55 Clack, 'Industrial Relations', p. 253.

56 Hartmann, p. 31.

57 *RDM*, 23 September 1980.

58 Carter, p. 77. *SA Digest*, 29 April 1983.

59 L. Schlemmer, *Privilege, Prejudice and Parties* (SAIRR, 1973), p. 12; and 'Change in South Africa' in Price and Rosberg, p. 254.

60 *Olson, Rise and Decline*, p. 25.

61 Schlemmer, *Privilege, Prejudice*, p. 24, and 'Change in South Africa', p. 261.

62 Schlemmer, 'Change in South Africa', p. 259ff.

63 Half as many votes were required to elect a SWA MP.

64 Clack, 'Industrial Relations', p. 205.

65 Carter, *Politics of Inequality*, pp. 302ff. Robertson, *Liberalism*, pp. 51 ff.

66 A. Sachs in Thompson and Butler, p. 233.

67 Gerhart, *Black Power* (cited in footnote 15 above), Chapter 1 and pp. 220ff.

67a L. Schlemmer, 'The Stirring Giant' in Price and Rosberg, p. 100.

68 R. Dahrendorf, *Society and Democracy in Germany* (Weidenfeld and Nicholson, 1971).

69 On this see also Sachs in Thompson and Butler. Adam, *Modernizing Racial Domination*. On the erosion of the rule of law see A. S. Matthews, *Law, Order and Liberty in South Africa* (Juta, 1971), and J. Dugard, *Human Rights and the South African Legal Order* (Princeton, 1978).

70 Ballinger, *Union to Apartheid*, pp. 434ff. *Survey 1961*, p. 9ff and 63ff. J. de Gruchy, *The Church Struggle in South Africa* (Philip, 1979), Chapter 3.

71 W. D. Wilson of AAC in *Optima*, Vol. 25, No. 2, of 1975.

72 Reserve Bank, *Quarterly Bulletins*. Houghton, *South African Economy*, p.

179. *Organization and Structure of the Metal and Engineering Industries in South Africa* (Seifsa, undated), pp. 26ff. Lachman (cited footnote 27 of Chapter 8 above). On food prices see Brand (cited in footnote 2 of Chapter 4 above). On steel *F.M.*, 8 November 1974.

73 Houghton, *South African Economy* (2nd edition, 1967), pp. 203ff. Reserve Bank, *Quarterly Bulletins*.

74 Du Plessis in Litvak and Maule (cited in footnote 1 above). J. de Villiers Graaff, 'Alternative Models of South African Growth', *SAJE*, 1962, Vol. 30, pp. 47ff.

75 Their aims were set out in rightwing journals like *Veg, SA Observer* and, later, *Die Afrikaner*.

76 For example, *Star*, 3 October 1970.

77 For example, Hertzog's 'Calvinism' speech in *HAD*, Vol. 26 of 1969, cols. 3876ff. See also J. H. P. Serfontein, *Die Verkrampte Aanslag* (Human & Rousseau, 1970).

78 H. Lever, *The South African Voter* (Juta, 1972), p. 25.

79 M. Weber, *Economy and Society* (Bedminster, 1968).

80 Lipton, 'Independent Bantustans'; and Schrire (cited in footnotes 31 and 37 of Chapter 2). Ballinger, *Union to Apartheid*, p. 459.

81 Muller's estimate in *RDM*, 15 March 1979. Incomes from Adam and Giliomee, *Rise and Crisis*, p. 174.

82 Schlemmer, 'Change in South Africa' in Price and Rosberg, pp. 244ff.

83 *Op cit*, p. 262. T. Hanf *et al, South Africa: prospects of peaceful change* (Collings, 1981), pp. 110ff, 157ff and 337.

84 On the press see E. Potter, *The Press as Opposition* (Chatto & Windus, 1975). Serfontein, *Verkrampte Aanslag*, Chapter 9.

85 This analysis is based on my interviews and on extensive reading of the press.

86 *Financial Times* (London), 31 January 1983.

87 *HAD*, Vol. 30 of 1970, col. 3636. *S.T.*, 18 October 1970. *RDM* throughout October 1970. *Beeld* and *Dagbreek en Landstem* cited in *RDM*, 12 October 1970.

88 *Viljoen Report*.

89 1964 interview with Oppenheimer cited in Bunting, *South African Reich*, p. 391.

90 See Wassenaar's book (cited footnote 50 above). Speeches by Wessels in *RDM*, 19 February 1974, and W. B. Coetzer in *RDM*, 24 June 1971.

91 *F.M.*, 6 June 1975.

92 Schlemmer, *Privilege, Prejudice*, Chapter 2, and 'Change in South Africa', pp. 252ff.

93 *Survey 1979*, p. 440.

94 *The Economist* (London), 16 May 1981.

95 *Die Transvaler*, 12 May 1973. *Financial Times*, 25 February 1975. Also London *Daily Telegraph*, 2 April 1971.

96 My interviews. *RDM*, 30 March and 27 April 1971. *S.T.*, 28 March and 4 April 1971.

97 The use of the Bureau for State Security (Boss) against the HNP was confirmed by Boss defectors Arthur McGivern and Gordon Winter; see the latter's *Inside Boss: South Africa's Secret Police* (Penguin, 1981).

98 Jan Steyn, Director of the Urban Foundation, at an on-the-record Chatham House meeting, 25 April 1979.

99 *HAD*, Vol. 66 of 1977, cols. 783–90.

100 Interviews in 1978 with businessmen who readily discussed their lobbying on behalf of P. W. Botha.

101 For example, C. Leys, 'What is the problem about corruption' in *Journal of Modern African Studies*, Vol. 3 of 1965. For a different view see R. Wade, 'The System of Administrative and Political Corruption: Canal Irrigation in India' (I.D.S., Sussex University, 1982).

102 *Rapport* poll, cited *F.M.*, 22 December 1978.

103 *Star (w)*, 5 February 1983. *SA Digest*, 6 August 1982.

104 *Sunday Tribune* survey, cited *SA Digest*, 7 May 1982.

105 *S.T.*, 4 September 1983. L. Schlemmer in *Indicator*, 1983, Vol. 1, No. 3.

106 Gerschenkson (cited in footnote 54 of Chapter 4 above), pp. 287ff.

107 HNP views from *Survey 1982*, pp. 13f. *SAF News*, May 1982. *The Times* (London), 28 October 1981. *Financial Times* (London), 9 October 1981. SA Institute of International Affairs opinion poll cited in *Star (w)*, 20 November 1982.

108 On the military see S. Jenkins in *The Economist*, 16 July 1983. K. W. Grundy, *Rise of the South African Security Establishment* (SA Institute for International Affairs, 1983). R. Jaster, *South Africa's Narrowing Security Options* (IISS, 1980).

109 *Survey 1980*, p. 289.

110 Statement by Lawrence, President of the Chamber of Mines, quoted in 1981 *Business International South Africa*.

111 *The Military Balance 1982/3* (International Institute for Strategic Studies, 1983).

112 As in footnotes 13 and 91 of Chapter 3.

113 Reserve Bank, *Quarterly Bulletin*.

114 *Star*, 5 February and 4 April 1980.

115 My interviews. *F.M.*, 23 March 1979.

116 *RDM*, 4 October 1982. Lipton, *Optima*, Section 5.

117 See reports to the 1981 Black Sash Conference. Koornhof in an interview in BBC-TV series, 'The White Tribe of Africa' (broadcast in January 1979).

118 *Survey 1963*, p. 17. P. Mayer, 'The Origin and Decline of The Rural Resistance Ideologies' in *Black Villagers in an Industrial Society* (OUP, 1980).

119 *RDM*, 15 June 1978.

120 Lipton, *Optima*, p. 125.

121 S. Huntington, *Political Order in Changing Societies* (Yale, 1968), p. 157.

122 J. Lombard, *Freedom, Welfare and Social Order* (Benso, 1978). 'A verligte Manifesto' by W. de Klerk, editor of Die Transvaler, reprinted in *SAF News*, September 1981.

123 *Die Vaderland*, cited in *SA Digest*, 7 March 1980.

124 *Star (w)*, 5 February 1983. *SA Digest*, 1982. *RDM*, 2 September 1980.

125 Speech by the party leader, Jaap Marais, at the 1980 HNP Congress, *RDM*, 27 and 29 September 1980. See also *RDM*, 17 February 1974.

126 *RDM*, 19 September 1979 and 2 September 1980. See Treurnicht's book, *Credo van 'n Afrikaner*.

127 From his article in *Star (w)*, 30 October 1982.

128 *RDM*, 29 June and 11 July 1979 and 14 March 1980.

129 *Rapport*, 16 May 1982.

130 This was the assessment of many observers, for example, C. Hill, *Change in South Africa: Blind alleys or new directions?* (Collings, 1983).

131 S. M. Lipset, *Political Man* (Mercury, 1963).

132 On consociationalism see Slabbert and Welsh (cited in footnote 17 of Chapter

1 above), Chapters 4 and 6. The influence of consociational theories is evident in the Buthelezi and Quail Reports.

133 Glazer and Moynihan, *Beyond the Melting Pot*, p. lxii.

134 M. McGrath in *Indicator*, 1983, Vol. 1, No. 2.

135 My interviews. See Schwarz's articles in *S.T.*, 6 October and 8 December 1979. 'Report of the Economic Commission of the PFP' (mimeo, November 1981).

136 In a speech to the PFP's 1981 Congress in the party newsletter, *Deurbraak*, February 1983.

137 Van Zyl Slabbert in *Deurbraak*, July and September 1982.

138 *HAD*, Vol. 91 of 1981, col. 44; and his Durban speech, *RDM*, 15 September 1979.

139 Simkins (see footnote 61 of Chapter 3 above).

140 No Sizwe (see footnote 9 of Chapter 1 above).

141 K. Moodley, 'Inequality and Anxiety of Middle Groups in South Africa' in Price and Rosberg. Hanf, *South Africa*. E. C. Webster, 'The 1949 Durban Riots: A case-study in race and class' (roneo, Natal University).

142 Survey for the *Buthelezi Commission*, Vol. 1, Chapter 3. *SA Digest*, 30 September 1983.

143 *Report of the Commission of Inquiry into the Riots at Soweto and Elsewhere* (Chairman: Cellie) RP55/1980, Vol. 1, pp. 587ff.

144 *Quail Report* (Conference Associates 1979), Appendix 12.

145 *Statistical Review of Black Development*, 1980, p. 105. On the Bantustans see works cited in footnote 37 of Chapter 2 above.

146 Streek & Wicksteed, *Render unto Kaiser* (Ravan, 1981), Chapter 7.

147 *Southern Africa Report*, 22 July 1983.

148 M. G. Buthelezi, *White and Black Nationalism, Ethnicity and the future of the Homelands* (SAIRR, 1974); and *Power is Ours: Selected Speeches* (Focus, 1979). L. Schlemmer and T. Muil in Thompson and Butler. L. Schlemmer, 'The Stirring Giant' in Price and Rosberg.

149 In a speech to the National Council of Churches in New York, *RDM*, 12 September 1979.

150 *Buthelezi Report*, Vol. I, Tables 6 and 7. *RDM*, 14 April and 9 June 1980.

151 Statement by Joe Foster of Fosatu, *Survey 1982*, p. 184.

152 *Survey 1977*, p. 285. *RDM*, 31 October 1983. *F.M.*, 28 October 1983 (and see p. 206 above).

153 My interview with van der Watt in 1983. Also *F.M.* supplement, 16 September 1983.

154 *RDM*, 12 December 1983 and 9 February 1984.

155 *Survey 1982*, p. 158.

156 For example, Huntington, *Political Order* (cited in footnote 121 above), pp. 283ff.

157 Based on a survey of black workers cited in *F.M.*, 21 October 1983.

158 Gerhart, *Black Power*. Lodge, *Black Politics*. S. Nolutshungu, *Changing South Africa* (Manchester University 1982), Part 3.

159 *Ibid*. On the Soweto riots, see also J. Kane-Berman, *Soweto: Black Revolt, White Reaction* (Ravan, 1978).

160 Gerhart, p. 301.

161 Hanf, *South Africa*, p. 353.

162 For example, *Riekert Report*, p. 233. Heunis in speech to the Political Science Association of Southern Africa, cited in *SAF News*, October 1981.

163 Cited in K. Heard, 'Change, Challenge and Response – a view of the 1977 general election' in D. Anglin *et al, Conflict and Change in Southern Africa* (University of America, 1978).

164 South African police estimate, cited by Stanbridge in Price and Rosberg, p. 92.

165 Cited in *Washington Post*, 1 January 1984.

166 *Op cit*. See also S. Jenkins in *The Economist*, 16 July 1983.

167 This analogy was suggested in my 1972 paper 'Independent Bantustans' (see footnote 37 of Chapter 2 above).

168 *RDM*, 13 February, 20 October and 8 December 1980. See attack by the Minister of Police, Le Grange, *RDM*, 20 October 1980.

169 Memorandum by Judge Didcott to the Hoexter Commission, reprinted in *RDM*, 14 October 1980.

170 *RDM*, 3 September 1980 and 10 January 1981.

171 E. Gellner, *Spectacles and Predicaments: essays in social theory* (Cambridge, 1979), pp. 271–2.

172 On 'status inconsistency' see G. Lenski, *Power and Privilege* (McGraw Hill, 1966).

173 A de Tocqueville, *The Old Regime and the French Revolution*. For an analysis which predicts that these rising expectations will lead to revolution rather than evolution see M. Arnheim, *South Africa After Vorster* (Timmins, 1979).

174 Glazer and Moynihan, Introduction to the 2nd edition.

175 Hanf, pp. 319ff and 330ff.

176 Malcolm X, *Autobiography*.

177 My interviews. *Financial Times*, 22 February 1980.

178 My interviews. L. Douwes Dekker, 'Notes on International Labour Bodies and their relevance to South Africa' in *The South African Labour Scene* (SAIIA, 1980); and 'International Trade Secretariats' in *South African Journal of Labour Relations*, 1984, Vol. 8, No. 2. Information from Robin Smith of Durham University, from his forthcoming thesis on South African trade unions.

179 *F.M.*, 23 March 1984.

180 *RDM*, 2 July and 11 September 1980. *Star*, 24 May 1983.

181 My interviews. *RDM*, 25 October 1980.

182 In a speech to the Institute of Labour Relations, *RDM*, 1 December 1978.

183 Published in *Investment in South Africa: The Options* (Christian Concern for Southern Africa, London, 1976) and in *South African Labour Bulletin*, 1976. Attacks and replies cited in footnotes 6 and 18 of Chapter 1.

184 *The Times* (London), 27 September 1984.

185 On Western and African policies see C. Crocker, 'South Africa: Strategy for Change', *Foreign Affairs*, Winter 1980/1. R. W. Johnson, *How long will South Africa survive?* (Macmillan, 1977). W. Foltz, 'United States Policy towards Southern Africa: Economic and Strategic Constraints', *Political Science Quarterly* (Spring 1977). J. Barber, *The Uneasy Relationship – Britain and South Africa* (Chatham House, 1983). J. Mayall, *Africa: the Cold War and After* (Elek, 1971). C. Coker, 'South Africa and the Western Alliance 1949–81' in *Journal of the Royal United Services Institute for Defence Studies*, 127 June 1982. J. Spence, *Republic under Pressure* (OUP, 1965). D. Austin, *Britain and South Africa* (OUP, 1966). C. and M. Legum, *Crisis for the West* (Pall Mall, 1964). I. W. Zartman, 'The African States as a Source of Change' in C. Crocker and R. Bissell, *South Africa into the 1980s*.

186 *RDM*, 12 December 1983, 5 March and 13 June 1984.

187 *RDM*, 26 August 1980.

188 In a speech to the South African Political Science Association, cited in *SAF News* October 1981.

189 Heard (cited in footnote 2 above).

190 G. Lenski, *Power and Privilege*.

191 *SA Digest*, 21 May 1982.

192 Huntington, *Political Order*, pp. 154ff.

193 *Op cit*, pp. 288ff.

194 Hanf, *South Africa*, p. 319.

195 E. Feit, *African Opposition in South Africa* (Hoover, 1967), pp. 18ff. Hanf, Chapter 11.

196 HSRC Survey, cited in *The Times* (London), 16 July 1983. This finding was confirmed by a subsequent survey by L. Schlemmer, *Black Worker Attitudes: Political Options, Capitalism and Investment in South Africa* (Indicator, 1984).

197 P. Mayer, 'Class, Status and Ethnicity as perceived by Johannesburg Africans' in Thompson and Butler. See also the Hanf and Schlemmer surveys cited above.

198 *South African Statistics 1972*.

199 Cited in J. D'Oliviera *Vorster: The man* (Stanton, 1977), p. 290.

CHAPTER 10

1. A. G. Frank, *Capitalism and Underdevelopment in Latin America* (Monthly Review Press, 1969). A recent Marxist analysis more compatible with South African development is that by B. Warren, *Imperialism: Pioneer of Capitalism* (Verso, 1980).

2 R. Fogel and S. Engerman, *Time on the Cross* (Little Brown, 1974), pp. 244ff, especially Table 3.

3 O'Meara, 'Class, Capital and Ideology' (see footnote 56 of Chapter 6), pp. 69, 77, 191, 281, 313.

4 T. Nairn, *The Break-up of Britain. Crisis and Neo-Nationalism*, cited in Gellner, *Spectacles and Predicaments*, p. 270.

5 M. Weber, *General Economic History*. D. Apter, *Politics of Modernization* (Chicago, 1967).

6 Glazer and Moynihan, *Beyond the Melting Pot*, p. 310.

7 *Op cit*. Glazer and Moynihan, *Ethnicity* (Harvard, 1975). Nairn *op cit*. Gellner *op cit*. P. van den Berghe, *The Ethnic Phenomenon* (Elsevier, 1981).

8 Gellner, p. 273.

EPILOGUE

1 The manuscript was completed at the end of 1983. Subsequently, the proofs were briefly updated to take account of major events such as the Nkomati Accord, inauguration of the tricameral constitution etc.

2 This term is derived from my 1974 'Authoritarian Reform' paper, see p. 416 above.

3 In the *Annual Report of the Commission for Administration* (Chairman: J. de Beer, 1985).

4 For example, the 1985 Mthiya judgment of the Supreme Court, upholding the right of migrants to qualify for Section 10 rights; the 1985 Amendment easing requirements under Section 10 of the Black (Urban Areas) Consolidation Act; the extension of local government, including the establishment of Regional Services Councils on which representatives of the local councils of all races would serve jointly; the 1985 announcement that urban freehold property rights would be extended to Africans.

5 Dugard (cited above p. 451) p. 57.

6 These principles were spelt out in the Nationalists' typical step-by-step manner in the following speeches by President Botha: Addresses to Parliament on 25 January, 19 April and 19 June 1985; speeches to the 1985 National Party provincial congresses in Natal on 15 August, in the OFS on 11 September, and in the Cape on 30 September (roneos from Department of Information, SA Embassy, London). Report on Transvaal Congress in *SA Digest*, 27 September 1985.

7 Memorandum presented to Senator Edward Kennedy during his visit to SA in January 1985 by the AHI, ASSOCOM, Chamber of Mines, FCI, SEIFSA and NAFCOC.

8 *International Herald Tribune*, 20 September 1985

9 See their statement to this effect in *Star* (weekly), 29 July 1985.

10 For example, the recent conferences between SA and foreign companies at Leeds Castle and in London to draw up a joint strategy to oppose apartheid and to raise funds for the reform programme, which is their alternative to economic sanctions; see the *Financial Times*, 18 November 1985.

11 The leading advocate of this view was Dr F. du Plessis, Chairman of SANLAM.

12 See the November 1985 issues of the *Star* (weekly) and of the *Weekly Mail* (which replaced the *Rand Daily Mail*).

13 See e.g. *Guardian* of 9 October 1985 on their refusal to support a stayaway called without consulting them. On tensions between unions and community groups in the Eastern Cape see *Work in Progress*, 1985.

14 Quoted in *Quarterly Industrial Review*, 28 July 1985 (AAC, Johannesburg); see also 'Local Response to Disinvestment: No Simple Equation' in *Work in Progress* No. 37 of 1985.

15 *Financial Times*, 2 December 1985

16 On the ANC see T. Lodge, 'The Second Consultative Conference of the African National Congress', *SA International*, October 1985; D. Willers in *Finance Weekly*, 4 December 1985; *Africa Confidential* of 18 September and 30 October 1985; H. Adam & S. Uys 'Eight new realities in southern Africa', *Africa Notes*, No. 39 of 1985.

17 On ANC policy see *Render South Africa Ungovernable*: Message of the National Executive Committee of the ANC (8 January 1985, London); speech by Oliver Tambo, ANC President, at Chatham House (London) 29 October 1985; Anthony Heard's interview with Tambo in *Cape Times* of 4 November 1985; Lodge, *op cit*.

18 On these local initiatives see *Weekly Mail*, 11–17 October 1985.

19 See, for example, the editorial in the *New York Times*, 18 April 1985.

20 *SA Digest*, 1 February 1985.

21 In an interview in *Die Transvaler*, 25 March 1981.

22 R. Jaster, 'South Africa' in J. C. Snyder & S. Wells (Eds) *Limiting Nuclear Proliferation* (Ballinger, Cambridge, Mass, 1985).

Index

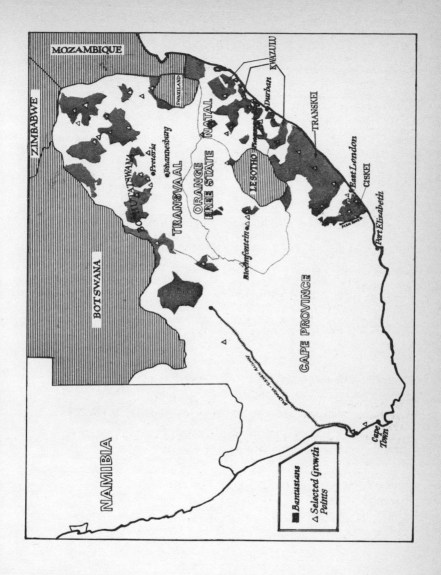

MOZAMBIQUE

ZIMBABWE

SWAZILAND

KWAZULU

Durban

NATAL

TRANSKEI

East London

CISKEI

Port Elizabeth

BOPHUTHATSWANA

Pretoria

Johannesburg

TRANSVAAL

ORANGE
FREE STATE

LESOTHO

Bloemfontein

BOTSWANA

ORANGE-FISH TUNNEL

CAPE PROVINCE

NAMIBIA

Cape
Town

■ Bantustans

△ Selected Growth
  Points